Max Siporin

FIVE FIELDS OF SOC   ICE

FIVE FIELDS OF SOCIAL SERVICE:

REVIEWS OF RESEARCH

Henry S. Maas, Ph.D., Editor

Professor, School of Social Welfare
University of California, Berkeley

National Association of Social Workers, Inc.
2 Park Avenue   New York, N.Y. 10016

The preparation of the material for this publication was made possible through the generosity
of the National Clearinghouse of Mental Health
of the National Institute of Mental Health.

Printed in the U.S.A.
January 1966

FOREWORD

The purpose of this book is to present critically what has been learned through systematic study, and may now be drawn upon for use in five fields of social service. This statement of purpose is a modification, in certain ways, of the call for an evaluative analysis of social work research issued in 1961 by the Executive Committee of the Research Section (now the Council on Social Work Research) of the National Association of Social Workers. This book is both more and less than the original conception.

It is more in so far as its chapters review some of the literature lying beyond the boundaries of social work research. Knowledge in many disciplines is useful to the social services. Thus, each author was invited to review, within a single field of service and without special regard for the disciplinary origins of a study, research on (1) those persons or groups toward whom the field directs its services; (2) the social organization of agencies set up to give the services; (3) the social policies that orient the services; (4) the social work methods used with clients; and (5) the outcome of the services. Though social work research was expected to provide the largest share of the literature under review, authors agreed to include studies in any of the sciences of man that bore directly upon the questions asked.

The book is less than originally planned in that it includes only five fields of service. All of these five are services organized directly under social welfare auspices. The prospectus for this book included eight fields of service. The three fields not included here are corrections, medical social work, and psychiatric social work. Each of these three fields is organized under host agency auspices, i.e., within legal or medical institutions. Efforts to prepare reviews of research in these three fields foundered in part because of the seemingly unresolvable problem of defining the boundaries of the literature to be studied. Lines could not be drawn clearly enough between knowledge germane to the total host agency's problems and those specific to the social services offered within the legal or medical facility.

The five reviews presented in this book will, hopefully, in the years ahead, periodically be brought up to date. Second efforts at reviewing research in the three fields of service omitted from this book may be more successful than the first. New fields of service may be added, and knowledge relevant to their operation may be analyzed. In this book, the National Association of Social Workers presents a first attempt at relatively comprehensive analyses in a single volume of the products of studies that contribute to the knowledge base for professional activity in social work.

In all of the chapters, authors have tried to synthesize what is now known, to examine critically with what degree of confidence social workers can make use of this knowledge, and to suggest where and how future research should proceed. The results should be of utility to social workers, to public officials, and to other socially responsible citizens concerned with social welfare problems and their empirical investigation.

This book could not have been prepared without help from the following persons and organizations, to whom the editor expresses his indebtedness: the Council on Social Work Research of the National Associ-

ation of Social Workers, for issuing a call for a review of research-based knowledge; an advisory committee, consisting of Scott Briar, Genevieve W. Carter, Alfred J. Kahn, and Roger Miller, all of whom helped especially in the early planning of the book and at critical junctures in its subsequent preparation; the National Clearinghouse for Mental Health Information, National Institute of Mental Health, Public Health Service of the Department of Health, Education and Welfare, for contracting with the National Association of Social Workers for the preparation of this book, and thus providing a modest source of funds to underwrite authors' basic expenses; and Marjorie J. Herzig, Associate Director, Department of Social Work Practice, National Association of Social Workers, for extremely able administrative help throughout and for overseeing the efforts of many from the beginning of the project to its conclusion.

The authors' extraordinarily difficult pioneer labors may be apparent to some readers. The value of their efforts should be apparent to all.

HENRY S. MAAS
Editor

June 1965

CONTENTS

FAMILY SERVICES

By SCOTT BRIAR

The family has long been one of the central concerns of social work. One reflection of this concern is seen in the important role played by private family agencies in the development of social work. From the early 1900's until quite recently, the private family agency was regarded as the true "home" of the social caseworker. With the exception of child welfare, all other types of agencies were considered "secondary" settings, or outposts in which caseworkers were attempting to find and establish a legitimate place for themselves. The central stream of casework theory—again until quite recently—has been developed either in family agencies or at least against the backdrop of family agency practice. It is not surprising then, as shall be seen in this review of research in the family field, that some of the major research endeavors in social work have been conducted in family agencies or have focused on problems of special concern to social workers in the family field.

Since the time of Mary Richmond, the degree of emphasis placed on the family per se by the caseworker in his practice has waxed and waned. There were periods in which this emphasis diminished to such an extent that one finds, paradoxically, some practitioners in family agencies arguing that it is inappropriate for the caseworker to regard the family as his client.[1] Over the past ten to fifteen years, however, there has been a strong resurgence of interest in the family, and the concepts of family-centered diagnosis and treatment are now permeating all fields of social work. This development has stimulated research activity designed to increase knowledge about the family and about family disorganization in particular.

[1] *See* Natalie F. Friedman, "The Changing Concept of the Family in Social Casework: From Mary Richmond to 1959." Unpublished master's thesis, Columbia University School of Social Work, 1959.

This review will examine social work research in the two general areas identified in the preceding paragraphs: research conducted in or about private family agencies; and social work research concerning the family per se. The breadth of these two areas, and the relatively large amount of research that could be subsumed in them, necessitates the following restrictions:

1. This review will not include studies concerned primarily with the family as a factor in the etiology of social and psychological problems such as delinquency and mental illness.

2. There will be no attempt to review the large body of research on the family that has been conducted in other disciplines. As Goode has noted, more research is reported each year concerning the family than in any other single substantive field of sociology; even the most cursory review of this vast literature would require a chapter in itself.[2] Occasional references, however, will be made to this literature, either to illustrate a point or to suggest a direction for research in social work.

3. Clinical reports will not be covered in this review unless they meet research criteria. One exception to these criteria has been made in the case of the literature on social policy regarding the family.

4. The review will be confined primarily to recent research in the fields to be covered. Some early studies will be mentioned, but no systematic review of them is attempted here. For an overview of the history of social work research in this area the interested reader is referred to Macdonald and especially to Shyne.[3]

5. The review is confined largely to research conducted in the United States, although some references will be made to studies in other countries.

6. For the most part the review is limited to published studies.

7. Finally, although this review is intended to be comprehensive in so far as major trends and developments are concerned, it is selective rather than exhaustive, especially in areas where a large number of studies have been reported, as in the case of research on the multiproblem family.

Within the above limitations, then, this chapter will review social work research related to: (1) the organization and operations of private family agencies; (2) methods of intervention in the family field; (3) family disorganization; and (4) social policy regarding the family.

The Private Family Agency

Social work research focused on the operations of the private family agency has tended to concentrate in two areas. The first area consists of research concerned essentially with problems of organizational efficiency, including principally studies of costs, distribution of staff time, and certain personnel problems. A second direction is seen in studies of the characteristic patterns of service in family agenices.

Organizational Efficiency

Cost analysis. Prompted by a variety of concerns regarding the administrative and fiscal operations of the private family agency, in 1951–52 Hill and Ormsby conducted a cost analysis of the Family Service of Philadelphia.[4] Essentially, what they did

---

[2] William J. Goode, "The Sociology of the Family," in Robert K. Merton, Leonard Broom, and Leonard S. Cottrell, Jr., eds., *Sociology Today* (New York: Basic Books, 1959), pp. 178–196.

[3] Mary E. Macdonald, "Social Work Research: A Perspective," in Norman A. Polansky, ed., *Social Work Research* (Chicago: University of Chicago Press, 1960), pp. 1–23; and Ann W. Shyne, "Casework Research: Past and Present," *Social Casework*, Vol. 43, No. 9 (November 1962), pp. 467–473.

[4] John G. Hill and Ralph Ormsby, "The Philadelphia Cost Study," *Social Work Journal*, Vol. 34, No. 4 (October 1953), pp. 165–168 and 176–177; and Hill and Ormsby, "The Philadelphia Time-Cost Study," in *Proceedings of the National Conference of Social Work* (New York: Columbia University Press, 1953), pp. 205–206.

was to apply well-established principles and methods of cost-accounting to the operations of a family agency, a feat which, as Hill commented later, was previously believed by many to be virtually impossible in social agencies because of the intangible nature of their services.[5] Thus, one of the major contributions of this study was to research methodology in that the investigators developed a systematic procedure for cost analysis of family agencies.[6] The original Philadelphia study was followed by cost analyses of the Family Service Association of Cleveland and the Jewish Family Service of Philadelphia, with strikingly similar findings in all three agencies.[7] Subsequently, cost analysis has been applied in other fields, and principally in child welfare by Schwartz and Wolins, using concepts and methods differing in some respects from those followed by Hill and Ormsby.[8] More recently, Wolins developed a computerized program for the cost analysis of institutions for children, thereby simplifying the mechanics of data-processing and increasing the range of possible analyses. Presumably, similar developments can be expected in the family service field.[9]

[5] John G. Hill, "Cost Analysis of Social Work Service," in Polansky, ed., *op. cit.*, pp. 223–224.

[6] *See* John G. Hill and Ralph Ormsby, *Cost Analysis Method for Casework Agencies* (Philadelphia: Family Service of Philadelphia, 1953); and John C. Hill, Ralph Ormsby, and William B. McCurdy, *Time Analysis Manual: Procedures for Time Analysis in Family Service Agencies, Including Those Which Provide Child Welfare Services* (New York: Family Service Association of America, 1962).

[7] Ralph Ormsby, "Cost Analysis in the Family Field," *Planning Social Services for Urban Needs, Papers on Community Organization at the National Conference on Social Welfare, 1957* (New York: Columbia University Press, 1957), pp. 102–111.

[8] Edward E. Schwartz and Martin Wolins, *Cost Analysis in Child Welfare*, Children's Bureau Publication No. 366 (Washington, D.C.: U.S. Department of Health, Education, and Welfare, Children's Bureau, 1958).

[9] Martin Wolins, *A Manual for Cost Analy-*

Ormsby predicted that the major contribution of cost studies may reside not so much in the information they provide about the costs of agency operations, nor even in the immediate adjustments agencies make in response to this information, but rather in the general questions cost data raise about the way things are done in family agencies and the stimulus this may give to the development of new and improved patterns of operation. The prediction appears to be substantiated by subsequent research developments in this area.

Recording. Perhaps the strongest reactions to the results of the family service cost studies were to the findings that consistently revealed that caseworkers devoted only about one-third of their time to interviews with clients, even though the time studies that produced these findings were a means and not an aim of the cost analyses. There seemed to be a widespread reaction that the proportion of caseworkers' time devoted to direct service to clients was too low, and that this proportion ought to be increased. Accordingly, attention was directed to workers' nondirect-service activities. Of these, the most important single category was recording, which represented from 28.2 to 31.3 percent of casework costs. This activity was examined in a major study of recording, which is reviewed below. Curiously, supervision, the next largest category of activities not involving direct service to clients, has not yet been subjected to systematic research—an omission that is even more surprising in view of some findings to be discussed shortly. In addition, these studies called attention to the cost of the high rate of staff turnover in family agencies—a problem that has since been examined in a major survey of staff losses.

A rather ambitious study of recording was conducted by Frings, Kratovil, and

sis in Institutions for Children, Part I (New York: Child Welfare League of America, 1962).

Polemis in two large family agencies in Chicago.[10] The study employed an experimental design in which three systems of recording were compared: (1) very brief, monthly recording on 6 x 9 cards; (2) brief recording at periodic intervals on 8½ x 11 forms; and (3) essentially traditional narrative-recording with no restrictions on length. These systems were randomly assigned to the nine district offices of the two agencies studied so that each system was tested in three offices. Several outcome measures were employed, including record use, amount of recording, staff satisfaction-dissatisfaction with the systems, and time devoted to the production, use, and discussion of records. The results revealed virtually no differences in the proportion of time workers devoted to recording under the three systems—approximately 24 percent of the workers' total working time. When workers were expected to record at greater length they responded, not by increasing the time they gave to recording, but by falling further behind in their recording. Thus it seemed that the caseworkers followed certain implicit work norms governing the proportion of time they would devote to recording, and expanded or contracted the amount of recording within this time depending on the system used—in what appears to be a special case of Parkinson's law.[11] This interpretation is reinforced by the investigators' observation that—in the eyes of caseworkers —to record with ease and dispatch is "not to belong" to the caseworker group.

Frings also found, as did Kogan and Brown in an earlier study, that caseworkers made very little use of case records for treatment planning.[12] For the worker, whatever values were seen in recording resided in the act of recording itself; the product—the case record—was prepared primarily for use by someone else. By and large, "someone else" was the supervisor, the prime user of case records. Moreover, although the caseworkers did not express a clear preference for any of the recording systems tested, the supervisors' satisfaction with workers' recordings increased in direct relation to the length of the recording. This preference on the part of supervisors is paradoxical, since as the expected length of workers' recording increased, the lag in recording also increased. Supervisors often had to rely on workers' verbal reports, and not their recordings, for information about current activities in their cases. The study findings also indicate that as far as the administrative uses of case records are concerned—such as case assignment and administrative review—brief recording in most instances was quite adequate and often was preferred. In sum, much of the time these caseworkers spent on recording was devoted to the production of material primarily of use to supervisors for nonadministrative purposes.

These findings raise an important and interesting question. Why do supervisors need detailed case-recording? Frings's report tells a great deal about the perceptions of recording by caseworkers, largely because the investigators conducted intensive interviews on the subject with a sample of caseworkers. But the report gives virtually no insight into the function of detailed case-recording for the supervisor. The authors report that they also planned to conduct intensive interviews with the supervisors and administrators, but abandoned the plan on the basis of the highly dubious assumption that supervisors and administrators would say the same things the researchers had heard from caseworkers.

---

[10] John Frings, "Experimental Systems of Recording," *Social Casework*, Vol. 38, No. 2 (February 1957), pp. 55–63; and John Frings, Ruth Kratovil, and Bernice Polemis, *An Assessment of Social Case Recording* (New York: Family Service Association of America, 1958).

[11] *See* C. Northcote Parkinson, *Parkinson's Law and Other Studies in Administration* (Boston: Houghton Mifflin Company, 1957).

[12] Leonard S. Kogan and Benjamin H. Brown, "Two-Year Study of Case Record Uses," *Social Casework*, Vol. 35, No. 6 (June 1954), pp. 252–257.

In view of the contradictions and paradoxes unearthed in this research, studies of the supervisor's role in the agency are not only sorely needed but appear to offer a promising avenue for subsequent research into the operations of family agencies.

Supervision. The need for research on the supervisor's role is reinforced by Tollen's study of what Ormsby called "that bugbear of all agencies, staff turnover." [13] Tollen conducted a survey of staff losses in child welfare and family service agencies throughout the United States. His sample included 2,120 workers in 256 voluntary family agencies that were members of the Family Service Association of America in 1957. A discussion of Tollen's findings will be restricted here largely to this part of his sample. Of all fields studied, the rates of resignation were highest in voluntary family service agencies; 24 percent for caseworkers and 19 percent for all professional staff.[14]

Tollen's report provides a detailed analysis of resignations by employee characteristics, including sex (turnover rates higher for men than women), age (rates higher among younger workers), training (rates greater for untrained), and marital status. One of the findings that should be of great concern to the family service field is that 69 percent of the resignees subsequently went into a field other than family service, and 56 percent of the resignees had no interest in re-employment in the family service field. While such findings obviously have implications for the family service field they also contribute to knowledge about the sociology of social work.

Tollen does, however, report other findings that bear directly on the operations of voluntary family agencies. One major finding, connected with the preceding discussion of Frings's research, is that dissatisfaction with supervision was third in frequency (after "to accept offer of better job" and "moved from community") among the basic reasons for resignation given by the workers studied. And among female caseworkers, when case aides are excluded from the analysis, dissatisfaction with supervision was the most frequently cited basic reason for resignation. Unfortunately, Tollen obtained very little data about the nature of this dissatisfaction, but the information he was able to collect suggests that a principal complaint may have been that supervision was too close and pervasive. Tollen believes that resignations based on dissatisfaction with supervision may be preventable, and if so this suggests a possible alternative to the dominant approach taken to the turnover problem thus far—the advocacy of increased salaries for caseworkers.[15] Tollen also advances a strong argument for research "to determine the significance of supervision for supervisors, those supervised, and for the social agencies," a suggestion which also has been made by Fanshel and others.[16] Such research would be especially timely in view of the questions many practitioners currently are raising about supervision.[17]

---

[13] William Tollen, *Study of Staff Losses: Child Welfare and Family Service Agencies*, Children's Bureau Publication No. 383 (Washington, D.C.: U.S. Department of Health, Education, and Welfare, Children's Bureau, 1960); and Ormsby, *op. cit.*, p. 109.

[14] Rate of resignation expresses the number of resignations during a period as a percent of the total number of employees on duty at the beginning of the period.

---

[15] *See* Nathaniel Goodman, "Salaries, Costs, and Workloads," *Social Work*, Vol. 4, No. 1 (January 1959), pp. 49–57; and Welfare Federation of Cleveland, *Pricing Casework Jobs* (Cleveland: Welfare Education, 1956).

[16] Tollen, *op. cit.*, p. 103; and David Fanshel, "Administrative Research in Social Welfare: A Review of Current Trends," in Fanshel, ed., *Research in Social Welfare Administration* (New York: National Association of Social Workers, 1962).

[17] *See* Lucille N. Austin, "Supervision in Social Work" in Russell H. Kurtz, ed., *Social Work Year Book 1960* (New York: National Association of Social Workers, 1960), pp. 579–586.

Characteristic Patterns of Service

A body of research findings gradually is being accumulated about the characteristic patterns of service in voluntary family agencies. Thus far, most of this research has been descriptive and much of it has consisted of unpublished self-surveys conducted by individual agencies.[18] However, some studies involving a number of agencies or employing more sophisticated methods have appeared in the literature.[19] One of the major results of these studies has been to focus attention on the length of casework service. A consistent finding of such studies has been the high proportion of cases that do not continue beyond the initial interview—53 percent in McCurdy's 1954 survey of 60 FSAA member agencies, and 55 percent in Beck's 1960 study of 280 family agencies—and the very small proportion of cases that continue in casework for five interviews or more—16 percent in the McCurdy study; and 20 percent in Beck's research. Findings such as these have stimulated a great deal of research focused on the correlates of client continuance-discontinuance in casework treatment. This research will be discussed later.

Surprisingly, although the "short-term" or "brief-service" case has attracted attention from researchers interested in problems of social casework, the finding that for most clients the period during which they are accessible to treatment is extremely brief does not appear to have received a like amount of attention from casework theorists. Their formulations still seem to be predicated, for the most part, on an assumption that the model, or at least the modal case is one in which treatment is more prolonged. This is not to say that the brief-service case has been completely ignored in casework theory, but only that work with these cases has received little attention relative to their numerical importance.

These studies also have presented data about the demographic characteristics of clients served by voluntary family agencies, and some studies, especially those of Beck, Fanshel, and Coleman, have investigated the relationships between some of these demographic characteristics and service patterns in the agency.[20] The characteristic that has received most attention is client social class—a focus undoubtedly stimulated by the findings of Hollingshead and Redlich.[21]

Briefly, to mention some illustrative findings of the Beck study, the occupational status distribution of family agency clients was remarkably similar to that found in the general population, although both the upper and lower extremes were slightly over-represented in the client group. As one might expect, highly unionized occupational groups were under-represented; there were, in fact, no referrals from labor unions in the client group studied (N of cases = 577; N of persons = 2,250). Client social class was found to be positively associated with worker-client agreement on the

---

[18] For examples of such studies, *see* the listing in *Research and Study Projects Reported by FSAA Member Agencies*, issued annually since 1957 by the Family Service Association of America.

[19] *See*, for example, Dorothy Fahs Beck, *Patterns in Use of Family Agency Service* (New York: Family Service Association of America, 1962); David Fanshel, "An Overview of One Agency's Casework Operation" (Pittsburgh: Family and Children's Services, 1958) (mimeographed); Fanshel, "A Study of Caseworkers' Perceptions of Their Clients," *Social Casework*, Vol. 39, No. 10 (December 1958), pp. 543–551; and William B. McCurdy, *Statistics of Family Casework, An Analysis of 1954 Data from 60 F.S.A.A. Member Agencies* (New York: Family Service Association of America, 1955).

[20] Beck, *op. cit.;* Fanshel, "An Overview of One Agency's Casework Operation"; Fanshel, "A Study of Caseworkers' Perceptions of Their Clients"; and Jules V. Coleman *et al.*, "A Comparative Study of a Psychiatric Clinic and a Family Agency," *Social Casework*, Vol. 38, Nos. 1–2 (January–February 1957), pp. 3–8 (Part I), and pp. 74–80 (Part II).

[21] August B. Hollingshead and Fredrick C. Redlich, *Social Class and Mental Illness* (New York: John Wiley & Sons, 1958).

problem, appropriateness of client expectations of service, number of interviews, and client initiative in termination; class was inversely related to the number of problems the worker saw in the case. In addition, associations were found between client social class and source of referral, types of problems reported by clients, and the kinds of services requested by the client. Most of Beck's findings with regard to social class are consistent with those reported earlier by Fanshel and Coleman.

A few studies have begun to focus on the important subject of the relationship between structural variations in agencies and service patterns. Thus, one of the aims of the Community Service Society's study of the aged is to test the relative effectiveness of providing services through a special unit serving only aged persons, versus the provision of services in nonspecialized district offices of the agency. A complete report of this project had not yet appeared at the time this review was written (1965), but preliminary reports indicate that the results significantly favor the specialized unit.[22]

Since alternative explanations for the findings are possible, additional research is needed before any definitive conclusions can be drawn regarding the relative advantages of specialized versus general practice settings. Beck, in the study cited above, compared agencies that used a waiting list with those that did not, and found that absence of a waiting list was associated with a decrease in the proportion of cases carried through to completion of service. In subsequent reports Beck has promised to report an analysis of differences in service patterns by size of agency, a variable that Thomas found to be important in his research on the public welfare agency.[23]

Future Research on the Family Agency

Research on the family agency has made little use of the conceptual tools and research methods developed for the study of organizations, a deficiency that also has been noted in other fields of social work.[24] Thus, there have been no studies of decision-making, communication, or staff conflict in family agencies, even though (1) some tools for studying these subjects are available and have been applied in other fields of social work, and (2) there is reason to believe—on the basis of the findings presented by Frings, Kratovil, and Polemis, for example—that such studies would be of value to the field. It seems especially unfortunate that as yet there have been no case studies of the family agency as an organization—a type of research of which one of the best known examples is *The Mental Hospital*.[25] Most studies of this type in the health and welfare fields have been conducted in institutions, but similar research could be done in noninstitutional settings. Such studies would help to explicate some of the paradoxes and problems identified by Frings, Tollen, and others.

Another major deficiency in this research area is the lack of studies dealing with questions about the goals and functions of family agencies vis-à-vis other fields of social welfare. One study that does bear on these questions is the comparison of a psychiatric clinic and a family agency conducted by Coleman.[26] Perhaps the most striking result of the Coleman study is the high degree of similarity between the two settings in the persons served and in certain patterns of service. One of the major points of difference between the settings, as reported by Coleman—that both staff and clients construe client problems in different terms in one setting as compared to the

[22] Institute of Welfare Research, *Annual Report, 1960–61* (New York: Community Service Society, 1961).

[23] Edwin J. Thomas, "Role Conceptions and Organizational Size," *American Sociological Review*, Vol. 24, No. 1 (February 1959), pp. 30–37.

[24] *See* Fanshel, ed., *op. cit.*

[25] Alfred H. Stanton and Morris S. Schwartz, *The Mental Hospital* (New York: Basic Books, 1954).

[26] Coleman *et al., op. cit.*

other—is intriguing and merits further examination.[27]

Two recently completed studies, one by Levin, and the other by Cloward and Epstein, have analyzed the changing functions of private family service agencies over time.[28] Both of these studies conclude that there is a strong and continuing trend in family agencies toward the provision of highly specialized and skilled services "to an increasingly upper-class level of society." [29] Commenting on this trend, Cloward and Epstein suggest that "the problem may be that the [family service] field has increasingly developed a strategy of help which is neither practicable for nor congenial to the needs and interests of the low-income person." [30] In any event, these studies raise important policy questions concerning the future of the family agency and its place in the spectrum of social welfare services.

Social Work Treatment in the Family Field

Research concerning methods of intervention in the family field has been concentrated thus far in three major areas: (1) treatment *outcome*, and especially the prob-

lems of measuring the results of casework service; (2) factors associated with client *continuance* in treatment and the characteristics of *brief-service* cases; and (3) *methods and techniques* of treatment. Some of the studies reviewed overlap more than one of these three areas, but for the purposes of this review it seemed useful to consider each area separately.

Measurement and Results

One of the predominant emphases in research concerning the outcome of casework treatment in the family field has been the attempt to develop tools and instruments for measuring change in clients, or essentially basic research on methodology. At first glance this strategy would appear to be a sound one, since research on the effectiveness of treatment is hardly possible unless change can be measured with a reasonable degree of reliability and validity. The results of these research efforts, however, raise some questions about the wisdom of this strategy at the present stage of social work knowledge, or at least about the value of the particular approaches taken to the solution of this measurement problem.

The Movement Scale. The most important research effort to date in this area —at least insofar as persistent effort and sheer volume of reported findings is concerned—is the work that has gone into the development and testing of the Movement Scale at the Community Service Society of New York.[31] The CSS approach to the measurement of change consists essentially of an attempt to standardize caseworkers' judgments so that they can be used as reliable measures of movement in clients.

Parenthetically, it should be noted that although the work on the Movement Scale

---

[27] For example, family agency clients tended to present their problems in social and interpersonal terms whereas psychiatric clinic patients were inclined to construe their difficulties as psychological ones. Comparable differences were noted between staff members in the two types of agencies. An important question is the degree to which these tendencies reflect (1) actual differences in the problems clients bring to these two types of agencies, or (2) differences in perceptual and cognitive orientations to similar phenomena.

[28] Herman Levin, "The Future of Voluntary Family and Children's Social Work: A Historical View," *Social Service Review*, Vol. 38, No. 2 (June 1964), pp. 163–173; and Richard A. Cloward and Irwin Epstein, "Private Social Welfare's Disengagement from the Poor: The Case of Family Adjustment Agencies" (New York: Columbia University School of Social Work, 1964) (mimeographed).

[29] Levin, *op. cit.*, p. 163.

[30] *Op. cit.*, p. 71.

[31] Research on the Movement Scale spans a period of some twenty years, from about 1943 when Dollard began to tackle the measurement problem to the present. *See* Edna Wasser, "Classified Bibliography: CSS Movement Scale" (New York: Community Service Society, 1960). (Mimeographed.)

can be classified—by virtue of its methodological aims—as basic social work research, some of the major research strategy decisions made in the course of developing the Movement Scale apparently were dictated by administrative rather than research considerations. Thus, for example, as both Hunt and Kogan have noted, the original impetus for the efforts that resulted in the Movement Scale came in the form of a directive from the agency board asking the Institute of Welfare Research "to determine and express how casework is carried on, at what cost, and with what success." [32]

Subsequently, when it was found that Dollard and Mowrer's Distress Relief Quotient, the first measure of movement developed out of the CSS effort, had only a low order correlation with workers' judgment of movement, a decision was made to abandon work on the DRQ in favor of an effort to refine workers' judgments so that they could be used as measures of change.[33] According to published reports, this decision appears to have been based primarily on administrative considerations, principally the much higher cost involved in use of the DRQ and the greater ease with which a measure based on workers' judgment could be made a routine part of agency operations. A second justification for this decision was the finding that workers' judgments were highly reliable, but since this was also true of the DRQ measure, reliability does not appear to have been the decisive factor. The intent of these remarks is not to discount the importance of such administrative considerations—in fact, one of the aims of the developers of the Movement Scale was to develop a measure that

could be used routinely in the agency—but rather simply to note that it is not clear what course the investigators might have followed if they had been guided entirely by research objectives. As a postscript, neither the DRQ nor the Movement Scale predicted movement in the CSS follow-up study, so that crucial questions about the validity of both measures still remain unanswered.

The Movement Scale studies established a pattern that has been followed, with relatively minor modifications, in most other attempts to assess the outcome of social work service in the family field. One feature of this pattern is the reliance on workers' judgments as measures for other variables, particularly client variables. Among the most frequently cited results of the Movement Scale studies are the findings that caseworkers can make reliable judgments and, moreover, that the reliability of their judgments can be increased appreciably by training and by using anchored judgment scales. These findings have been reaffirmed, with great regularity, in other studies employing this method of measurement, of which two particularly well-known examples are the St. Paul Family-Centered Project and the Motivation, Capacity, and Opportunity (MCO) studies at the University of Chicago.[34]

In general, it has been assumed—or at least investigators have proceeded as if

[32] J. McVicker Hunt, "Measuring Movement in Casework," *Social Casework*, Vol. 29, No. 9 (November 1948), p. 343. *See also* Leonard S. Kogan, J. McVicker Hunt, and Phyllis F. Bartelme, *A Follow-up Study of the Results of Social Casework* (New York: Family Service Association of America, 1953).

[33] John Dollard and O. H. Mowrer, "A Method of Measuring Tension in Written Documents," *Journal of Abnormal and Social Psychology*, Vol. 42, No. 1 (January 1947), pp. 3–32.

[34] Ludwig L. Geismar and Beverly Ayres, *Measuring Family Functioning* (St. Paul: Greater St. Paul United Fund and Council, 1960); Lilian Ripple, "Motivation, Capacity, and Opportunity as Related to the Use of Casework Service: Theoretical Base and Plan of Study," *Social Service Review*, Vol. 29, No. 2 (June 1955), pp. 172–193; and Lilian Ripple and Ernestina Alexander, "Motivation, Capacity, and Opportunity as Related to the Use of Casework Service: Nature of the Client's Problem," *Social Service Review*, Vol. 30, No. 1 (March 1956), pp. 38–54. The MCO studies do not, however, use judgments to measure the outcome or criterion variables, but judgments do constitute the principal measures for predictor variables. Many of the problems in the use of judgments as measures apply regardless of which variables the judgments are intended to measure.

they assumed—that high reliability coefficients vindicate the use of judgments as measures. Thus many researchers have taken pains to insure high coefficients of reliability, including steps such as the elimination of judges who do not agree with a criterion group of judges.[35] However, it has become increasingly difficult to be sanguine about the significance to be attached to high reliability coefficients per se in view of recent analyses of the relationship between judgment reliability and predictive validity, the pitfalls in the use of conventional correlation techniques to estimate judgment reliability, and the limits of the social worker as a processor of information.[36] Concern about these and other problems connected with clinical judgments has stimulated a number of studies in social work of the judgment process and the factors affecting it.[37]

A second feature of Movement Scale research, which also has been followed in many other studies—including the St. Paul and the MCO projects—is the use of case records as the raw data for judgment measures. Many problems have been raised in relation to the use of case records for research purposes, but one difficulty that has received less attention than it deserves is the degree to which case records accurately describe their subjects.[38] Since judgment measures based on case records consist, in fact, of judgments about other judgments, error in the initial judgment made by the author of a case record may well be amplified when filtered through the inferential screen of another worker whose judgments will be treated as measures of the original phenomena. Thus, although some studies have reported that judgments tend to be more reliable when based on reading than on listening or observing, these findings may reveal more about the limitations of judges than about the adequacy of the different media used.[39]

[35] *See* Ripple, *op. cit.*; and Ripple and Alexander, *op. cit.*

[36] *See* Donald N. Buckner, "The Predictability of Ratings as a Function of Interrater Agreement," *Journal of Applied Psychology*, Vol. 43, No. 1 (February 1959), pp. 60–64; Sol L. Garfield and D. C. Affleck, "Therapists' Judgments Concerning Patients Considered for Psychotherapy," *Journal of Consulting Psychology*, Vol. 25, No. 6 (December 1961), pp. 505–509; Charles D. Windle and Harvey F. Dingham, "Interrater Agreement and Predictive Validity," *Journal of Applied Psychology*, Vol. 44, No. 3 (June 1960), pp. 203, 204; Robert R. Bush, "A New Look in Measurement Theory," in *Use of Judgments as Data in Social Work Research* (New York: National Association of Social Workers, 1959), pp. 89–95; and Henry Miller and James Bieri, "An Informational Analysis of Clinical Judgment," *Journal of Abnormal and Social Psychology*, Vol. 67, No. 4 (October 1963), pp. 317–325.

[37] James Bieri, Ben Avis Orcutt, and Robin Leaman, "Anchoring Effects in Sequential Judgments," *Journal of Abnormal and Social Psychology*, Vol. 67, No. 6 (December 1963), pp. 616–623; Scott Briar, "Clinical Judgment in Foster Care Placement," *Child Welfare*, Vol. 42, No. 4 (April 1963), pp. 161–169; Scott Briar, "Use of Theory in Studying Effects of Client Social Class on Students' Judgments," *Social Work*, Vol. 6, No. 3 (July 1961), pp. 91–97; Miller and Bieri, *op.*

cit.; Roger R. Miller, "An Experimental Study of the Observational Process in Casework," *Social Work*, Vol. 3, No. 2 (April 1958), pp. 96–102; Harold L. Plotnick, "The Relation Between Selected Personality Characteristics of Social Work Students and Accuracy in Predicting the Behavior of Clients," unpublished doctoral dissertation, Columbia University School of Social Work, 1961; and Tony Tripodi and James Bieri, "Information Transmission in Clinical Judgments as a Function of Stimulus Dimensionality and Cognitive Complexity," *Journal of Personality*, Vol. 32, No. 1 (March 1964), pp. 119–137.

[38] Ann W. Shyne, "Use of Available Material," in Polansky, ed., *op. cit.*, pp. 106–124.

[39] *See* Helen Bourke and Donald W. Fiske, "Factors Influencing the Prediction of Behavior from a Diagnostic Interview," *Journal of Consulting Psychology*, Vol. 21, No. 1 (February 1957), pp. 78–80; J. McVicker Hunt, "On the Judgment of Social Workers as a Source of Information in Social Work Research," in *Use of Judgments as Data in Social Work Research*, pp. 38–53; and Joseph Luft, "Differences in Prediction Based on Hearing Versus Reading Verbatim Clinical Interviews," *Journal of Consulting Psychology*, Vol. 14, No. 2 (April 1951), pp. 115–119.

In view of these and other serious problems in the use of judgment measures, it is encouraging to note an increasing trend toward use of more objective data, including judgments based on first-hand observations and responses obtained directly from clients.[40] A plea for even wider use of more objective measures, including tests and other standardized instruments, has been voiced by Borgatta, Fanshel, and Meyer.[41]

Results. It is not yet possible to state any firm conclusions from the research literature about the general effectiveness of social work treatment in the family field. The studies that have been reported—such as the work on the Movement Scale, the St. Paul Family-Centered Project, and other similar but less ambitious efforts—admittedly have not incorporated the controls and sampling procedures required to separate the influence of social work service from other factors affecting outcome.[42]

With these reservations in mind, some interesting points of convergence in several of these studies can be noted.

In general, the results of many of these studies, with relatively minor variations, are consistent with each other. They follow a pattern typical of many global effectiveness studies in psychotherapy in finding that roughly one-third of the clients show substantial progress or movement, one-third show some progress, and one-third either show no change or become worse.[43] The Movement Scale studies and the St. Paul Family-Centered Project converge at a more specific level. Both projects used seven-step scales to measure movement, but apart from this the movement measures used in these two approaches differed markedly (e.g., movement in the St. Paul studies was measured by the difference between before and after ratings of adjustment, whereas in the CSS research movement per se was rated; and in the St. Paul project movement denoted change in *family* functioning not *individual* adjustment as in the CSS studies). Nevertheless, it is striking that the mean movement scores obtained in these two studies were nearly identical: .44 of a scale step in the St. Paul project as compared to .43 of a scale step in the components of movement study.[44] It would be premature, however, to draw any conclusions from what may prove to have been a coincidental similarity in movement scores.

Both the CSS and the St. Paul studies have attempted to relate movement to other variables. Ratings of initial adjustment at case-opening generally were not good pre-

[40] *See*, for example, Margaret Blenkner, "Part I—The Research Design and Preliminary Findings," in *Experimental Research in Social Work: Three Papers on the CSS Study in Services for the Agency* (New York: Community Service Society, 1959); Fanshel, "An Overview of One Agency's Casework Operation," and "A Study of Caseworkers' Perceptions of Their Clients"; and Henry J. Meyer and Edgar F. Borgatta, "Social Agency and School as the Context for Studies of Mental Health: Research in Progress," *Social Work*, Vol. 5, No. 1 (January 1960), pp. 21–26.

[41] Edgar F. Borgatta, David Fanshel, and Henry J. Meyer, *Social Workers' Perceptions of Clients* (New York: Russell Sage Foundation, 1960).

[42] *See* Kogan, Hunt, and Bartelme, *op. cit.*; Ludwig L. Geismar and Beverly Ayres, *Patterns of Change in Problem Families* (St. Paul: Greater St. Paul United Fund and Council, 1959); A. A. Heckman, "Measuring the Effectiveness of Agency Services," *Journal of Social Casework*, Vol. 29, No. 10 (December 1948), pp. 394–399; Leonard S. Kogan, "Evaluative Techniques in Social Casework," *Social Service Review*, Vol. 26, No. 3 (September 1952), pp. 305–309; Malcolm Preston, Emily Mudd, and Hazel B. Froscher, "Factors Affecting Movement in

Casework," *Social Casework*, Vol. 24, No. 3 (March 1953), pp. 103–111; and Preston *et al.*, "Some Results from Research at the Marriage Council of Philadelphia," *Marriage and Family Living*, Vol. 12, No. 3 (Summer 1950), pp. 104–105.

[43] *See*, for example, H. J. Eysenck, "The Effects of Psychotherapy: An Evaluation," *Journal of Consulting Psychology*, Vol. 16, No. 5 (October 1952), pp. 319–324.

[44] Ayres, *op. cit.*; and Ann W. Shyne and Leonard S. Kogan, "A Study of Components of Movement," *Social Casework*, Vol. 39, No. 6 (June 1958), pp. 333–342.

dictors of movement, although the St. Paul research found a low-order negative correlation between opening status and change. In both sets of studies significant relationships were found between movement and *selected components* of adjustment at case-opening. In the Shyne-Kogan study the number of interviews was found to have a low (.20) positive correlation with movement, thereby reaffirming a finding reported by Blenkner in an earlier CSS study.[45] The latter study suggests, however, that the nature of the relationship between number of interviews and movement is rather obscure. Blenkner found five factors that were related to movement but not to number of interviews and, conversely, four factors found to be predictive of number of interviews were unrelated to movement. This subject is further confounded by the finding in the Shyne-Kogan study that number of interviews is unrelated to change in level of adjustment from case-opening to closing, even though change in adjustment level and movement are highly correlated with each other. Apart from a variety of ad hoc explanations, the theoretical significance of these findings is not clear—a point made by Macdonald in a critique of the Shyne-Kogan study.[46]

More generally, outcome studies in the family field typically have not been systematically articulated to theory. For this reason the findings have been interpreted on an *ex post facto* basis, and there is a strong possibility that some of the associations reported may be spurious, especially those derived from correlation analyses. It may be that the untheoretical character of this research also accounts in part for the fact that it has had little visible influence on casework practice and theory.[47]

Attempts to validate outcome measures and to determine the permanence of change during treatment by means of follow-up studies were remarkably similar in that both types of studies found: (1) the gains made during the course of treatment generally were sustained in the period from case-closing to follow-up; and (2) movement from closing to follow-up was not associated with movement during treatment, as measured by the scales developed in these projects (i.e., the Movement Scale in the case of CSS, and the Family Functioning Scale in the St. Paul project). However, movement from closing to follow-up was found to be related to other variables, including level of functioning at closing and workers' predictions of movement from closing to follow-up. Thus, these studies were unsuccessful in their attempts to validate the movement measures used as predictors of client functioning subsequent to treatment. However, as the investigators point out, it probably is not reasonable to expect a linear relationship between movement during treatment and the subsequent course of the client's functioning, because—to mention just one of several reasons—of the many other factors that may influence client adjustment following treatment. Some other attempts to establish the concurrent validity of the Movement Scale in relation to other measures have met with more success, such as the high correlation between judged movement and change in level of functioning from case opening to closing reported by Kogan, Hunt, and Bartelme; and the successful attempts by Koret and Rubin, and Davids and Talmadge to relate change as measured by the movement scale to client responses on the Rorschach.[48]

---

[45] Margaret Blenkner, "Predictive Factors in the Initial Interview in Family Casework," *Social Service Review*, Vol. 28, No. 1 (March 1954), pp. 65–73.

[46] Macdonald, *op. cit.*

[47] For one of the few exceptions to this statement, *see* Nathaniel Goodman, "The Use of the Movement Scale with Brief Recording," *Social Casework*, Vol. 39, No. 5 (May 1958), pp. 282–285.

---

[48] Kogan, Hunt, and Bartelme, *op. cit.*; Sidney Koret and Eli Z. Rubin, "Utilization of Projective Tests as a Prediction of Casework Movement," *American Journal of Orthopsychiatry*, Vol. 27, No. 2 (April 1957), pp. 365–374; and Anthony Davids and Max Talmadge, "Utility of the Rorschach in Predicting Movement in Psychiatric Casework," *Journal of Consulting Psychology* (in press).

Many of the methodological weaknesses in the studies reviewed above appear to have been overcome in two major studies of effectiveness still in process, namely, the CSS study of services to the aged, directed by Margaret Blenkner, and the Meyer and Borgatta study of preventive treatment of adolescent girls, a project involving cooperation between a high school and a family agency.[49] Both studies are noteworthy for their use of carefully conceived experimental designs, including control groups, and for the use of other measures in addition to the judgments of social workers.

Continuance-Discontinuance and the Short-Term Case

In recent years, interest in global measurement and assessment of over-all effectiveness has been supplanted by studies of continuance in casework treatment. That is, investigators in the latter area argue that continuance in treatment is a necessary condition for its successful use—the client cannot be treated *in absentia*. Thus, even though continuance is not equivalent to successful use of treatment, knowledge about the correlates of continuance-discontinuance contributes directly to an understanding of the determinants of success and failure in treatment. Or, to put it differently, continuance and discontinuance constitute outcomes of treatment, at least in the early phases, and these outcomes posses an advantage over other outcome indicators, such as the Movement Scale,

in that they can be objectively defined. Thus, the studies in this area represent efforts to examine more specific and delimited aspects of treatment effectiveness, a strategy that also has been followed increasingly in research on psychotherapy.[50]

Since several excellent reviews of research on continuance and short-term cases are available, one by Levinger, a selective review by Shyne, and a somewhat more delimited review by Rosenfeld, the present discussion will be confined to an examination of some of the general characteristics of continuance research and of some convergences in the findings of these studies.[51]

Continuance studies. The typical approach in studies of continuance has been to compare a group of continuers with a group of discontinuers on a variety of variables and attributes in an effort to identify items that discriminate significantly between the two groups. Continuers are defined as clients who continue beyond an arbitrarily fixed number of interviews, ranging from one interview in some studies to five in others, and conversely, the discontinuers consist of clients who leave treatment before the fixed number of interviews (clients who discontinue early *by plan* are typically treated separately or excluded from these studies). Studies of continuance in social work usually rely on social workers' judgments as measures of the var-

---

[49] Margaret Blenkner and Julius Jahn, "A Research and Demonstration Project in Services for the Aging" (New York: Community Service Society, 1956) (mimeographed); *Experimental Research in Social Work: Three Papers on the CSS Study in Services for the Aging* (New York: Community Service Society, 1959); Julius Jahn, *The Design of an Experiment to Measure the Effectiveness and Costs of Programs of Services for Aging Persons* (New York: Community Service Society, 1957); and Meyer and Borgatta, *op. cit.*

[50] *See* E. A. Rubinstein and M. B. Parloff, eds., *Research in Psychotherapy* (Washington, D.C.: American Psychological Association, 1959); and Hans H. Strupp and Lester Luborsky, eds., *Research in Psychotherapy*, Vol. 2 (Washington, D.C.: American Psychological Association, 1962).

[51] George Levinger, "Continuance in Casework and Other Helping Relationships: A Review of Current Research," *Social Work*, Vol. 5, No. 3 (July 1960), pp. 40–51; Ann W. Shyne, "What Research Tells Us About Short-Term Cases in Family Agencies," *Social Casework*, Vol. 38, No. 5 (May 1957), pp. 223–231; and Jona Michael Rosenfeld, "Strangeness Between Helper and Client: A Possible Explanation of Non-Use of Available Professional Help," *Social Service Review*, Vol. 38, No. 1 (March 1964), pp. 17–25.

iables expected to discriminate between continuers and discontinuers. Some of the major problems in these studies can best be illustrated by examining one of the continuance projects in detail, namely, the Motivation, Capacity and Opportunity (MCO) studies conducted by Ripple, Alexander, and Werble.[52]

The MCO project constitutes the most ambitious and sophisticated study of continuance in social work to date. Although the final report of this project has not yet appeared, several preliminary reports have been published. The design of the MCO studies incorporates several advantageous features usually not found in other studies of continuance in social work:

1. The MCO studies were conducted within a theoretical framework that stipulated the major factors expected to discriminate continuers from discontinuers, i.e., motivation, capacity, environmental opportunity, and service opportunity. Thus, the measurement instruments used consist of items developed for their relevance to the theoretical framework and not an assortment of essentially unrelated items selected on an ad hoc basis.

2. A stringent definition of continuance was used, so that continuers were clients who continued beyond the fourth interview and had at least a fifth interview. This cutting point was selected on the basis of the finding that while the client dropout rate continues to be high to the fourth interview, after the fourth interview the rate drops off sharply, thus pointing to an empirically meaningful cutting point for defining continuers and discontinuers.[53]

3. Although the MCO studies rely on workers' judgments as measures of the major discriminating variables—as have most other studies of continuance in social work—elaborate steps were taken to prevent judges from knowing whether the client being judged was a continuer or a discontinuer.

4. Finally, and perhaps most important, a concerted effort was made to push beyond the discovery of items that discriminate the two groups to the construction of a typology related to continuance and therefore, hypothetically, to use of treatment.

The typology developed by Ripple and Alexander deserves some discussion, if for no other reason than that it is widely known and used by practitioners and teachers of casework practice. Moreover, in view of the importance of diagnostic typologies in the development of social work theory, the construction of a typology that is discriminating when applied to a phenomenon as important as continuance would represent an achievement of considerable theoretical and practical importance.[54]

The Ripple-Alexander typology is essentially a classification into two categories of problems for solution: (1) external problems, and (2) psychological problems. Each of these categories is further divided into subtypes of external and psychological problems. Clients in the external problems category were found to have a significantly higher rate (55 percent) of continuance than clients in the psychological problems group (33 percent). Analysis of the items measuring the motivation, capacity and opportunity variables revealed that some factors associated with continuance in one of the two major problem categories were not always associated with continuance in

---

[52] Lilian Ripple, "Factors Associated with Continuance in Casework Service," *Social Work*, Vol. 2, No. 1 (January 1957), pp. 87–94; Ripple, "Motivation, Capacity, and Opportunity as Related to the Use of Casework Services: Theoretical Base and Plan of Study"; Ripple and Alexander, *op. cit.*, and Beatrice Werble, "Motivation, Capacity, and Opportunity in Services to Adolescent Clients: Major Findings," *Social Work*, Vol. 3, No. 4 (October 1959), pp. 22–30.

[53] Ripple, "Motivation, Capacity, and Opportunity as Related to the Use of Casework Services: Theoretical Base and Plan of Study," pp. 176–177.

[54] *See* Ernest Greenwood, "Social Science and Social Work: A Theory of Their Relationship," *Social Service Review*, Vol. 29, No. 1 (March 1955), pp. 20–33.

TABLE 1. CONTINUERS AND DISCONTINUERS BY PRESENCE OR ABSENCE OF NEGATIVE
FACTORS AND TYPE OF PROBLEM [a]

Group	Total	Continuers	Discontinuers	Proportion of Continuers
Negative Factors Present [b]	198	26	172	.13
Psychological Problems	150	21	129	.14
External Problems	48	5	43	.10
Negative Factors Absent	153	118	35	.77
Psychological Problems	71	51	20	.72
External Problems	82	67	15	.82

[a] Based on data presented in Tables 1 and 2 of Lilian Ripple, "Factors Associated with Continuance in Casework Service," *Social Work*, Vol. 2, No. 1 (January 1957), pp. 92, 94.
[b] This group includes group IV in Table 1 and groups III and IV in Table 2 of Ripple.

the other category. Subsequently, an attempt was made to construct subclassifications in each category by various combinations of continuance-discriminating items, and in 1957 Ripple reported four such subgroups for each of the two major problem categories.[55] Graduated differences in the proportion of continuers were reported for these subgroups, thus suggesting a typology with considerable power to differentiate continuers from discontinuers.

Secondary analysis of the data provided by Ripple suggests, however, that continuance actually is *unrelated* to problem classification per se, and that the relation between type of problem and continuance reported by Ripple can be attributed to a set of factors that appear to be differently distributed in the external and psychological problems groups. Specifically, the four subgroups that Ripple constructed in each of the two major problem categories (i.e., external and psychological problems) include subgroups distinguished solely by the presence of some "negative factors" (i.e., cases in which the client was judged to have negative motivation *or* the worker was rated as not encouraging *or* the environment was judged to be restrictive and unmodifiable).[56] Examination of the num-

ber of clients judged to have some of these negative attributes in the external and psychological problems groups reveals a much higher proportion of such clients in the psychological problems category (68 per cent) than in the external problems group (37 percent). When continuance is analyzed by problem with the presence of negative factors held constant, as shown in Table 1, the relationship between problem and continuance disappears.

Table 1 indicates that the differences found in continuance rates, which Ripple associates with problem, can be attributed to the presence or absence of negative factors. Moreover, the absence of negative factors alone approaches the maximum discriminative power of Ripple's subgroups. This analysis raises another question: why is the incidence of negative factors greater in the psychological than in the external problems group? One possible answer is provided by the fact that worker and client are more likely to differ in their definitions of the problem in the psychological problems group than in the external problems group. Such differences between client and worker have been found to be related to continuance in a number of studies.[57]

Subsequently, Werble attempted to develop another problem classification for

[55] See "Factors Associated with Continuance in Casework Service."
[56] *Ibid.*, pp. 92–94. The specific subgroups identified here are subgroup IV in the external problems category, and subgroups III

and IV in the psychological problems category.
[57] See, for example, Rosenfeld, *op. cit.*

prediction of continuance in adolescent clients. Werble's scheme consisted of two basic categories: (1) behavior resulting in social conflict; and (2) little evidence of social conflict. Each category was divided into two subgroups. Although, as Werble noted, there are evident differences in continuance trends between Werble's basic categories, analysis of the data reported reveals that these trends are not statistically significant.[58] Nevertheless, Werble proceeded to conduct separate analyses within each major diagnostic category. The major discriminating variable reported by Werble is not presence or absence of a set of negative factors, but motivation scores, which were found to be significantly associated with continuance in both of the major problem categories. Secondary analysis of Werble's data—along lines similar to that reported above for Ripple's data—reveals no differences in continuance by problem when motivation scores are controlled. Rather, the differences reported appear to be attributable to motivation scores alone.

While it is not suggested that the above problems appear in all studies of continuance in social work, the tendency in most other continuance studies to use a large array of loosely related factors in the expectation that some will discriminate increases the risk of obtaining spurious findings. The use of a conceptual framework, as in the MCO studies, provides a safeguard against this risk, although not a perfect one. Thus Ripple reports that when judges could not rate the role played by other people in the case because of insufficient information, the client was likely to be a discontinuer, and Werble notes that adolescents tended to continue if "the adolescent and the study judge were in agreement on the problem."[59] The behavior of the study judge vis-à-vis the case cannot conceivably have any direct influence on client continuance. Thus, the reason

for even reporting such findings is unclear unless there is some basis for thinking that the responses of the judges reflect meaningful characteristics of the clients or workers.

The MCO studies can serve to illustrate another difficulty in studies of continuance: a biased judgment can be introduced if the judge knows the continuance status of the client. If the judge does have this information, his judgments may simply reflect his assumptions about continuers and discontinuers compounded by a halo effect, which might lead him to find negative factors for discontinuers and positive factors for continuers. As noted earlier, the MCO studies attempted to eliminate such biases by several procedures, and principally through the use of "decoy" cases.[60] Since continuers were defined as clients who continued beyond the fourth interview, if the judge received a case to rate in which only two or three interviews were held, he would know automatically that the client was a discontinuer (a separate set of judgments were made at the end of the first interview for all clients in the sample). To reduce this problem decoy cases were constructed, or cases "for which the judge was given only two or three interviews although, in fact, the client had four interviews."[61] This device was designed to keep the judges off balance so that when they received a case with only two or three interviews they could not know whether the client was a discontinuer or a decoy. While this procedure would prevent the judge from reliably identifying the discontinuers, it does not deal with the strong possibility that the judges were able to identify the continuers. According to Ripple, of those clients expected to continue after the first interview, only about 30 percent continued for four interviews, a dropout rate of approximately 70 percent.[62] Of those clients who had a

---

[58] For the data presented, *see* Werble, *op. cit.*, p. 25, Table 1; $\chi^2 = 5.94$, d.f. $= 3$, $.20 > p > .10$.

[59] *Ibid.*, p. 28.

[60] *See* Ripple, "Motivation, Capacity, and Opportunity as Related to the Use of Casework Service: Nature of the Client's Problem."

[61] *Ibid.*, p. 185.

[62] *Ibid.*, pp. 176–177.

fourth interview, however, over 90 percent continued for at least a fifth interview. In other words, nine out of ten of the clients who had four interviews were continuers. On the basis of this information, which the judge may have learned from the project or from his own experience, the judge could safely assume—consciously or unconsciously—that nearly all clients who had four interviews were continuers.

It is unlikely, however, that this source of bias has been present in the MCO findings reported thus far, since all published analyses have been based on judgments of the first interview—judgments were made before the judges were given any information about subsequent interviews. On the other hand, another form of bias, more subtle and difficult to control, may have been present. There exists the possibility that the case records contained information on factors *other* than motivation, capacity, and opportunity, from which the experienced practitioner-judges could infer the probability of continuance. It is difficult to evaluate this possible source of bias since, for example, no information is provided about the ability of the judges to predict continuance beyond one interview from data about the first interview. Krause reported that caseworkers can predict continuance only slightly better than chance, but in his study the predictions were based on information obtained in telephone intakes, a more limited source of data than the first in-person interview.[63]

Results. Summarization of research findings in this area is difficult because the studies tend to be discrete and atheoretical, thus typically yielding "significant" associations between continuance and some rather loosely connected predictor variables. Nevertheless, several points of convergence can be seen in the findings of these studies:

1. *The degree of congruence between the worker and client* in their definitions of

the client's situation has been found to be strongly associated with continuance in all studies that have examined this factor.[64] Similar findings also have been reported in other fields.[65] Moreover, Rosenfeld, in his review of the research findings bearing on this topic, suggests that many of the other factors found to be associated with continuance can best be understood as reflections of an underlying congruence or lack of congruence factor, or what he calls *strangeness* between helper and client. This view suggests, for example, that the explanation for the finding that continuance is related to the social class of the client may reside in the lack of congruence between the views of worker and client occasioned by the social class distance between them.[66] Some suggestive support for this interpretation is found in Beck and Werble, and in Briar's finding that social work students tend to perceive greater dissimilarity between themselves and the client as social class distance between worker and client

[63] Merton S. Krause, "Predicting Client Discontinuance at Intake," *Social Casework*, Vol. 43, No. 6 (June 1962), pp. 308–312.

[64] *See* Beck, *op. cit.*; Blenkner, "Predictive Factors in the Initial Interview in Family Casework"; Fanshel, "An Overview of One Agency's Casework Operation"; Fanshel, "A Study of Caseworkers Perceptions of Their Clients"; Ripple and Alexander, *op. cit.*; Shyne, "What Research Tells Us About Short-Term Cases in Family Agencies"; Ivor Svarc, "Client Attitudes Toward Financial Assistance: A Cultural Variant," *Social Service Review*, Vol. 30, No. 2 (June 1956), pp. 136–146; and Werble, *op. cit.*

[65] *See,* for example, Jerome D. Frank *et al.*, "Why Patients Leave Psychotherapy," *Archives of Neurology and Psychiatry*, Vol. 77, No. 3 (March 1957), pp. 283–299; Martha Lake and George Levinger, "Continuance Beyond Application Interviews at a Child Guidance Clinic," *Social Casework*, Vol. 41, No. 6 (June 1960), pp. 303–309; and Philip Lichtenberg, Robert Kohrman, and Helen MacGregor, *Motivation for Child Psychiatry Treatment* (New York: Russell and Russell, 1960).

[66] The relation between continuance and social class is noted in Beck, *op. cit.*; Coleman *et al., op. cit.*; Fanshel, "An Overview of One Agency's Operation"; and Fanshel, "A Study of Caseworkers' Perceptions of Their Clients."

increases. The congruence or strangeness hypothesis could also be applied to other factors associated with continuance, and particularly to those factors that may reflect points of divergence between the belief systems of worker and client: adequacy of communication between worker and client; client's attribution of responsibility for the problem to himself rather than to others; and appropriateness of the client's attitudes and expectations regarding the worker and treatment.[67] While it is unlikely that the congruence hypothesis can account for all the variance in the above factors (e.g., it is possible that the association between social class and continuance is partly related to the fact that lower-class clients face greater practical obstacles to continuing treatment than do middle- and upper-class clients), it does provide a way of ordering some otherwise discrete and unrelated findings and, as Rosenfeld has indicated, suggests a promising direction for future research.[68]

2. *A second point of convergence is the apparent importance of client motivation in continuance.* Appropriate or "high" moti-

---

[67] For a discussion of adequacy of communication, *see* Blenkner, "Predictive Factors in the Initial Interview in Family Casework"; Fanshel, "An Overview of One Agency's Operation"; Fanshel, "A Study of Caseworkers' Perceptions of Their Clients"; Leonard S. Kogan, "The Short-Term Case in a Family Agency," *Social Casework*, Vol. 38, Nos. 5–7 (May-June 1957), pp. 231–238 (Part 1), pp. 296–302 (Part 2), and pp. 366–374 (Part 3); Shyne, "What Research Tells Us About Short-Term Cases in Family Agencies"; and Werble, *op. cit.* For client's attribution of responsibility, *see* again Kogan's three-part article, and Howard E. Mitchell, Malcolm G. Preston, and Emily H. Mudd, "Anticipated Development of Case from Content of First Interview Record," *Marriage and Family Living*, Vol. 15, No. 3 (August 1953), pp. 226–231. For appropriateness of the client's attitudes and expectations, *see* again Blenkner and Kogan.

[68] *See* Jerome D. Frank, *Persuasion and Healing* (Baltimore: Johns Hopkins University Press, 1961); and Rosenfeld, *op. cit.*

vation tends to lead to continuance, whereas clients with inappropriate, low, or negative motivation tend to be discontinuers.[69] However, the meaning of these findings is not entirely clear, because the term motivation has been used to refer to at least five different phenomena: (a) *what* the client wants from help; (b) *how much* he wants it; (c) the *appropriateness* of what the client wants; (d) how much *discomfort* the client experiences as a result of the problem(s) for which he is seeking help; and (e) how much *hope* the client feels about treatment.

In most continuance research, instructions for judging motivation tend to emphasize the appropriateness dimension.[70] Thus, what these judgments may measure is not so much what the client wants from treatment and how much he wants it, but rather the degree to which what the client wants corresponds to what the judge thinks the client *should* want. The latter judgment will be recognized as another indicator of congruence or strangeness. Thus, it is possible that a client could be highly "motivated" to achieve certain goals in treatment and still be judged as having low or even negative motivation because his goals are considered to be inappropriate by the judge. On the other hand, judgments of client discomfort and hope would seem to be less influenced by discrepancies between client and worker belief systems, and both factors have been found to be related to con-

---

[69] *See* Kogan, "The Short-Term Case in a Family Agency," Parts 1–3; Ripple, "Factors Associated with Continuance in Casework Service"; Ripple and Alexander, *op. cit.*; Shyne, "What Research Tells Us About Short-Term Cases in Family Agencies"; Beatrice Werble, "Current Research on Motivation," *Social Casework*, Vol. 39, Nos. 2–3 (February-March 1958), pp. 124–130; and Werble, "Motivation, Capacity, and Opportunity in Services to Adolescent Clients: Major Findings."

[70] *See*, for example, the instrument described in Ripple, "Motivation, Capacity, and Opportunity as Related to the Use of Casework Service: Theoretical Base and Plan of Study."

tinuance, although for both factors the effects appear to be nonlinear and tend to vary in relation to the nature of the client's problem.[71]

3. The final convergence to be suggested in this review is the *relation between client problem and continuance*. A number of continuance studies have reported associations between continuance and type of problem presented by the client.[72] However, the findings have not always been consistent. Thus, Blenkner found that clients presenting psychological and interpersonal problems were more likely to be continuers than clients with other problems. Ripple, on the other hand, found that clients presenting psychological problems had lower continuance rates than clients presenting external problems, although as noted earlier in this section this difference appears to be related more to the differential distribution of negative factors among these two problem groups than to the problem per se. Nevertheless, the MCO studies of Ripple, Alexander, and Werble have identified a number of interaction effects between type of problem and other factors in association with continuance. Werble found a series of quite specific problem categories that were related to continuance. Thus, subsequent research on continuance needs to consider possible variations as a function of client problem, although no adequate theoretical formulations have yet appeared that attempt to account for and predict rela-

tions between type of problem and continuance.

There are several striking gaps in the research reported on continuance thus far:

1. Virtually nothing is known about the influence of agency policy, structure, and operations on continuance. The evidence from studies of the effects of organizational factors on the treatment of mental hospital patients suggests that similar factors may be important in extramural settings as well.[73]

2. Little attention has been given to possible relationships between continuance and personal characteristics of the caseworker; such studies also have been rare in research on psychotherapy. One notable exception is Ripple's finding that continuance is related to encouragement by the worker. Another is the Pfouts and Rader study of the interactions between the personality characteristics of medical students, their perceptions of their patients, and the patient's perceptions of the student.[74] Although this study was not conducted in the family field, it suggests a promising direction for research on the caseworker.

The most extensive research on the practitioner thus far has been that focused on caseworkers' judgments. Briar's studies of the effect of client social class and agency setting on caseworkers' judgments; Roger Miller's study of the observational process in casework; the investigations of caseworkers' channel capacity by Miller and Bieri, and Tripodi and Bieri; Bieri, Orcutt, and Leaman's analysis of anchoring effects in judgment; and Plotnick's investigation of the influence of certain personality characteristics of caseworkers on their judg-

---

[71] *See* Blenkner, "Predictive Factors in the Initial Interview in Family Casework"; Ripple, "Motivation, Capacity, and Opportunity as Related to the Use of Casework Service: Theoretical Base and Plan of Study"; Rosenfeld, *op. cit.*; and Werble, "Motivation, Capacity, and Opportunity in Services to Adolescent Clients: Major Findings."

[72] *See* Blenkner, "Predictive Factors in the Initial Interview in Family Casework"; Ripple, "Factors Associated with Continuate in Casework Service"; Ripple and Alexander, *op. cit.*; and Werble, "Motivation, Capacity, and Opportunity in Services to Adolescent Clients: Major Findings."

[73] *See* Milton Greenblatt, Daniel J. Levinson, and Richard H. Williams, *The Patient and the Mental Hospital* (Glencoe, Ill.: Free Press, 1957).

[74] Jane H. Pfouts and Gordon E. Rader, "The Influence of Interviewer Characteristics on the Initial Interview," *Social Casework*, Vol. 43, No. 10 (December 1962), pp. 548–552.

ments represent substantial contributions to knowledge about the process by which case-workers perceive and assess their clients.[75] Moreover, as noted earlier, these studies have implications for the use of casework-ers' judgments in research. In view of the importance attached to the worker's per-sonal attributes in casework theory, this dimension should receive more attention in continuance research.

3. Environmental and situational factors have received limited investigation in con-tinuance research, although such factors were among those most commonly cited by clients as reasons for discontinuance in the follow-up study reported by Kogan.

4. Finally, one fact that research on con-tinuance has highlighted is the numerical importance of short-term services. In view of the fact that the great bulk of clients in family service agencies are seen two or three times at most, there is need for ex-perimental projects aimed at developing and testing new casework approaches designed to increase the help that can be given in brief contacts. Such projects have been conducted in other fields, and some be-ginning efforts have been made in the fam-ily service field.[76] The point of view im-plicit in most continuance studies, however, is that with the exception of planned early closings (which consist mostly of cases re-ferred elsewhere), short-term contacts gen-erally are less desirable than long-term contacts. In the MCO studies, in fact, five interviews are explicitly assumed to be a

necessary, although not sufficient, condition for the effective use of casework service. However, the universality of these assump-tions is questionable in view of: (a) Ko-gan's findings that worker and client valu-ations of service in short-term cases were unrelated to number of interviews, and that client valuations of service did not differ for planned as compared to unplanned clos-ings; and (b) the absence of relationship between frequency of interviews and out-come of psychotherapy reported by Lorr.[77] Studies of methods and techniques of brief service would seem to have considerable potential for making a direct contribution to casework theory and practice.

Research on Treatment Methods and Techniques

When practitioners periodically call for studies of practice, they usually have in mind not studies of outcome and continu-ance but research on methods and tech-niques, and on the processes of treatment.[78]

[75] Briar, "Use of Theory in Studying Ef-fects of Client Social Class on Students' Judgments"; Briar, "Clinical Judgment in Foster Care Placement"; Roger R. Miller, *op. cit.*; Henry Miller and Bieri, *op. cit.*; Tripodi and Bieri, *op. cit.*; Bieri, Orcutt, and Leaman, *op. cit.*; and Plotnick, *op. cit.*

[76] See B. Kalis *et al.*, "Precipitating Stress as a Focus in Psychotherapy," *Archives of General Psychiatry*, Vol. 5, No. 3 (September 1961), pp. 219–226; Ralph A. Garcia and Olive Irwin, "A Family Agency Deals with the Problem of Dropouts," *Social Casework*, Vol. 43, No. 2 (February 1962), pp. 71–75; and Anita Gilbert, "An Experiment in Brief Treatment of Parents," *Social Work*, Vol. 5, No. 4 (October 1960), pp. 91–97.

[77] Maurice Lorr *et al.*, "Frequency of Treat-ment and Change in Psychotherapy," *Journal of Abnormal and Social Psychology*, Vol. 64, No. 4 (April 1962), pp. 281–292.

[78] One might argue that the distinction be-tween studies of outcome and studies of method and process is a false one, in the sense that any study of treatment must per-force also be an outcome study. It is possi-ble, however, to study treatment without asking the question: Does it work? In the first place there is the distinction drawn by Martin Wolins between studies of *effect* and studies of *effectiveness*. See his "Measuring the Effect of Social Work Intervention," in Norman A. Polansky, ed., *Social Work Re-search* (Chicago: University of Chicago Press, 1960), pp. 247–272. The outcome and, to a lesser extent, the continuance studies ask the question: Is treatment effective? Studies of effect, on the other hand, might focus on (1) the specific, or more microscopic effects of *particular* interventions and (2) *how* treat-ment works rather than *whether* it works at all. Finally, an equally legitimate area of re-search inquiry consists of *descriptive* studies of treatment processes in which the investi-gator may not be concerned directly with questions of effect or effectiveness.

Although this point was made over fourteen years ago in a survey conducted by Herzog, it appears to have had little effect on the subsequent course of social work research in the family field.[79] The great bulk of the professional literature on casework methods and techniques, apart from purely theoretical essays, continues to consist of case reports. Few studies have delved systematically into the intricate mysteries of the therapeutic process. There are many explanations for this state of affairs, some of which will be considered later in this section.

In recent years, however, some beginning efforts have been made to subject practice to more systematic scrutiny. Most of these endeavors have taken the form of "demonstration" or "experimental" projects in which either new methods of treatment were employed or more traditional approaches were applied under special conditions, such as reduced case loads or particular types of clients. Among other things, these projects usually have aimed at demonstrating the value of the methods used and/or developing new or modified treatment methods and techniques adapted to the special conditions addressed by the project.

Actually, many projects of this sort in the family field cannot be considered research ventures, even by rather liberal criteria. For instance, perhaps one of the best known examples of this type of project to appear in recent years is the one reported by Reiner and Kaufman.[80] Although described by the authors as a research study, the report of this project bears none of the essential earmarks of research (e.g., the authors do not describe the characteristics of the study sample or their research methods), and thus the report is essentially a theoretical essay

with illustrative case material.[81] Nor is this an isolated example.

In recent years, one area—the multiproblem family—has been the focus for a substantial proportion of the demonstration projects conducted in the family field.[82] In a survey conducted in 1962 of all communities of 100,000 or more in Canada and the United States, Lagey and Ayres found that 60.1 percent of those communities reporting (91.5 percent of the population studied) were either planning, operating, or had recently concluded special programs for multiproblem families.[83] Various types of projects were reported, the most frequent being programs emphasizing an intensive casework approach to multiproblem families.

A rough analysis of the forty-four "intensive casework" projects, using the descriptions obtained by Lagey and Ayres, reveals that: (1) in ten, or about one-fourth of these projects, no research was planned; (2) eight of the projects planned to assess the value of the program through conference or committee discussions; (3) of those projects incorporating some specific research plan (about one-half of the projects), more than half planned to rely on workers' ratings of their own cases as the basis for assessing the value of the program; and (4) only two programs appeared to incorporate one of the features, i.e., con-

[79] Elizabeth Herzog, "What Social Casework Wants of Social Science Research," *American Sociological Review*, Vol. 16, No. 2 (February 1951), pp. 68–73.

[80] Beatrice Simcox Reiner and Irving Kaufman, *Character Disorders in Parents of Delinquents* (New York: Family Service Association of America, 1959).

[81] A good contrast to the Reiner and Kaufman volume is provided by the recently published report of the Multiple-Impact Therapy project by MacGregor *et al.*, *Multiple Impact Therapy with Families* (New York: McGraw-Hill Book Co., 1964), which incorporates many of the features lacking in the Reiner and Kaufman report.

[82] A large number of projects of a similar nature also have been conducted in Great Britain.

[83] Joseph C. Lagey and Beverly Ayres, "Community Treatment Programs for Multi-Problem Families," in Benjamin Schlesinger, ed., *The Multi-Problem Family* (Toronto: University of Toronto Press, 1963), pp. 55–71; and Joseph C. Lagey and Beverly Ayres, *Community Treatment Programs for Multi-Problem Families* (Vancouver, B.C.: Community Chest and Councils of the Greater Vancouver Area, 1962).

trol groups, essential to any rigorous assessment of program effectiveness. Of course, this state of affairs can be viewed simply as a reflection of the fact that research of this sort is now in an embryonic, exploratory stage. On the other hand, the project descriptions obtained by Lagey and Ayres contain some disquieting indications that the limitations inherent in some of these projects are not always recognized, as exemplified in the following statement obtained for one project in response to a question about evaluation plans: "There is no plan for evaluation and research. However, the program has proven to be most effective, and it is anticipated that some time in the near future it will be expanded." [84]

The limitations of these projects, insofar as measuring effectiveness is concerned, could be overlooked if they provided systematic knowledge about the *processes* of treatment. Although many of these demonstration projects have aspired to study treatment methods and processes, few have succeeded in moving beyond the level of illustrative case reports. A good example of this is provided by the St. Paul project, probably the most carefully researched multiproblem family project to date. In the *Casework Notebook* and other publications, Overton and Tinker set forth the principles and methods advocated for use by caseworkers in the St. Paul project, supporting their contentions with selected case illustrations.[85] Subsequently, in a systematic study of 30 cases randomly selected from 150 cases studied in the St. Paul project, Tinker attempted to determine the

extent to which the concepts and methods advocated were in fact applied by the workers in their treatment of families in the project sample.[86]

The findings of Tinker's study are rather disappointing. They are concerned with questions that seem trivial or at best incidental, relative to the treatment concepts and principles advocated by Overton and Tinker. That is, Tinker analyzed the thirty cases in relation to topics such as (1) the relative frequency with which workers made their initial approach to the family via letter or telephone; (2) the number of face-to-face contacts with family members; (3) the number of interviews with fathers; (4) the proportion of interviews conducted in the home versus the office; (5) the frequency distribution of topics discussed with family members; (6) contacts with other agencies; and (7) the number of conferences with consultants.

The theoretical and practical significance of many of the findings is not clear. One example will suffice. Tinker notes that the project had "advocated extensive use of home visits as the *sine qua non* in developing and maintaining a family-centered approach." [87] It was found that 27.6 percent of all interviews were conducted in the home. Does this proportion constitute "extensive use" of home visits? Under what conditions were home visits used and not used? Tinker offers some speculations in relation to the latter question, but there is no indication that any attempt was made to identify these conditions in the study of case records.

Subsequently, Geismar and Ayres attempted to relate some of the factors studied by Tinker to other case characteristics.[88] This effort apparently met with limited success, since Geismar and Ayres report only two significant findings in this area. One

[84] Lagey and Ayres, *Community Treatment Programs for Multi-Problem Families*, p. 92.

[85] Alice Overton and Katherine H. Tinker, *Casework Notebook* (St. Paul: Greater St. Paul United Fund and Council, 1959) ; Alice Overton, "Resistance in Serving Families at Odds with the Community" (St. Paul: Greater St. Paul United Fund and Council, 1957) (mimeographed) ; and Katherine H. Tinker, "Casework with Hard-to-Reach Families," *American Journal of Orthopsychiatry*, Vol. 29, No. 1 (January 1959), pp. 165–171.

[86] Katherine H. Tinker, *Patterns of Family-Centered Treatment: A Descriptive Study of 30 FCP Closed Cases* (St. Paul: Greater St. Paul United Fund and Council, 1959).

[87] *Ibid.*, p. 18.

[88] *Patterns of Change in Problem Families.*

is the finding of a positive relationship between the subjects discussed by caseworker and client, and the problem areas identified in the case. In other words, the caseworkers tended to talk with the client about those areas of the client's life in which he was considered to be experiencing difficulties. Second, movement was found to be associated with the frequency with which certain areas of family functioning were discussed.

Although many of the practice demonstration projects in the family field suffer from the kinds of deficiencies noted above, a small but encouraging number of studies of practice methods and processes have been reported that have gone substantially beyond the level of the speculative essay illustrated with case material. These studies have not yet appeared in sufficient numbers to be classified into substantive categories, and consequently they will be reviewed here in one group.

A number of studies have attempted to describe a specific service or the patterns of service offered to certain types of clients. Examples are the Community Service Society study of extended homemaker service; a number of the multiproblem family projects, such as the St. Paul project and the Roxbury project in Boston; Fanshel's studies of service patterns in a family agency; and Wiltse's studies of the use of social casework with ADC recipients.[89] Studies of this type are of considerable value to practitioners, since they often describe the principles and procedures for providing the service being studied in sufficient detail that workers could apply them in their own practice if they wished to do so.

Overton took the bold step of interviewing clients to obtain their perceptions of the good caseworker vis-à-vis multiproblem families.[90] In earlier studies, Polansky and Kounin, and Chance also interviewed clients to obtain their perceptions of the worker or therapist.[91] The results of these beginning explorations—especially Polansky and Kounin's finding that willingness to continue in the treatment relationship and feelings about being influenced by the worker are separable and possibly independent components of the client's assessment of the worker—suggests that this is a promising avenue for further investigation.

Some studies have been conducted concerning various procedural aspects of social work practice. A few descriptive studies of fee-charging and of workers' attitudes toward use of fees have been reported.[92] For the most part, however, the authors of these reports often seem more intent on making a case for charging fees rather than answering such basic questions as what are the different effects of use and non-use of fees and are these effects what practitioners believe them to be? The issue of fees touches on the more basic question of the effects of money—whether as a fee paid by the client or assistance given by the

---

[89] Community Service Society, *Report of the Extended Homemaker Service Project* (New York, 1958); Tinker, *Patterns of Family-Centered Treatment: A Descriptive Study of 30 FCP Closed Cases*; Edward Stone et al., *The Place of Darkness* (Boston: United Community Services, 1962); Fanshel, "An Overview of One Agency's Casework Operation"; Fanshel, "A Study of Caseworkers' Perceptions of Their Clients"; Kermit T. Wiltse, *Social Casework in Public Assistance: Testing Method and Skill Applied to a Selected Caseload* (Sacramento: State of California Department of Social Welfare, 1952); and Kermit T. Wiltse, "Social Casework Services in the Aid to Dependent Children Program," *Social Service Review*, Vol. 28, No. 2 (June 1954), pp. 173–185.

[90] Alice Overton, "Taking Help from Our Clients," *Social Work*, Vol. 5, No. 2 (April 1960), pp. 42–50.

[91] Norman A. Polansky and Jacob Kounin, "Clients' Reactions to Initial Interviews: A Field Study," *Human Relations*, Vol. 9, No. 3 (1956), pp. 237–264; and Erika Chance, *Families in Treatment* (New York: Basic Books, 1959).

[92] Family Service Association of America, *Fee Charging in a Family Agency* (New York, 1944); Ruth Fizdale, "A New Look at Fee Charging," *Social Casework*, Vol. 38, No. 2 (February 1957), pp. 63–69; Tina Claire Jacobs, "Attitudes of Social Workers Toward Fees," *Social Casework*, Vol. 33, No. 5 (May 1952), pp. 198–202.

worker—in treatment or, more generally, in interpersonal influence situations. This question seems amenable to systematic investigation, both in field and laboratory studies, and research in this area could have profound implications for practice.

Some systematic experimentation with the waiting list problem has been reported.[93] The importance of further experimentation in this area is underscored by the relationships found by Beck between use of waiting lists and certain outcome factors. Pollak's carefully designed study of the relative advantages of assigning one versus two caseworkers in marital counseling cases furnishes one model for studies of treatment procedures, although Pollak's findings are open to interpretations other than those he suggests.[94] His paper also is a model for the courageous reporting of findings that appear to run counter to cherished theoretical convictions. There are, of course, many other procedural aspects of practice that should be examined. One example is the referral and steering process, and as Kogan has shown, variations in this process differ greatly in effectiveness.[95]

The widespread and growing interest in family treatment has not led as yet to the publication of much systematic research on this practice development. A notable exception is the report of the Multiple-Impact Therapy project mentioned earlier.[96] This report, which could well serve as an example of its kind, describes in detail the sample and the treatment procedures used. The design of this project also incorporated a careful follow-up of each case.

Perhaps the most promising development

in recent years has been the appearance of several studies attempting to study casework treatment in a systematic and rigorous manner. These studies include Thomas' imaginative use of an actress to simulate casework interviews, Reid's experimental investigation of methods used in casework, Pollak's experiment comparing use of one versus two workers in marriage counseling cases, and the attempts by Maas and by Briar and his students to explicate the assumptions invoked by caseworkers to guide their actions.[97]

At the beginning of this section it was suggested that the relative paucity of research on the methods and processes of treatment in social work can be attributed to a number of factors. Space does not permit a full discussion of these factors, but a few comments about two of them may be in order. One of the most common explanations for the lack of research in this area is the sheer difficulty of studying treatment because of the inherent complexity of the phenomena. This explanation, however, is not entirely convincing. First, the treatment situation seems no more complex than many other human interaction situations that have been studied. Second, vigorous and increasingly sophisticated research activity in this area is occurring in other fields, notably psychology, and one of the results of this activity is the development of improved tools for investigating the treatment process. Some of these tools could be used in research on social case-

---

[93] *See* Beck, *op. cit.*; and Catherine M. Bitterman, "Serving Applicants When There is a Waiting List," *Social Casework*, Vol. 39, No. 6 (June 1958), pp. 356–360.

[94] Otto Pollak, "Worker Assignment in Casework with Marriage Partners," *Social Service Review*, Vol. 37, No. 1 (March 1963), pp. 41–53.

[95] Leonard S. Kogan, "The Utilization of Social Work Research," *Social Casework*, Vol. 44, No. 10 (December 1963), pp. 569–574.

[96] *See* MacGregor *et al.*, *op. cit.*

[97] Edwin J. Thomas, Donna L. McLeod, and Lydia F. Hylton, "The Experimental Interview: A Technique for Studying Casework Performance," *Social Work*, Vol. 5, No. 3 (July 1960), pp. 52–58; William Reid, "An Experimental Study of Methods Used in Casework Treatment" (unpublished doctoral dissertation, Columbia University School of Social Work, 1963); Pollak, *op. cit.*; Henry S. Maas, "Case Workers' Perceptions of Clients' Cues" (Berkeley: University of California, 1960) (mimeographed); and Harold Barnett *et al.*, "Selected Factors in Judgments About Foster Care Placement: II" (unpublished master's thesis, University of California, School of Social Welfare, Berkeley, 1962).

work. A more compelling explanation for the current state of social work research on treatment is the apparent failure, on the part of the profession and the professional schools, to foster the development of practitioner-researchers who would make a long-range investment of their energies in research on treatment.[98]

Family Organization and Disorganization

In his address to the National Conference of Social Work in 1919, Stuart Chapin issued a plea for social workers to serve essentially as laboratory workers for the sociologist.[99] Chapin's suggestion sprang partly from his belief that social workers—and he had in mind caseworkers primarily—had unique access to valuable data about the lives of persons and families of special interest to sociologists. Although Chapin's proposal attracted few supporters, his belief that social workers have an unusual opportunity to collect data that could contribute to the advancement of social science has been echoed repeatedly by social workers themselves.

For a number of years, in fact, social workers often bemoaned the failure to make use of the vast amounts of information that presumably could be mined from case records in social agency files. This lament still is heard occasionally, although it has long since been recognized that extracting data from social case records is fraught with

such difficult problems (e.g., the noncomparability of records) that it usually is more efficient and often essential to collect fresh data. Nevertheless, the belief persists that social workers are in an advantageous position to add to knowledge about family organization and disorganization. This section will assess the extent to which this promise has been fulfilled.

The Multiproblem Family

For obvious reasons, social workers' interest in the family has been focused primarily on disorganization and pathology, and this preoccupation is reflected in social work research on the family. Thus, with very few exceptions, recent research on the family in social work has been concerned with family dysfunctioning. Moreover, most of the research on family pathology has been concentrated on one subject: the multiproblem family.[100]

Current interest in the multiproblem family has many antecedents. The study of the Kallikak family is only one of several well-known examples that could be cited of the long-standing concern with families who are chronically beset by multiple social, economic, and health problems, sometimes extending over several generations.[101]

However, the present spurt of social work research activity in this area appears to have been stimulated largely by Bradley Buell's study in St. Paul.[102] Buell found that (1) of the families served in St. Paul social agencies in November 1948, 6 percent received approximately 50 percent of the professional services given, and (2)

---

[98] A recent development that may help to meet this deficiency is the establishment of research centers in schools of social work and in some family agencies. *See*, for example, Leonard S. Kogan and Mildred Kilinski, "An Experimental Center for Social Casework Research," *Social Casework*, Vol. 42, No. 9 (November 1961), pp. 446–450, for a discussion of the practice research center created at the Community Service Society in New York City.

[99] F. Stuart Chapin, "The Relation of Sociology and Social Case Work," *Proceedings of the National Conference of Social Work* (Chicago: National Conference of Social Work, 1920), pp. 358–365.

[100] The reader is reminded that research on the role of the family in the genesis of individual pathology is not covered in this review.

[101] *See* Henry Goddard, *The Kallikak Family* (New York: Macmillan Company, 1912).

[102] This refers to the United States only; parallel activities in Great Britain have a different history. *See* A. F. Philp and Noel Timms, *The Problem of the Problem Family* (London: Family Service Units, 1957).

this small group of families was characterized by the presence of multiple problems.[103] Buell and the Community Research Associates (CRA), whom he represents, have continued work in this area, concentrating their efforts on problems of identification, classification, and organization of services for problem families.[104]

Since the initial CRA efforts, there has been a proliferation of multiproblem family projects, many of which are modeled after the CRA approach. Some indication of the extent of this proliferation is provided by the Lagey and Ayres survey, mentioned earlier, which found projects of this sort in 60.1 percent of the communities they surveyed. Lagey and Ayres did not collect data about the cost of these projects, but assuming that each project required a minimum expenditure of at least $25,000, the 143 projects described represent, conservatively, a total investment of more than 3.5 million dollars.[105] Another indication of the volume of activity is provided by the bibliography on the multiproblem family compiled by Schlesinger. It contains 307 titles, few of which bear a date prior to 1952, the year in which Buell's initial St. Paul study was published.[106]

For several reasons, no attempt will be made here to conduct an extensive review of the literature on the multiproblem family:

1. Several reviews of this literature are already available, including those by Spencer, Kasius, and Philp and Timms.[107] Although the Kasius summary is quite selective, Spencer's review is thorough and comprehensive in its coverage of recent materials. The Philp and Timms volume provides an excellent review and critique of the British literature.

2. As noted earlier, many of the multiproblem family projects have not incorporated any systematic plan of research and therefore fall outside the scope of this review.

3. Some of the projects incorporating a research design have not as yet published a sufficiently detailed description of their methods and procedures to permit an intelligent analysis of these projects from a research perspective. The most conspicuous example of the latter problem is the work of Bradley Buell and his associates who have been subjected to severe criticism for, among other things, their failure to publish a full account of their research methods.[108] Because of these considera-

---

[103] Bradley Buell and associates, *Community Planning for Human Services* (New York: Columbia University Press, 1952).

[104] *See* Bradley Buell, "Preventing and Controlling Disordered Behavior," *Mental Hygiene*, Vol. 39, No. 3 (July 1955), pp. 365–375; and Bradley Buell, Paul T. Beisser, and John M. Wedemeyer, "Reorganizing to Prevent and Control Disordered Behavior," *Mental Hygiene*, Vol. 42, No. 2 (April 1958), pp. 155–194.

[105] This is, of course, an arbitrary estimate that could only be verified by more extensive research than was possible for this review. To the reader who may think the figure too high, it should be noted that most projects of this type extend over more than one year and often involve hidden costs, such as agency staff time not funded by the project.

[106] Benjamin Schlesinger, ed., *op cit*. The pre- and post-1952 distribution of items in this bibliography partly reflects the compiler's orientation and his method of search, since this listing does not include some earlier

works that should be of interest to the student of the multiproblem family. However, the point of the present discussion is the volume of activity in the area since 1952.

[107] John Spencer, "The Multi-Problem Family," in Benjamin Schlesinger, ed., *op. cit.*, pp. 3–54; Cora Kasius, "Family Disorganization and the Multi-Problem Family," in *Children and Youth in the 1960's* (Washington, D.C.: Golden Anniversary White House Conference, 1960), pp. 233–241; and Philp and Timms, *op. cit.*

[108] *See* Council on Social Work Education, *Concepts of Prevention and Control: Their Use in the Social Work Curriculum* (New York, 1961); Irving Lukoff and Samuel Mencher, "A Critique of the Conceptual Foundation of Community Research Associates," *Social Service Review*, Vol. 36, No. 4 (December 1962), pp. 433–443; Henry S. Maas, "Family Casework Diagnosis: An Essay Review," *Social Service Review*, Vol. 36, No. 4 (December 1962), pp. 444–450; Martin

tions, this review will focus primarily on one major multiproblem family project that can serve as an exemplar and as a springboard for discussing research problems in this area.

The Family-Centered Project of St. Paul. Begun in 1952, the FCP was a direct outgrowth of Buell's St. Paul study.[109] The St. Paul project still is in operation and thus represents twelve years of continuous research and demonstration activity.[110] FCP has published detailed accounts of its research methods and is widely regarded as the single most important project in this substantive area.

The FCP has had two components: (1) a demonstration project providing intensive family-centered treatment to a sample of multiproblem families; and (2) a research component closely related to the demonstration project but also with some aims of its own. Research in the FCP on treatment methods was reviewed in the preceding section; consequently, discussion in this section will be limited to research in this project on the family per se.

A major problem that has beset all multiproblem family projects, including FCP, is that of defining the object of investigation, i.e., the multiproblem family. As Philp has observed: "This term [the "problem family" is the British equivalent of "multiproblem family"] occurs so freely that one forgets how loosely it is used and that there is no general agreement as to what a 'problem family' is." [111] None of the

projects reviewed has developed more than a vague and loose definition of the concept "multiproblem family." Most attempts at definition include two principal elements: (1) the presence of multiple social, psychological, economic, and/or health problems afflicting one or more individuals in the family group; and (2) the problems presented by family members do not respond to conventional methods of intervention.[112] Some of the difficulties involved in applying these criteria can be seen by examining one attempt to use them.

The St. Paul FCP provides a good case in point for discussing this problem, since the project has used criteria that are as stringent and explicit as those of any multiproblem family project published to date. The FCP criteria consist of three elements, *all* of which must be present to classify a family in the multiproblem category.[113]

1. Either neglect, delinquency, or other behavior problems must be present and must have been verified by an official agency, e.g., by court activity in the case of delinquency.

2. A known health and/or economic problem must be present.

3. If the first two criteria are satisfied, the family must be one in which a child is judged to be in clear or present danger, physically or emotionally.

Although these criteria seem fairly specific—with the exception of the third condition—interjudge agreement in applying

Wolins, "Letter to the Editor," *Social Service Review*, Vol. 37, No. 2 (June 1963), pp. 220–221; and Martin Wolins, "Readers' Exchange," *Children*, Vol. 2, No. 5 (September–October 1955), p. 199.

[109] Charles Birt, "The Family-Centered Project of St. Paul," *Social Work*, Vol. 1, No. 4 (October 1956), pp. 41–47.

[110] Greater St. Paul United Fund and Council, *Report to Supporting Foundations: Family Centered project, 1961–1964* (St. Paul, 1964).

[111] A. F. Philp, *Family Failure* (London: Faber and Faber, 1963), p. 15.

[112] *See*, for example, Kenneth Dick and L. Strand, "The Multiproblem Family and Problems of Service," *Social Casework*, Vol. 39, No. 6 (June 1958), pp. 349–355; Berta Fantl, "Integrating Psychological, Social, and Cultural Factors in Assertive Casework," *Social Work*, Vol. 3, No. 4 (October 1958), pp. 30–37; Ralph Ormsby, "Defining the Problem Family," *Social Work*, Vol. 4, No. 1 (January 1959), p. 109; Philp and Timms, *op. cit.*; Spencer, *op. cit.*; and Kermit T. Wiltse. "The Hopeless Family," *Social Work*, Vol. 3, No. 4 (October 1958), pp. 12–22.

[113] *See* Ludwig L. Geismar, *Report on Check List Survey* (St. Paul: Greater St. Paul United Fund and Council, 1960).

them left much to be desired. Geismar reports that interjudge error (or disagreement) was as high as 38 percent for the first criterion, 30 percent for the second, and 25 percent for the third. He offers several explanations for the low interrater reliabilities in applying these criteria. For example, he notes that judges made a binary present or absent judgment for each criterion, but since judges were not given an opportunity to indicate the adequacy of information for making a judgment, a judgment that a condition was absent could mean either that the judge found sufficient information to determine that the condition was not present in the case, *or* that there was insufficient information for making any judgment at all. Geismar argues that the addition of an "insufficient information" judgment category would increase reliability, but this remains to be seen.

Even assuming that these criteria, or others designed to identify multiproblem, intractable families, could be applied reliably, another more fundamental problem remains. In FCP, and in most multiproblem family projects surveyed for this review, an assumption is made, sometimes explicitly but always implicitly, that these families form a homogeneous *family* type.[114]   That

is to say, multiproblem intractable families are presumed to be at least more similar to each other, *as families,* than they are to non-multiproblem families who respond to conventional methods of intervention. This assumption may or may not be valid, but the point is that no theoretical rationale for making this assumption has appeared. In fact, it should be emphasized that until this assumption is made explicit and stated in the form of hypotheses that are linked to some conception of family types, multi-problem family projects rest on a dubious and shaky conceptual base.[115]   For there is no reason to believe, *a priori*, that families presenting similar problems—at least as gross as those used to identify the multi-problem family—form a homogeneous family type. On the contrary, one of the striking findings reported in a variety of studies is the variation among families beset by common situational problems.[116]

---

[114] For one of the exceptions, *see* Philp, *op. cit.* Philp and Timms, *op. cit.*, found that this assumption also was prevalent in the British literature on the problem family.

Often underlying the notion of homogeneity is the equally questionable assumption that the determinants of the social problem called "multiproblem families" are to be found primarily within the families themselves. As several writers have noted, the social problems ascribed to the multiproblem family arise from the way in which social services are organized and, more generally, from the structure, values, and norms of the society. *See* Lukoff and Mencher, *op. cit.*, and Philp and Timms, *op. cit.* As Philp and Timms observe on p. 68 of their study:

It is generally considered that these are neglectful parents; but we have difficulty in describing this neglect, because we have no very clear idea of what we consider adequate motherhood nor what relationship we expect between working class mothers and children at different stages of

infancy, childhood, and adolescence. Problem family parents are known as bad managers and misspenders; but we have very little knowledge of how other families organize their budgets or of how they come to make their choices in a society of changing habits and values. It is said that problem family parents fail to respond to the help offered by social workers; but there is very little knowledge of what in fact is the general response of the population to, for instance, the health visitor's services, and caseworkers have hardly begun to consider in detail what happens when they help, or fail to help, a client.

[115] One such attempt has been made by Alice L. Voiland and associates, *Family Casework Diagnosis* (New York: Columbia University Press, 1962), but as pointed out in Spencer, *op. cit.*, p. 15, virtually all multiproblem families would, by definition, fall into *one* of Voiland's categories so that this typology probably is insensitive to possible differences *among* multiproblem families. Moreover, Voiland's typology is so value-laden and based on such questionable research methods (Voiland claims that her typology was constructed empirically) as to mitigate its utility as a framework for research. For an excellent and penetrating critique of Voiland's work, *see* the essay review of her book by Maas, *op. cit.*

[116] *See,* for example, Reuben Hill's study of familial responses to military separation, *Families Under Stress* (New York: Harper & Brothers, 1949) ; Bernard Farber's researches

The common elements that have emerged relate to the disruptive processes set in motion by the problems of the families involved, and the measures families take in an effort to counteract these disruptions.[117] The concepts of distorting and counteracting family processes, formulated most clearly by Farber, provide a promising framework for more sophisticated studies of the multiproblem family. At the very least, this framework offers the advantage of conceptualizing the phenomena to be investigated at the level of family behavior rather than individual functioning—and despite aspirations to the contrary, in social work literature the multiproblem family is perceived, and in fact, defined, in terms that refer to individual, not family, behavior and pathology.

It would be easier to answer some of the questions raised above if adequate descriptive studies of multiproblem families were available that analyzed these families with reference to family-life variables. Although Spencer observed that "the multiproblem family is much easier to describe than to define," he must have had in mind the case summaries and reports that have appeared.[118]

These reports have serious limitations for research purposes.[119] In the first place, most of them consist of interpretations rather than observations and thus are difficult to treat as raw data about the families they describe.[120] A good example of this problem is provided by the Schedule of Family Functioning used in the St. Paul FCP.[121] This schedule provides an outline for workers to organize their observations of a family, but the instructions and the completed schedules that have been published indicate that workers essentially report their interpretations rather than a description of their observations. Social workers, like all other observers, attend to and therefore report the phenomena they assume to be most salient. Since social work theory still tends to emphasize psychological over social processes—or at least has adopted more sophisticated theoretical tools for analyzing phenomenon in psychological rather than social terms—the reports of multiproblem families reflect this emphasis. As a result, even when written descriptively, the reports are deficient in their attention to phenomena that would permit an analysis according to family-life variables. The FCP Schedule of Family Functioning does direct the worker to attend to some of the latter variables, but the impres-

---

on families with retarded children, "Family Organization and Crisis: Maintenance of Integration in Families with a Severely Mentally Retarded Child," *Monographs of the Society for Research in Child Development*, Vol. 25, No. 1 (1960), Serial No. 75; and Fred Davis' investigation of the impact of polio on family life, *Passage Through Crisis* (New York: Bobbs-Merrill Co., 1963). *See also* the studies of families with unemployed fathers: Mirra Komarovsky, *The Unemployed Man and His Family* (New York: Dryden Press, 1940); E. Wight Bakke, *Citizens Without Work* (New Haven: Yale University Press, 1940); and Ruth Cavan and Katherine Ranck, *The Family and the Depression* (Chicago: University of Chicago Press, 1938).

[117] For an elaboration of this point, *see* Bernard Farber, *Family: Organization and Interaction* (San Francisco: Chandler Press, 1964), pp. 388–440.

[118] *Op. cit.*, p. 7. *See*, for example, C. P. Blacker, *Problem Families: Five Inquiries* (London: Eugenics Society, 1952); New

York City Youth Board, *Reaching the Unreached Family*, Monograph No. 5 (New York, 1958); Overton and Tinker, *op. cit.*; Philp, *op. cit.*; Tom Stephens, ed., *Problem Families* (London: Victor Gollancz, 1946); and Stone *et al.*, *op. cit.*

[119] Philp and Timms (*op. cit.*, pp. 7–8), reviewing the British literature, make the following comments about descriptive studies of the problem family:

The absence of detailed studies of actual cases is one of the most serious gaps in the literature. Those already published are totally inadequate; they . . . give no idea of family relationships or the dynamics of family life.

[120] There are, of course, exceptions; *see*, for example, Political and Economic Planning, *Family Needs and the Social Services* (London: George Allen & Unwin, 1961).

[121] For a sample copy of this schedule, completed for one family, *see* Geismar and Ayres, *Measuring Family Functioning*.

sionistic, interpretive quality of the reports limits their usefulness for other investigators.

In general, then, multiproblem families have not been described adequately from a research perspective. In defense of researchers in this area it might be noted that description of these families has not always been a central concern of their investigations, except with regard to such gross characteristics as the number and types of problems afflicting the individual family members, and the number and kinds of agencies serving them. Important as such information may be for other purposes, it contributes relatively little to an understanding of the multiproblem family.

Rather than description, a main thrust of research effort in this area has been toward the development of measures of family functioning that could be used to detect change in studies of the effectiveness of treatment programs for multiproblem families. The St. Paul Family Centered Project can again be used as an example. The researchers in this project reasoned, along lines suggested earlier by the developers of the Movement Scale at CSS (who, in fact, served as consultants to FCP in its early stages), that a first step in research on the multiproblem family should be the development of tools for measuring change in family functioning.[122] The FCP investigators, however, were not satisfied with only a relative measure of change, as represented by the Movement Scale; instead, they wanted to develop a measure that would permit comparison of families according to the absolute level of functioning they had achieved. These efforts led to the development of (1) the Schedule of Family Functioning, mentioned earlier, consisting of nine "levels" of family functioning; and (2) the Profile of Family Functioning,

composed of ratings on each level.[123] Three major claims for the Profile of Family Functioning have been made—claims that, if valid, commend it as an extremely valuable instrument:

1. The Profile of Family Functioning forms a unidimensional scale. This claim is based on a Guttman-type analysis of the scale, resulting in reproducible coefficients that approached the level required of unidimensional scales.[124] This claim is not entirely convincing for two reasons. In the first place, Guttman-type scale analysis does not establish unidimensionality; it simply asserts that *if* there are sound logical or theoretical grounds for believing that a scale is unidimensional then it should achieve a specified level of reproducibility. FCP has not provided a systematic rationale for the assumed unidimensionality of the nine levels of family functioning. Second, each of the nine levels of functioning represents a judgment by a rater. Thus, the finding of similar contours on the Profile of Family Functioning for families selected from different populations may reflect the intercorrelations among these "levels" in the minds of the judges rather than the actual relationships between those levels in the families studied.[125]

---

[122] The logic here is not inexorable. The emphasis on measuring change, both in FCP and at CSS, represents the choice of one strategy from an array of equally viable research strategies.

[123] The nine levels are (1) care and training of children; (2) individual behavior and adjustment; (3) family relationships and unity; (4) relationship to social worker; (5) use of community resources; (6) social activities; (7) economic practices; (8) health conditions and practices; and (9) household conditions and practices.

[124] Ludwig L. Geismar, "Applying an Operational Definition of Family Functioning in Determining Need for Services" (New Brunswick, N.J.: Rutgers University, undated) (mimeographed); Geismar and Ayres, *Measuring Family Functioning;* and Geismar, Beverly Ayres, and Michael LaSorte, "Measuring Family Disorganization," *Marriage and Family Living,* Vol. 24, No. 1 (February 1962), pp. 51–56.

[125] This possibility is made more difficult to discount by the fact that the nine levels of functioning were not judged independently. When a judge rated a case, he rated it on all nine levels. Also, the explanation suggested above is not inconsistent with high

2. A second claim made for the Family Functioning Scale is that of relative freedom from social class bias. The importance of this claim can hardly be overemphasized, because if valid it would mean that the scale is value-free, at least so far as class differences are concerned. In support of this claim, Geismar reports a rank order correlation of .20 between mean-summated profile scores for five groups of families and the relative socioeconomic status of these groups. However, examination of Geismar's data reveals that this low order correlation is primarily attributable to the high mean profile scores achieved by one lower-class group. When this group, consisting of AFDC families, is removed, then $\rho=.75$. Moreover, there is reason to believe, based on Geismar's report, that raters had less adequate and possibly less reliable information about the AFDC families than was available for the other groups of families.

3. The levels of functioning scheme is supposed to represent an integrated framework that is systematically related to family role structure and the societal functions of families. At present, this claim must be considered more a hope than a reality. The rationale for selecting the specific levels included in the scale rather than others, and the articulation of these levels to a theory of family role structure and to a conception of the societal functions of the family have not been adequately developed. Nevertheless, one of the major achievements of the Family Centered Project has been the emphasis it has placed on these conceptual objectives, and the FCP researchers have taken some important initial steps toward the achievement of these aims. But attempts to evaluate the over-all effectiveness of FCP, discussed earlier, have been at the least disappointing, and at best inconclusive.

interjudge reliability, since judges working closely together on the same project often develop a high degree of consensus, especially when they have had comparable professional training.

In summary, the multiproblem family has been an unusually active focus of research, which thus far suffers from three major failings: (1) an extremely loose and vague definition of the phenomena to be studied; (2) a lack of adequate descriptive studies of multiproblem families; and (3) a failure to conceptualize research problems in terms of some theory of family behavior and disorganization. It seems that until some of these deficiencies are remedied, the heavy emphasis on effectiveness research in this area may be premature.

Other Studies of Family Disorganization

A search for recent social work studies of family disorganization, apart from research on the multiproblem family, yields only a few isolated and scattered investigations. This state of affairs may, in fact, be partly a consequence of the multiproblem family approach, which attempts to subsume all varieties of family disorganization under the umbrella of one concept.

Marital adjustment and divorce. Until quite recently, the only systematic study of marital conflict in social work was the one reported by Hollis in 1949.[126] In fact, social work research in this area, which, by contrast, is probably the most extensively researched area in family sociology, may have been inhibited by Hollis' finding that "personality factors lay at the root of the marriage conflict" in the families she studied, and by her conclusion that marriage conflict is not a special problem requiring the development of special treatment approaches.[127]

The possibility of increased research in

[126] Florence Hollis, *Women in Marital Conflict* (New York: Family Service Association of America, 1949).

[127] *Ibid.*, pp. 9, 219. For a discussion of research in family sociology, *see* F. Ivan Nye and Alan E. Bayer, "Some Recent Trends in Family Research," *Social Forces*, Vol. 41, No. 3 (March 1963), pp. 290–301.

marital conflict is suggested by two recent studies by Meyer and Levinger. Meyer employed the concept of complementarity— a much-used, and some have suggested overused, concept in research on marital adjustment—in a study of marital role relations.[128] Levinger's research, still in process, is an attempt to examine some of the correlates of marital satisfaction.[129] His approach is noteworthy as an attempt to link the study to family theory. As noted above, a number of studies in this area have been conducted by sociologists and social psychologists; two examples are Goode's study of divorce and Bernard's investigation of remarriage.[130]

Separation. Separation has been the focus of extensive study, and several reviews of research have appeared.[131] For the most part, however, these studies have been concerned primarily with the effects of separation on child development and, as noted earlier, these studies will not be reviewed here. An exception, from a field other than social work, is Reuben Hill's study of the effects of military separation on family life.[132] Davis' investigation of familial responses to polio includes an analysis of the effects on the family of separation occasioned by hospitalization of a child.[133] A variety of social welfare settings would seem to be strategically situated for research on family separation; obvious examples are Red Cross Home Service Units and certain hospital settings.

Neglected areas of study. In view of the extent to which social workers are expected to deal with many varieties of family disorganization, it is striking that several major kinds of disorganization have received virtually no research attention in social work. One such neglected area is that of family mobility and the strains associated with it. Schorr and Van Valen have pointed to the importance of this topic.[134] Desertion is another manifestation of family disorganization that is of special concern to social workers in public welfare, but except for some early studies it has received little systematic study.[135] An exception is McKeany's study of the absent father.[136] This, however, is an analysis of policies and programs pertaining to families in which the father is absent (for a variety of reasons including desertion), and it is not a study of these families per se. The disorganizing effects on the family of unemployment and poverty were studied in an exploratory way by Bakke, Cavan and Ranck, Komarovsky, and others; but these

---

[128] Carol Meyer, "Complementarity and Marital Conflict: A Development of a Concept and its Application to Casework Practice." Unpublished doctoral dissertation, Columbia University School of Social Work, 1957.

[129] George Levinger, "Instrumental and Expressive Functions in Marriage" (Cleveland: Western Reserve University, School of Applied Social Sciences, 1963). (Mimeographed.)

[130] William J. Goode, *After Divorce* (Glencoe, Ill.: Free Press, 1956) ; and Jessie Bernard, *Remarriage* (New York: Dryden Press, 1956).

[131] *See*, for example, Marian Radke-Yarrow and Leon J. Yarrow, "Child Psychology," *Annual Review of Psychology*, Vol. 6 (Palo Alto, Calif.: Annual Reviews, 1955), pp. 1–28; and Robert F. Winch, "Marriage and the Family," in Joseph B. Gittler, ed., *Review of Sociology: Analysis of a Decade* (New York: John Wiley & Sons, 1957).

[132] *Op. cit.*

[133] *Op. cit.*

[134] Alvin L. Schorr, "Mobile Family Living," *Social Casework*, Vol. 37, No. 4 (April 1956), pp. 175–180; and Martha Bushfield Van Valen, "An Approach to Mobile Dependent Families," *Social Casework*, Vol. 37, No. 4 (April 1956), pp. 180–186.

[135] *See* Lilian Brandt, *Five Hundred and Seventy-Four Deserters and Their Families* (New York: Charity Organization Society, 1905) ; Joanna C. Colcord, *Broken Homes: A Study of Family Desertion and Its Social Treatment* (New York: Russell Sage Foundation, 1919) ; and Earle Edward Eubank, *A Study of Family Desertion* (Chicago: Department of Public Welfare, 1916).

[136] Maurine McKeany, *The Absent Father and Public Policy in the Program of Aid to Dependent Children*, University of California Publications in Social Welfare, Vol. 1 (Berkeley: University of California Press, 1960).

studies were conducted during or shortly after the Depression and bear replication and elaboration, not only because social conditions have changed but also because these studies raised at least as many questions as they answered.[137]

These examples of family disorganization and of situational conditions affecting family life could be extended considerably, but for the most part social work research in this general area has been limited and scattered. Perhaps the most promising recent development is the attempt, as seen in the works of Farber and Hill in sociology and Parad and Caplan in social work, to develop a general theory that would be applicable to all or at least most varieties of family crises.[138]

Family Structure and Process

Social work research on the family has followed the social worker's preoccupation with family pathology. Thus, there has been a substantial amount of research activity focused on problem families but few studies concerned with the basic structure and dynamics of family functioning—whether in "normal" or "pathological" families. This emphasis on the problem family probably stems not only from the realities of practice, which have forced social workers to be concerned with pathology, but also from the distinction that has been drawn between basic and applied research—the former regarded as the province of the social sciences and the latter presumably the domain of the professions.[139]

Since social work has reported few basic studies of the family—some are currently in process—this section will be limited to a brief discussion of general directions of inquiry that social work research might profitably pursue, with selected references to relevant studies in the social sciences.

The family unit in relation to its environment. Virtually no recent empirical studies of ecological influences on family life—such as housing patterns, neighborhood characteristics, physical environment, and so on—have been conducted in social work. However, social work research in this area may be stimulated by the attention students of family policy have directed to the possible importance of these influences in shaping family life and in the etiology of family problems.[140] Ecological influences have not been totally ignored, as seen, for example, in the studies of the effects of housing patterns on family life by Schorr, Young and Wilmott, Rosow, and Wilner and Walkley, and in Gans's analysis of the importance of the neighborhood

---

[137] Bakke, *op. cit.*; Cavan and Ranck, *op. cit*; and Komarovsky, *op. cit.*

[138] Farber, *Family: Organization and Interaction*; Reuben Hill, "Social Stress in the Family, I. Generic Features of Families Under Stress," *Social Casework*, Vol. 39, Nos. 2–3 (February–March 1958), pp. 139–150; and Howard Parad and Gerald Caplan, "A Framework for Studying Families in Crisis," *Social Work*, Vol. 5, No. 3 (July 1960), pp. 3–15.

[139] For a particularly lucid discussion of

this distinction, *see* Greenwood, *op. cit.* This is not the place for a full discussion of the difficulties involved in maintaining a distinction between basic and applied research, but an attempt to allocate these two types of research activity to different disciplines could have some unfortunate consequences. For one thing, if applied rigidly this policy would foreclose possible contributions to basic science by social work researchers and, conversely, additions to applied fields by social scientists. Second, and more important, it tends to sharpen a distinction—between basic and applied research—that in reality is at best blurred and indistinct. This is not to argue that basic research on the family should be a *primary* emphasis of social work research in the family field, but rather that free movement between the basic and applied domains should be permitted and even encouraged. Thus, this reviewer is encouraged to note the appearance of some more basic research in social work on the family.

[140] *See* Alvin L. Schorr, "Family Policy in the United States," *International Social Science Journal*, Vol. 14, No. 3 (1962), pp. 452–467.

in urban family life.[141]   Such studies have provided some of the kinds of data needed for the formulation of sound family policy. The possibility that adjustments in the ecology can produce major changes in family life, and perhaps even reduce the incidence of certain family problems, underscores the crucial importance of expanded research activity in this area.   Even if social work researchers do not conduct major studies of ecological influences per se, perhaps some applied research in the family field could incorporate such variables in the study design and thereby attempt to relate the findings to general theory.

Subcultural variations in family behavior.   In sociology considerable attention has been paid to social class differences in family life.   The most familiar examples to social workers of such studies probably are those of class variations in child-rearing practices.[142]   Class differences in other aspects of family life have been the subject of some excellent recent studies, including, for example, those by Rainwater, Miller and Swanson, and McKinley.[143]   The

McKinley volume should be especially useful to social workers, since it summarizes previous research findings regarding class differences in family behavior.

Ethnic and religious subgroup patterns of family life have received somewhat less systematic attention than class variations, although some of the findings in this area have found their way into the social work literature.[144]   One conspicuous gap in this area is knowledge about family patterns in different racial groups, and especially among Negroes.   Few really significant studies of the Negro family have appeared since the publication of Frazier's rather impressionistic work over twenty years ago.[145]   Several writers on social work practice have stressed the importance for the practitioner of knowledge about subcultural patterns of family life—especially in the lower class and among Negroes.[146] As yet, however, social work research has not made any major contributions in this area.   This is unfortunate, not only because of the value of such knowledge to practitioners, but also because social workers do have strategic access to information about families in some subgroups for which adequate knowledge is lacking.   The current wave of interest in the problems of poverty may stimulate some research on families affected by poverty, in the tradition of the Depression-period studies by Bakke, Ginsberg, and others.[147]   If so, it would seem both appropriate and desirable for some of this research to be conducted within social work.

[141] Alvin L. Schorr, *Slums and Social Insecurity* (Washington, D.C.: Social Security Administration, 1963) ; Michael Young and Peter Wilmott, *Family and Kinship in East London* (Glencoe, Ill.: Free Press, 1957) ; Irving Rosow, "The Social Effects of the Physical Environment," *Journal of the American Institute of Planners*, Vol. 32, No. 2 (May 1961), pp. 127–133; Daniel M. Wilner et al., *The Housing Environment and Family Life: A Longitudinal Study of the Effects of Housing on Morbidity and Mental Health* (Baltimore: Johns Hopkins University Press, 1962) ; and Herbert J. Gans, *The Urban Villagers* (New York: Free Press of Glencoe, 1962).

[142] *See*, for example, Urie Bronfenbrenner, "Socialization and Social Class Through Time and Space," in E. Maccoby, T. Newcomb, and E. Hartley, eds., *Readings in Social Psychology* (New York: Holt, Rinehart & Winston, 1958), pp. 400–425.

[143] Lee Rainwater, *And the Poor Get Children* (Chicago: Quadrangle Books, 1960) ; Daniel R. Miller and Guy E. Swanson, *The Changing American Parent* (New York: John

Wiley & Sons, 1958) ; and Donald G. McKinley, *Social Class and Family Life* (New York: Free Press of Glencoe, 1964).

[144] *See* James N. Morgan *et al.*, *Income and Welfare in the United States* (New York: McGraw-Hill Book Company, 1962).

[145] E. Franklin Frazier, *The Negro Family in the United States* (Chicago: University of Chicago Press, 1939).

[146] *See*, for example, Fantl, *op. cit.*

[147] Bakke, *op. cit.*; and Eli Ginsberg, *The Unemployed* (New York: Harper & Brothers, 1943).

Kinship structure. Another aspect of the nuclear family's relations with its environment, which has received considerable attention from students in sociology and especially in anthropology, is the area of kinship structure. Only recently, however, has this body of knowledge been thought to have more than a general and indirect relevance to social work practice. One study that has helped to demonstrate the significance to social workers of knowledge (or, more accurately, lack of knowledge) about kinship patterns is Leichter's investigation of the kin networks of families served by Jewish Family Service of New York. The final report of this study has not yet appeared, but preliminary papers have described two major findings that appear to have direct implications for practice.[148] Specifically, Leichter found that social workers often were unaware of the extent and intensity of their client-family's kinship ties, and typically tended to discourage kinship ties when they were aware of them.

Leichter's findings assume added significance in view of the studies by Litwak, Sussman, Sussman and Burchinal, and others showing that, contrary to widespread belief, many "isolated" urban nuclear families actually maintain strong ties to extended kin, and that these ties provide considerable material aid and less tangible supports that play a crucial role in the maintenance of the nuclear unit.[149]

Leichter's work will have served a useful purpose if it does no more than sensitize practitioners and researchers to the importance of the kinship network in family life.

Structure and dynamics of the nuclear family. Increasingly, social workers have come to realize that general knowledge about the structure and dynamics of the nuclear family group is relevant to their work. A prominent theme running through the voluminous literature on family diagnosis and treatment is the need for family theory to aid the social worker in his attempt to understand and help the family as a unit. In view of these appeals, it is likely that the near future will witness an expansion of research and theory construction in this area. These developments already are under way in related disciplines —as exemplified by the recent appearance of a new journal, *Family Process,* devoted to clinical reports, theoretical essays, and research on the family group in relation to clinical practice—and some signs of parallel developments are emerging in social work. In addition to studies mentioned earlier by Levinger, Meyer, and Parad and Caplan, Mayer's ongoing investigations at CSS of family privacy, Glasser's study of changes in family equilibrium during psychotherapy, and the work by Brier and his students on role conflicts in the family represent attempts to extend theory about the structure and dynamics of the family unit.[150]

---

[148] Hope J. Leichter, "Kinship and Casework," a paper presented at the Groves Conference, Chapel Hill, North Carolina, April 6, 1959 (mimeographed) ; Hope J. Leichter, "Life Cycle Changes and Temporal Sequence in a Bilateral Kinship System," a paper presented at the annual meetings of the American Anthropological Association, Washington, D.C., November 20, 1958 (mimeographed) ; and Hope J. Leichter and Judith Lieb, "Implications of a Research Experience with Caseworkers and Clients," a paper presented at the annual meeting of the National Conference of Jewish Communal Service, Pittsburgh, May 31, 1959 (mimeographed).

[149] Eugene Litwak, "Geographical Mobility and Extended Family Cohesion," *American Sociological Review,* Vol. 25, No. 1 (February 1960), pp. 385–394; Marvin B. Sussman, "The Help Pattern in the Middle Class Family," *American Sociological Review,* Vol. 18, No. 1 (February 1953), pp. 22–28; and Marvin B. Sussman and Lee Burchinal, "Kin Family Network: Unheralded Structure in Current Conceptualizations of Family Functioning," *Marriage and Family Living,* Vol. 24, No. 3 (August 1962), pp. 231–240.

[150] John C. Mayer, "Family Privacy: A Pilot Study" (New York: Community Service Society, 1962) (mimeographed) ; Paul Glasser, "Changes in Family Equilibrium During Psychotherapy," *Family Process,* Vol. 2, No.

As yet, however, these efforts in social work still are too scattered and embryonic to identify common themes and problems. Fortunately, a great deal of methodological and theoretical spade work has been done in these areas by investigators in other disciplines. Thus, some conceptual and technical tools are available for the study of a number of important dimensions of family behavior including, for example, decision-making, power and authority, and role conflict.[151] For the serious investigator in this area, Straus has abstracted and classified existing techniques for measuring family behavior.[152] Mention also should be made of the annual reviews of family research published in *Marriage and Family Living*, providing ready access to the voluminous literature in the family field. With the impetus provided by the growing interest in family dynamics on the part of social work practitioners, social work research in this area has an opportunity not only to advance family diagnosis and treatment but also to make a contribution to basic knowledge about the family.

Finally, it might be well to return to a question raised at the outset: Has social work research capitalized on social workers' strategic access to information about family organization and disorganization? The answer, at present, must be a qualified "no." Some possible explanations for this

failing have been suggested: (1) the preoccupation with studies of effectiveness; (2) reliance on loose, global, and essentially atheoretical concepts, such as the multiproblem family; and (3) the failure to use and relate social work research on the family to available theory and methods developed in other disciplines. The qualification attached to this negative answer refers to the dawning realization, on the part of social work practitioners and researchers alike, of the practical value of basic knowledge about family structures and processes, and to the emergence of social work research reflecting this realization.

Social Policy and the Family

Most if not all of the research reviewed earlier has implications for social policy on the family, but research bearing directly on such policy has, to date, been relatively limited. Moreover, major policy studies, such as Schorr's, are more in the tradition of historical or philosophical analysis than of quantitative social science, although they draw upon the findings of quantitative studies.[153] This is not to say that these policy studies are not "research," but rather that they represent a different type of research.

A problem, then, in reviewing social policy materials is that the standards for evaluating policy research are not entirely clear. Even in the case of empirical research, when one might expect that evaluative criteria would be the same as for research in the social and behavioral sciences generally, some have suggested that research directed to policy questions should follow a different logic of research strategy than is generally accepted in social science. Thus, for example, Freeman suggests that independent variables in policy research should be selected not for their theoretical relevance but for what he calls their "influ-

---

2 (September 1963), pp. 245–264; and Aura Aguirre *et al.*, "Toward Diagnostic Typology for the Family," unpublished master's thesis, University of California, School of Social Welfare, Berkeley, 1960.

[151] *See* Robert O. Blood and Donald M. Wolfe, *Husbands and Wives* (Glencoe, Ill.: Free Press, 1960); David Heer, "The Measurement and Bases of Family Power: An Overview," *Marriage and Family Living*, Vol. 25, No. 2 (May 1963), pp. 133–139; and Jack V. Buerkle and Robin F. Badgley, "Couple Role-Taking: The Yale Marital Interaction Battery," *Marriage and Family Living*, Vol. 21, No. 1 (February 1959), pp. 53–58.

[152] Murray A. Straus, *Family Measurement Abstracts* (Minneapolis: University of Minnesota Family Study Center, 1961).

[153] *See*, for example, Schorr's *Slums and Social Insecurity*.

ence potential." [154] And for policy analysis studies, no explicit canons have been formulated by which one can evaluate these studies, other than such obvious considerations as the adequacy of the evidence cited by the analyst and the soundness of his logic.

There is no better way to begin a review of family policy analysis in social work than with Schorr's excellent essay on family policy in the United States.[155] In this lucid and carefully reasoned paper, Schorr argues that the United States—including especially the social welfare system—lacks a coherent and explicit family policy, by which he means "consensus on a core of family goals, towards the realization of which the nation deliberately shapes programmes and policies." [156] Schorr traces this lack to certain deep-rooted traditions in American culture, including individualism, minimal government intervention, and cultural pluralism. Consequently, policies affecting families are adopted without adequate consideration of family need, and frequently on the basis of the questionable assumption that "families are served if people are served." [157]

This assumption appears to guide policy decisions in many social welfare programs and, as Schorr points out, "because family policy is not the foremost consideration and has not even been formulated, damaging family effects may inadvertently be produced." [158] Thus, for example, in response to concern about the social problem correlates of slum housing, public housing projects are created on the assumption that improved housing facilities for people are beneficial for families, but without consideration of the possible deleterious consequences of relocation and project housing design on family life. In short, Schorr's paper is an eloquent plea for the formulation of family policy and for the research that this formulation will require. Similar pleas have been made earlier by Frank and Hill.[159]

Schorr himself has done as much if not more than anyone in social work toward filling the gaps identified in his paper. He has published studies analyzing public policy in three crucial areas. *Filial Responsibility in the Modern American Family* reviews the research on relations between parents and their adult children and analyzes policy in social security programs requiring adult children to assume responsibility for their parents.[160] Schorr notes that the requirement of filial responsibility has developed since medieval times, does not exist in American common law, and is inconsistent with contemporary family norms and with the emphasis on adult independence and autonomy in American culture. He identifies a number of undesirable consequences of this policy and concludes that the major deleterious effects are the restrictions it can impose on the independence of families and their freedom of choice regarding living arrangements.

In *Slums and Social Insecurity* Schorr turned his attention to the effects of the physical ecology, and particularly housing, on family life and to a consideration of housing policy to promote family life.[161] After marshaling the available evidence on the effects of housing and neighborhood on family life, on attitudes, and on poverty, Schorr shows that for the most part physical planning has failed to consider these effects. With Gans, Schorr argues that

---

[154] Howard E. Freeman, "The Strategy of Social Policy Research," *Social Welfare Forum, 1963*, Proceedings of the National Conference on Social Welfare (New York: Columbia University Press, 1963), p. 152.
[155] "Family Policy in the United States."
[156] *Ibid.*, p. 452.
[157] *Ibid.*, p. 457.
[158] *Ibid.*, p. 462.

[159] Laurence K. Frank, "A National Policy for the Family," *Marriage and Family Living*, Vol. 10, No. 1 (Winter 1948), pp. 1–4; and Reuben Hill, *Families Under Stress*.
[160] Alvin L. Schorr, *Filial Responsibility in the Modern American Family* (Washington, D.C.: U.S. Department of Health, Education, and Welfare, 1960).
[161] *Op. cit.*

for poor families maintenance of housing is more important than new housing, but that existing codes and tax laws discourage maintenance. His general conclusion is that a socially conscious housing policy must be a crucial component of any program that hopes to prevent poverty and family disorganization effectively.

Schorr's analysis of certain policies in the ADC program consists of an examination of known effects of the program measured against its implied and explicit objectives.[162] He reaches four conclusions regarding damage done to families by the program:

1. The program "operates selectively to serve families who are not only disadvantaged economically but who meet with social disfavor"; moreover, these families "receive less favored treatment than other public assistance recipients." [163]

2. The ADC program gives the mother little effective choice regarding whether she will or will not work. She feels pressured to work but work brings her little or no financial advantage.

3. Although the ADC program focuses on the whole family when the family consists of a mother and children, the program operates so as to divide the father from his wife and children.

4. Because of several important uncertainties in the program—the work dilemma and the absent father policy—"the ADC program operates to add to the instability characteristic of the troubled families who receive grants." [164]

Actually, these conclusions, as well as the conclusions of Schorr's other two studies, should be considered hypotheses and, in fact, Schorr presents them in that form. More generally, one of the values of policy analyses of this sort is that they identify gaps in the knowledge base on which sound policy must rest and generate additional

questions regarding the possible effects of alternative policies. In fact, Schorr's studies are a gold mine of problems for research.

McKeany's study of the absent father provisions of the ADC program is a carefully documented analysis.[165] Her thesis is that "the provisions of the ADC legislation with reference to children deserted or abandoned by their fathers is a manifestation of a conflict between two public policies—the policy of meeting the economic needs of children, and that of forcing this responsibility upon fathers who do not perform their duty of support." [166] The monograph traces the background of this conflict, examines its manifestations in policy and legislation, reviews the states' experiences with these policies, and considers alternative policy resolutions. Her study reveals that broad public policy decisions in this area typically have not moved much beyond an essentially regulatory concern with methods of requiring fathers to meet their responsibilities. When combined with Schorr's observations regarding the tendency of the ADC program to isolate fathers from their families, McKeany's analysis highlights the importance of research on policy alternatives in this area.

The influence of economic policy on family life, and especially the role of these policies in the genesis and perpetuation of poverty, has received considerable attention recently, although most of the studies have been conducted outside social work.[167] One of the more sophisticated studies in this area is the one conducted at the University of Michigan Survey Research Center by Morgan *et al.*[168] This complex study can-

---

[162] Alvin L. Schorr, "Problems in the ADC Program," *Social Work*, Vol. 5, No. 2 (April 1960), pp. 3–15.

[163] *Ibid.*, p. 7.

[164] *Ibid.*, p. 15.

[165] *Op. cit.*

[166] *Ibid.*, p. 5.

[167] *See,* for example, John K. Galbraith, *The Affluent Society* (Boston: Houghton Mifflin Company, 1958); Michael Harrington, *The Other America* (New York: Macmillan Company, 1962); Morgan *et al., op. cit.*; and Richard M. Titmuss, *Income Distribution and Social Change* (London: George Allen & Unwin, 1962).

[168] Morgan *et al., op. cit.*

not be summarized briefly; instead, this review will be limited to one aspect of the study particularly pertinent to family policy.

In their study, the investigators assumed —and offer findings to support their assumption—that certain voluntary family decisions, such as choices regarding the allocation of family resources, are significant intervening variables in determining family income. That is, family income is not predetermined by socioeconomic factors external to the family, but is partly determined by choices made within the family unit. Accordingly, some of the policy implications of this study acknowledge the importance of family choices in the attainment of economic and welfare objectives. Thus, for example, the authors imply that a choice strategy designed to increase educational attainment may, at least in the long run, reduce poverty because of the potency of education as a determinant of family income. On the other hand, some analyses of employment opportunities indicate that pressuring youth, and especially youth in minority groups, to advance their educational status may in fact only increase the frustrations of those youths most in need of upgrading.[169] This specific problem illustrates a major difficulty in social policy analysis: the need to juxtapose different domains of analysis—a task that requires familiarity with a broad range of knowledge.

Students of family policy in social work have not yet confronted fully and directly the policy questions posed by the major changes occurring in the American family system. Scholars are not entirely in accord as to what changes have occurred; they agree even less in their interpretations of these changes, and they differ considerably in their projections of the future evolution of the American family. Social work re-

search can hardly be expected to resolve these differences, but it should be concerned with the implications of these changes for welfare policies.

Several discussions of the changing American family have appeared in the social work literature.[170] They all adopt an optimistic stance regarding the future of the American family and thus do not adequately reflect the views of some important but less sanguine students of the family.[171] Moreover, while some of these essays refer to the policy implications of changes in the family, they go little beyond the admonition that welfare policy should be adapted to these changes.

Policy research still is a comparatively young field in social work. The vigor and quality of the work completed thus far in the realm of family policy augur well for the future of this research area.

Conclusions

Four broad areas of the family field have been reviewed. Since a wide range of material was covered, it may be useful at this juncture to summarize the major conclusions.

1. Social work research on the private family agency has thus far been focused

---

[169] Harry Brill, "Educating Youth: The Cruel Solution," *The Nation*, Vol. 198, No. 13 (March 23, 1964), pp. 296–297; and Ben B. Seligman, "Automation and the State," *Commentary*, Vol. 37, No. 6 (June 1964), pp. 49–54.

[170] *See* Leon Eisenberg, "The Family in the Mid-twentieth Century," *Social Welfare Forum, 1960*, Proceedings of the National Conference on Social Welfare (New York: Columbia University Press, 1960); Phillip Fellin, "A Reappraisal of Changes in American Family Patterns," *Social Casework*, Vol. 45, No. 5 (May 1964), pp. 263–267; Charles Frankel, "The Family in Context," in Fred Delliquadri, ed., *Helping the Family in Urban Society* (New York: Columbia University Press, 1963); Reuben Hill, "The Changing American Family," *Social Welfare Forum, 1957*, Proceedings of the National Conference on Social Welfare (New York: Columbia University Press, 1957), pp. 68–80; and Milton J. Yinger, "The Changing Family in a Changing Society," *Social Casework*, Vol. 40, No. 8 (October 1959), pp. 419–428.

[171] *See*, for example, Farber, *Family: Organization and Interaction*.

primarily on studies of organizational efficiency and patterns of service. While these efforts have produced practical, usable results, perhaps their main contribution has been to raise questions about family agency operations—questions on which further research is needed. Thus, for example, studies of caseworkers' use of time, of case recording, and of staff turnover have highlighted a need for studies of supervision—a subject that has received virtually no systematic attention from social work researchers. This seems a rather striking gap in view of the importance attached to this activity in social work agencies. By and large, studies of the family agency have made limited use of the conceptual and methodological tools of organizational analysis. This seems unfortunate in view of the valuable findings that have resulted from the application of these tools in studies of institutional settings. While it is well known that the services and clientele of family agencies have changed over time, with some notable and recent exceptions, the implications of these changes for the role and function of the family agency in the social welfare community have received little systematic study.

2. The voluntary family agency has been the focus of many important studies of methods of intervention conducted in social work. Until recently, systematic research on methods of intervention in the family field has been almost exclusively occupied with the problem of effectiveness, and particularly the task of constructing techniques for measuring change in clients. To be sure, a practicing profession must inevitably be concerned with this problem, but it is appropriate to question the amount of research attention it has received. These efforts have not succeeded in demonstrating unequivocally the effectiveness of social work treatment, or shed much light on the ingredients of client change. Moreover, even though the primary emphasis of the major studies of this problem has been avowedly methodological, there has been little inclination to experiment with alternative techniques for measuring treatment outcome. Rather, investigators have shown a strong predilection to rely on clinical judgment, in spite of a growing body of evidence indicating its limitations as a measure of client variables. If measurement is a major problem in the study of treatment outcome, it would seem wise for methodological research systematically to explore and compare alternative methods of measurement, including techniques developed in related disciplines.

One method of dealing with the problem of measuring effectiveness that has received considerable attention from social work researchers is the use of continuance in treatment as an indicator of outcome. Some convergences in the findings of continuance studies were noted, especially the relationships reported between continuance and (1) congruence between the belief systems of worker and client, (2) client motivation, and (3) client problem. Thus far, continuance research has neglected a number of possibly important factors, particularly the effects of (1) agency policy and structure, (2) personal characteristics of the social worker, and (3) environmental and situational factors in the client's life situation. A more fundamental weakness of continuance studies is the assumption that continuance is a necessary prerequisite to the effective use of casework service. Not only is the validity of this assumption in doubt (on the basis of some empirical findings), but it also diverts attention from one of the most well-documented facts about family agency services—their predominantly short-term character. The continuance studies imply that the task is to find out how short-term cases can be helped to become long-term ones. Another approach, and one that may be more consistent with service realities, is to ask what can be done to increase the effectiveness of short-term casework.

A more general issue, insofar as the study of treatment is concerned, is whether at the present stage of social work outcome research should be emphasized at the expense of other vantage points, such as studies of treatment methods and processes, for the study of intervention.[172] A variety of potentially transferable methods for the study of treatment have been developed in related disciplines, and it is encouraging to note signs of a growing interest in other approaches to the study of treatment among social work researchers. One of the obstacles to the development of more sophisticated and diversified research activities in this area has been the profession's failure to promote the development of a larger number of practitioner-researchers with a career interest in studying social work treatment.

3. As might be expected, studies of the family in social work have been concerned primarily with family pathology and disorganization. In recent years, social work research on family disorganization has been dominated largely by the multiproblem family. In retrospect, selection of the multiproblem family as the orienting concept for research in this area may have been unfortunate. Loosely defined to begin with, the concept has not been clarified appreciably, in spite of years of active research effort. In fact, researchers working with the multiproblem family have shown little interest in conducting the kinds of descriptive studies that need to be done before the term can be defined more precisely. But vagueness is not the only weakness. As yet, the multiproblem family has not been explicitly connected to a theory of family disorganization, although current usage of the term often implies certain questionable assumptions about the determinants of the social problems it subsumes. The inclusiveness of the concept may inhibit studies of specific and more easily defined aspects of family disorganization.

There are some recent indications that the widespread and growing interest in family diagnosis and treatment among practitioners may stimulate more delimited and theoretically meaningful studies of family behavior. In such studies, social work could capitalize on its virtually unique access to certain groups of families and thereby contribute not only to practice but to the general fund of knowledge about family life.

4. Social policy regarding the family has received comparatively little research attention in social work. The excellence of some recent studies in this area is encouraging, and hopefully signals increased activity in the future. One of the virtues of policy analysis studies is that they highlight important gaps in knowledge, and thus provide guides for research that can make strategic contributions to the planning of social welfare programs. One of the gaps in this area is that policy analysis has yet to come to grips with a problem of central importance to the family field—the implications for social welfare of the profound changes occurring in the American family.

Throughout this review, the tendency to conduct research in seeming isolation from the relevant theory and research techniques of other disciplines has been noted. This practice is unfortunate and wasteful. It has meant reliance on crude concepts and research tools when more sophisticated ones were available—as, for example, in the case of research on the family. In part this may reflect a misguided provincialism that can be detected here and there in the literature. Many believe that because social work has a unique concern with certain human problems and has developed its own methods for dealing with them, social work needs to formulate its own theory and fashion research tools especially suited to its needs. These are laudable and desirable aims, but they should not pre-empt other more important objectives, such as the need to increase understanding of the problems of concern to social workers and to enhance social workers' effectiveness in ameliorating them. Knowledge relevant to the latter objectives should be utilized whenever it can be found.

---

[172] In other words, if existing outcome measures are inadequate, and *if* we do not know how to improve them, then perhaps serious attempts to demonstrate effectiveness should be deferred or at least soft-pedaled until the necessary methodological research has been done.

An applied profession must cultivate its relationship to the basic sciences.

In spite of the faults of social work research in the family field, the over-all impression is one that should give the profession grounds for optimism about the future of research in this vital area. The volume of research activity is remarkable in view of the slow development of organized research in social work and the small number of persons engaged in research activity. Although the work that has been done thus far has produced precious little

in the way of solid, usable knowledge, social workers have learned a great deal about how they should proceed to acquire the knowledge needed by their profession.

To be sure, research is not a panacea for the problems confronting the profession, but these problems will not be solved without it. Since an essential dynamic in the growth of a profession is the expansion of its knowledge base, there can hardly be a more important or more practical task in social work than the conduct of sound and meaningful research.

PUBLIC WELFARE

By SAMUEL MENCHER

The responsibility of public welfare in society is so vast that it is not possible to encompass, in a review of this scope, all the research bearing on the many kinds of practice and services that constitute public welfare. This review will therefore concentrate on, although not limit itself to, research on economic assistance, because this is the primary responsibility of public welfare today, and many of the other public welfare functions are closely related to or determined by this responsibility. Even within the scope of economic assistance, only selected studies can be considered.

The research reviewed is related to (1) the characteristics of public assistance clients, (2) the effects of public assistance programs, (3) the administration of public assistance, and (4) the economics of public welfare.

Characteristics of Public Assistance Clients

Historically, the nature of public assistance policy has been controversial. As a result, many reports of studies of public assistance are polemical documents rather than scholarly appraisals. One of the earliest and most famous was the English Poor Law investigation of the 1830's, preceding the Poor Law Reform of 1834. A national survey with a lengthy and complex schedule "proved" the influence of relief on dependency, illegitimacy, and a wide variety of individual and social ills. More recently, the federal Aid to Families with Dependent Children (AFDC) study is an illustration of an examination of assistance programs under public pressure.[1] A great number of state and local studies occur under similar circumstances. The variety of reports on AFDC and illegitimacy attest to the continued partisan interest of state legislatures and the public generally.

More frankly than most, the report of a 1963 study of AFDC in Detroit sponsored by the local chapter of the National Asso-

---

[1] U.S. Department of Health, Education, and Welfare, "Eligibility of Families Receiving Aid to Families with Dependent Children" (Washington, D.C., 1963). (Mimeographed.)

ciation of Social Workers (NASW) stated
its purpose to be:

Interpretative—to incite the people of Michigan to take action against an end . . . It
may be noted that the national attention
gained by the study is not due to its exceptional scientific merit but to the recent increase in interest in the "Other America,"
and most of all to the efficiency of . . . a
professional public relations firm.[2]

Another large group of studies, also conducted by official bodies, reflects the ongoing attempts to assess program and solve
policy problems. While perhaps not so
polemical as the studies noted above, they
cannot be considered entirely objective in
their approach or sophisticated in their research methods. Even when a private organization such as Community Research
Associates (CRA) has conducted studies,
its involvement in policy and program pre-
vents total objectivity. A higher level of
objectivity may be achieved when the outside body is not program involved, as in
the Greenleigh Associates study of the
AFDC program in Cook County.[3] Rarest,
and from a research point of view most
valuable, are independent studies as, for
example, the two American Public Welfare Association studies of the AFDC program.[4] While the study of public assistance
and public welfare generally would be
greatly advanced by an increasing quantity
of independent research, discriminating use
of the large amount of available material
can provide valuable dividends.

Most current studies of characteristics of
the assistance population have concentrated
on the aged and AFDC families. They are
the largest of the categorical programs (approximately 90 percent of all federally
aided assistance recipients), and present
the most complex problem for policy-making. While the Old Age Assistance (OAA)
and AFDC populations have been reported
upon in full-scale characteristic studies,
knowledge of the other categories is often
obtained as by-products of other kinds of
research. Thus, while this section will review formal characteristic studies limited
to the OAA and AFDC populations,
throughout this review as a whole knowledge of these and other populations will be
supplemented from data produced in other
types of studies. For example, efforts to
determine the extent of fraud in public assistance often reveal much about the clients,
as do examinations of eligibility requirements, rehabilitation, and relative responsibility.

It is noteworthy that the general assistance cases, the major population on which
there is least information, are also among
the most complex and the most poorly cared
for. Apart from what may be gathered from
the CRA reports and a few local studies,
there is little else other than the monthly
statistics of those state agencies involved
in general assistance. Perhaps the heyday
of general assistance research occurred in
the early 1930's before the federal categorical programs, when the federal government took general relief responsibility.[5]
These studies at times achieved a depth of
analysis and detail rarely attempted in the

---

[2] Charles N. Lebeaux, "Life on ADC in
Detroit, 1963," *Metropolitan Detroit NASW
Chapter Newsletter*, Vol. 1, No. 3 (November
1964), p. 1.

[3] Greenleigh Associates, "Facts, Fallacies
and Future, A Study of the Aid to Dependent
Children Program of Cook County, Illinois,"
and "Addenda to Facts, Fallacies and Future" (New York, 1960). (Mimeographed.)

[4] Gordon W. Blackwell and Raymond F.
Gould, *Future Citizens All* (Chicago: Ameri-
can Public Welfare Association, 1952); and
Elaine M. Burgess and Daniel O. Price, *An
American Dependency Challenge* (Chicago:
American Public Welfare Association, 1963).

---

[5] *See*, for example, E. Wight Bakke, *Citizens Without Work* and *The Unemployed
Worker* (New Haven: Yale University Press,
1940); and Elizabeth W. Gilboy, *Applicants
for Work Relief* (Cambridge: Harvard University Press, 1940); Elizabeth W. Gilboy,
"The Expenditure of the Unemployed," *American Sociological Review*, Vol. 3, No. 6 (December 1938), pp. 801–814; and Mirra Komarovsky, *The Unemployed Man and His Family*
(New York: Dryden Press, 1940).

current emphasis on broad-gauge descriptive statistics.

The Old Age Assistance Population

The federal Bureau of Public Assistance conducted two national surveys, in 1953 and 1960, on characteristics of OAA recipients.[6] Comparative analysis of these reports provides trend data for the OAA population, as well as indications of the divergence between this group and the aged in the general population. One of the major findings of the 1960 study was the increasing physical limitations among the aged on assistance since 1953, and the greater incidence of these handicaps among assistance recipients as compared to all aged. The proportion of bedridden had increased slightly from 3.5 to 4 percent, but those with limited mobility increased from 14.3 percent to 18.6 percent. This was particularly true of the white aged and, according to the study, reflected the relatively higher average age among white recipients. This difference does not appear sufficient to account for the much greater increase among whites requiring care from others. The greater coverage of whites by Old Age, Survivors and Disability Insurance (OASDI) may be an important factor in leaving a residue on OAA of those of the white aged who for reasons of health or other limitations had poor work histories. In this as in other programs, the characteristics of the population are strongly affected by the eligibility requirements of the program and by the changing environment of related programs that concentrate on or

siphon off specific elements of the population.

This phenomenon is reflected in the much greater proportion of noninstitutionalized aged confined to their homes among the OAA aged as compared to the general aged population: 13.9 percent to 4.4 percent. In addition to the OASDI effect noted above, there is also the likelihood that greater confinement to home on OAA may result not from absolute physical limitations alone, but also from the absence of the concern and care of relatives, which may be associated both with eligibility requirements and with the effect of handicapping conditions.

The living conditions of OAA recipients not in institutions improved between 1953 and 1960. As measured by access to telephones, electric lights, refrigeration, and running water, there was a general advance for the aged on assistance. Some of these gains reflected more liberal budgetary policies of assistance agencies in 1960. A somewhat higher proportion of aged in 1960 were living alone in their own homes (30.4 percent) as compared to 1953 (26.5 percent). The proportion living in institutions, however, increased from 4.7 percent to 8.8 percent.

Few aged were receiving financial contributions from their children in 1960. Less than one-fourth of the aged with non-dependent children received such help. The proportion of those receiving help from children living in the same household was much greater than for those who lived separately. The 1953 and 1960 reports summarize other useful demographic data on the aged on assistance including sex, race, age, and place of residence.

[6] U.S. Department of Health, Education, and Welfare, Bureau of Public Assistance, "Recipients of Old-Age Assistance in Early 1953," Part I—State Data, Public Assistance Report No. 26 (Washington, D.C., 1955) (mimeographed); and "Characteristics and Financial Circumstances of Recipients of Old-Age Assistance, 1960," Part I—National Data, Public Assistance Report No. 48 (Washington, D.C., 1961) (mimeographed).

The AFDC Population

As noted above, widespread research interest has centered on the AFDC case load. Innumerable small studies have been conducted on state and local levels, although in many the absence of any explicitly reported research procedures or the limited regional relevance of the data greatly reduce the value of their contributions. Selected findings of several AFDC studies are reviewed below as illustrative of the strengths and limitations of these studies, as well as studies of client characteristics generally.

Parents in AFDC families. On the basis of a national sample of 5,517 closed AFDC cases, in which all but eight states were represented, Burgess and Price collected a wealth of data on AFDC families. Since much of the schedule was comparable to that used in the 1950 study of Blackwell and Gould, trends in population and program could be examined. Burgess and Price's findings supported the general thesis of the continuity of deprivation and dependency among segments of the population. Of those of the sample for whom the information was given (77 percent), over 40 percent of the mothers and/or fathers had themselves come from homes in which public assistance had been received. AFDC parents were found to have little education and vocational skill.[7]

These findings are corroborated by studies conducted in California and Oklahoma.[8] The Oklahoma study of a 10 percent sample of open cases (1,885) in one month reported most fathers as unskilled or semiskilled, and only one-half of the mothers had finished the ninth grade. The California study, based on a 4 percent sample of the fifteen largest counties with more than 80 percent of the total state case load, also emphasized the lack of education, work experience, and work skills of the mothers.

The nationwide study of AFDC families conducted by the U.S. Bureau of Family

Services in late 1961 provided further evidence of the low educational and vocational preparation of mothers and fathers in these families.[9] Compared to 35 percent of all men, only 3 percent of AFDC fathers were in white-collar occupations. By comparison, 34 percent of AFDC fathers were in unskilled work as contrasted with 7 percent nationally. Similar differences were reported for mothers, who had on the average 3.3 years less schooling than the average of women in the general population. These findings suggest, moreover, that AFDC fathers are more like the general population than they really are. A large proportion of the fathers in the Bureau of Family Services survey, though reporting a vocation, were unemployed at the time of the study and some may never have had full-time employment.

Nature of family life in AFDC cases. As several studies of public assistance clients point out, the eligibility practices of public assistance agencies so influence the selection and, therefore, the reported characteristics of the families aided that any study may as much reflect official attitudes toward who should be helped as any indigenous nature of the dependent group itself. This becomes even more striking in comparisons over time when differences in policy may well account for the changing characteristics of the client population. For example, one of the differences between AFDC families in 1960 and 1950 is the proportion of those in which the major crisis precipitating dependency was the death of the father. In 1960, 4.5 percent of the total were so affected whereas in 1950 it had been 18 percent.[10] This difference is accounted for by the expansion of OASDI; families of deceased fathers no

---

[7] Burgess and Price, *op. cit.*, pp. 158–159.

[8] California Department of Social Welfare, "Social and Economic Characteristics of Aid to Needy Children Families, March 1960" (Sacramento, 1961) (mimeographed); and Oklahoma Department of Public Welfare, "Aid to Dependent Children Families, December 1961" (Oklahoma City, undated) (mimeographed).

[9] U.S. Department of Health, Education, and Welfare, Bureau of Family Services, "Characteristics of Families Receiving Aid to Families with Dependent Children, November–December 1961" (Washington, D.C., 1963). (Mimeographed.)

[10] *See* Burgess and Price, *op. cit.*, p. 40; and Blackwell and Gould, *op. cit.*, p. 21.

longer relied so heavily on AFDC. Similarly the recent inclusion of families with able-bodied fathers in AFDC will result in significant changes in characteristics of the families served, by comparison with data for 1950 and 1960.

The major factors contributing to families requiring AFDC in 1960, according to Burgess and Price, were incapacitated father, desertion by father, unmarried motherhood, and father in a penal institution. While these were the major crises for both white and Negro families, the order of importance varied. Unmarried motherhood and desertion were more prevalent among the Negro families, and incapacity of the father among the white.[11]

Approximately one-half of the families in the Burgess and Price study were reported as having some kind of "adult behavior difficulty"—marital conflict, desertion, unmarried parenthood, promiscuity, or drinking.[12] The Greenleigh study of a sample of 1,010 active cases in Cook County in the same period found 81 percent of families in the Chicago area to have no problem behavior—alcoholism, drug addiction, truancy, or delinquency.[13] The definition of the problem behavior may in itself account for the difference (although the use of an active case load by Greenleigh and closed cases by Burgess and Price may be of significance, as may the other differences in the samples and methodologies of the studies). The definition of behavior difficulty by Burgess and Price does no more, however, than repeat the terms of eligibility for most families.

The extent of illegitimacy among AFDC families has been the cause of much public concern. The concept of major crisis used by Burgess and Price does not measure prevalence, but rather the single most instrumental factor influencing dependency. Thus in 10.3 percent of the cases, mother unmarried was listed as the major crisis,

but the study reported unwed motherhood in 20 percent of the families.[14] Saul Kaplan estimated that families of unwed mothers in 1955 were 22.7 percent of all AFDC families, and found a substantial increase in the number of unwed mothers and their children between 1948 and 1955.[15]

Although the proportion of unwed mothers and illegitimate children is certainly high, this in itself does not answer the question of the extent to which illegitimacy is a significantly unique phenomenon of the AFDC case load or is relatively representative of the population at risk. There has been some tendency in studies attempting to deal with the issue merely to compare general population rates with AFDC rates and conclude that there is a vast difference between the two groups. Apart from questions about the comparable accuracy of reporting for both populations, serious difficulties arise. As the report of the California Aid to Needy Children (ANC) Task Force noted:

Illegitimacy rates cannot be compared to those in the general population. ANC recipients are a selected population who meet eligibility requirements and who are in need. Also the majority of ANC mothers are divorced, separated or single; and the ANC rate would have to be compared to the rate of illegitimacy among similarly situated women rather than with the rate among all women—single or married—in the general population.[16]

Care of children. While the behavior of parents has frequently been considered the measure of the welfare of the children on AFDC, several studies have examined the welfare of children directly. Some light

---

[11] Burgess and Price, *op. cit.*, p. 40.
[12] *Ibid.*, p. 135.
[13] "Facts, Fallacies and Future," p. 14.

[14] Burgess and Price, *op. cit.*, pp. 40, 139.
[15] U.S. Department of Health, Education, and Welfare, Bureau of Public Assistance, *Support from Absent Fathers of Children Receiving ADC: 1955*, Public Assistance Report No. 41 (Washington, D.C., 1960).
[16] California Department of Social Welfare, "Illegitimacy in the Aid to Needy Children Program" (Sacramento, 1960), p. 5. (Mimeographed.) ANC was the title of the AFDC program in California.

on the relationship of adult behavior and child care was provided by the operations of the Florida suitable home law. Of 5,927 cases reviewed in the first year because of alleged unsuitability, 98.9 percent were reported as providing improper moral environment, but abuse of child, physical or mental, applied to only 0.5 percent; exploitation of child, 0.2 percent; neglect of needs of child, 1.2 percent; neglect of care of child, 3.1 percent.[17] These categories were not mutually exclusive and the percentages are not additive. While these reports were part of an administrative review, rather than a formal research project, the marked discrepancy between judgments of "stable moral environment" and evidence of child neglect was striking.

Burgess and Price reported child neglect and abuse to be present in 8 percent of their sample of families, and 4 percent were reported as not using their grants "primarily" for their children.[18] The latter, however, can be questioned as a valid criterion of neglect, for the freedom of parents to determine their own family goals is one of the purposes of the program. In the Greenleigh study of Cook County, only 3 percent of the families had been the subject of complaints about child neglect and only one-half of these were found to be valid complaints.[19]

Criteria such as school attendance and performance, health, and delinquency have also been used to measure the level of welfare of children on AFDC. Of all reported AFDC children 6–17 years of age and eligible to attend school, according to the Bureau of Family Services survey, 96.3 percent were attending in 1961, and physical and mental incapacity accounted for an additional 1.2 percent.[20] Burgess and

Price found great differences between the educational progress of AFDC and other children. For example, only 30 percent of AFDC children, 18–24, had completed high school as compared to 62 percent in the general population.[21] Some analysts, however, have not considered these differences excessive. In Greenleigh's Cook County study only one-half of the children in AFDC families were in their proper grade; nevertheless the study concluded that this was remarkable in view of the mother's educational level, mobility of the families, economic deprivation, and poor schools attended.[22] Referring specifically to out-of-wedlock children on the AFDC case load, the Oklahoma Department of Welfare study found no "notable" school retardation when compared to other children on assistance.[23]

The extent of physical and mental impairments, when remediable, among children in AFDC families may also be considered relevant to the care received. The Bureau of Family Services survey reported about 11 percent of children in AFDC families having one or more mental or physical defects. However, only a small proportion of the sample was diagnosed by expert opinion, and thus this may not have been the true rate.[24] No mention is made of the proportion whose conditions were remediable. The Oklahoma study of out-of-wedlock children on AFDC found that neglected physical or mental impairments were no more prevalent than among other children on the AFDC case load. In the age group 6–17, the illegitimate children had 9.1 per-

---

[17] Florida Department of Public Welfare, "Suitable Home Law," Preliminary Report (Jacksonville, 1960), Table 7. (Mimeographed.)
[18] *Op. cit.*, p. 139.
[19] "Facts, Fallacies and Future," p. 12.
[20] U.S. Department of Health, Education,

and Welfare, Bureau of Family Services, *op. cit.*, Table 35.
[21] Burgess and Price, *op. cit.*, pp. 106–107.
[22] "Facts, Fallacies and Future," p. 15.
[23] *Op. cit.*, p. 10.
[24] *See*, for example, Robert H. Mugge, "Aid to Families with Dependent Children: Initial Findings of the 1961 Report on the Characteristics of Recipients," *Social Security Bulletin*, Vol. 26, No. 3 (March 1963), pp. 7–8.

cent fewer impairments and among these children one was more "apt to find these needs met." The percentage of all children 6–17 on AFDC with physical or mental impairments was 18.4. However, the source of diagnosis was not indicated.[25]

Delinquent behavior is another indication of parental interest, although like other factors its incidence cannot be totally attributed to parental influence. In the Burgess and Price national AFDC sample, 5 percent of all children, Negro and white, were reported delinquent.[26] In Cook County, of 391 families with children 12 years or older, the Greenleigh study found less than 5 percent with children known to the court and most had only one child before the juvenile court.[27] The Burgess and Price criteria for delinquency were broader than Greenleigh's, but they concluded that the rate was lower than might have been expected among children of AFDC families. Speaking of all the factors in the lives of these children they state:

They all add up to a general, though not completely consistent picture of many of the more undesirable environmental conditions and inadequate opportunities in the lives and ADC homes of most of the delinquent children—absent mother, poorly educated homemaker, inadequate supervision, concentration in large urban centers, school retardation, poor economic and employment opportunities, etc. On the basis of the available data and keeping their limitations in mind, it is felt that the incidence of juvenile delinquency is far lower than might be expected among children from such disadvantaged backgrounds, and still below the estimated national rate for all children.[28]

The General Assistance Population

Among the few reports on general assistance clients is a study conducted by the Cook County Department of Public Aid in 1961 to determine the effect of automation on a group of general assistance recipients.[29] Of persons included in the study, from a random sample of 3,000 general assistance cases, there were initially 138 considered to have had skilled or semiskilled occupations. However, out of this small number, data collected subsequently during this study resulted in reclassifying 44 percent of these as unskilled.[30] Filtering out so few who could possibly be considered semiskilled or skilled was probably the most significant finding of the study. It indicated the employment potential of this total general assistance population. The study collected much additional data on the small group interviewed, but the size of the sample and the interview techniques used raise questions about reliability. The data were representative of neither the total general assistance population nor any considerable segment, but showed that even the most highly skilled members of one metropolitan assistance population fell below the general population in median education and had a recent history of extremely irregular employment.

An earlier study conducted by the University of Chicago used a random sample of Chicago assistance applicants in a six-week period between January and March 1959.[31] This sample was more representative of the total general assistance population, although the particular time of the year selected may have introduced some bias. Of the 1,412 cases in the sample, 59.2 were reported as seeking assistance because of insufficient employment income and 40.8 percent because of social, psychological, or

---

[25] Oklahoma Department of Public Welfare, *op. cit.*, p. 19.

[26] *Op. cit.*, p. 119.

[27] "Addenda to Facts, Fallacies and Future," p. 47.

[28] Burgess and Price, *op. cit.*, pp. 123–124.

[29] Cook County Department of Public Aid, "A Study to Determine the Possible Impact of Automation on a Selected Group of General Assistance Recipients in Chicago" (Chicago, 1961). (Mimeographed.)

[30] *Ibid.*, p. 20.

[31] Cook County Department of Public Aid, "A Study of General Assistance Applications to Determine Causes of Dependency" (Chicago, 1959). (Mimeographed.)

physical factors. Based on interviewers' observations, 14.7 percent of applicants for employment reasons suffered from mental limitations and 15.0 percent from physical handicaps. Of those with insufficient employment income, 84.1 percent were requesting assistance because unemployment compensation benefits had not been present or were insufficient. This finding clearly demonstrates the relationship of the insurance and assistance systems and indicates that the problem of growing assistance rolls may frequently reflect inadequacies in the basic economic security structure. This assumption is supported by the study's finding that 61 percent of those applying because of unemployment were new applicants, not chronic relief recipients.[32]

In general, the group of applicants for employment reasons were marked by little skill and education. Only 16.3 percent were classified as skilled workers, and 62.7 had no more than eighth-grade education. Age, alcoholism, mental and physical handicaps, and language difficulties did not account for the absence of employment income. The great majority were below 45 years of age.[33] The study concluded that low education and skill were responsible for the limited employment of these applicants. As in the study noted above, the reliability of data based either on the applicant's reporting or the interviewer's observations has evident limitations. Until empirical results indicate that the error factor from these study methods is negligible, not much confidence can be placed on investigations relying on information given by assistance applicants and on the judgments of interviewers in such matters as alcoholism and mental and physical disabilities.

General Critique

The unco-ordinated and noncumulative nature of the characteristics studies completed

to date make for large gaps in knowledge of entire client groups and of significant aspects of groups about whom some data have been collected. It is assumed that until public agencies have a thorough knowledge of the nature of the client groups whom they serve, it is unlikely that they can serve them as effectively as they might.

Administrative statistics of operating agencies irregularly supplemented by special studies involve more effort for fewer results than a well-constructed and routinized collection of data geared to immediate and long-term policy needs. The development of uniform schedules that will make possible comparisons among regions as well as trend studies is essential. The development of sound scientific procedures for the regular collection and analysis of essential data on clients may well obviate some of the need for highly charged, emergency studies at critical moments in the course of public programs.

Knowledge of client characteristics cannot, however, be supplied entirely through more efficient agency data collection of the conventional kind. This must be supplemented by studies in depth of the lives of families on assistance. Current data provide at best crude silhouettes of the populations at risk. In view of the close contact that many agencies maintain with clients, there is every possibility of following up a small sample of families in depth so that a clearer understanding may be gained of psychological and social characteristics of assistance recipients.

Current studies of assistance populations have been limited in their usefulness by a dearth of comparable data on relatively similar groups in the general population.[34]

---

[32] *Ibid.*, pp. 2, 3, 7.
[33] *Ibid.*, pp. 6–7.

[34] A recent contribution in this direction has been made in a study, under the direction of Sydney E. Bernard, of low-income, female-headed families. He compared the characteristics of a small sample of "never-users," "low-users," and "high-users" of AFDC. *See* Bernard, "The Economic and Social Adjustment of Low-Income Female-Headed Families." Unpublished doctoral dissertation, University of Michigan, 1964.

Although, on the whole, the uniqueness or comparability of the assistance population is unknown, there has not been a dearth of strong opinions on the subject. Studies of the poor in the total population may help in understanding much about the assistance population, or it may be found that the latter have only superficial resemblances to other low-income groups. The recent renascence of interest in poverty may result in a fuller knowledge of low-income groups generally than has been available for perhaps a generation and it may provide norms for measuring the assistance population.

Studies of the kind envisaged must be guided, however, by a well-planned behavioral scientific focus if they are to be at all useful. The present collection of disconnected data and irrelevant case materials must be superseded by purposeful probing. The problem of understanding the economically dependent population is too complex to be left to simple measurement and description, which is too often stimulated by partisan expectations. Answers are needed to such questions as these: Who requires assistance? Who gets assistance? Why do some people in need seek assistance and not others? What does the experience of seeking assistance entail? What effect does relief have on recipients? How do some people manage without assistance? Who leaves assistance and becomes economically independent? What factors account for the differences among those studied with regard to these questions? Characteristics studied should be policy related and invested with variables with potential for dividends in policy improvement.

Some Effects of Economic Assistance Programs

One of the major questions affecting economic assistance policy since the inception of aid, public or private, has been the relationship of relief and dependency. To what extent does the presence of programs of economic aid stimulate reliance on external help rather than the use of available capacities and resources of the individual and his family? Several types of research are related to this question: (1) research on attitudes toward the acceptance of relief; (2) research on the economic potential of those on relief; and (3) research on the tendency toward continuation on relief rather than finding independent alternatives. Recent studies, particularly of AFDC clients, that have examined the justification for some families or individuals receiving assistance, do not illuminate the problem of dependency, but rather are examinations or quality checks on eligibility practices. Studies solely of administrative practice should clearly be distinguished from studies of the client population, although frequently there is the implicit assumption that liberally administered aid encourages dependency.

Attitudes Toward Acceptance of Relief

Most studies of relief are restricted to a population who are or have been recipients of assistance. Such samples, of course, cannot throw light on the significance of relief to the general population or, more broadly, its reaction to need. An example of the larger approach is E. Wight Bakke's *Unemployed Worker*.[35] This research was based on an intensive and extensive survey of unemployed families and others in New Haven during the period from 1932 to 1939. Of a sample of 2,000 New Haven families, 988 individuals were unemployed in 1933. A follow-up two years later showed that only 24 percent had applied for relief, although 68 percent of the unemployed workers had been unemployed over one year by 1933.[36] Among resources available to those with insufficient wages

---

[35] *Op. cit.*
[36] *Ibid.*, pp. 363–364.

for support, direct relief was found to be the least desired of ten types of aid, and represented the greatest violation to the sense of independence of the workers.

Acceptance of relief, according to Bakke, threatened the workers' self-respect and status arising from earning their own living.

No rationalization and no modification of relief procedures enabled him [the unemployed] to escape the fact that the new relationship to the community has separated him in this respect from his fellows. Since satisfactory living is inhibited by that separation we should expect great resistance to it.[37]

Bakke added that the above statement was not a judgment of faith, but that "the actual records of the unemployed justified the conclusion that relief was for the great majority a last resort in the losing battle to remain 'normal.' "[38]

There has been a great paucity of recent studies on the unemployed or the experience of economic deprivation. A study of about 1,500 unemployed conducted by Cohen, Haber, and Mueller during the 1958 recession provided some evidence on the nature of dependency, at least in relation to unemployment benefits.[39] The authors found that reliance on unemployment insurance did not discourage thrift. Savings were the primary source of supplementing unemployment benefits. Although the possible effect of assistance policy and procedures was not taken into account, only a small proportion of families in the study turned to relief, and these generally after at least thirteen weeks of unemployment.

Acceptance of relief is a function of both emotional and cognitive factors. While these are interrelated, they can be examined separately, and the cognitive elements are more clearly identifiable and simpler to study. There has been much concern about the emotional factors affecting dependency but little attempt to find out what the public generally, low-income groups, and assistance recipients think or know about public assistance. The lack of such studies would almost suggest a fear of recognizing public assistance as respectable enough for the kinds of surveys related to other aspects of public policy.

There have been several studies of public knowledge of the social insurance. If the level of familiarity with these programs is at all indicative, cognitive factors may play a very significant part in public assistance. Bakke in the 1930's found that only two-fifths of his sample of eligibles for unemployment insurance "understood even vaguely their rights to benefit and the process by which the amount and duration of benefit were determined."[40] More recently, Janowitz surveyed 764 households in Detroit in the first four months of 1954.[41] Of the persons interviewed, 21 percent gave answers that could only be considered "incorrect," "inadequate," or displaying "no knowledge" of social security benefits. At most, 26 percent demonstrated correct knowledge, and, as might be expected, level of knowledge was positively correlated with social class position. Thus, those likely to benefit most were least acquainted with the program.

Under these circumstances the fact that less than one-fourth of poor families in the Morgan study received public assistance may be accounted for to some extent by lack of knowledge.[42] For in public assistance it is the client who initiates eligibility, and awareness of the program alone may

[37] *Ibid.*, p. 363.

[38] *Ibid.*

[39] Wilbur J. Cohen, William Haber, and Eva Mueller, *The Impact of Unemployment in the 1958 Recession, A Report of Nationwide Surveys of Unemployment, Unemployment Insurance, and Attitudes of the Unemployed,* Eighty-sixth Congress, second session (Washington, D.C.: U.S. Government Printing Office, 1960).

[40] *The Unemployed Worker*, p. 313.

[41] Morris Janowitz, "Public Perspectives on Social Security," *Social Work,* Vol. 1, No. 3 (July 1956), pp. 94–101.

[42] James Morgan *et al., Income and Welfare in the United States* (New York: McGraw-Hill Book Co., 1962), p. 216.

extend or limit the number of applicants. On the other hand, the small survey conducted by Charles Lebeaux for the Detroit chapter of the National Association of Social Workers (NASW) with a sample of ninety-three mothers in AFDC families indicated that knowledge may act as a deterrent to seeking help since sophistication about restrictive policies may discourage expectation of aid.[43]

Potential for Independence of Assistance Recipients

Potential for economic independence at any particular time is a combination of internal or personal factors and external or market demand. For such groups as the aged or handicapped there is relatively little expectation of current efforts to achieve independence. On the other hand, for the able-bodied adults on general assistance or AFDC there is strong pressure for employment even though the economic market may not be favorable to a considerable proportion of all workers. What, then, do these adults bring competitively into the employment market?

The Burgess and Price study of AFDC families addressed itself to this question. The parents in these families, according to their study, have the kinds of background that mark the least successful occupational careers in society. Almost half of the homemakers had eight or fewer years of schooling. Less than 16 percent of the homemakers possessed skills or training desired on the job market.[44]

In their 1956 Minnesota project, covering three counties in the state, the Community Research Associates (CRA) reported on the proportion of their population having rehabilitation potential and the proportion of this group responding to intensive services. The sample, a total of 2,027 cases, was classified as "Alpha" or "Beta." "Alpha" cases were "those who needed and could benefit from intensive agency service" while "Beta" were "those in which only basic ameliorative services were necessary or possible."[45] While rehabilitation potential, as the report of the study indicated, did not necessarily mean that the Alpha group were better than the Beta group, analysis of the groups pointed to the fact that "the prospects for improvement in this group [Alpha] were markedly better than for Beta."[46]

Of the total 2,027 cases, 12.9 percent were classified as Alpha type. The report stated that this was probably a "conservative" estimate since other CRA projects had indicated greater prognosis for improvement. While 87 percent of all the cases received some public assistance and 81 percent had dependency as the major problem, only 40 percent of the latter were included in the Alpha group. These were primarily cases on AFDC and general assistance: 47 percent of the AFDC and 20 percent of the general assistance load. The dependency cases were heavily concentrated in the Beta or low-potential-for-improvement group.

The Alpha cases were given intensive casework services. At the end of twelve months, 28 percent of the total group showed improvement, and 25 percent of the "dependency as a major problem" group improved. Beta cases showed an over-all improvement of 12.8 percent. While the study had not planned to measure the specific influence of service, an opportunity was presented when all the Alpha cases could not be accommodated in special case loads. Although the "Alpha-assigned" showed more improvement than the less-served cases, the differences were not great or statistically significant.

---

[43] *Op. cit.*

[44] Burgess and Price, *op. cit.*, p. 159.

[45] Donald B. Glabe, Leo J. Feider, and Harry O. Page, "Reorientation for Treatment and Control," *Public Welfare*, Vol. 16, No. 2 (April 1958), Special Supplement, p. vii.

[46] *Ibid.*, p. xi.

Despite the CRA's efforts to justify the value of increased services, the study did not provide evidence supporting the rehabilitation potential of financially dependent clients. In all, 97 cases of 1,648 whose major problem was dependency were considered as rehabilitatable, and only 24 of those showed improvement. The absence of reported indicators for classification of the cases, the unorganized approach to the selection of the sample, the absence of intensive service for the Beta cases as a control, and the lack of objective methods of measuring improvement raise questions as to the validity of the study's findings.

Continuation on Relief

In view of the handicaps—physical, mental, and emotional (their poor educational and vocational background, the restrictive policies of assistance agencies, and the general state of the job market)—of many persons on relief today, it is difficult to judge the extent to which continued relief validly reflects dependency. Bakke, in his 1930's study, when the unemployed were probably more representative of the general working population, concluded, "Out of our six years of attempts to find cases of refusal of jobs . . . we have developed a thorough conviction that this state of affairs is so unusual as to be of no real concern for public administration." [47]

In general, Bakke found that being unemployed did not change values and aspirations, but the structuring of the relief situation might influence adaptation. If relief were sufficiently widespread within the community, it could become a way of life for the group and lose its stigma. The administration of relief was also effective in creating attitudes toward the continuation of relief. Where the control and restrictive policies of the administration were most prevalent, according to Bakke, greater energies were invested by recipients in manipulating the situation, even to the point of demonstrating need at the expense of maintaining their interest in employment. [48]

Elizabeth W. Gilboy, in a study of work relief cases, also in the 1930's, confirmed Bakke's general conclusion that the weaker the "culture" of relief, the less the dependency. [49] Comparing the sample of those remaining on work relief with those leaving or separated from work relief, Gilboy found that those who left work relief had, even during the period of their eligibility, been less conditioned to relief throughout as a way of life. They had maintained more normal standards, with greater personal debts, property, and income derived from private employment. The less the family became wholly reliant on relief, the less the probability that it would be continuously dependent.

Gilboy found no evidence to support the belief that relief recipients would refuse jobs if they were available. Gilboy cited her own study and one conducted by the Works Project Administration Division of Research to suggest the hypothesis that receiving relief over any duration becomes correlated with being marginal in the labor market even if workers were not marginal originally. Only the "upper stratum" of cases had any chance of private employment, and even those would continue to require relief.

Some of the strain toward independence was evidenced by Burgess and Price in their study of AFDC cases. In 60 percent of these families, efforts were made, but unsuccessfully. The remainder farmed, or raised produce to supplement their income. These families, as compared to those who made no effort, were favored by better education, and by generally less acute problems and more socially acceptable behavior. [50]

---

[47] *The Unemployed Worker,* p. 369.

[48] *Ibid.,* pp. 315–316, 325–327, and 383–385.

[49] *Op. cit.*

[50] Burgess and Price, *op. cit.,* pp. 162–164.

Responsibility of Relatives

The degree to which relatives may be held responsible for more indigent family members has been a major issue in economic assistance programs. The enforcement of relative responsibility has sometimes been assumed to prevent dependency by discouraging those who might otherwise accept help. Some research has been done on several aspects of the question of relative responsibility. How do American families view financial responsibility for their relatives, particularly the aged? What is the potential of responsible relatives for support of assistance clients?

A survey conducted by the National Opinion Research Center, under the direction of Ethel Shanas, collected data on attitudes toward responsibility of the aged, responsible individuals, and the general public.[51] The study found some particularly significant differences among the kinds of responsibilities that respondents expected could be assumed toward the aged. A variety of situations were posed to respondents: provision of a home for an aged mother, priorities between children's own affairs and help needed by parents, and financial help to the aged. Of all, financial responsibility was the least expected responsibility by each of the groups in the sample. For example, 44 percent of older people, 46 percent of responsible individuals, and 46 percent of the general public favored moving mother in with the family in times of crisis, while only 26 percent of older people, 40 percent of responsible individuals, and 33 percent of the public considered children or relatives as financially responsible for dependent aged. Both the aged and the general public thought that government had greater responsibility for financial security.[52]

The Shanas study points to the fact that responsibility is not monolithic or defined by a single attribute. While close ties with the aged may be favored, this does not necessarily mean financial support, which may be viewed as a relatively impersonal issue.

The study summarized its findings: "A majority of older people, and of the public generally believe that adult sons and daughters must assume certain responsibilities toward their aged parents. These responsibilities are largely in the area of interpersonal relationships." While it was generally believed that children should make some adjustments to accommodate the needs of the elderly, there was some conflict in priority between the demands of the children's own lives and those of the parents.

As for financial responsibility, the study concluded that the elderly want to be independent. When the elderly had not provided for themselves, they felt that the government should establish income maintenance programs. Sons and daughters of the elderly were more likely to favor financial support than the elderly themselves who, it may be assumed, felt that financial help would undermine affectional bonds.[53]

The complexity of attitudes and behavior toward the elderly was examined by Morgan and his associates in a Michigan Survey Research Center study. As in the Shanas study, the Michigan survey revealed a strong acceptance of the general notion of relative responsibility, but found little willingness to provide in specific situations. Responsibility of relatives generally for older people in need was supported by two-thirds of the spending-unit heads interviewed. An equal proportion, however, were opposed to having aged parents live with their children.[54] As the study pointed out: "The extent to which people definitely

[51] Ethel Shanas, *Family Relationships of Older People* (New York: Health Information Foundation, 1961).
[52] *Ibid.*, pp. 17, 29.

[53] *Ibid.*, pp. 37–38.
[54] Morgan *et al., op. cit.*, pp. 158, 275.

expect to care for their own parents in the future seems to be related only slightly to their attitude toward general responsibility for the aged." Expectations about caring for one's own parents were not related either to favoring relative responsibility or favoring government responsibility for the aged. Neither group planned to participate to any extent in the care of their own parents. For example, of those favoring sole or primary responsibility of relatives, 13 and 11 percent, respectively, "will give them general financial help" as compared to 8 and 14 percent, respectively, of supporters of sole or primary government responsibility. Low earnings were positively associated with favorable attitudes toward government responsibility. On the other hand, people most able to afford providing for the aged in their own household were most opposed to it.[55]

Research on relative responsibility reflects the changing patterns of American family life and the changing significance of financial aid as a familial function. Current research suggests that independence may be weakened rather than strengthened by the policies of some assistance agencies emphasizing dependence on relatives.[56]

The national surveys conducted by the Bureau of Public Assistance reported that approximately 15.7 percent of the aged on assistance in 1953 were living in the homes of sons or daughters; in 1960, the figure was 15.5 percent.[57] It may be noted that only 23 percent of the Morgan sample of adult spending units favored to any degree older people living with their chil-

dren (favorable, 8 percent; favorable, qualified, 5 percent; depends, 10 percent).[58] According to the bureau's 1960 survey, the item most frequently contributed by children was shelter, and items other than cash were provided usually in conjunction with shelter. Children living in separate households contributed much less frequently than those in shared homes. Only one in every six recipients received some contribution from children outside their home as compared to two out of every five in a common living arrangement.[59]

With the growth of AFDC, support by the fathers has become a pressing issue of public assistance policy. In 1955, the Bureau of Public Assistance surveyed the responsibility undertaken by fathers in AFDC families. The major categories of the sample were (A) fathers married and (B) fathers who had never been married to the mothers. The limitations of paternal support were emphasized in the findings of the study. The whereabouts of the father were unknown in 57 percent of the cases: 55 percent in the A group and 61 percent in the B group. Only 14.8 percent of all fathers contributed: A, 18.3 percent; B, 10.2 percent. Apart from absence, the main distinguishing characteristic of the fathers was low income. Of those whose income was known, two-thirds had an income below $200 per month. However, those with known income were only a small proportion of the total number of fathers and were probably not representative of the whole. The effect of income on family contribution was indicated in the A group by the fact that 26.6 percent of contributing fathers, as compared to 4.1 percent of the noncontributing, had an income of $200 or more per month. In the case of fathers with $200 or more known income

---

[55] *Ibid.*, pp. 159–161, 278.

[56] *See* Robert J. Havighurst and Ruth Albrecht, *Older People* (New York: Longmans, Green & Co., 1953); and Ethel Shanas, *op. cit.*

[57] U.S. Department of Health, Education, and Welfare, Bureau of Public Assistance, "Recipients of Old-Age Assistance in Early 1953," and "Characteristics and Financial Circumstances of Recipients of Old-Age Assistance, 1960."

[58] Morgan *et al., op. cit.*, p. 160.

[59] U.S. Department of Health, Education, and Welfare, Bureau of Public Assistance, "Characteristics and Financial Circumstances of Recipients of Old-Age Assistance, 1960," p. 5.

only 14.9 percent were not contributing, although able to provide support. Other factors, such as closeness of location of father to home, length of absence of father, and the nature of support agreement between father and mother, also influenced the degree of support. While the study pointed out that in both A and B groups some arrangement was necessary if the father was to contribute, the more informal the nature of the agreement the greater the likelihood that the contribution would be made.[60]

In general, research on relative responsibility for the aged and for children indicates that the degree of responsibility assumed is heavily determined by informal factors. The Greenleigh study in Cook County supported this hypothesis by its findings on the limited nature of parental relationships in AFDC cases. In only 4 to 5 percent of AFDC families, in the opinion of case analysts, was there any possibility of reuniting father and mother. The study concluded that "in light of indifference and hostility toward the father and the number of families which had had no contact with the father," these findings were not "surprising." [61]

Illegitimacy and Relief

Several studies have attempted to examine the relationship of relief and illegitimacy. Note has already been made earlier of the difficulties of comparing populations so that the question of whether or not families on assistance have higher rates of illegitimacy has itself not been settled. However, some studies have tried to establish evidence directly relating the existence of the AFDC program to the incidence of illegitimacy. Three such studies—Burgess and Price's national AFDC survey, Lansdale's analysis of the Florida suitable home law statistics, and South Dakota's examination of its AFDC load in 1958—all question the assumption of a positive relationship between illegitimacy and AFDC.[62]

Three lines of evidence are presented in these studies: (1) the delay in asking for AFDC; (2) the number of illegitimate children born to AFDC mothers for whom no aid is asked; and (3) the reduced number of illegitimate births after receiving AFDC. The South Dakota study found that 57 percent of the children were six months old or more, and 20 percent were two years old or more before the first AFDC payment was made. While some delay might be assumed in the new applications, the study hypothesized that when the mother was already on AFDC, if she wanted more assistance, she would only go through the formality of verification to have the additional child added to the budget. Thus, the length of time between birth and aid for the child was assumed to indicate that assistance was not instrumental in encouraging illegitimacy.[63]

A sizable group of children are born out-of-wedlock to AFDC mothers for whom no aid is provided. Among Negro children assisted, according to Burgess and Price, less than 10 percent had been born out-of-wedlock after the family received AFDC, while of those not assisted 35 percent were illegitimate and born after the beginning of AFDC. Thus, a large group of such children received no financial aid. For white children, the proportions were 2 and 10 percent, respectively.[64] To what extent

---

[60] U.S. Department of Health, Education, and Welfare, Bureau of Public Assistance, *Support from Absent Fathers of Children Receiving ADC: 1955*, pp. 4, 5, 11, 18, 22, 32, and 35.

[61] Greenleigh Associates, "Facts, Fallacies and Future," p. 17.

[62] Burgess and Price, *op. cit.*; Robert T. Lansdale, *The Florida Suitable Home Law* (Tallahassee: Florida State University, 1962); and South Dakota Department of Public Welfare, "Does ADC Encourage Illegitimacy?" (Pierre, 1958) (mimeographed).

[63] South Dakota Department of Public Welfare, *op. cit.*, pp. 1–2.

[64] Burgess and Price, *op. cit.*, p. 36.

the delay in seeking aid in the South Dakota study and the absence of assistance above were reflections of local policy and other factors rather than parents' decisions is, of course, pertinent. If one assumes, however, that there is awareness of restrictive local relief practices, continuing illegitimate births would indicate that expectation of relief was not the dominant factor.

Alternate policies and programs need also to be examined. While AFDC itself may not be given, alternate forms of public responsibility may have the same effect in encouraging dependency. For example, examination of the small sample of South Dakota cases that were not included in the AFDC grant indicated that adoption and foster care were provided for a large number.[65] Thus parental irresponsibility may be fostered by other programs, and AFDC may be merely one and not the most influential of a larger category of programs that encourage illegitimacy through removing or sharing with parents their responsibility for out-of-wedlock children.

The third factor emphasized is the incidence of illegitimacy after receipt of AFDC. Both Burgess and Price and the Florida suitable home study provided evidence of decreasing incidence of illegitimacy in these families. In Florida, 60.1 percent of the families had illegitimate births only prior to the receipt of assistance.[66] Burgess and Price found that the proportion of illegitimate births in their population decreased after the first AFDC payment. For the white population, approximately three times as many illegitimate births had occurred before as after receiving AFDC; in Negro families, approximately twice as many.[67]

Further evidence of the decreasing rate of illegitimacy on AFDC is indicated by the tendency of the proportion of illegitimate births to decrease with the increasing size of the family. For example, 20 percent of the children in white two-person families in the Burgess and Price sample were illegitimate as compared to 4 percent in ten-or more-person families.[68] This also conflicts with the hypotheses that AFDC has made illegitimacy "a way of life" for some families and that it has subsidized continuing "immorality" for a relatively small segment of the population.

Migration and Relief

Residence requirements have been an almost universal part of American public assistance administration and have reflected a desire on the part of communities and states to protect themselves from indigent migrants and settlers. Research in the broad area of social and economic aspects of mobility is pertinent to understanding motivation and trends affecting the movement of low-income persons and families. However, the salience of the issue of residence for public welfare departments has resulted in several studies being wholly or partially oriented to the effect of residence restrictions or settlement on assistance.

These studies have examined length of residence to determine how much the assistance population represents recent migrants who have responded to liberal relief policies. A study conducted in Shelby County, Tennessee, between 1957 and 1959, with a sample of 932 AFDC families reported that approximately two-fifths of the white mothers and three-fifths of the Negro mothers had been in the county prior to 1940.[69] In a survey of AFDC families in Cuyahoga County, Ohio, 87 percent of

---

[65] South Dakota Department of Public Welfare, *op. cit.*, Table 2.

[66] Lansdale, *op. cit.*, p. 78.

[67] Burgess and Price, *op. cit.*, p. 267.

[68] *Ibid.*, pp. 94–95.

[69] Tennessee Department of Public Welfare, "Report on Shelby County ADC Project, July 1957–June 1959" (Nashville, undated), pp. 7, 36. (Mimeographed.)

all the children were born in the county. The report states: "This is contrary to a popular belief that illegitimate children are brought to Cleveland because of the higher Aid to Dependent Children benefit." [70] The Greenleigh study of AFDC families in Cook County found that over 75 percent of the children and 25 percent of the mothers were born in Illinois. Less than 1 percent of the families were in Cook County for fewer than two years, and only 10 percent were in Illinois for fewer than five years.[71]

The Louisiana Department of Public Welfare, in 1957, made a "study of residence status of its old age assistance caseload for the purpose of determining the extent to which aged persons have moved into Louisiana in order to receive assistance." [72] The study was based on a 10 percent sample of old age cases certified after May 1, 1953. This was the date of liberalization of OAA residence to five years. The study found that 76.8 percent of recipients had lived in Louisiana all their lives; another 22.3 percent had lived in the state before 1948; and less than 1 percent had moved to Louisiana after May 1948—the date that would make them eligible for the new 1953 residence law. In addition, the number of post-1948 migrants into the state was balanced approximately by a similar number leaving the state.

The New York State Department of Social Welfare conducted a series of studies of state-charge assistance recipients (less than one year in the state) during 1957 and 1958.[73] These studies reported that

of an estimated sixteen million persons who come into the state annually, a monthly average of 7,229 required hospital care, foster care, or public assistance during 1957. In the first half of 1958 state charges constituted about 1.5 percent of the total public assistance population, and were declining in New York City and leveling off in upstate New York. The report concluded that the absence of residence requirements in New York had not affected the rate of in-migration, and pointed to such factors as economic opportunity, educational advantages, standard of living, and climate as instrumental in influencing mobility.[74]

While the limited number of newcomers on assistance casts doubt on the prevalent belief that relief attracts migrants, it is not sufficient evidence. Since those studied were already on assistance rolls, there is no knowledge of those who were refused assistance. Even in a state like New York, without a residence requirement, administrative practice may deter new migrants from applying.

Some studies also assume that whatever factors explain migration in the general population necessarily apply to the relief population. While this may be true, it has not been validated. Two of the studies noted above have collected data on the issue. In the Shelby County sample, less than 8 percent of the mothers coming into the county since 1940 were from cities of more than 50,000; almost 75 percent came from rural localities and mostly from farms.[75] This would indicate that the AFDC mothers may have represented the less adequately prepared participants in the general mobility pattern from rural to urban areas.

The Cook County study of Greenleigh Associates reported that only 8 percent of AFDC mothers who came to Illinois as adults could specify no reason for migrating. Of the others (1) 17 percent heard

[70] Cuyahoga County Welfare Department, "The Story of Phantom Fathers, Unwed Mothers, Ill-starred Children" (Cleveland, 1960), pp. 7–8, 37. (Mimeographed.)

[71] "Facts, Fallacies and Future," p. 9.

[72] Louisiana Department of Public Welfare, "Report on the OAA Residence Study" (Baton Rouge, 1957). (Mimeographed.)

[73] New York State Department of Social Welfare, "The Movement of Population and Public Welfare in New York State" (Albany, 1958). (Mimeographed.)

[74] *Ibid.*, pp. 2, 3, 16.

[75] Tennessee Department of Public Welfare, *op. cit.*, p. 8.

about jobs, including 0.9 percent who came through prearrangement with an employer; (2) 38.2 percent came to be near relatives; (3) 21.6 percent came to be with their husbands; and (4) 15.2 percent came to have a change, or for better living conditions. Among those who had moved to Illinois in their adult years, 11 percent said that they had received public assistance within the two years prior to coming to Illinois and 3.5 percent said that they had applied but had been rejected. (Among those coming after May 1955, only 5 percent had been on assistance elsewhere.) The opinion of 45 percent of the total group of migrants was that it was easier to get support for their children in Illinois than in their former states; 22.7 percent felt that it was about the same; and 3.1 percent that it was harder.[76] While the reliability of assistance clients' responses in officially sponsored interview surveys is generally open to some question, the data do not indicate that assistance acted as the primary influence on migration.

General Critique

Research on the effects of economic assistance programs is still in its most elementary stage. Since much of public assistance policy is founded on the simple assumptions of early nineteenth-century utilitarian hedonism, much research energy has been expended in testing the fundamental premises of pleasure-pain psychology. While, no doubt, those supportive of more humane welfare services see the need of confuting popular and official prejudices about assistance recipients, there is little scientific gain in entering into this dispute about the nature of human nature. The questions are rarely framed in refined terms. They are so global that the studies merely clarify relationships among relevant variables.

The lines of inquiry that are more valid

in contemporary social policy disputes are those that (1) clarify the situation on a descriptive level, e.g., the proportion of relief recipients who use help for a short period or make efforts to be independent; (2) demonstrate the similarity of the assistance population to the general population, e.g., in regard to relative responsibility, illegitimacy rates; and (3) evaluate specific policy alternatives. Attempts, however, to support hypotheses about the effect of general administrative measures on broad areas of social behavior result in research conclusions often as naive as the positions attacked. On the basis of current knowledge about the characteristics of assistance recipients there is little evidence to support popular beliefs about the consequences of assistance policies. Predicted characteristics are not widely found in assistance populations or do not differ from the characteristics of populations who have not undergone the assistance experience. However, much more accurate data are needed before it is possible to speak with any certainty.

On the other hand, much greater emphasis needs to be placed on research evaluating the effects of policy alternatives in terms of feasibly measurable consequences. Specific policies having predictable effects, or containing variables closely connected to the variables to be influenced, may be examined in a variety of carefully observed, if not controlled, situations. For example, what effects do extra assistance allowances for working adolescents have on their seeking employment or remaining in school? Given a realistic choice, do mothers in AFDC households prefer employment to grants? What factors control or influence the selection of either course? What are the effects of work relief on maintaining morals, developing skill, stimulating employment? What are the consequences of different approaches to work and relief? These questions are illustrative, but even they may be too ambitious at the present stage of evaluating public welfare policy.

---

[76] Greenleigh Associates, "Facts, Fallacies and Future," pp. 9–11.

Administrative Standards and Practices

This section focuses on research evaluating the effectiveness of administration or the execution of policy. The dispensing of public funds is perhaps the most sensitive area of public welfare administration, and there have been a variety of efforts to appraise the effectiveness of performance. Most of these are but beginning attempts in the use of research designs and systematically collected data for the purpose of program evaluation. Among the areas of major inquiry have been (1) quality checks on maintaining standards explicitly or implicitly defined; and (2) evaluations of the adequacy of assistance standards themselves.

Quality Controls

The maintenance of standards of efficient performance in administering relief has been measured largely by three criteria: (1) the specific practices of agencies to estimate the degree of deviation from expected performance; (2) the amount of client fraud; and (3) the presence of recipients who, though not fraudulently eligible, could meet need without agency help.

Although closely connected, these are three separate subjects of investigation. Efficiency of the agency might be seen as including detection of fraud and avoidance of unnecessary relief. However, misrepresentation by clients can also be seen as distinct from the agency's own failure, and, in a co-operative process of eligibility, represents immoral, if not criminal, behavior on the client's part. Finally, ultimate tests of the validity of client need are difficult, if not impossible, under usual circumstances. According to the agency's standards the client may be eligible and he may not be misrepresenting, but there may be resources that neither he nor the agency have explored. How frequently do such situations occur?

Efficiency of agency practice. The most extensive recent quality control check in public assistance was undertaken in regard to AFDC by the U.S. Department of Health, Education, and Welfare at the request of the Senate Committee on Appropriations.[77] The report prepared by the department from a sample of over 21,000 cases, with representation from all states, provided a useful beginning at quality control checking in public assistance. The eligibility review found that 5.4 percent of the families were ineligible according to the federal and individual state standards used. There was a range among the states from 0.8 to 17.3 percent of total case load ineligible. About one-fifth of the states had below 2 percent ineligible and an equal proportion had above 10 percent.[78] While the study examined the numbers incorrectly eligible, it did not study the numbers who should have received assistance considered ineligible by the states.

The Greenleigh Associates study of Cook County's AFDC program examined the correctness of decisions of initial rejection and later closings on the grounds of ineligibility. Based on a small sample of cases not receiving any kind of assistance at the time of the survey, the study concluded that in 32 percent of the cases the reasons for rejection in the record were "invalid" or "questionable" according to state policy. On the basis of a sample of 207 cases removed from the rolls over a five-month period, the study estimated that about one-quarter were closed for "invalid or questionable reasons." [79]

The federal review also surveyed the proportion of families eligible for assist-

---

[77] U. S. Department of Health, Education, and Welfare, "Eligibility of Families Receiving Aid to Families with Dependent Children" (Washington, D.C., 1963). (Mimeographed.)

[78] *Ibid.*, p. 11.

[79] "Facts, Fallacies and Future," pp. 56–57.

ance who were receiving more or less than the correct budgetary allowance. Although the amount of deviation was not noted, the proportion of incorrect payments, positive and negative, was substantial. The range by states was from 3.4 percent to 80.6 percent. The overpayments ranged from 2.6 percent to 42.4 percent and the underpayments from 0.8 percent to 60.6 percent.[80] The study sought to distinguish between those families who were ineligible as a result of agency practice and those ineligible because of other factors. In nearly all states errors in agency practice—inadequate determination of eligibility, failure to follow up on changes in circumstances, misinterpretation of policy, and other errors—accounted for the majority of ineligible families receiving assistance.[81]

Client fraud. Intentional concealment or misrepresentation of facts in the AFDC eligibility study accounted for only a small proportion of the reasons explaining determination of ineligibility. In only eight states did concealment or misrepresentation occur in more than 3 percent of the total number of families on the AFDC load.[82] Similar low estimates of client fraud were made as a result of two other studies. A study conducted by the Department of Social Welfare of California in the fiscal year 1958–59 led to an estimate of 1.5 percent of the total California ANC load as receiving assistance fraudulently.[83] (In 1963 the federal study estimated 0.8 percent for California.) The 1960 study of AFDC in Cook County by the Greenleigh Associates examined ineligibility on

two counts: undisclosed income and the presence of "absent" fathers, comparable to the concept of fraud used in the other studies. In less than 2 percent of the cases was ineligibility actually determined or suspected.[84] (This may be compared with the 1.6 percent of the 1963 federal study for Illinois.)

Validity of need. Historically, one of the assumed measures of the reality of need has been the development of more restrictive conditions for assistance as a test of need. The most famous was the workhouse test of the English Poor Law of 1834. English Poor Law boards after 1834 pointed to the reduced population on assistance thereafter as proof of the unnecessary laxness of previous Poor Law administration. However, the absence of follow-up studies of the population leaving or removed from the rolls always left some questions about the official interpretation in the minds of skeptics.

Recently the suitable home law has been looked upon by some as offering an experimental situation to test depth of need. For example, Lansdale, in his discussion of the analysis of the effects of the Florida law, remarks on the fact that nearly three-fourths of the families withdrawing during the first year of the law had not reapplied. "How these families managed," he states, "is, of course, not known. That they did not take advantage of their right to reapply for so long a period suggests that many may have made satisfactory arrangements." [85] On the other hand, the reasons for their withdrawal suggested sufficient cause for reluctance to reapply; i.e., unwillingness to risk placement or loss of children, 65 percent, and not wanting involvement with court, 14 percent.[86]

In the small sample of ninety-three AFDC

---

[80] U.S. Department of Health, Education, and Welfare, "Eligibility of Families Receiving Aid to Families with Dependent Children," p. 19.

[81] *Ibid.*, p. 16.

[82] *Ibid.*

[83] California State Department of Social Welfare, "Fraud in the Aid to Needy Children Program" (Sacramento, 1960). (Mimeographed.)

[84] "Facts, Fallacies and Future," p. 55.

[85] Lansdale, *op. cit.*, pp. 87–88.

[86] *Ibid.*, p. 99.

families in the NASW Detroit study, sixty-five received a routine budget cut. Less than one-half, however, complained to the city welfare department. Did this indicate that the others were able to get along on the smaller budget? The responses quoted in the study do not support this assumption. Most mothers stated that they knew "it would be useless to try." [87]

A follow-up study of a sample of 104 families removed from the Washington, D.C., AFDC program in 1955, as a result of a suitable home amendment, provided some evidence of the resources used as alternatives to public aid.[88] There was an increase in the number of children and mothers working. More aid-in-kind and general help were obtained from maternal relatives, neighbors, and friends. Private agencies also contributed cash and aid-in-kind. Relatives of the father helped. The number of "acting husbands" contributing increased from sixty-five to eighty-one. The median income of these families was estimated to have improved by about $25 per month. After termination of the grant, 10 percent of the children were removed from the homes studied: approximately one-half were placed by the public welfare department and half by the mother through informal arrangements.[89] Some of these consequences appear desirable and others undesirable, from both personal and social perspectives, but until an over-all evaluation is made of the consequences in regard to the total welfare of the family unit, no valid conclusion can be drawn as to whether or not the program was catering to families who could get along without government aid.

---

[87] Lebeaux, *op. cit.*

[88] District of Columbia Department of Public Welfare and the National Catholic School of Social Service of Catholic University, "Children in 104 Families Who Became Ineligible for ADC" (Washington, D.C., 1956). (Mimeographed.)

[89] *Ibid.*, Tables 4, 6, and p. 8.

Adequacy of Standards

The level of living provided recipients of assistance, although a major issue of social policy, has not been the subject of regular reporting by official agencies, state or federal. Studies seeking to measure the adequacy of assistance standards have used such approaches as (1) comparison of level of assistance grants and/or total income with some standard budget; (2) comparison of actual assistance grants with total income or assistance standards of the state; and (3) examination of the level of living of assistance recipients on the basis of such indexes as housing, sanitary facilities, and telephone.

The comparison of assistance grants with an established standard was used for assessing the adequacy of state grants by the Committee on Long-Range Work and Relief Policies in its 1943 report to the National Resources Planning Board.[90] The committee selected as its standard for families on public assistance the "emergency-level" budget constructed by the Works Progress Administration. This budget was selected because of its minimal standards to avoid any "unrealistic" and "exaggerated" notions of the level of government support, and yet at the same time to provide some reasonable base of assistance. Its emergency nature was emphasized by the fact that it was assumed to be hazardous for families to subsist on this budget over long periods of time. The budget was applied to the relief standards of fifty-nine cities throughout the nation for which costs of budget items were available.

The second problem for the committee was the determination of a comparable and reliable measure of assistance standards. Average grants were rejected because they did not reflect the variety of circumstances that gave them differing significance in different localities. The committee selected

[90] U.S. Congress, Committee on Long-Range Work and Relief, *Security, Work and Relief Policies* (Washington, D.C., 1943).

instead a standard family of four with no resources, and the local agencies were asked to indicate their relief grant to this family.

Comparison of the cost of the "emergency" budget for the standard family was made with the general relief allowances specifically by the agencies and with general allowances supplemented by surplus foods, the practice in most communities. In none of the fifty-nine cities was the relief grant alone sufficient to maintain the "emergency" level. While the addition of surplus commodities substantially raised the proportion of budget met, there were still some sixteen cities that fell below 50 percent of the standard.[91]

Comparison of assistance grants and total income of recipients with standards of the state has been used in other studies. The Burgess and Price survey of AFDC families used the concept of "total budgeted monthly requirements" or "income deemed necessary" by the budgeting authority. For all cases in the sample the median was just over $146 per month, or $43 per person. However, the median actual total monthly income of the families in the study was $133 or $13 less than the budgeted requirement. Of the total sample, 31 percent had incomes below budgeted need.[92]

In addition to the amount of deviation, Burgess and Price surveyed the factors correlated with adequacy of budget standards. The 1943 study of the Committee on Long-Range Work and Relief Policies had found region and size of community related to the adequacy of general assistance grants.[93] Burgess and Price also found size of the community related directly to the size of the AFDC grant, budgeted monthly requirements, and total income for both Negro and white families. Regional standards in their AFDC study were highest in

the Far West.[94] The northeastern states had held this position for the 1943 relief programs studied by the committee.

Burgess and Price, like Blackwell and Gould in their earlier study of AFDC, examined the relationship of such factors as race, education of homemakers, nature of family crisis, and size of assistance group to total income, AFDC payments, and budgeted requirements.[95] Income and payments tended to be higher for white families and for families where the homemaker had more education. The latter finding was also true in the 1950 study.[96] The fact that AFDC payments as well as total income were related to higher education may, according to Burgess and Price, reflect urban-rural or Negro-white differences as well as administrative bias in favor of recipients with initially higher levels of living.[97]

Size of family was found to affect strongly per person income and AFDC payments, and was assumed to reflect the administrative practice of reducing per capita grants with increasing family size. The Blackwell and Gould study had found that the presence of younger children tended to keep monthly income per person lower, and attributed this to less employment of the mother of younger children as well as the greater employment opportunities for older children.[98]

Study of the relationship of the crisis accounting for presence on AFDC to size of income and assistance grants offers opportunities for examining those situations that are treated least and most generously, and to note changes or trends in such treatment. For example, whereas the median per person income in 1950 was

---

[91] *Ibid.*, pp. 160–168.
[92] Burgess and Price, *op. cit.*, pp. 60, 66, 150.
[93] *Op. cit.*, pp. 166–168.

[94] *Op. cit.*, pp. 68, 74.
[95] Burgess and Price, *op. cit.*, chap. 4; and Blackwell and Gould, *op. cit.*, chap. 4.
[96] Burgess and Price, *op. cit.*, p. 91; and Blackwell and Gould, *op. cit.*, p. 89.
[97] *Op. cit.*, p. 76.
[98] Burgess and Price, *op. cit.*, pp. 72–73; and Blackwell and Gould, *op. cit.*, pp. 89–90.

highest for families in which the father was incapacitated, per person income was almost the lowest for both Negro and white families with incapacitated fathers in 1960, and the dollar income was actually less in the later period. Families of unmarried mothers were among the highest per assisted person income in 1960 whereas they were among the lowest in 1950.[99] While a great deal more detailed statistical analysis must be made on these data to uncover all the significant relationships among variables, this is a fruitful approach to the analysis of agency policy.

The study of old age assistance recipients in 1953 also noted the disparity between budgetary requirements and income. Need was defined as "the amount of assistance that would be necessary to provide the level of living contemplated by states' standards." The difference between payments and need for a selected month between December 1952 to May 1953 was reported. Of recipients with no spouse or with a spouse not receiving OAA, 73.2 percent received payments equal to need; 11.9 percent received payments of $10 or more less than need. Of recipients living with a spouse also receiving OAA, 72.8 percent had payments equal to need, and 13.8 percent had payments of $10 or more below need.[100]

The difficulty of obtaining maximum advantage from data on the proportion of need being met is heightened by the absence of accepted or common standards so that comparisons over time or between regions cannot validly be made. On the other hand, even the proportion of need met, based on different local standards, is an improvement over comparisons and trends currently drawn from the average grant data in federal reports on operating statistics, where there is not even a relative concept of need. Such an approach has been illustrated for

OAA recipients by the Bureau of Family Services.[101]

A third approach to measuring the adequacy of assistance uses level-of-living criteria.[102] Both Burgess and Price and the 1953 study of old age recipients, noted above, used level-of-living indexes to study the well-being of their populations. The OAA study provided national and state data on the proportion of recipients having cooking facilities of some type (95 percent), electric lights (88.1 percent), telephones (35.7 percent), refrigeration (75.4 percent), and sleeping-room crowding (8.5 percent sharing with at least one other person, not a spouse).[103] The last percentage probably reflects the larger proportion of OAA recipients who live alone.

Burgess and Price employed a variety of indexes to assess the level of living of the AFDC families in their sample: housing, home ownership, housing conveniences, and ownership of such appliances as car, washing machine, refrigerator, and television. Comparisons were made with the national population, and while the standards of the 1960 AFDC families improved over 1950, there were still important differences between the AFDC population and the national average. For example, in overcrowding, the 1960 AFDC families were slightly better off, but were still far below the national median, which had improved at a much greater rate between 1950 and 1960 than had the median for AFDC families. As for family appliances, the range was from 29.1 percent of AFDC families owning a car or truck to 89.9 percent having a refrigerator, and the national proportions

---

[99] Burgess and Price, *op. cit.*, p. 262.

[100] U.S. Department of Health, Education, and Welfare, Bureau of Public Assistance, "Recipients of Old-Age Assistance in Early 1953," p. 38.

[101] "Meeting Financial Needs Under Old-Age Assistance," *Welfare in Review*, Vol. 1, No. 6 (June 1963), pp. 1–6.

[102] *See* Margaret J. Hagood and Louis J. Ducoff, "What Level of Living Indexes Measure," *American Sociological Review*, Vol. 9, No. 1 (February 1964), pp. 78–84.

[103] U.S. Department of Health, Education, and Welfare, Bureau of Public Assistance, "Recipients of Old-Age Assistance in Early 1953," pp. 17–18.

were 78.0 and 98.0 percent, respectively. Within the AFDC population, Negro and rural families fared worst.[104] Generally speaking, the comparisons would have been more meaningful if the AFDC and national population figures had been standardized by similar demographic subcategories, since the AFDC population is not representative of the national population.

A promising approach to judging the adequacy of assistance standards was Elizabeth N. Gilboy's study of the effect of reduced income owing to relief.[105] The sample studied was of low educational and occupational level, and could be considered to represent the lowest level of independent income prior to being unemployed. A comparable employed population was selected to represent the normal or previous expenditure pattern of the unemployed. The major shortcoming of the study was the question of the comparability of these "matched" populations.

Gilboy found an attempt by assistance recipients to maintain the previous level of living, particularly in food consumption. Economies were practiced in other areas— clothing and transportation—to keep up food expenditure. The proportion spent on housing was relatively constant, but the lower actual amount meant less-adequate housing. Many families went into debt and resorted to credit. Rent, doctors' bills, and in some cases grocery bills went unpaid so that the diversity of previous consumption patterns might be maintained. Studies of this type provide a reality check on assumptions of budget standards and, as with Gilboy's sample of recipients, point to the unfortunate effects of neglected needs, such as clothing, as well as the precarious position of families falling into increasing indebtedness.

The Detroit NASW chapter study of AFDC also sought to assess the adequacy of assistance both in terms of the actual living conditions of recipients and the deviation from state budgetary standards.[106] The report pointed out that the difference between budgetary requirements and maximum allowable grants varied from $31 in a family of a mother and one child to $128 in families of seven or more children. In addition to describing the living standards of recipients the study used such criteria as rent and utilities arrears and the amount of cash and food stamps on hand over the duration of one month. Sixteen families of the ninety-three were in arrears in rent, and twenty-five were in arrears in utilities. Thirty-one families had four dollars or less on hand to last from three to fourteen days. Data on the adequacy of assistance standards need to be examined with respect to short- and long-term need. The significance of small budgetary deficiencies increases greatly with the length of the period on assistance.

General Critique

Research on administrative standards and practices, while of direct significance for evaluating performance whatever the policies, has not reached the point where, as a fairly routine operation, agencies (1) know what they are doing; (2) can compare what they are doing with their own past performance and similar functions carried on elsewhere; and (3) can keep their public informed. Every now and again "revelations" about welfare practices appear in popular media, but rarely are agencies so knowledgeable about their own operations that they can clearly justify their practices. Regular and special agency reports, from the point of view of scientific criteria, are rarely supported by sufficient or appropriate evidence. Size of sample, classifications, standards and methods of evaluation, control or comparison techniques, among other criteria make agency studies of dubious value. The reliance without safeguards on

---

[104] Burgess and Price, *op. cit.*, pp. 83–84, 90.

[105] "The Expenditure of the Unemployed."

[106] Lebeaux, *op. cit.*

staff personnel for qualitative judgments is standard procedure. Beyond superficial counts, few of the many state and local agency reports and studies of practice can be considered serious contributions to the knowledge of public welfare. This, in turn, affects independent studies, which frequently rely on agency data.

The Economics of Public Welfare

The social policy of a society may be broadly gauged by the amount and kinds of welfare services it provides. While a variety of more sensitive measures may be developed for particular services, the most general and most applicable for comparative purposes has been expenditure analysis.

Expenditure Studies

Two expenditure studies will be examined to illustrate differences in problems and approaches encountered in this type of research: "Social Welfare Expenditures" developed by Ida C. Merriam and the staff of the Division of Research and Statistics of the Social Security Administration, and *The Cost of the National Health Services in England and Wales* by Brian Abel-Smith and R. M. Titmuss.[107] The Merriam reports annually organize official expenditure figures for a broad view of the nation's welfare. The Abel-Smith and Titmuss study was a single detailed analysis of one service for the purpose of estimating the cost to British society of the new national health program. The Merriam reports have relied

on expenditure statistics from a variety of agencies, and have, in addition, the problem of maintaining some consistency over time for deriving trend data. The National Health Service study concentrated on determining the best absolute measure of cost since cost was the controversial policy issue and the period covered was relatively short. The authors did not accept official cost, as does Merriam, but sought "true" costs and projected these costs to indicate the continuing investment British society may be expected to make if present use and population trends prevail. The Merriam reports are a summary of past direction rather than an indication of future welfare commitments.

One of the major issues in analysis of national expenditures is the definition of welfare services. Merriam makes the "distinguishing characteristic" of social welfare "direct concern with the economic and social well-being of individuals and families."[108] However, there is recognition of a "wide borderline area" that is open to interpretation and often follows traditional classification. The major categories included are the income maintenance programs, health, veterans' programs, education, public housing, and other welfare services.

While the type of service defines whether it comes under the category of welfare, in the Merriam analysis sponsorship of the service determines whether it is classified as "public" welfare. The Merriam reports include as public expenditure costs of programs that are not necessarily supported by tax funds, but are under legal mandate. For example, workmen's compensation and temporary disability payments are included under statutory programs even though the payments may be made from private insurance companies. Similarly, the inclusion of social insurance generally under public programs has been questioned, at least to the extent that benefits represent contributions of the beneficiaries rather than tax

---

[107] Merriam, "Social Welfare Expenditures, 1962–63," *Social Security Bulletin*, Vol. 26, No. 11 (November 1963), pp. 3–14; and Abel-Smith and Titmuss, *The Cost of the National Health Services in England and Wales* (Cambridge, Eng.: Cambridge University Press, 1956).

[108] Merriam, *op. cit.*, p. 14.

funds.[109] The detailed categories of the reports, however, permit reorganization of the data for purposes of analysis.

There is value, on the other hand, in obtaining the most complete view of social welfare investment, whatever the source. The total social expenditure is an important indicator in trend and comparative analysis. Frequently the tendency is to consider governmental expenditures exclusively, and this underestimates the investment of countries with a large voluntary or private sector. The Merriam analyses in the areas of health, education, and income maintenance are useful in providing estimates of private expenditure.

The total expenditure, public and private, for health, education, and welfare, according to the Merriam studies was $100 billion in 1962–63. Of this, two-thirds were in the public sector, and one-third in the private sector. In the public sector, the total expenditure was 11.7 percent of the gross national product, with the social insurances and education accounting for 4.5 and 4.0 percent, respectively. Per capita, the total was $347.01, and in constant 1962–63 dollars this represented approximately a fivefold increase per capita since 1928–29. The major changes were in the social insurances (hardly present in 1928–29), and in education. Since 1949–50, the rate of increase has been slower than in preceding years.

In 1962, social welfare expenditures represented 38.5 percent of all governmental expenditure, federal, state, and local. However, if budgeted or tax revenue expenses are considered alone, the total is 29.5 percent: 15.9 percent of federal and 54.8 percent of state and local expenditures from general revenue. The proportion of federal funds has decreased sharply since 1949–50, although most of this has been in veterans' programs. The rest has taken

between 7 and 10 percent of the federal budget. The state and local proportion of total revenue spent on welfare has remained relatively constant during the last twenty years. Including the insurances, state and local funds currently account for about one billion dollars more of social welfare expenditure than do federal government funds. The differences have narrowed with the growth of the federal OASDI program.

In health and medical care, the 1962–63 total of $33 billion was shared one-fourth public and three-fourths private expenditure. Public funds accounted for 21.3 percent of personal health expenditure, health insurance was almost 25 percent, and the remainder were direct payments. In both public and insurance expenditures there were sizable increases: in 1928–29, direct payments by consumers had accounted for 88 percent of the personal health bill. Income maintenance has become a predominantly public field with private philanthropy providing services rather than material aid. The only significant change has been in the growing role of employee benefit plans, which, apart from health insurance benefits, accounted for 80 percent of private expenditure in income maintenance and welfare services.

While the optimum proportion of the national product to be devoted to social welfare may be greatly influenced by philosophical considerations, reports by bodies such as the International Labour Office permit comparative analysis of national policies. International statistics are generally limited by differences in definitions of categories, but rough comparisons can be made. In proportion of national income devoted to social security expenditures, the United States ranks among the lowest of the large industrial nations.[110]

Margaret S. Gordon, noting the inconsistent relationship between national income and expenditures on social security in the

---

[109] *See* Frank G. Dickinson, "The Growth of Private and Public Philanthropy," in Dickinson, ed., *Philanthropy and Public Policy* (New York: National Bureau of Economic Research, 1962), pp. 21–26.

[110] International Labour Office, *The Cost of Social Security, 1949–1957* (Geneva, 1961).

United States, remarked on a tendency for countries with the oldest programs of modern type to spend larger proportions of their incomes on social welfare.[111] Thus, the United States, a relative newcomer in the social security field, spent 6 percent of its national income on social security in 1956–57, as compared to 11.9 percent in the United Kingdom, 10.1 percent in Norway, and 13 percent in New Zealand.[112] In addition to the more general liberal benefit systems in these other national programs, the larger proportional expenditures, Gordon observes, occur because as programs mature their obligations become greater.[113]

The Abel-Smith and Titmuss study of the cost of the British health service between 1948 and 1954 was undertaken, as noted above, to obtain the most valid picture of cost, trends in cost, and future projections of cost. Originating as evidence for a government committee on the rising cost of the health services, the study had important policy implications. The study is technically interesting for its contribution to the very complex area of cost analysis, and significant for its clarification of the controversial issue of cost of the national health service.

For practical purposes the establishment of a "less ambiguous and more consistent concept of cost" and the development of effective policy are closely interrelated. As the authors stated:

We do not suggest that statistical and accounting intelligence in combination with *ad hoc* research modifies in any way the need for skilled administration. But we do believe that administration at most levels—regionally, locally and at the centre—is capable of some improvement if aided with the results of a discriminating statistical service. The diversity of the National Health Service makes it particularly dangerous to assume that any unit or any piece of activity is typical of the whole. We often found in pursuing this study that commonly held opinions were disproved when the appropriate facts were collected and analyzed in a meaningful way. It was also instructive to see how our inquiries stimulated an interest in the exploration of various fields of Health Service activity which had hitherto not been examined in any detail.[114]

Cost was defined as "all current productive resources administered by the Service" and paid for by public and/or private funds, depending on whether or not the total cost or the public cost only was desired. The increase of charges during the period studied resulted in a small but growing proportion of the gross cost being paid privately. As a result of redefining and reorganizing the cost statistics, the study made yearly adjustments in the nature of £70–80 million to the official costs as reported.[115]

Trend in cost of the services was of major concern. The study, using actual prices, found a much more regular trend in public cost with a gradual flattening of the curve. In terms of the gross national product, both the total and public costs decreased between 1949 and 1954 by 10 and 14 percent respectively. On the basis of 1948–49 prices, there was an actual decrease in the public cost of the service from a high of £388.3 million in 1950 to £380.8 million in 1953.[116]

The development of indexes based on 1948–49 prices was itself a complex procedure, since general price measures were not resorted to, but analysis was made of the price trends for the unique items in the health budget. In 1948–49 prices, the gross cost rose about £32 million between 1948–49 and 1953–54, and the major changes were £25 million on wages and salaries and £24 million on drugs and medical goods. A decrease of £20 million on

---

[111] Gordon, *The Economics of Welfare Policies* (New York: Columbia University Press, 1963), p. 16.

[112] International Labour Office, *op. cit.*, pp. 205–210.

[113] Gordon, *op. cit.*, p. 16.

[114] Abel-Smith and Titmuss, *op. cit.*, p. 73.

[115] *Ibid.*, pp. 10, 73.

[116] *Ibid.*, pp. 25, 60, 63.

dentures and spectacles occurred during the same period. Analysis of the trend of expenditure on the various items of the total services led to an examination of such problems as needed capital investment in hospitals. In terms of replacement cost and the rate of obsolescence it was concluded that the rate of hospital expenditure was less than half that needed to maintain the present supply.[117]

The effect of the charges introduced in 1951 and 1952 has been of particular interest to the health system, as well as of policy significance for welfare services generally. In both the dental and ophthalmic services, there was reduction in the gross expenditure. However, this was largely attributed in the study to a decline that had already set in before the introduction of charges, and represented a saturation of the demand existing prior to the introduction of the National Health Service.[118]

In predicting future costs of the health service, present use of the service was plotted against population trends. Anxiety over mounting costs rested to a large extent on the assumption that a growing aged population would result in an enormous increase in health expenditure. However, age was not found to play an important role, at least for hospital costs, but age associated with living alone was the major factor in the use of hospital facilities. Relevant to social class differences, the study pointed up that younger men of the higher socioeconomic classes made greater use of hospitals than did semiskilled and unskilled men of similar ages.

Generally speaking, in regard to further expenditure the data of the study indicated:

Irrespective of the changing incidence of disease, concepts of ill-health, standards of diagnosis and treatment and attitudes to medical care, all these "social" factors of age, sex, family, relationships, class and income play a variety of roles in determining the pattern of demand. They do not all work in the same

direction; more old people may mean more demands on some services but not on others; more children and a higher birthrate affect the different branches of the Service in different ways; less hospitalized sickness may mean more expenditure on welfare services; a larger proportion of the population with middle-class standards and aspirations may mean more *expressed* demand for some forms of medical care; a lower marriage rate and smaller families may mean increased demands for hospital care; changes in the proportion of men and women who are single, widowed, divorced and childless may represent in the future more important factors influencing demand for medical care than any foreseeable changes in the age structure of the population as a whole.[119]

Redistribution Effects

Studies of the cost of welfare services give one perspective on the nature and extent of the welfare function. Another measure of the welfare function, particularly since the growth of welfare economics in this century, has been the redistribution effect of welfare programs. The impact of welfare programs can be gauged by the modifications effected in the distribution of personal income. Research on redistribution is at present relatively primitive, but like other areas of research more refinement will come from increasing attention and productivity. The few studies undertaken have been greatly hampered by the very same factors that have complicated research on income distribution, for the latter provides the raw data for redistribution analysis.[120]

---

[117] *Ibid.*, pp. 53, 66.
[118] *Ibid.*, pp. 40–45.

---

[119] *Ibid.*, p. 70.
[120] *See* Conference on Economic Progress, *Poverty and Deprivation in the United States* (Washington, D.C., 1962); Martin David, "Welfare, Income, and Budget Needs," *Review of Economics and Statistics*, Vol. 41, No. 4 (November 1959), pp. 393–399; John K. Galbraith, *The Affluent Society* (New York: Mentor Books, 1958); Selma Goldsmith *et al.*, "Size Distribution of Income Since the Mid-Thirties," *Review of Economics and Statistics*, Vol. 36, No. 1 (February 1954), pp. 1–32; Gabriel Kolko, *Wealth and*

International comparisons of expenditures on welfare indicate, as noted above, that the United States spends a smaller proportion of its gross national product on welfare functions than most other industrialized states. That relatively more of the national product is involved in transfers in other countries, however, does not necessarily indicate greater redistribution or equalization of income through social policy. Welfare transfers may favor all, may

---

Power in America (New York: Frederick A. Praeger, 1962); Simon Kuznets, *Shares of Upper Income Groups in Income and Savings* (New York: National Bureau of Economic Research, 1953); Robert J. Lampman, "Recent Change in Income Inequality Reconsidered," *American Economic Review*, Vol. 44, No. 3 (June 1954), pp. 251–268; Lampman, "Taxation and the Size Distribution of Income," *Tax Revision Compendium*, Vol. 3 (Washington, D.C.: U.S. House Committee on Ways and Means, 1959), pp. 1537–2382; Lampman, "The Low Income Population and Economic Growth," Study Paper No. 12 (Washington, D.C.: U.S. Congress Joint Economic Committee, 1959); Herman P. Miller, *Income of the American People* (New York: John Wiley & Sons, 1955); Miller, "Is the Income Gap Closed? 'No!'" *New York Times Magazine* (November 11, 1962), p. 50; Miller, "New Definition of Our 'Poor,'" *New York Times Magazine* (April 21, 1963), p. 11; James Morgan, "The Anatomy of Income Distribution," *Review of Economics and Statistics*, Vol. 44, No. 3 (August 1962), pp. 270–283; James Morgan, Review of *Shares of Upper Income Groups in Income and Savings* by Simon Kuznets, in *Review of Economics and Statistics*, Vol. 36, No. 2 (May 1954), pp. 237–239; Morgan et al., op. cit.; National Bureau of Economic Research, Conference on Research in Income and Wealth, *Studies in Income and Wealth: An Appraisal of the 1950 Census Income Data*, Vol. 23 (Princeton, N.J.: Princeton University Press, 1958); National Bureau of Economic Research, *Studies in Income and Wealth*, Vol. 13 (New York, 1951); Richard M. Titmuss, *Income Distribution and Social Change* (London: G. Allen and Unwin, 1961); and U.S. Department of Commerce, Bureau of the Census, *Trends in the Income of Families and Persons in the United States: 1947 to 1960*, Technical Paper No. 8 (Washington, D.C., 1963).

transfer income from one period of life to another, may effect transfers within groups, and may seemingly favor particular income classes that, in reality, merely contain the greater proportion of those suffering from the risks provided for. As Titmuss has pointed out, in the health services there may even be a differential use of services that results in relatively greater resources being consumed by upper-income groups. Peterson, in his study of transfers through social security programs in France, points out that the beneficiaries of these programs pay for most of its cost indirectly, through higher consumption costs. Thus for nearly all income groups direct social security payments are more than balanced by the size of the benefits themselves.[121] Cartter, comparing England with the United States and using a broader range of welfare programs than did Peterson, concluded that both before the war and immediately after, redistribution of income was greater in England than in the United States, and there was less inequality of income in England.[122]

In the United States, as Lampman points out, transfer payments have had a radical effect on spending units in the lowest fifth among the income classes.[123] However, as Morgan and his associates note, most of those transfer payments are not between or among income classes. Rather, they are transfers over time from earning years to retirement years. Nor is Morgan as impressed as Lampman with the extent or numbers affected by redistribution.[124] While both studies agree that about one-half of low-income units benefit from transfers, Lampman considers this a positive advance while Morgan and his associates are more impressed by the large unsatisfied need.

---

[121] Wallace C. Peterson, *Welfare State in France* (Lincoln: University of Nebraska Press, 1960).

[122] A. M. Cartter, *The Redistribution of Income in Post-War Britain* (New Haven: Yale University Press, 1955).

[123] "The Low Income Population and Economic Growth," p. 30.

[124] Morgan et al., op. cit., p. 217.

The proportion of income replaced by redistribution is another indicator of the extent of welfare programs. For example, Lester has examined the amount of wage loss compensated in unemployment insurance, and found that on the average no more than 20 percent of wage loss from total unemployment is recovered. If all public programs are taken into account, about 23 percent of wage loss is compensated.[125] Again, as with other indicators, there is theoretical disagreement as to optimum compensation, but such research is important if the validity of any assumption is to be tested by the operations of current practice. The range of most assumptions on compensation, however, rarely starts as low as the proportion found by Lester, and the deviation between the actual and the expected is important for social policy development.

General Critique

Research on the balance sheets of welfare programs is both interesting and significant. At present, however, much of the official data upon which such studies are based is questionable, and assumptions about the classification of services, the incidence of taxes, and the division of benefits require more standardization before comparative studies can be effectively undertaken. Even more complex than the illustrations given above is research on redistribution through other than direct income transfers. In programs such as health, education, recreation, or housing, the recipients are less clearly identified than in income maintenance. A great deal more research needs to be done on the actual beneficiaries of such programs, despite popular assumptions that the beneficiaries are known. The private field of philanthropy, a major field of

welfare in the United States, has not been subject to redistribution analysis. It would be of great value to know, for example, in view of the spread of "democratic" giving under the community chests, who are the ultimate gainers in the philanthropic balance sheet of benefits and contributions.

Conclusions

While this review has not attempted a comprehensive survey of knowledge in or pertinent to the field of public assistance, the research reviewed points up major limitations and problems. The amount of usable knowledge available for current welfare policy and program belies the long history of the field.

Public welfare has neither produced nor stimulated a body of knowledge applicable in any significant measure to many contemporary issues. For immediate policy purposes knowledge is currently inadequate with respect to (1) the nature of the client group to be served—actual and potential; (2) the nature of the programs presently in operation and previously attempted; (3) the effect of policy or program on the client group; and (4) the public welfare system as a social institution—its internal structure, its environment, and the relationship of these factors to its functioning.

Methodologically, few of the studies cited may be considered as meeting even minimal criteria for sound research. The lack of specific studies clearly oriented to significant questions points to the need for reassessing the direction of research in public welfare. While fact-collecting in itself is important for a field that must stay abreast of social trends, the facts quickly lose importance when they cannot be related to any framework that interprets their significance. For example, what does it signify that more mothers on assistance are working, that more communities are providing work relief, or that fewer old people on assistance are being helped by relatives? The essential variables for clarifying these and other

[125] Richard A. Lester, "The Economic Significance of Unemployment Compensation, 1948–1959," *Review of Economics and Statistics,* Vol. 42, No. 4 (November 1960), pp. 359–360.

questions have not been pursued to the point where hypotheses may be stated with any degree of confidence. The significant variables affecting public welfare practice must be delineated and their interaction studied in research oriented to hypothesis formulation and testing.

The fundamental questions of public welfare are not unique. They are questions in the mainstream of social welfare generally and closely interlinked with the chain of the applied and basic behavioral sciences. Yet seldom does research in public welfare give evidence of its kinship with cognate practical and theoretical fields. The assumptions underlying public welfare inquiry more often reflect traditional values and contemporary political controversies. For example, the relationship of relief and dependency that underlies many current studies and demonstration projects rarely increases theoretical understanding of the contemporary phenomenon of dependency or expands practical capacity for dealing with current aspects of the phenomenon. It is vitally necessary for public welfare to distinguish between immediate needs for defensive action, as in Newburgh, and the long-run demand to establish a sound rationale for public welfare policy. Too long have these objectives been confused. Industry generally separates its advertising and public relations departments from its fundamental research operations.

Contemporary policy issues as generally stated are, on the whole, far too complex for the production of sound research. The value components must be siphoned off, and the residue must be broken down into concrete and identifiable units. Studies of dependency, for example, often compound a variety of types of psychosocial relationships, of which some may be positive or functional in society. However, all have been grouped indiscriminately as dysfunctional under the influence of earlier philosophies that have dominated public assistance policy for so long. Increasing education on the one hand, and early retirement on the other, have drastically shortened the period of independent action for the whole population. Research in public welfare, however, has not freed itself sufficiently from concern with the stigma of dependency to provide guidelines for a society in which independence will more clearly be a function of a sound structure of social supports. Perhaps a proportion of the public welfare budget should be set aside for pure research—research unrelated to marketing the contemporary product.

Whatever the research question, such scientific standards as adequate sampling, objective collection of data, and logical analysis must be followed. These are obvious and simple tenets. Nevertheless they have frequently been overlooked in public welfare research. The complexity of the public welfare clientele requires the development of a detailed scheme of categories reflecting the diversity of the population. Rarely, however, are the subclasses in studies sufficiently large for significant statistical analysis. In fact, the impression is frequently given that the classification of the population is an afterthought rather than an essential aspect of the design. Much public welfare data are a combination of observations and evaluations of public welfare personnel. Rarely do public welfare studies consider the problems of reliability that such data collections present. To compound the matter further, national studies are often a compilation of local and state data, and the lack of uniformity among these data complicates the picture. Thus far, no quality control study of research has been done to estimate the deviance or error factor introduced by following such research procedures.

The public welfare population must be related to parallel or similar categories in the general population if the public welfare data are to be of maximum value. Comparisons made with the general population on illegitimacy, education, and other criteria are of extremely limited significance since the public welfare population, and public assistance recipients particularly, include only a narrow range of the total population. Public assistance families cannot be compared to average-income families, southern Negro families on AFDC to Negro families generally, and children on public assistance to children in the nation as a whole. Do assistance clients differ significantly from others of the same general socioeconomic type, or do they look different merely because they are being compared to the wrong people?

If they do differ, how and why do they differ? Here, faulty logic is often applied to satisfy preconceived explanations. Since assistance is the only assumed variable, receiving assistance is made to account for the differences, and the assistance family becomes the source of low education, ill health, and immoral behavior. Correlations become confused with causation, if not explicitly, often implicitly, when comparative standards are applied to the assistance population. Underlying these explanations is the assumption that dependence on public assistance causes differences in ways that are significant for the problems studied. Thus far, no causal relationship has been established between the receipt of assistance and an increase in personal or social disorganization.

During the depression of the 1930's, Bakke and others studied the effect of unemployment and economic dependency on the life-style of workers.[126] At the end of the 1930's, Stouffer and Lazarsfeld produced a research memorandum suggesting some fruitful lines of inquiry on the effect of economic crisis on marriage and the family.[127] However, other than a scattering of social science studies examining the distinctive culture of low-income groups in American society, there have been few contemporary additions to scientific knowledge of the poor, the conditions of poverty, and its social and psychological antecedents or consequences.[128] The low-income groups upon whom some of the research has been done, moreover, are not necessarily representative of the groups who are, or who become, the clients of public assistance agencies. There are, for example, several types of poor and several kinds of poverty: (1) the poverty of the partially or insufficiently employed; (2) the poverty of those temporarily unemployed owing to small- or large-scale business crisis; and (3) the poverty of those isolated from the economy, such as the uneducated and elderly, or residents of rural and depressed areas.

What are the different effects of each type of poverty? What does experiencing inadequate income mean in each situation? What is the nature of the cycle of becoming poor, moving into economic dependence, and either remaining dependent or becoming self-supporting again? What factors make for differences in the experiencing of poverty, dependence, and independence? There is need for much greater knowledge in depth of the phenomenon of poverty before public welfare programs can be rationally geared to the needs of the variously impoverished. An impressionistic account like Caudill's *Night Comes to the Cumberlands* approaches the subject of poverty and public aid with much perception and provides insightful clues for research hypotheses.[129] Scientific studies of different kinds

[126] *See* the following studies, all cited in full at the beginning of this review: Bakke, *Citizens Without Work*; Bakke, *The Unemployed Worker*; Gilboy, *Applicants for Work Relief*; and Komarovsky, *The Unemployed Man and His Family*.

[127] Samuel A. Stouffer and Paul F. Lazarsfeld, *Research Memorandum on the Family in the Depression* (New York: Social Science Research Council, 1937).

[128] *See*, for example, Ely Chinoy, *Automobile Workers and the American Dream* (New York: Doubleday & Co., 1955); Albert K. Cohen, *Delinquent Boys* (Glencoe, Ill.: Free Press, 1955); August B. Hollingshead, *Elmtown's Youth* (New York: John Wiley & Sons, 1949); August B. Hollingshead and Fredrick C. Redlich, *Social Class and Mental Illness* (New York: John Wiley & Sons, 1958); and Frank Reissman, *The Culturally Deprived Child* (New York: Harper & Row, 1962).

[129] Harry M. Caudill, *Night Comes to the Cumberlands* (Boston: Little, Brown & Co., 1963).

of poverty following Caudill are needed.

The experience of public welfare practice, broadly defined, has hardly been recorded or analyzed. Not only is there a paucity of knowledge about new or experimental practices, but even the conventional or usual practices of public welfare are poorly documented. The last full-scale analysis of economic assistance programs was in the 1943 Report of the Committee on Long-Range Work and Relief Policies.[130] *The American Social Security System* by Eveline M. Burns, although narrower in scope, was also a thorough and scholarly survey, but it, too, was published over fifteen years ago.[131]

While good descriptive studies themselves make a valuable addition to current knowledge, the goal should be studies that include at least some evaluation of the consequences of policies and programs. Only through searching analysis of public welfare practice will a science of public welfare administration develop. There has been much criticism of the anachronistic or repetitive nature of some aspects of public welfare. This is not entirely the fault of public attitudes and cultural lag, as is sometimes stated. The responsibility must also be placed on the field's accumulated knowledge, which is not yet sufficient to provide relatively reliable answers about practices often almost four centuries old.

Programs and policies must be explicitly defined and their results evaluated objectively if the field is to learn from its own experience. Comparative studies permitting observation of similar programs under varying conditions provide rough models of experimental designs as, for example, Gladys M. Krammerer's recent *British and American Child Welfare Services*.[132] The many jurisdictions within the United States with different environments and different ways of administering welfare are an excellent source of field studies. While much may be learned through comparative studies under natural conditions, there is also need for carefully devised experiments with planned variations.

While research on policy and programs is important, there must also be better understanding of the instrument for carrying out policy, and of the factors that affect its operation. Little is known about the public welfare department as a social organization. How does it formulate policy? What are its most influential forces? How is policy translated into programs and practice? What is the relationship of the department to its client group and the public generally? What is the significance for a public welfare organization of different kinds of personnel—trained, untrained; specialist, generalist; social work, administrative?

Knowledge of workers' attitudes and behavior is lacking. A contemporary analysis comparable to Grace F. Marcus' evaluation of family relief practices in a private casework agency in 1929 would be of great value for the understanding of worker-client relationships today.[133] Alan Keith-Lucas, in *Decisions About People in Need*, has attempted to classify and weight the factors influencing social workers' actions in AFDC cases.[134] It is surprising, however, that a profession generally so sensitive to interpersonal relationships should be so tardy in examining the pattern of its own administrative behavior.

What are the effects of differing internal structures and environment? *Children in Need of Parents* demonstrates the value of examining the interplay of forces within the welfare system and between the system and its environment for understanding how

[130] U.S. Congress, Committee on Long-Range Work and Relief Policies, *Security, Work and Relief Policies.*

[131] Boston: Houghton Mifflin Company, 1949.

[132] Detroit: Wayne State University Press, 1962.

[133] *Some Aspects of Relief in Family Casework* (New York: Charity Organization Society, 1929).

[134] Chapel Hill: University of North Carolina Press, 1957.

welfare services are provided.[135] Blau has made interesting observations on the informal system of the welfare agency and its consequences for professional performance.[136] Some of the contrasts between "manifest" and "latent" factors in the functioning of the welfare structure may become clearer through organizational analysis.

These are specific substantive areas of concern for research in public welfare. Together, however, they indicate the general need for developing public welfare into a more disciplined field of practice through expansion of its knowledge base. Program data developed and reported by public agencies should be geared to the accretion of knowledge for program development. Much current official data are irrelevant or require the interpolation of too many unknown factors to be useful for policy determination. Emphasis on significance for practice will lead to further refinement of both data and practice. In effect, the qualitative and quantitative knowledge in public welfare, as in other areas of social welfare, should be formulated with the

[135] Henry S. Maas and Richard E. Engler, *Children in Need of Parents* (New York: Columbia University Press, 1959).

[136] Peter M. Blau, "Orientation Toward Clients in a Public Welfare Agency," *Administrative Science Quarterly*, Vol. 5, No. 3 (December 1960), pp. 341–361.

long-range goal of improving services, not merely reporting activities. Gradually the disparate pieces of knowledge from the social sciences, administration, public welfare practice, and other related fields may be woven together into appropriate generalizations for policy-making.

The impetus for such research and knowledge formulation must come from many sources, but it is reasonable to assume that the government will play a major role, whether through directly administering its own research or sponsoring research undertaken elsewhere. Progress in this direction has already been made. The research proposals currently supported by the U.S. Bureau of Family Services indicate a higher standard than previous research in the field.

Whatever the mechanism, there must be opportunity for critical assessment of present practices. Public welfare today is primarily administered by the states and localities, and it is at these levels that there is the greatest dearth of objectives and well-designed studies. The advance of knowledge in public welfare, the exploration of policy, and the testing of policy against practice will depend to a great extent on a research strategy that will make available the service experience of operating units at federal, state, and local levels.

CHILD WELFARE

By DAVID FANSHEL

The expansion of child welfare research during the past decade must be regarded as a healthy portent for a science-based practice. This important development has received its thrust from a number of sources, not the least of which has been the availability of funds and research personnel.[1] In fixing the bounds of this review of current research, the writer has chosen to focus upon those findings that deal with the provision of care or protection of children by persons other than their natural parents. The need for such service may stem from the absence, physical illness, psychological impairment, or social deviancy of the parents. Thus, children who are reared away from their own homes in foster family homes or in institutions are included within this presentation. Similarly, children who are placed with adoptive parents not biologically related to them will come within the purview of this review. An attempt will also be made to scrutinize research dealing with the care of children away from their own homes on a less total basis, viz., through various forms of day care arrangements. The common thread of concern will be with children who are the products of families unable to provide adequate care and who, therefore, require organized child welfare services.

It has not been an easy task to limit the scope of this review because many forces impinge upon children who require organized child welfare services. For example, the recent national interest in the problems of poverty and the problems of minority racial groups, particularly Negroes, covers ground that is very germane to the life-chances of children who are known to child welfare agencies. Also, research dealing with the effects of public welfare programs such as Aid to Families with Dependent Children has a very tangible relevance for the practitioner in child

[1] David Fanshel, "Research in Child Welfare: A Critical Analysis," *Child Welfare*, Vol. 41, No. 10 (December 1962), pp. 484–507.

welfare. These topics, however, will not be covered in this review. Research that has been undertaken in connection with the problems of unmarried motherhood might be considered relevant here, since children born out of wedlock are a major source of clientele for child welfare agencies. However, it has been deemed more efficient to focus attention upon the research directly related to children, rather than on the behavior of their parents. Finally, in the list of areas excluded is the rather sweeping category called "service to children in their own homes."

Several points should be made about the basis for selecting research for coverage in this review. First, while occasional reference is made to foreign studies, this chapter is essentially an overview of child welfare research carried on in the United States. It was felt that there had been such an expansion of research in this area on the American scene as to represent a sufficiently large task for one reviewer. Second, the bulk of the research covered here has been executed during the past decade. This reflects the extreme paucity of research undertaken in child welfare prior to this recent period. Finally, most of the coverage has been restricted to empirical studies involving some use of quantitative techniques. Individual case analyses or exclusively theoretical articles have not been considered appropriate for coverage in this particular chapter.

The major emphasis of this review, therefore, will be on adoption, foster family care, institutional care and other forms of group living, and daytime care of children away from their own homes. The review will be concerned with the characteristics of these children, what is known about the decision-making processes that result in their coming to the attention of organized social agencies, the forces that help shape the kinds of services they receive, and the consequences of these services for their over-all adjustment. It will include what is known about some of the major actors in the placement drama, such as foster parents and cottage parents. Finally, evaluation as a major research task will come under scrutiny, and a number of follow-up studies will be summarized.

Maternal Deprivation

A major source of theoretical orientation and knowledge about children who have been deprived of care by their parents has stemmed from the work of a fairly impressive number of investigators concerned with an area of research about the human (and animal) species known as "maternal deprivation." While significant studies in this area had made their way into the literature of several professions (i.e., psychiatry, psychology, and social work) subsequent to World War II, a high point was reached in the publication of John Bowlby's classic monograph, *Maternal Care and Mental Health,* published in 1951.[2]

This publication constituted a summary statement of much of the research that had previously been reported about children deprived of their natural parents and reared in nurseries, institutions, hospitals, and other types of group care settings. The publication of this monograph had a profound impact upon child welfare agencies throughout the world, and a particularly receptive audience was found among child welfare workers in the United States. The latter had already been sensitized to the problem by the research reports of Spitz, Goldfarb, and others.[3] After scrutinizing many studies, Bowlby came to the conclu-

---

[2] (Monograph Series No. 2; Geneva: World Health Organization, 1951.)

[3] *See,* for example, René A. Spitz, "Hospitalism: An Inquiry into the Genesis of Psychiatric Conditions in Early Childhood," *Psychoanalytic Study of the Child,* Vol. 1 (1945), pp. 53–74; and William Goldfarb, "Psychological Privation in Infancy and Subsequent Adjustment," *American Journal of Orthopsychiatry,* Vol. 15, No. 2 (April 1945), pp. 247–255.

sion that children who were deprived of maternal care for an extended period in their early lives were in grave danger of showing serious deleterious effects in the subsequent development of their personalities.

While Bowlby's pronouncements were unequivocal and based upon an impressive marshaling of research findings, it was not long before a plethora of questions arose about the adequacy of his formulations in the light of a number of variables that he had not taken into account. It became apparent that the task of spelling out the consequences of maternal deprivation was more complex than was at first assumed by pioneer investigators. Rather than being the final word on the subject, Bowlby's monograph became instead the springboard for considerable further research; and the processes of clarification of concepts, goals, and research procedures are still unfolding at the present time.

It is not the purpose of this review to cover the basic types of studies that have been developed in the area of maternal deprivation. This has already been adequately accomplished by a number of scholars and the reader is referred to these summary articles and monographs for systematic treatment of the subject of maternal deprivation.[4] A reading of these reviews makes clear how profoundly complex is the task of sorting out the effects of various types of depriving experiences children

encounter through the absence of maternal figures or through suffering interaction with highly disturbed and inadequate parents. In reviewing recent findings, Ainsworth makes the following commentary:

An examination of the evidence should leave no doubt that maternal deprivation in infancy and early childhood indeed has an adverse effect on development both during the deprivation experience and for a longer or shorter time after deprivation is relieved, and that severe deprivation experiences *can* lead in some cases to grave effects that resist reversal. This conclusion is essentially the same as Bowlby's in 1951. Research both during the last ten years and previously, however, makes clear that these adverse effects differ in nature, severity, and duration, and that these differences are themselves related to qualitative and quantitative differences in the deprivation experience. The nature and the severity of the deprivation experience are now known to be determined by an interacting and complex set of variables, although much further research is required before the relationship between antecedent depriving conditions and their effect can be specified in detail.[5]

Some of the alleged complexity of this research is explained by the fact that various investigators have studied different types of maternal deprivation. It has become apparent that deprivation can actually be as severe in situations in which the child remains within his own family as when he is totally deprived of his biological family. In discussions of "deprivation," there is often a confounding of "insufficient," "discontinuous," and "distorted" kinds of maternal care. Investigators are also aware that children vary in the degree to which they are adversely affected by the same kind of depriving experiences. Some children apparently escape serious ill effects after being exposed to pathological handling by their parents, while others succumb to this same type of handling.

Children also seem to vary in the ways in which they manifest the effects of deprivation; some youngsters show the effects of deprivation in the area of intellectual

[4] *See Deprivation of Maternal Care: A Reassessment of Its Effects* (Geneva: World Health Organization, 1962), and especially Mary D. Ainsworth's superb review article, "The Effects of Maternal Deprivation: A Review of Findings and Controversy in the Context of Research Strategy." *See also* Leon J. Yarrow, "Maternal Deprivation: Toward an Empirical and Conceptual Re-Evaluation," *Psychological Bulletin*, Vol. 58, No. 6 (November 1961), pp. 459–490; and Leon J. Yarrow, "Separation from Parents During Early Childhood," in Martin L. Hoffman and Lois Wladis Hoffman, eds., *Review of Child Development Research* (New York: Russell Sage Foundation, 1964).

[5] Ainsworth, *op. cit.*, p. 142.

functioning; others may show it with respect to other cognitive areas such as concept formation; and still others may show aberrations in personality and character development. There is also the problem that some effects are not visible until many years after the deprivation has been experienced and might be described as showing a "sleeper effect." It is also apparent that although many children may suffer severe damage as a consequence of deprivation, some may show impressive improvement in functioning due to intensive psychotherapy or radical improvements in environmental conditions. All in all, however, there has been a rather imposing array of findings indicating that inadequate mothering, in the aggregate, has a serious impact upon infants and young children.

Yarrow has pointed up similar complexities in maternal-deprivation research. He notes:

It is apparent that the data on maternal deprivation are based on research of varying degrees of methodological rigor. Most of the data consists of descriptive clinical findings arrived at fortuitously rather than through planned research, and frequently the findings are based on retrospective analyses which have been narrowly directed toward verification of clinical hunches.[6]

He suggests that longitudinal studies currently under way may offer better data on the persistence of the effects of various depriving experiences than do retrospective studies.

A number of investigators concerned with the problems of maternal deprivation have, in recent years, focused upon the very early experiences of the human infant (and animals as well), in order to understand the capacities of the newborn for developing social responsiveness to a variety of types of parental care.[7] Rheingold, one of the investigators at the Tavistock Clinic conference, reported on research dealing with the responsiveness of infants to experimental forms of stimulation. Surprisingly, she found that institutionalized infants were more positively responsive to a person and to toys with which they had no prior experience than were infants cared for in their own homes by their mothers.[8] Her research, as well as that of others at the same conference, has suggested that much of the concern about maternal deprivation might well be more finely focused upon the problem of sensory deprivation than exclusively upon the loss of the mother figure. This is an area that until recently was not adequately highlighted by those responsible for the care of infants in institutional settings.

Children in Foster Care

In the United States there are approximately a quarter of a million children without homes of their own. These are the children who reside in foster family care or in institutions under the supervision of social agencies. For a long time, there was a serious lack of information available about the characteristics of these children. Not infrequently, in the daily press and in the popular journals, assertions by professionals and laymen could be found about the fate of children languishing in foster care who ought to be adopted and assured of families.

In response to these expressions of concern, and because these children had not been studied and described in any systematic fashion, a major effort was undertaken by the Child Welfare League of America from October 1957 to August 1958. A milestone project by Maas and Engler involved scrutinizing the characteristics of

---

[6] "Maternal Deprivation: Toward an Empirical and Conceptual Re-Evaluation, p. 485.

[7] *See* the report of a study conference sponsored by the Tavistock Clinic in London, B. M. Foss, ed., *Determinants of Infant Behavior* (New York: John Wiley & Sons, 1961).

[8] Harriet L. Rheingold, "The Effect of Environmental Stimulations Upon Social and Exploratory Behavior in the Human Infant," in B. M. Foss, ed., *op. cit.*

children in care in nine selected communities in the United States, "varying in size from rural counties to big cities of close to a million, and in location from Atlantic to Pacific shores and from the Gulf to the Great Lakes, with way stations in between." [9] Two research teams, each composed of a child welfare worker and a sociologist, carefully examined these nine communities with respect to the kinds of organizational arrangements that had been developed locally for the care of dependent and neglected children. Through interviews with key informants they sought to develop understanding of (1) the placement resources available for dependent children; (2) the legal systems that provided the means by which many of these children came into placement and influenced the type of care they received; and (3) the network of agencies that served these children and their families, with emphasis upon the co-operation among agencies. Simultaneously, the children receiving care in each of these communities were carefully studied in order to gain greater knowledge about their adjustment as foster children.

Maas and Engler found differences in the way dependent families were defined and reacted to in the communities studied. In each of the communities, they saw differing patterns in the way children were legally removed from neglectful parents and variations in the availability of foster homes, adoptive homes, and institutions—both in quality and volume. They also found variations in the degree of co-operation among groups responsible for the care of these children. For example, most of the 110 children in two rural communities were without homes of their own, and only a few were moving into adoptive families or back to their own parents. Of these two communities, it was found that the one with a more integrated network linking agencies together moved proportionately more children into adoption. In the less well-integrated rural community, the children either returned home or spent their childhood years in foster care.

Similarly, in the two small urban communities studied, there was a stark contrast in the kinds of care provided dependent children. In one community, 90 percent of the children in foster care were in institutional placements, while in the contrasting community of similar size 85 percent of the children were in foster family care. When two metropolitan areas were studied, it was found that in one community, 64 percent of the children were in institutional care, with 30 percent going into foster family care and 6 percent into adoptive homes. By contrast, the other metropolitan area had only 20 percent in institutional care, with 58 percent going into foster family care and 22 percent into adoptive homes. Less striking differences were found when the investigators studied two big cities.

In reporting on the children in these nine communities, Maas and Engler found that most of those in foster care were separated voluntarily from their parents. Where involuntary separation was high, marital—and not economic—problems were the major source of the difficulty. Almost half the children in foster care in each of the nine communities were separated from their parents because of neglect and abandonment, death, illness, or economic hardship. Maas and Engler found that "as precipitators of parent-child separation, the less purely physical and more clearly psychological parental problems seemed to increase in importance with the complexity of the community and/or the professional character of the services provided." [10] Of the nine communities studied, five offered social contexts in which foster family placement was clearly the dominant type of placement, while three communities were considered to offer preponderantly insti-

[9] Henry S. Maas and Richard E. Engler, Jr., *Children in Need of Parents* (New York: Columbia University Press, 1959).

[10] *Ibid.*, pp. 349–350.

tutional care. One community was in transition toward greater use of foster family care.

Most of the children in the Maas and Engler study were first separated from their parents as preschoolers, and a majority of them remained in care for two- to five-year periods. The children who were able to return to their own families tended to be those who had been in care a shorter time, on the average, than those who remained in foster care. The authors emphasized that *time* was perhaps the most important factor in the movement of children out of foster care; if a child stayed in a setting beyond a year and a half, his chances of not being adopted or of returning home were greatly increased. A most telling finding was that in 42 percent to 77 percent of the cases in each community, the parental housing arrangements at the time of the field study were so bad that there was either no space available for the child, or he would have been compelled to share a room with an adult. Also of significance was the fact that while the economic circumstances of the parents were seldom comfortable, they were not primarily situations of destitution.

Maas and Engler found that the forces aligned against a child's return home seemed to stem from a combination of social and psychological conditions. The child who was fortunate enough to secure a permanent family of his own through adoption was typically under 2 years of age and had formed no relationships with natural parents or with natural brothers and sisters. These infants and toddlers were, almost uniformly, a healthy group and free from symptoms of psychological or intellectual impairment. However, many of the remaining children studied in this major research undertaking were faced with the prospect of most likely spending all of their childhood years in substitute care.

One of the limitations of Maas and Engler's data stems from the fact that their study was undertaken from the vantage point of an *ex post facto* perspective of the experiences of children in care. Thus, the field investigators had the difficult task of obtaining information about events that may have taken place a considerable number of years earlier. Some questions might be raised about the firmness of the data entered into the case-reading schedules used by the field teams. While the percentage of item-by-item agreements of the four field workers tended to be quite high, case records are notorious for having major gaps in information, particularly when they have not been specifically prepared for research purposes. In order to meet this kind of criticism, future studies of children in care will no doubt seek to use prospective designs in which the children are studied as significant events take place in their lives.

Further analysis of the data reported in *Children in Need of Parents* was undertaken by Fanshel and Maas.[11] A factor analysis of the data drawn from the case records of the children in care again pointed up the factor of *time in care* as a crucial and dynamic variable affecting the life-chances of children in foster care. It was also found that the four categories of outcome of placement (i.e., remaining in institutional care, remaining in foster family care, being placed for adoption, and returning home) were associated with somewhat different causes leading to the original placement. Those children who returned home tended to be the ones who were placed because of parental illness or a parent's death. Children in large families where there were affectionate relationships with siblings and where parent-child relationships were maintained also tended to return home. The child going into an adoptive home placement tended to be the infant requiring care because of an out-of-wedlock birth. By contrast, the children

[11] David Fanshel and Henry S. Maas, "Factorial Dimensions of the Characteristics of Children in Placement and Their Families," *Child Development*, Vol. 33, No. 1 (March 1962), pp. 123–144.

remaining with foster families or in institutional care were those who were placed because of (1) marital conflict, when the family was legally intact; or (2) came from broken homes where the mother either manifested serious psychosocial problems or was living with a mate other than the father.

A forerunner to the larger investigation of Maas and Engler was conducted by Boehm in a New England community.[12] This investigation pointed up striking differences in the age, health, race, intelligence, and emotional adjustment of children who were placed for adoption as contrasted with those who were retained in foster care. Assigning weights to each deterrent in accordance with its importance in discriminating between the children remaining in care and those placed for adoption, Boehm found that there was a high concentration of foster children with lower range scores, i.e., those where the deterrants tended to loom large. With a highest possible score of 430, it was found that a cut-off point of 350 marked the score that discriminated most accurately between the children placed in adoption and those retained in foster care. Thus, although adoption seemed to be appropriate in approximately one-third of the cases studied in the total foster care case load of this community, it became evident that very few of the children in care might be considered adoptable under the prevailing circumstances. Typically, a child with a very low score would be a nonwhite child, 4 years or older, whose intelligence was lower than normal and whose health was less than excellent. This child would typically manifest conflict in his attitude toward his own parents and would evidence symptomatic signs of behavioral problems. By way of contrast, the child at the top of the scoring system would be a white child, 3 years of age or less, with at least normal intelligence and excellent health. A child in this category would manifest no conflict in his attitude toward his own parents and would show no symptoms of behavioral problems. Boehm noted that her data suggest that the most effective service to a "hard-to-place" child is to prevent his becoming hard to place! This would entail undertaking more preventive work in helping children to remain with their own families. Of further interest in this study was the finding that the children who were placed in adoptive homes received more adequate casework, as revealed by rating of case record material, than was true of their counterparts in foster care. In this study, as was subsequently reported for the Maas and Engler undertaking, a major implication of the data for practice was seen in the overwhelming importance of the length of time in care. Boehm notes:

We see this revealed in many of the study findings. Opportunities for adoption diminish as the child grows older, not only because he is no longer the tiny infant that most families prefer but because at the same time he begins to develop other problems which complicate adoptive placement. We have seen that for the child in foster care emotional difficulties tend to increase with the passage of time. We find a growing incidence of behavior problems and of conflict and confusion in regard to parental relationships. As he grows older, the child begins to sense his difference from children who live with their own families and develops relationships and values which make it more difficult for him to become totally incorporated into the new adoptive family. Placement in foster care for a period of more than two years is the factor which discriminates most highly against adoptability.[13]

Adequacy of Families

A study by the State Charities Aid Association in New York City was undertaken, along lines similar to Maas and Engler's, to shed light upon the status of children in foster care and to make a determination

[12] Bernice Boehm, *Deterrents to the Adoption of Children in Foster Care* (New York: Child Welfare League of America, 1958).

[13] *Ibid.*, p. 28.

about the adoptability of children.[14] Professional judgments were made about the child's adoptability from a legal view, from the standpoint of family ties, from the perspective of the child's ability to form a satisfactory relationship to adoptive parents, and with respect to his physical and emotional health. The potential adoptability status of these children was examined at three periods of the child's life: (1) when first known to the agency at the time of initial placement; (2) two years after the child was first known to the agency; and (3) at the time the study was undertaken in 1958.

The study reveals that 45 percent of these foster children were at some point in their placement experience presumptively adoptable, but as of 1958, only 13 percent of the youngsters had achieved this status. The study also revealed that the children had been in care for the greater part of their lives and there was a substantial degree of emotional disturbance among them. The majority of these children had, at best, a tenuous relationship with their own parents. The study also showed that seventy-seven of the one hundred children in the sample had families who were so markedly disturbed and socially incompetent as to render them, in all probability, "beyond the hope of salvage for the particular child." This agency has raised the question whether the social work profession needs to re-evaluate what it means by "family ties." It also has expressed doubt whether the presence of one or more siblings in the child's life, and the desire to keep them together, ought necessarily exclude an adoptable child from adoptive placement.

A major issue that has occupied the attention of child welfare workers over the years concerns the degree to which families of children who are placed away from home constitute viable units that can eventually reabsorb these children. One early

study was carried on at the Jewish Children's Bureau of Chicago.[15] The case records of 158 unmarried mothers whose children were known to the agency from January 1, 1930, through December 1, 1939, were examined. The material suggested that the families of these children offered little in the way of resources for their care.

Forty-six percent of the unmarried mothers' own families were broken by death, desertion, or divorce. The parental relationship was judged to be unhappy in almost three-fourths of the families. The unmarried mothers themselves were seldom secure enough to offer dependable care to their children. As determined by psychometric tests, 36 percent of the subjects presented problems of mental limitations ranging from somewhat less than average intelligence to pronounced feeblemindedness. Psychiatric examination of more than one-third of the mothers revealed that they were emotionally disturbed individuals. The outlook for treatment was not considered hopeful. One-third of the mothers kept their children but review of their cases led the agency to surmise that the plan was questionable or contraindicated in all except a few cases. The outlook for the normal growth and development of the children returned to these mothers seemed most unfavorable.

The removal of a child from his own home is not infrequently the recommendation of child guidance clinics after unsuccessful efforts have been made to treat the emotional disorders of children who have been reared in essentially unwholesome family environments. There has been little research undertaken to determine the consequences of this decision for the parents and the siblings. Professional writers are aware that feelings of guilt and unworthiness may be intensified in parents as a consequence of the decision to place a child

---

[14] State Charities Aid Association, *Adoptability: A Study of 100 Children in Foster Care* (New York, 1960).

[15] Jewish Children's Bureau of Chicago, *The Care of Children of Unmarried Parents* (Chicago, 1943).

away from his home, but this is a matter for further systematic study. It is not known under what conditions the separation experience results in the parents developing lessened identification with the child or when respite from the burdens of parental care results in subsequent strengthening of parental capacity.

One study reported by Ricketts involved a follow-up study of nineteen parents who had placed their children following the recommendation of the clinical staff of the Institute for Juvenile Research in Chicago.[16] Although most of the parents expressed relief that the burden of caring for the child had been removed, they also revealed feelings of intense loneliness, emptiness, and guilt. The experience also appeared to be an upsetting one for the siblings who remained at home. For them, the threat of placement in similar fashion seemed very real.

Foster Children and Their Foster Families

Child welfare professional literature indicates widespread concern about what happens to the legally adoptable child who is not placed for adoption. Does denial of legal adoption mean depriving the child of a meaningful family life? Kadushin studied all children under 10 years of age not placed for adoption and who had been under the care of the Division of Children and Youth of the Wisconsin State Department of Public Welfare for five or more months by June 1, 1957.[17] He constructed a questionnaire that was sent to the child welfare workers responsible for the children defined as eligible for the study. Subsequent data

were also obtained from structured interviews with those who worked with some of the children and from reading samples of the records.

For 215 children who had been under care for more than five months, it was found that in 91.5 percent of the cases a limited number of factors—race, age, physical and mental disability—were principally responsible for the delay in placement. Kadushin raised question as to whether these children considered and felt themselves to be part of the family group with whom they were living. Question also arose about the degree to which the children were identified with the foster family. Seventy-three percent of these children had been living in the same foster home since the guardianship commitment. One hundred and fifty-one of the children had been under guardianship for two years or longer; of these 88 percent were in the same home for two years or more.

In examining the adjustment of these children, the workers responsible for supervising the child in the foster home were asked to respond to a list of symptoms of maladjustment, such as stealing, truanting, thumb-sucking, nail-biting, temper tantrums, and nightmares. Kadushin also sought to obtain an "educated opinion" about the adjustment of these children from the professional person who was acquainted with each child's behavior on the basis of regular contacts. His findings suggested that most of the children—68 percent— fell in the middle range of behavioral adjustment categorized as "fair," with 15 percent in the "good," and 17 percent in the "poor" adjustment categories. With respect to the quality of the child's integration in the foster home, the ratings indicated that 38 percent of the children showed "good" integration, 56 percent showed "fair" integration, and only 6 percent showed "poor" integration. Reflecting upon his findings, Kadushin commented: "Perhaps we need to reassess the respectability of long range boarding home care for hard to place children." He also raised for dis-

---

[16] Betty M. Ricketts, "Child Placement and Its Effect on the Child and His Family." Unpublished master's thesis, Smith College School for Social Work, 1959.

[17] Alfred Kadushin, "The Legally Adoptable Unadopted Child," *Child Welfare*, Vol. 37, No. 9 (December 1958), pp. 19–25.

cussion consideration of a program for subsidized adoptions on a selective basis, noting:

The data add up to something else. They demonstrate empirically that there are parents who want these children, however different, however handicapped. They may not, for a variety of reasons, want them as their legal sons and daughters, but they do want them, and have accepted them as their own in their minds and in their hearts.[18]

Weinstein undertook to study the adjustment of foster children at the Chicago Child Care Society.[19] He was concerned with the degree of clarity developed by children in foster family homes regarding their status as foster children and their understanding of the agency's role. He posed the following questions: "How well do foster children understand the placement situation? How do they view themselves in relation to the situation? With whom do they identify? What conditions in the placement situation tend to promote or attenuate the child's ability to function effectively in it?" The investigator interviewed sixty-one children under the agency's care, tape-recording the interviews to allow for subsequent coding. This represents one of the few studies reported in the child welfare literature where the research investigator was granted direct access to children in care.

The findings of Weinstein's study have considerable significance for practice. On the basis of the data, it was suggested that continuing contact between the child and his own parents had an ameliorative effect on the otherwise detrimental consequences of long-term foster care. The average well-being of youngsters whose parents visited them regularly was significantly higher than children who did not have contact with their natural parents. This was true even when the children had been in foster care

for long periods. His data do not make clear, however, whether visits by the natural parents after placement per se result in the children's apparent well-being or whether they received better care prior to placement. Weinstein also concluded, on the basis of responses from the children, that those who predominantly identified with their natural parents had the highest well-being ratings of any group in the study. Those who identified most with their foster parents or who had mixed identifications achieved significantly lower ratings. He also concluded that adequate conceptions of the meaning of foster status and the role of the agency were important for the child's well-being. A significant correlation was found between a child showing a sense of well-being and his understanding of his foster status. A corresponding association was also found for his understanding of the function of the agency. Failure to clarify the role of the agency in the child's life seemed to reflect a weakness in the kind of casework provided.

Further information about the adjustment of foster children has been provided by Mech, who studied the problem of anxiety shown by children in foster care.[20] The Children's Manifest Anxiety Scale was administered to 114 children in foster family care. Mech found that the extent of a child's contact with his own family was positively correlated with evidence of anxiety. This was particularly pronounced in girls. This finding runs counter to the one reported by Weinstein and suggests the possibility that anxiety is not a variable reflecting negatively upon the child's adjustment in placement, but rather is appropriate to the living conditions he encounters.

A creative study of the problems of "breakdown" of foster home placements of children in England has been reported by

---

[18] *Ibid.*, p. 18.
[19] Eugene A. Weinstein, *The Self-Image of the Foster Child* (New York: Russell Sage Foundation, 1960).

[20] Edmund Mech, "Manifest Anxiety in Foster Children." Unpublished master's thesis, Bryn Mawr College, Graduate Department of Social Work and Social Research, 1959.

Trasler.[21] He compiled a study sample of fifty-seven children who had experienced at least one failure in a foster home and contrasted them with children who were identified as more happily placed (i.e., enjoying satisfying relationships with their foster parents and with their emotional, intellectual, and material needs met as fully as possible). Eighty-one placements uniformly assessed as "excellent" by multiple judges constituted this second group. It was found that children previously separated from their mothers before reaching the age of 3 years formed a higher proportion of the study sample (73 percent) than of the more satisfactorily placed contrast group (60 percent), but this was not a statistically significant difference (p = 0.15). Looked at another way, however, it was found that two-thirds of the children who were placed in their current foster homes before they reached the age of 4 years achieved a good adjustment to their foster homes, suggesting that stability of placements of young children might be an important factor in their long-term adjustment. Children placed between the ages of 7 and 13 were not able to sustain the placements; almost 70 percent of these were later removed. Trasler's findings support the view that under certain conditions young children can accept substitute parents more readily than those who are older.

Emotional Disturbance in Foster Children

Significant findings have been reported by Eisenberg about children who have shown emotional disturbance while in foster care.[22] During a five-year period in which he served as psychiatric consultant to the foster care division of a large urban welfare department, this investigator saw some four hundred children who required clinical appraisal for emotional disturbance. He compared children seen in the first year of the clinic and in the fourth year (n = 140) with characteristics of all the foster children in the state during the intervening period. In contrasting clinic cases with the larger population of foster children, Eisenberg found a number of noteworthy differences. In looking at the family backgrounds of the disturbed youngsters he found that only about half of the parents were married, as contrasted with a 70 percent legitimacy rate in the statewide foster child population. Further, the family experiences of the referred children at the time they were committed were considerably more unfavorable than those of the general foster care population with respect to availability of parents. Less than 10 percent of the mothers of the clinic cases visited regularly and not more than another 10 percent visited at all. The visitation patterns of the fathers were even lower. It seemed clear that the foster children referred for psychiatric care were far more often abandoned by their parents than was true for the typical foster child. Also, the children who required this special attention had been in placement for more extended periods than their counterparts in the larger state case load. Sixty four percent of the clinic cases had been under care for at least three years, as contrasted to 48 percent of the state case load. Most telling in its impact was the finding that more than half of the clinic cases had experienced three or more placements—about three times the proportion of the statewide case load.

When Eisenberg compared these children with another contrast group—children receiving psychiatric attention in city and county clinics—it was found that there were few substantial differences between them except for the tendency for personality disorders to appear somewhat more frequently among the foster children. The

[21] G. Trasler, *In Place of Parents: A Study of Foster Care* (London: Routledge and Kegan Paul, 1960).

[22] Leon Eisenberg, "The Sins of the Fathers: Urban Decay and Social Pathology," *American Journal of Orthopsychiatry*, Vol. 32, No. 1 (January 1962), pp. 5–17.

preponderance of referrals for these children were for aggressive and nonconforming behavior. Generally, it was found that foster children referred for psychiatric attention showed a reluctance to verbalize, and it was Eisenberg's view that their lack of verbal facility reflected a subculture in which feelings tended to be expressed by doing rather than by talking. They also showed little capacity for insightful introspection and displayed poor orientation to time, place, and person.

Eisenberg's experience with children in foster care has caused him to raise piercing questions about needed changes in the care of children away from their own homes:

Is it not time that we re-examine the very nature of foster care itself? The instability of foster homes, the shortage of adequate homes, the inability to provide continuity of worker, supervisor, and foster parent—all these factors combine to suggest that group homes deserve to be given more weight in planning.[23]

Eisenberg's comments find an echo in the research report of DeFries, Jenkins and Williams.[24] Their research stemmed from a rather heroic effort to help emotionally disturbed children in foster care. The study was undertaken in 1961 by the Westchester Children's Association, with the co-operation of the Westchester County Department of Public Welfare. A group of seriously disturbed children was the target of intensive therapy and casework services. The basic orientation of the action-research staff was an attempt to overcome "the trauma of separation and the inherent confusion in the foster care situation through a therapeutic plan which sought to help the children develop a better sense of identity, and a more realistic appraisal of their life situation." [25]

Matched pairs of disturbed foster children on the public welfare case load were assigned alternately to an experimental and to a control group. The former received a variety of therapeutic innovations in care while the latter received the usual services of the Westchester County Department of Welfare. One of the serious problems encountered by the staff was that the majority of the foster parents "entirely rejected the idea of therapy, and many were openly in opposition to it." [26] Not one foster parent actually brought a child to the agency for treatment and other travel arrangements had to be made. Children's problems were typically either denied entirely by the foster-mother or substantially exaggerated. In reporting upon this action-research, the investigators noted that the measures of improvement emerging from the study did not favor the children in the experimental group. "In view of the expenditure of special services," they commented, "changes appear to be minimal." [27] They suggested that perhaps some disturbed foster children may be better served in group living situations than through foster family care arrangements.

Williams of Guy's Hospital in London reported on children who were placed in a reception center following removal from their foster homes.[28] These were children who had experienced a breakdown in fostering due to an unsatisfactory relationship with their foster parents. Fifty-four such foster children were identified in a five-year period. The foster homes were rated on a five-point scale by a senior caseworker and by a psychiatrist. The foster homes from which the children had been removed were judged to be of at least average quality as a home for normal children. While the author did not give specific data about the

---

[23] *Ibid.*, p. 15.

[24] Zira DeFries, Shirley Jenkins, and Ethelyn C. Williams, "Treatment of Disturbed Children in Foster Care," *American Journal of Orthopsychiatry*, Vol. 34, No. 4 (July 1964), pp. 615–624.

[25] *Ibid.*, p. 616.

[26] *Ibid.*, p. 619–620.

[27] *Ibid.*, p. 623.

[28] Jessie M. Williams, "Children Who Break Down in Foster Homes: A Psychological Study of Patterns of Personality Growth in Grossly Deprived Children," *Journal of Child Psychology and Psychiatry* (London), Vol. 2, No. 1 (June 1961), pp. 5–20.

reliability of the ratings, it would appear that the independent judgments tended to show consensus. A control group was developed of children who had come into the reception center for short stays during the same period as did the children in the breakdown group. These short-stay children came from their own homes and were placed temporarily in care because of a crisis that rendered their parents unable to care for them for a time. While these children had suffered some trauma, it was felt that differences between the control children and the breakdown group would point to factors other than those arising from the temporary effect of such an experience.

The results of the application of the Children's Apperception Test (CAT) showed that breakdown children 5 and 6 years of age gave stories that conveyed no sense of family and gave significantly more stories where the kinds of punishment meted out to children by parents were completely unrealistic in severity. The main themes were loneliness, rejection, and desertion. When the Rorschach Test findings were examined for the same age group, it was found that the breakdown children expressed more sinister feelings and showed more recourse to escapist fantasy (autistic responses). The author notes, however, that despite expressions of the sinister and of blackness, the children at this age demonstrated resilience—even though conditions were heavily weighted against them. At the 7- and 8-year level some shifts in Rorschach results were noted, indicating that the child, as he grew older, came to face the reality of his world as a place in which it was not safe to allow too much feeling. For both age levels there was manifested a significantly lower performance by the foster children in verbal IQ and in verbal-performance IQ. In the 9- to 11-year-old group, the Rorschach revealed that the breakdown child could be seen as one who "in process of coming to terms with his circumstances, has hardened into a character reaction pattern and in doing so has become a limited and emotionally impoverished person." [29]

Studying Foster Parents

A key person on the child welfare team serving the dependent and neglected child is the foster parent. He is given the major share of responsibility in substituting for the care normally provided by the child's natural parents. Until recently, almost all that was known about foster parents as a specialized group of persons had been derived from the clinical experience of child welfare workers with foster families known to them in the course of supervising the placement of foster children. Little systematic investigation of the characteristics of foster parents and their performance in a very complex status position had been undertaken. There has fortunately been a sudden acceleration of research interest in this area in recent years.

Fanshel undertook to study 101 foster families who constituted the roster of families caring for the children who were the wards of a large voluntary social agency in Pittsburgh, Pennsylvania.[30] Systematic data were derived from standardized interviews conducted by caseworkers with the foster parents and from an attitude questionnaire administered to the foster-mothers. In addition, professional judgments were obtained from the caseworkers who had supervised children in the foster homes.

One of the findings of this study was that a basic dichotomy existed between those foster parents who cared primarily for infants and those who cared for older children. In examining their reported satisfac-

---

[29] *Ibid.*, p. 14.
[30] David Fanshel, "Studying the Role Performance of Foster Parents," *Social Work*, Vol. 6, No. 1 (January 1961), pp. 74–81; and David Fanshel, "Specialization Within the Foster Parent Role: A Research Report," *Child Welfare*, Vol. 40, Nos. 3 and 4 (March and April 1961), pp. 17–21 and 19–23.

tions in assuming the foster parent role, Fanshel found some interesting variations in the sources of role satisfaction for the two groups. Those caring for infants appeared primarily oriented to private gratifications, in contrast to the more social gratifications of those caring for older children. For example, "enjoying a cuddly baby" was the item most frequently selected by those caring for infants but this was ranked only seventh for the group caring for older children. By way of contrast, "knowing I am doing something useful for the community" emerged as the highest ranking satisfaction for those foster-mothers who cared for older youngsters. This satisfaction ranked only seventh for those caring for infants. Fanshel also uncovered a basic orientation of some foster parents whose responses on a Guttman-type scale called "Benefactress of Children" was indicative of a somewhat overbearing, self-inflated approach to the foster parent role. This orientation was shown to be highly correlated with a negative social outlook as measured by Srole's Anomie Scale and to a number of pathogenic attitudes shown by foster-mothers on the Parental Attitude Research Instrument (PARI)—an instrument developed by Schaefer and Bell.[31]

The rating instrument utilized by caseworkers in Fanshel's study showed fairly poor reliability. This deficiency seemed related to a number of factors, such as the tendency of caseworkers to be influenced by a "halo effect" in making ratings of foster parents in which the quality of care given a single child in the foster home tended to be a major determinant in shaping ratings about the usefulness of the home for other types of children. The fact that pairs of raters had varying periods of contact with the foster families and different kinds of interaction with them seemed to impair further the reliability of the rating procedures.

Of interest in examining the judgments of the caseworkers was that a factor analysis of their ratings revealed a number of dimensions of foster parent behavior that resembled those that have emerged from studies dealing with natural parents. For example, a factor accounting for a large number of ratings described the foster parent's ego strength or parental competence. A second factor concerned the degree to which a foster family was democratically or autocratically oriented. Of interest to the child welfare practitioner was the finding that there seemed to be two types of foster parents: those who could tolerate children with biological deficits, such as mental retardation or physical handicaps, and those who were able to care for the "acting-out" youngster.

When the ratings of several caseworkers for each foster family in Fanshel's study were consolidated, it was found that 60 of the 101 foster families were regarded by the worker-raters as having uniformly performed well with the children who had been placed with them. The remaining 41 did less than well. When these low and high performance groups were compared with respect to their scores on the Parental Attitude Research Instrument, it was found that they were significantly differentiated from each other on six of the scales of this instrument. For each of these scales the high performance group tended to repudiate pathogenic attitudes and the low group tended to support them. Fanshel suggests that the PARI may have potential usefulness as an aid in screening new applicants for the foster parent role.

A somewhat unusual study of the role performance of foster parents was reported by Stanton.[32] A special emergency situation in Chicago made it necessary for an agency to undertake drastic methods for finding homes for illegitimate Negro children born at Cook County Hospital. Some

[31] Earl S. Schaefer and Richard Q. Bell, "Development of a Parental Attitude Research Instrument," *Child Development*, Vol. 29, No. 3 (September 1958), pp. 339–361.

[32] Howard R. Stanton, "Mother Love in Foster Homes," *Marriage and Family Living*, Vol. 18, No. 4 (November 1956), pp. 301–307.

of these babies had remained at the hospital for six months or more partly owing to the agency's inability to find foster homes. The typical recruiting system of the agency had failed to make headway in meeting the problem. A new method of recruitment was developed that involved having a social worker approach selected people in the community. These people were asked to refer the worker to Negro families believed to be very desirable as parents. A caseworker visited these "low-motivated" parents and attempted to interest them in the care of a Negro baby. While Stanton reports that only a small number of such homes were recruited, he nevertheless came up with the intriguing finding that the couples recruited in this novel manner performed as well as couples who had been recruited in the traditional way. Using as an evaluative criterion the ability of a foster family to sustain the placement of a child, he found that removal of the foster child was required in only one out of six cases in the experimental group and in four out of the twenty-one regular foster homes. Stanton concludes that prior motivation, particularly as manifested through self-application to a social agency for the foster parent role, did not appear to be essential for the development of later identification with the foster child.

A series of studies of foster parents conducted at the Astor Home for Children at Rhinebeck, New York, was reported by Colvin.[33] In one study, it was found that the Thematic Apperception Test developed by Henry Murray was useful in identifying the characteristics of foster-mothers who were successful in their role performance. These foster-mothers showed the following traits: (1) *achievement*—a need to overcome obstacles, to exercise power, and to strive to do something difficult as well and as quickly as possible; (2) *nurturance*—a need to nourish, aid, or protect the child, to express sympathy, and to "mother" the child; and (3) *play*—a need to relax, amuse oneself, seek diversion and entertainment, and to "have fun."

In another study reported by Colvin, the characteristics of the most—and least—adequate foster families revealed the following findings:

1. The most adequate parents were younger than the least adequate.

2. The most adequate parents had more children of their own than did the least adequate foster parents.

3. Success of placement was associated with neither race nor nationality of parents.

4. In comparing the success of parents of Italian and Irish descent with no children of their own, Italian parents showed a significantly greater tendency to succeed with foster children than did the Irish parents.

5. Whereas the most adequate foster parents showed no preference for either boys or girls, the least adequate parents showed a significantly greater preference for girls.

6. Least adequate parents showed a significantly greater tendency to choose children of the same sex as the preponderance of their own children.[34]

An interesting piece of action research designed to measure the impact of a thirty-two-week educational program for foster parents conducted at a school of social work was undertaken by Soffen.[35] Since the basic aim of the program was to alter the attitudes and behavior of foster parents, an attempt was made to measure change in behavior associated with exposure to this program. Twenty foster parents completed the educational program and constituted the experimental group, and fifty-four foster parents not exposed to the educational experiment were utilized as a control group. Soffen reports that the education program

---

[33] Ralph Colvin, "Toward the Development of a Foster Parent Attitude Test," in *Quantitative Approaches to Parent Selection* (New York: Child Welfare League of America, 1962), pp. 41–53.

[34] *Ibid.*, p. 47.

[35] Joseph Soffen, "The Impact of a Group Educational Program for Foster Parents," *Child Welfare*, Vol. 41, No. 5 (May 1962), pp. 195–201.

had an apparent impact in some areas and not in others:

The experimental group showed significant change in comparison with the control group in seven areas: relationship to agency, understanding the growth needs of children, ability to respond to their growth needs, understanding the meaning of difficult behavior, ability to respond appropriately to difficult behavior, and ability to respond appropriately to children's needs. Significant improvement was not noted in relationship to caseworker, motivation, climate in family, adequacy of home, and potential response of home to receiving foster children.[36]

The ability of child welfare workers to understand the motivations and attitudes of foster parents has been seen as a critical task. Nevertheless, there has been a paucity of research dealing with basic child-rearing attitudes of those who provide substitute care for children. A recent study by Dingman and others sought to test whether social workers practicing in a California institution for mental defectives could predict the child-rearing attitudes of a group of child care personnel who filled out the Parental Attitude Research Instrument (PARI).[37] The social workers were asked to fill out the form in two ways: as they themselves felt, and as they believed each caretaker whom they were supervising would answer it. It was found that the family caretakers who had been rated as "good" by supervising social workers in the institution were those whose attitudes corresponded rather closely with the social workers who had regular contact with them. It also appeared that social workers were able to predict the responses of caretakers only when these individuals were responding on the PARI as they did. When the caretaker revealed attitudes that did not coincide with the social worker's predictions of his own attitudes, this disagreement was strongly related to the supervisor's judg-

ment about the "goodness" of the home. The authors concluded that social workers should receive training that would lead them to understand and deal more satisfactorily with the attitudes and motivations of people with backgrounds quite unlike their own.

By and large, foster parents appear to be recruited from the lower socioeconomic groups. Because of the scarcity existing in most communities of foster families for children needing placement, some agencies have sought to obtain applicants from the middle classes. Simsarian undertook a study of sixty housewives residing in the Bethesda and Kensington areas of Montgomery, Maryland.[38] These represented 68 percent of the women who were approached from a registry secured from two Protestant churches. Only a third of the families studied had incomes of less than $10,000 a year. Simsarian concluded from an analysis of data obtained from standardized interviews with these subjects that while none of the women was overtly critical about social work or social workers, they were obviously uninformed about social agency programs. While more than two-thirds knew of someone who had provided full-time or daytime foster care for a child, only two knew how the youngsters had come to the families. This investigator was impressed with the possibilities available for recruiting foster parents in high-income areas. Thirty-seven of the sixty women interviewed expressed some interest in taking responsibility for a child not their own. Of this group, fourteen said they would possibly be interested when their children were older or when they had a larger house; twenty-three expressed a definite current interest in providing child care as a "sponsor" of a child, as a foster day care mother or as a full-time foster-mother. There were eight women in the latter category.

---

[36] *Ibid.*, p. 199.

[37] Harvey F. Dingman *et al.*, "Prediction of Child-Rearing Attitudes," *Child Welfare*, Vol. 41, No. 7 (September 1962), pp. 305–307, 327.

[38] Frances P. Simsarian, "Foster Care Possibilities in a Suburban Community," *Children*, Vol. 11, No. 3 (May–June 1964), pp. 97–102.

As suggested in some of the previously cited studies, there is a growing sentiment in child welfare circles that the typical foster home is not well suited to withstand the stress of living with impulsive, aggressive foster children. Disturbed youngsters tend to wear out the tolerances of foster parents and often experience several foster home placements before being assigned to institutions as a last resort. In studying fifty foster parents who were caring for disturbed foster children in Detroit, Ambinder and his associates found that most of the foster parents they interviewed were vague about the respective roles they, the caseworker, and the agency were to play in the lives of the children under their care.[39] A good many of the subjects emphasized the surveillance aspect of the casework role, suggesting an anxious anticipation of criticism that, according to the researchers, might have reflected the fear that if they did not "measure up" to the caseworker's standards, the child would be removed. On the basis of their research, the authors urged the necessity of constructing a clear role image for all participants in the foster family care system.

The need for more basic research about foster parents has been voiced by Reid:

A concerted effort is also needed to discover —in part through more intensive and systematic study and in part through better use of existing knowledge—the kinds of foster parents who are able to provide a relatively enduring family life for children with emotional difficulties. Identifying the motivation that makes of parents good foster parents and then seeking out such families can do much to reduce the numbers of re-placements in foster care which emotionally disturbed children are subjected to and the extent of disturbance among such children which is reinforced by their repeated changes in homes. We need to determine what services foster parents require in order to be more accepting of these children, including such mundane things as regular baby-sitting services financed by the agency to enable foster parents to have sufficient freedom to maintain their own emotional health.[40]

Follow-up Studies of Foster Children

It has long been considered necessary for a proper evaluation of child welfare services to conduct studies that will determine how well children adjust after they have left the care of an agency. Because studies of this kind are extremely difficult to execute, reports of such undertakings are relatively rare in the professional literature. Follow-up studies pose many problems: location of the subjects, obtaining their cooperation, developing reliable and valid measures of their adjustment, and designating appropriate control groups with whom the subjects can be compared. The complexity of attempting to link back to the foster care experience some of the variations in the child's current adjustment is also viewed as a formidable problem.

A classic follow-up study in the social work research literature was the one undertaken by the State Charities Aid Association in 1922 and reported by Sophie van Senden Theis in her monograph, *How Foster Children Turn Out*.[41] Between 1898 and 1922, the State Charities Aid Association placed some 3,363 children in foster homes. The group that came under the direct research scrutiny of the follow-up team consisted of 781 foster children all those of the 3,363 who were 18 years of age or over by January 1, 1922, and who had been under the care of the organization for at least one year. These children were scattered throughout New York State and some were in other parts of the country; 129 children could not be found. The agency was interested in developing a portrait of the adjustment of these former

---

[39] Walter Ambinder *et al.*, "Role Phenomena and Foster Care for Disturbed Children," *American Journal of Orthopsychiatry*, Vol. 32, No. 1 (January 1962), pp. 32–41.

[40] Joseph H. Reid, "Actions Called For— Recommendations," in Henry S. Maas and Richard E. Engler, Jr., *op. cit.*, p. 390.

[41] New York: State Charities Aid Association, 1924.

foster children and used a simple, perhaps primitive, method of classifying them. The agency point of view was stated as follows:

In spite of differences of family background and temperament among the subjects, certain facts about their managing of their lives could be made the basis of classification. Those who supported themselves honestly and adequately, worked steadily, were law-abiding, who lived in accordance with the better standards of their community and had good social and personal ethics were rated *capable*. Those who failed to get on either because of irresponsibility or lack of general ability were, on the other hand, *incapable*. These failures ranged from persons unable to get on because of physical capacity to those who are lawless or immoral.[42]

Of the foster children covered by this survey, 77.2 percent were classified as capable, whereas 22.8 percent were classified as incapable. The latter category included 89 children who were regarded as "harmless," 47 who were described as "harmful," 26 who were "on trial" and 20 who were in institutions. Thus, a major finding of the study was that three out of four of all the subjects who had lived in foster care were found to be able to manage their own affairs with "average common sense, to keep pace economically with their neighbors, and to earn the respect and good will of their communities. In other words, these subjects had 'made good'." [43]

The philosophy of Social Darwinism, which pervaded American philanthropy during the period of this study, is typified by the description of the eighty-nine subjects who were labeled as "harmless." This group was said to include those who were "irresponsible or shiftless individuals of inferior capacity or inferior character, or those who are incapacitated but who are not antisocial." The forty-seven subjects who were described as "harmful" tended to be those who were socially deviant and in conflict with the law. Nineteen of this group had been openly in conflict with the law and fourteen had illegitimate children.

"The rest are considered 'harmful' because of their general misbehavior and inferior traits of character." [44]

Another finding of interest from the Theis study was that 50 percent of the children had satisfactory relationships with their foster parents and formed ties that were described as firm and lasting. The ties were said to be hardly distinguishable from the natural relationship of parent and child. The study also found that the younger the child at placement the more apt he was to make a satisfactory social adjustment and to grow up without serious personal difficulty.

The study suffered from a substantial number of methodological limitations that reflected the state of research techniques at the time. Nevertheless, it has remained a beacon light for agencies to emulate, since the accomplishment of making contact with such a large sample of former foster children and the basic effort to portray their pattern of living at the time of follow-up represented a rather Herculean undertaking. More than three decades were to pass before any field study comparable to the Theis study would be undertaken.

A promising continuation of work in following up foster children, albeit on a smaller scale than the previously mentioned study, is represented by the recent research of Meier, who conducted a follow-up study of foster children in the state of Minnesota.[45] Her subjects were between the ages of 28 and 32 at the time of follow-up and were individuals who had been under the care of public or voluntary agencies in Minnesota for no less than five years. While the original size of Meier's target population was eight-two subjects, this was reduced to sixty-six owing to losses from various causes. The basic effort was to obtain

---

[42] *Ibid.*, pp. 22–23.
[43] *Ibid.*, p. 26.

[44] *Ibid.*, p. 43.
[45] Elizabeth Gertrude Meier, "Former Foster Children as Adult Citizens." Unpublished doctoral dissertation, Columbia University School of Social Work, 1962.

through a detailed interviewing schedule a multifaceted picture of the adjustment of these former foster children.

Meier chose to focus upon two major aspects of adjustment: social effectiveness and a sense of well-being. Within the area of social effectiveness, several aspects of social functioning were examined: home surroundings and housekeeping standards, employment and economic circumstances, health, support and care of children, and social behavior outside the family group. Ratings were made by the interviewer in each of these areas. The distribution of ratings among the subjects in the study were as follows: of the 24 men, 15 had positive ratings in all areas in which they were functioning, 4 had a negative rating in one area, 4 had negative ratings in two areas, and 1 man had negative ratings in three areas. Of the 42 women in the sample, 24 had positive ratings in all areas in which they were functioning, 10 had a negative rating in one area, 6 had negative ratings in two areas, and 2 had negative ratings in three areas.

Contrary to the investigator's prior expectations, it was found that individuals who had been placed in foster care prior to the age of 5 did not achieve lower ratings in social effectiveness in adulthood when compared with those who were placed after 5 years of age. Trasler's previously cited findings in England were similar. Those individuals who had experienced no more than three foster home placements during their entire placement experience did not achieve better ratings of social effectiveness than did those who had far more placements regardless of the causes for replacement. These are findings of considerable interest for practitioners and run counter to those reported by Maas and others for children still in care.[46] When Meier re-examined her data with respect to specific areas of functioning, however, it was found that four men in the sample with negative social behavior outside the home

were among the eleven men who had three or more living arrangements prior to the age of 5, whereas such behavior was not characteristic of any of the thirteen who had fewer arrangements.

In developing the concept of well-being, the author utilized the following operational criteria:

A feeling of adequacy in performing the functions for which the individual is responsible and the experience of pleasure in carrying out the activities in the various areas of adaptation. Ratings in each area are derived from indicators of the feelings of adequacy and pleasure. The overall score for well being is derived from the sum of the ratings. In using the scores, adaptation in a wide range of areas is accredited; constriction in the range of areas is debited.[47]

In developing these ratings, the investigator was hampered by the fact that full cooperation was obtained from only nineteen of the twenty-four males in her sample, in contrast to forty of the forty-two women who were available for the study.

In examining the relationship between a sense of well-being and some of her major independent variables, Meier found that contrary to her hypothesis there was no association whatever for the women of the sample between the current sense of well-being and the age of entry into foster home care. With the men, some difference, not statistically significant, was revealed according to the age when they went into care, but this was opposite to the direction hypothesized. Specifically, those who had entered foster home care after 5 years of age showed a better sense of well-being at follow-up. There were no statistically significant findings with respect to the number of placements the women had experienced and their current sense of well-being. The smallness of the number of men made statistical analysis of this factor difficult.

From a global standpoint, Meier's study supports the view that generally these foster children are functioning quite well. She notes:

---

[46] *See* Maas and Engler, *op. cit.*

[47] Meier, *op. cit.*, p. 389.

It is found that with few exceptions these young men and women are self-supporting individuals, living in attractive homes and taking good care of their children. In so far as comparison with the general population is possible with such a small sample, it appears that broken marriages are somewhat more common among this group than the general population. On the other hand due to the fact that among the women there are none who had never married, the proportion of women currently living with the spouse is higher than among the general population of their age range. But among the men, several had never married and others had experienced broken marriages so that a smaller proportion are currently living with a spouse than is true for the general population of their age range.[48]

A large proportion of the subjects designated the last placement they had been in as their "most influential home." However, there were some who regarded as most influential a home other than their last foster home. It was found that a significantly higher proportion of the persons who had lost their most influential home suffered an impaired sense of well-being. One of the most startling findings of Meier's study pertained to those persons who had lived in only one foster home or who remembered only one home. These individuals were more inclined to say that they would not place a child in that home than were the persons who had experienced more than one home placement. At the same time, Meier found that many of these former foster children continued to maintain meaningful relationships with their former foster parents. She suggests for future research and practice consideration that agencies consider examining policies from a "child's-eye" point of view.

Gil has reported research that seeks to remedy a deficit characteristic of the few follow-up studies that have been undertaken in child welfare in the United States.[49] In the past, these studies have generally been "one-shot" enterprises in which the adjustment of children has been studied some years subsequent to their departure from foster care and without reference to their prior modes of adjustment. Gil set forth a procedure for evaluating a child's adjustment at the time of follow-up in terms of his developmental potential as evidenced at the time he came into placement.

Using a small sample from a voluntary agency, he classified subjects into the following four categories: (1) those with good preadmission developmental potential realized to a considerable extent subsequent to their under-care experience; (2) those with good potential realized only to a limited extent; (3) those with fair preadmission developmental potential realized to a considerable extent; and (4) those with fair preadmission potential realized to a limited extent. Gil found that of fourteen subjects whose preadmission development potential was judged fair, four succeeded in realizing their potential to a considerable extent, whereas ten realized it to only a limited degree. On the other hand, of eleven subjects whose preadmission developmental potential was judged good, eight realized it to a considerable extent and three realized it to a limited extent. He notes:

These findings indicated that marked associations existed for this particular study group, under the particular circumstances of agency service to which they were exposed, between good pre-admission developmental potential and considerable extent of realization of it, and between poor pre-admission developmental potential and limited extent of realization.[50]

He also found that contrary to widely held assumptions in the child welfare field, there were no marked associations between such variables as number of re-placements and achievement of developmental potential. A low number of re-placements was not associated with considerable realization of

---

[48] *Ibid.*, pp. 522–523.

[49] David G. Gil, "Developing Routine Follow-up Procedures for Child Welfare Services," *Child Welfare*, Vol. 43, No. 5 (May 1964), pp. 229–240.

[50] *Ibid.*, p. 235.

developmental potential. This coincides with Meier's finding.

A variable in Gil's study that correlated highly with realization of potential was the quality of the foster homes used. Placement in positively evaluated homes tended to be significantly related to the achievement of developmental potential. This study suggests some routine procedures that can be built into regular agency practice which will result in more systematic evaluation of the consequence of the placement experience for children.

Temporary Foster Care

A problem of particular cogency in child welfare concerns the children who come into care on an unexpected and emergency basis because of some crisis situation that has struck their families. Often, these placements are hastily arranged and there is little time to prepare the children for the radical alteration in living circumstances they experience.

Some years ago, a New York City agency undertook to study the records of a group of children who had received such temporary care and were then returned to their own families.[51] There was concern that perhaps these children might have remained in their own homes if homemaker service could have been provided. A careful review was made of the record of a hundred families who had placed 229 children in temporary care to determine why emergency care was required. In forty-two of these families the mother had found it necessary to go to a hospital for emergency or planned operations; the mothers in sixteen other families had entered hospitals for confinement. In twelve families the children were deserted by their parents. In six, the mother became mentally ill. In three cases, the mother was not able to care for her children when she returned home,

and in three other cases the mothers were affected by illness in the home, acute fatigue, and emotional disturbance. The remaining families had miscellaneous difficulties requiring the use of temporary care. On the basis of case readers' judgments, it was estimated that if homemaker service had been available, 143 children in sixty-one families could have remained in their own homes. There were only forty-six children in twenty-one families where the problems were deemed so acute that placement seemed unavoidable.

The characteristics of deprived children known to a reception center in England have been reviewed in detail by Lewis.[52] The center received children needing care and made dispositions of them after thorough studies of their situations. The following portrait was developed for the five hundred children admitted between October 1947 and July 1950: 25 percent were found to be normal in behavior and in general mental condition; 21 percent showed slight and 18 percent showed severe neurotic symptoms; 32 percent were delinquent to some degree and 4 percent were either psychotic or psychopathic. Twenty-eight percent had IQ's below 90 and almost 20 percent were in poor physical condition. The conspicuous behavioral symptoms before admission were anxiety, enuresis, pilfering, and wandering. The social behavior of the children was classified and it was found that 10 percent conformed to the pattern of "unsocialized aggression"; 11 percent to the pattern of "socialized delinquency"; and 16 percent to the pattern of "overinhibited neurosis." Only 24 percent of the children were judged to be showing normal behavior. A study of their backgrounds revealed that parental rejection was significantly related to unsocialized aggression in the children. A major finding was that unless separation of the child from the mother had occurred before the age of 2 years and had been lasting (in which

---

[51] Children's Aid Society, *Study of Children in 100 Families Who Were Returned Home from Temporary Care* (New York, 1958).

[52] Hilda Lewis, *Deprived Children* (London: Oxford University Press, 1954).

case there was some greater indication of disturbance), it bore no statistically significant relation to the child's mental state at the time of admission.

A follow-up study of the children two years after they had been admitted to the reception center showed that 39 percent were showing a very good adjustment; 36 percent fair; 23 percent poor adjustment; and 2 percent very poor adjustment. Compared with their condition at the time they entered the reception center, almost two-thirds showed some improvement. The children who had been separated from their mothers at some previous occasion before they came to the reception center seemed less satisfactory in their adjustment at follow-up than those who had not.

Changes in Foster Care

In a number of cities throughout the United States a substantial change over the past three decades has been reported in the kinds of children requiring placement away from their own homes. One of the more thorough studies of such change is *To Serve the Children Best*, the report of the Federation of Jewish Philanthropies in New York City.[53] This report carefully traced the changes in the numbers and kinds of children coming into placement. With respect to sheer numbers it was noted that in 1955 there were 63 percent fewer children in placement than in 1940. The greatest reduction occurred in the number of children in institutional care—owing mainly to the closing of many large congregate facilities. In 1955 the institutional facilities of this organization accommodated only 20 percent of the children served in 1940. There was also a substantial reduction in the number of children in foster home placement—30 percent of those accommodated in 1940. It was found that

the average length of stay of children in care was shorter at the time of the study than it was in the late 1930's or early 1940's. In one large agency, the average length of stay in the institution was five years in that period; in 1954 the average length of stay was three and one-half years. In 1940, the average length of stay in foster homes was somewhat more than five years; in 1954 it was three and one-half years. The most telling finding relates to the change in the types of children being cared for.

The children who need our placement services today are far different from those we helped in the past. Formerly, we placed children because their family could not provide for them. But today, children are placed for two main reasons—their behavior is so difficult that they cannot remain at home or their home situations are too disturbing to permit their normal development. The number of disturbed children in placement continues to increase even as the number of children in placement decreases.[54]

Institutional Care

In 1960 there were an estimated 81,000 children in institutions for dependent and neglected children in the United States; this constituted 28.3 percent of all children in foster care.[55] While the trend in this country has been strongly away from institutional care as a preferred form of care for the less troubled foster child, increasing appreciation has developed for the specialized use of this care for children who cannot make use of the opportunities that family living offers or whose behavior cannot be tolerated in a family or in the community. Wolins has pointed out that institutional care is much less frowned upon for the so-called normal child in a number

---

[53] New York: Federation of Jewish Philanthropies, 1956.

[54] *Ibid.*, p. 13.
[55] Letter from U. S. Children's Bureau, Division of Research, to the Child Welfare League of America, October 31, 1961.

of countries with cultural orientations different from those in the United States.[56]

Institutional Care for Young Children

The research by Gavrin and Sacks has brought into question the commonly held assumption of professional practitioners that institutional care will always tend to be deleterious for the very young child.[57] They describe how the facilities of a hospital-institution, formerly a research and treatment center for young children with rheumatic fever, were opened in 1957 for dependent and neglected children in New York City desperately needing interim care. The children, primarily Negro and Puerto Rican, were awaiting foster home placement or return to their own families.

Research was conducted at the institution to determine whether changes in intellectual level might be detected for these youngsters, aged 2 through 7. The children were tested with the revised Stanford-Binet Scale (Form L) when they first came into the program; a Spanish language edition was used with Spanish children. The second testing took place about two weeks before discharge or after a stay of nine months if the child was not yet scheduled to leave. Reporting on a sample of ninety-four children, it was found that initially these youngsters showed a mean IQ of 89.0. At the termination examination the mean IQ had climbed to 97.58—a statistically significant climb in test scores. These children had remained in the institutional setting for an average of 8.72 months and the mean age of the group when first tested

was 4.08 years. The magnitude of the increment seemed directly associated with the length of time the children were in the institution, but the optimal level appeared to taper off at approximately one year. Children remaining longer than this time did not show significantly greater improvement. Interestingly, the children who remained at the institution for less than six months showed relatively little improvement in intellectual functioning, suggesting that there was first required a period of settling down at the institution before the child could take advantage of opportunities in the environment.

Gavrin and Sacks also noted that the children who appeared to gain most from the institutional placement were those who were functioning far below their ability because of deprivations in their physical and emotional environment. Thus, the Puerto Rican children, who often came from particularly disorganized home environments, tended to show unusually large increments in IQ. One suggested explanation for the improvements was that this was an institutional environment that took pains to ensure a low ratio of children to staff personnel and sought to develop stable contacts between the children and the staff. The particular setting seemed to provide more opportunity and stimulation for growth than did the homes from which the children came.

A recent study by Provence and Lipton sought to develop further the evidence presented by Bowlby, Spitz, Goldfarb, and others about the assumed damaging effect of institutional care upon the developing personalities of infants and young children.[58] Little prior attention had been given to the variety of symptoms that might be subsumed under the rubric of "hospitalism." These investigators sought to shed light upon the effects of a uniform type of

[56] Martin Wolins, "Some Theory and Practice in Child Care: A Cross-Cultural View," *Child Welfare*, Vol. 42, No. 8 (October 1963), pp. 369–377, 399.

[57] Joseph B. Gavrin and Lenore S. Sacks, "Growth Potential of Preschool-Aged Children in Institutional Care," *American Journal of Orthopsychiatry*, Vol. 33, No. 3 (April 1963), pp. 399–408.

[58] Sally Provence and Rose C. Lipton, *Infants in Institutions* (New York: International Universities Press, 1962).

deficit in maternal care by looking at seventy-five institutionalized infants and comparing their development with that of infants living in family settings.

The focus of the study was upon the child's first year of life and the study included only babies who were admitted to the institution under three weeks of age. These babies were examined periodically with tests that included the Gesell Developmental Examination and the Hetzer-Wolf Baby Test from the Viennese Scale. Physical and neurological examinations were also administered, and measurements of growth were systematically recorded. Direct observation provided supplementary information, and persons who cared for the babies were interviewed about their developmental progress. It was the investigators' belief that the poverty and infrequency of personal contact were the outstanding deficits to be noted in the experience of the institutionalized babies. The atmosphere as it appeared to the observer was mainly that of quiet, tranquility, and blandness.

Provence and Lipton found that the earliest deviation of the institutionalized children from normally developing infants was a minimal capacity during the second month to make postural adjustments to being held or carried. In the third and fourth months there appeared a discrepancy in the functioning of the upper and lower extremities, which suggested a lack of sensory stimulation in care as an "energizer" of motor functioning. The control of the head in the pull-to-sit situation, the development of sitting erect, of moving from sitting to prone, and of the capacity to rise into a sitting position were uniformly delayed. The institutionalized babies were also reported to be backward in pulling themselves to a standing position, walking with support, and in walking alone.

It was also determined that there was a diminished impulse to reach out and move toward people and toys, and this was easily visible from the eighth month onward. Further, there was significant impairment in the baby's ability to use motor skills to seek pleasure, avoid displeasure, to initiate a social interchange, to exploit the environment for learning, and to express feelings. In reacting to people, the earliest signs of deficit (second month) were diminished output of vocalization in responding to persons in the environment and a failure to adapt to holding. The responsive (social) smile, however, appeared at the normal time. It was reported that for some babies the responsive smile remained evidenced for several months while others became more sober. It was also found that there developed early a strong visual interest and this persisted throughout the year. However, this intense looking was not accompanied by development of normal discriminatory behavior and there was a delay in signs of visual discrimination in response to the face of the adult. There was also a reversal in the usual sequence of events in that institutionalized infants recognized the nursing bottle at an earlier age than they recognized the nurse. The investigators reported that the tenuousness of emotional ties was striking and there were no signs of increasing attachment to a particular person. The smile and constricted repertoire of feelings and the impoverishment of affective expressions were conspicuous findings.

In the development of speech, institutionalized babies showed signs of poor development early, and this became progressively worse. The investigators reported that speech was the most severely retarded of all the functions that could be measured by the test procedures. There was a continued scantiness of both responsive and spontaneous vocalization throughout the first year and a failure to develop a system of communicative vocal signals. The authors concluded that speech development was an area particularly vulnerable to the conditions of the environment in which these babies lived. Retardation in the developmental age or general maturity level as expressed through a developmental quotient was progressive through the first year.

In a follow-up of fourteen children who

had been institutionalized from the first month of life, and who were subsequently placed in foster family homes, Provence and Lipton found a number of areas of improvement, including gains in weight, improved affect, and a change in motor activity. Many of these children were said to have "blossomed." Language development was the area displaying the greatest continued retardation, as measured by tests, during the period of institutional living, and it was found that it also took a longer period of family living for significant improvement to take place.

The Provence and Lipton study represents an important research contribution to the literature on the development of children who have been exposed to institutional care and who, therefore, represent examples of clear-cut maternal deprivation. A possible limitation of the study is its failure to set forth the characteristics of the children who constituted the control group. Aside from the fact that they were reared in families, little is known about the backgrounds of these children—particularly the socioeconomic status of their families. It is possible that sociocultural factors may have served to confound the differences found by Provence and Lipton between the developmental patterns of institutionalized children and those reared in families.

A Follow-up Study of Early Group Care

Maas was interested in studying the adjustment of adults who had been children during wartime in London, and who had been evacuated during the bombing raids in 1939.[59] He pursued a follow-up study in a resourceful manner. Using rosters from three quite different wartime residential nurseries, his design was calculated to allow

for comparison of the adjustment of a modest sample of children according to their age when placed in the nursery and the type of nursery experience to which they had been exposed.

An interviewing schedule was developed with items obtained from the literature on early childhood separation. Five areas were covered: feeling life, inner controls, relationships with people, performance in key social roles, and intellectual functioning. The twenty adults who constituted the sample were rated on a five-point scale for each of twenty-four items dealing with the five major areas covered. In addition to the interview, each person was asked to tell stories in response to fourteen Thematic Apperception Test (TAT) cards. Part of the sample also completed the California Psychological Inventory. Visits were arranged with the parents of all but two of the twenty subjects. Final sources of information were the records of social and medical agencies and of the nurseries themselves. Some of the major findings reported by Maas are as follows:

1. Although the twenty subjects may have been seriously damaged by their earlier experience, "most of them gave no evidence in young adulthood of any extreme aberrant reactions. . . . To this extent, the data support assumptions about the resiliency, plasticity and modifiability of the human organism rather than those about the irreversibility of the effects of early experience."

2. Where there were evidences of individual cases of aberrant adjustment, in almost every case the data on the families seemed sufficient to explain this behavior.

3. The data support the prediction that children who are placed in residential nurseries during the first year of life would show evidence of damage in their young adult years. Every test given by these investigators show that this age group fared the worst of the four groups. Again, however, there is some indication that inadequate parenting partially explains the adjustment of these children. For the children

[59] Henry S. Maas, "The Young Adult Adjustment of Twenty Wartime Residential Nursery Children," *Child Welfare*, Vol. 42, No. 2 (February 1963), pp. 57–72.

who were placed at age 4 or over, the evidence does not support the view that separation and group care starting at this period are followed by enduring damage that is evident in young adulthood.[60]

Another interesting finding of the Maas study is that the adjustment of the young adults did not seem to be related to whether they were reared in a "somewhat firm, if not stern, and suppressive small nursery" or, by contrast, in a "psychologically sophisticated and much larger residential nursery." Finally, this study did show that 2-year-olds seem to have faired better in later years than those who were placed at 3 years of age. The suggested explanation for this is that, developmentally, the 2-year-olds are closer to the autonomy phase, whereas the 3-year-olds are beginning to become involved in Oedipal alignments with parents. In assessing the Maas study, Yarrow notes:

The results of Dr. Maas' study emphasize the importance of later life experiences in reinforcing or ameliorating the impact of an earlier separation experience. The findings on the children placed in the nursery under 1 year of age indicate that a single experience that might be labeled traumatic is probably not in itself a *sufficient* condition for later personality distortion, but that this condition increases the likelihood of personality damage in the presence of later reinforcing life experiences.[61]

Institutions As Treatment Settings

There has been a marked increase in research dealing with the problem of treating emotionally disturbed children in children's institutions. A series of studies dealing with the accessibility of children to treatment in an institution have been reported by Polansky, Weiss, Blum, and Appelberg.[62] Their research was conducted at Bellefaire, a residential treatment center in the Cleveland, Ohio, area. A key formulation in their concept of "accessibility" was that the child be able to involve himself verbally in a treatment-interviewing situation. It was believed that the best indication that a child was showing himself available to treatment would be if he were free to communicate painful, anxiety-laden material to his caseworker and permit the caseworker to talk with him about such content.

Using Guttman's scale analysis technique, the investigators found that there was an ordering among the indices developed for measuring the concept "freedom to communicate feelings." This order was as follows:

1. A child would at first communicate freely about other adults in the institution, since these were assumed to be relatively neutral.

2. Next, he might feel free to talk about feelings toward the caseworker.

3. After that, he would feel free to discuss painful feelings. It was assumed that least accessible would be the highly charged feelings toward his family and about himself as a person.

The investigators found that this ordering achieved a fairly high coefficient of reproducibility (96 percent at one time and 93 percent at another). Of particular interest was the finding that freedom to communicate feelings after fifteen months in treatment could be predicted from psychometric data obtained shortly after admission. It was found that eleven Rorschach factors distinguished between the high versus the low groups with respect to ability to communicate feelings. This communication scale was also found to correlate posi-

---

[60] *Ibid.*, pp. 66–67.

[61] *Ibid.*, p. 75.

[62] Norman A. Polansky and Irwin S. Weiss, "Determinants of Accessibility to Treatment in a Children's Institution," *Journal of Jewish Communal Service*, Vol. 36, No. 2 (Winter 1959), pp. 130–137; Arthur Blum and Norman A. Polansky, "Effect of Staff Role on Children's Verbal Accessibility," *Social Work*, Vol. 6, No. 1 (January 1961), pp. 29–37; and Esther Appelberg, "Verbal Accessibility of Adolescents," *Child Welfare*, Vol. 43, No. 2 (February 1964), pp. 86–90.

tively with the child's age at admission, with the older children seeming more accessible to casework. When the boys residing in the institution were directly queried about their behavior in casework treatment, their responses proved encouraging. Those who reported themselves as open about more areas of their life situations were also rated by the caseworkers as being verbally accessible. Thus, it would appear that the two main actors in the treatment situation showed substantial agreement about the child's accessibility.

In studying the child's use of confidants at Bellefaire, it was found that the selection of cottage staff, caseworkers, or others by the child as persons to whom he could reveal himself seemed most influenced by the degree of the adult's involvement in the cottage's direct care functions. With respect to the resources available in the institution for communication about meaningful matters, it was found that it was possible to create a situation within this setting that would enable the child to make clear discriminations about what kinds of problems he would bring to a particular staff person. It also became apparent, however, that even with special efforts to educate the child, specific attachments were apt to occur with persons directly charged with care functions and these relationships could serve to complicate the most intensive individual work with the child.

The importance of group processes in shaping the lives of institutionalized children has been graphically demonstrated by Polsky in his monograph, *Cottage Six.*[63] Through the technique of participant observation, this investigator was able to discern the main patterns of interaction in a cottage and to develop an illuminating portrait of the hierarchical "pecking order" that prevailed in this basic institutional living unit. He was able to discern the formation of subgroups and cliques, characterizing these by Damon Runyonesque terms

such as "toughs," "con-artists," "quiet types," "bush boys," and "scapegoats." These constituted the social system of the cottage.

Polsky observed that power was located in a few hands at the top of the social hierarchy, with toughness being the major ingredient required for acquiring status. These statuses seemed rigidly fixed and each boy in the cottage was treated according to the position assigned to him by the social system of the cottage. Within each clique there were "pecking orders" which were miniature reproductions of the cottage social organization. The principal way a boy could change his status was by challenging a boy of higher status to a fight.

A substantial finding reported by Polsky was that the cottage parent reinforced the delinquent subculture by "manipulating the boys' social hierarchy, wooing the leadership, and dominating weak members." Explanation for this behavior was attributed to the cottage parent's personality predispositions, his isolation from the professional staff, and the intense interaction with the disturbed delinquent boys. These factors resulted in a role adaptation that served to alienate the cottage parent from the relevant professional structures and the philosophy of the treatment institution.

Lacking an alternative status reference group, the cottage parent becomes dependent upon, and conforming to, the boys' delinquent orientation and eventually adjusts to it by taking over and utilizing modified delinquent techniques. The extreme concern with cottage loyalty and the violent condemnation of "ratting" cements the cottage parents to the boys' subculture and perpetuates a vicious circle which insulates the cottage from the rest of the therapeutic milieu.[64]

Staffing Arrangements

It has been made apparent at several points in this review that many of the children

---

[63] Howard Polsky, *Cottage Six* (New York: Russell Sage Foundation, 1962).

[64] *Ibid.*, p. 135.

in institutional care have emotional problems requiring treatment. These youngsters are often extremely demanding, and agencies are hard put to find personnel who can tolerate their acting-out behavior. Adults are required who will help provide these children with the kind of care that will permit them to overcome some of the gross inhibiting experiences they have encountered in the past.

Goodrich and Boomer report an effort to ascertain some of the qualities required of staff in residential treatment settings.[65] Using the Critical Incident Technique developed by Flanagan, these investigators interviewed the staff members at the residential treatment program established by Redl at the National Institute of Mental Health.[66] The staff members were asked to relate in their own words an actual incident involving a child and an adult in which the adult did something the respondent felt was either good or bad for the child in terms of the over-all goals of residential treatment. Some 240 episodes were gathered by this procedure and these were ordered under 31 separate principles of therapeutic intervention with hyper-aggressive children (the kind of children being cared for in this program).

The principles included:

1. Promoting personality change by helping the child to learn to view his own behavior evaluatively (e.g., by accepting temporary regressive modes of relatedness as the necessary step toward growth, by gently pointing out the self-defeating aspects of recent symptomatic behavior of the child, and so on).

2. Promoting ego growth (by welcoming and encouraging instances of positive or affectionate relatedness, by fostering rapport within the child by responding to his manifest interest, and so on).

3. Supporting existing ego control (by avoiding threats to existing controls, by helping the child maintain ego controls under special stress, or by helping the child regain such controls after temporary failure).

4. Managing one's own conduct as a staff person (by attempting to recognize, accept, and deal with one's own anxieties as nondestructively as possible, by freely admitting one's own limitations in the face of the child's uncompromising demands, and so on).[67]

Goodrich and Boomer concluded that the dimensions of staff behavior identified in their study could be embodied in a staff selection instrument, and also that these episodes could be useful in orienting and training new staff members.

Allerhand reported on a study that attempted to establish a more clear-cut method of evaluating the performance of cottage parents.[68] Through group discussions with the supervisors of cottage personnel, a series of the most important factors used in such evaluations was compiled. The factors, in order of the relative weights developed by three child care specialists, were personality, ability to work with other staff members, enjoyment in participating with children in a group, intellectual curiosity, ingenuity, personal standards, leadership qualities, ability to organize, program skills, and orientation toward child's schoolwork. When a sample of counselors was rated by two supervisors acquainted with their functioning, interrater reliability was found to be high. Allerhand developed a questionnaire based upon the ten factors that could be filled out by applicants for the cottage parent

[65] D. Wells Goodrich and Donald S. Boomer, "Some Concepts About Therapeutic Interventions with Hyperaggressive Children," *Social Casework*, Vol. 39, Nos. 4 and 5 (April and May 1958), pp. 207–213 and 286–292.

[66] John C. Flanagan, "The Critical Incident Technique," *Psychological Bulletin*, Vol. 51, No. 4 (July 1954), pp. 327–358.

[67] Goodrich and Boomer, *op. cit.*, pp. 211–212, 286–289.

[68] Melvin E. Allerhand, "Selection of Cottage Personnel," *Child Welfare*, Vol. 37, No. 9 (December 1958), pp. 14–18.

position. The results of testing this questionnaire with already employed cottage parents were quite promising in discriminating between those rated as high and those rated as low performers.

In addition to the special skills required of individual staff members there is a need to examine the total treatment milieu of children's institutions. It is generally accepted that the capacity of child welfare agencies offering institutional care to help their charges achieve adequate functioning largely depends upon the ability of the personnel within these settings to integrate their efforts. In this connection, research reported by Piliavin on the oft-reported conflict between caseworkers and cottage parents in children's institutions is of considerable interest.[69] He sought to determine how cottage parents and caseworkers evaluated each other in two types of institutional settings. In one, the agency took a number of steps to reduce cottage parent and caseworker conflict through a variety of procedures including higher remuneration, financing of cottage parents' training at institutes given by schools of social work, weekly case conferences for clinic and cottage personnel, and so on. In the second institution, the cottage parents were supervised only in administrative matters and contacts between them and the caseworkers were virtually nonexistent.

The data in the study was based upon focused interviews with cottage parents and clinic workers. The difference in orientation of the cottage parents in the two types of institutions was made evident by the fact that eleven of the fourteen cottage couples in institution A, the more professionalized institution, and only three of the fifteen couples in institution B believed that an individualized treatment approach was the preferred means to rehabilitating delinquent boys. The remaining couples

in both agencies believed this goal could be achieved only by training and discipline. It was a matter of surprise, however, to find that the mutual perceptions of caseworkers and cottage parents in the two institutions were essentially similar in that these were negatively charged in both settings. In each institution, a large segment of the caseworkers took a dim view of the operations of the cottage parents, regarding them as inadequate in the tasks they had to perform. In turn, the attitude of the cottage parents in institution B, the less professional setting, was essentially one of indifference, but those in institution A showed considerable anger toward the caseworkers. A great majority of them felt that the caseworkers were either unrealistic in their treatment of youth or in their appraisal of the possibilities of implementing the goals of the program within their cottages. An additional noteworthy finding was that even on the informal level, communication was rare between cottage parents and caseworkers at both of the institutions studied. Piliavin's research suggests the dysfunctional consequences that such rifts between key personnel in institutional settings can have with respect to the problem of achieving treatment goals for disturbed children.

Children in Residential Treatment Centers

A vital resource for children who are emotionally disturbed and need treatment away from their own homes is a type of institutional setting identified as a "residential treatment center." These institutions have expanded significantly in the past two decades and are considered by many practitioners to be an important placement resource that often serves the function of saving children from hospitalization in state institutions.

A major national survey of the programs of such centers and the children served by them was undertaken in the early 1960's

[69] Irving Piliavin, "Conflict Between Cottage Parents and Caseworkers," *Social Service Review*, Vol. 37, No. 1 (March 1963), pp. 17–25.

by Hylton.[70] Her study included twenty-one well-established residential treatment centers and two day schools caring for emotionally disturbed children. During the period of the study, some 923 children were in treatment in these residential centers and 47 were in the day care centers. It was found that 53 percent of the children in the residential centers and 26 percent of those enrolled in the two therapeutic day schools had received some kind of therapy for their emotional problems before entering these centers.

Hylton created a special typology that enabled the clinical staffs to characterize the children in treatment. Analysis of the data showed that one-fifth of the children were rated by the staff members as "extremely aggressive." Almost one-fourth were considered "disoriented." One in three was rated "difficult to reach." According to the modal categories of ratings, the typical child in residential care was characterized as being a moderately to well-oriented and accessible child. There was some association between the type of disturbance exhibited by these children and the costs involved in their treatment.

Generally, it is recognized that these residential treatment centers reach only a very small proportion of the emotionally disturbed children in the United States today. Hylton quoted from a number of national reports to provide the following estimates of the size of the problem of emotional disturbance in children:

For each hundred thousand people under 18 years of age, 135 are under care in in-patient psychiatric institutions and over 355 are served by out-patient clinics. Further, an estimated 2.4 million children—5% of the 148 million under 18 years of age—become involved with law enforcement agencies during a year.[71]

One of the few attempts to evaluate the results of intensive work with emotionally disturbed children in a residential treatment center was reported over a decade ago by Johnson and Reid.[72] Study of the response to treatment of 339 children accepted for treatment at the Ryther Center in Seattle revealed that three out of four seriously disturbed children were restored to what was regarded as normal functioning. An interesting finding of the study was that the younger the child when he came into the institution, the better his adjustment appeared upon follow-up.

A study by Bloch and Behrens of the referrals of emotionally disturbed children for residential treatment in New York State was begun in 1955.[73] They were interested in the kinds of referrals that had been made to three new residential treatment centers that had been set up by New York State as well as to three other centers. Using a seventeen-page questionnaire, these investigators elicited information about the disposition of each of the referrals. One of the important findings reported by Bloch and Behrens was that a major aspect of the problems faced by children referred for residential treatment care was that they required placement out of their own homes. In addition to their emotional problems, many of these children simply could not be cared for in their own homes. Of the original group of 961 cases referred to the six centers, only 60 cases (6.2 percent) had not been placed in some kind of institution by the time the follow-up was undertaken in 1957. A year later, this was reduced to 4 percent. Of those not placed, very few were estimated to have improved. In common with findings from

[70] Lydia Hylton, *The Residential Treatment Center: Children, Programs and Costs* (New York: Child Welfare League of America, 1964).

[71] *Ibid.*, p. 1.

[72] Lillian J. Johnson and Joseph H. Reid, *Evaluation of Ten Years Work with Emotionally Disturbed Children* (Seattle: Ryther Child Center, 1947).

[73] Donald A. Bloch and Marjorie L. Behrens, "A Study of Children Referred for Residential Treatment in New York State" (New York State Interdepartmental Health Resources Board, 1958).

other studies, the ratio of boys to girls in this sample of referrals was about five to one. Among the boys, the heaviest concentration was in the 9- to 12-year grouping; girls were referred at a more even rate per age year.

In attempting to look at the diagnostic categories within which these children might be placed, Bloch and Behrens relied mainly upon three categories: schizophrenia, behavior disorders, and neuroses. They occasionally used the categories of organic brain disease and mental retardation. A major finding of the investigation was that the study population was comprised of children who were diagnostically heterogeneous. Among the boys, about 23 percent could be categorized as suffering from schizophrenia; among the girls this was true of 34 percent. Twenty-two percent of the boys and 20 percent of the girls fell within the behavior disorder category and 17 percent of the boys and 10 percent of the girls fell in the neurotic classification. Three percent of each sex was said to suffer from organic brain damage. Thirty-seven percent of the boys and 33 percent of the girls could not be classified.

When the families of these children were studied, using a scale called the "Multi-Problem Family Index," only 15 percent of the families showed no negative information in any of the six problem areas. Half of the families were afflicted with difficulties in three or more problem areas, including marital relationships, parent-child relationships, social pathology, physical illness, mental illness, and financial dependency. Generally, the families were riddled with pathology. Fewer than 25 percent of the children had lived only in their natural homes, while 40 percent had lived in four or more foster homes or institutions before the application for residential treatment center care was made. Approximately 60 percent of the children did not have a continuous relationship with both parents. It was also found that these children and their families had been known to many

agencies, with an average of six agencies per family, over a three- to five-year period. A poignant finding of the over-all study was that the residential treatment centers were able to admit only about 20 percent of the children for whom application had been made.

Follow-up Studies of Residential Treatment

Research concerned with the postdischarge fate and experiences of children from an institution that treats emotionally disturbed children has been reported by Allerhand, Weber, and Polansky.[74] Among other purposes, the study was designed to assess the relationship of postdischarge adaptation patterns to the predominant type of treatment received in the institution, and to measures of the verbal accessibility obtained while they were in residence.[75] Fifty boys discharged from the Bellefaire institution in Cleveland after January 1958 constituted the study sample. The study included a relatively unstructured one-and-a-half- to two-hour electronically recorded interview with each youngster. In addition, a series of tests were administered to the child. Interviews with the parents of the subjects were also a source of data for this study.

Allerhand has reported some preliminary findings relating to a number of evaluative measures.[76] At the point of discharge, 70 percent of the subjects were functioning successfully from the perspective of achieving minimal adequacy. It was the evaluation of the institution staff that 90 percent of the discharged children

[74] Melvin E. Allerhand, Ruth E. Weber, and Norman A. Polansky, "The Bellefaire Follow-Up Study: Research Objectives and Method," *Child Welfare*, Vol. 40, No. 7 (September 1961), pp. 7–13.

[75] *See also* Polansky and Weiss, *op. cit.*

[76] Melvin E. Allerhand, "Success—A Many Splendored Thing" (Cleveland: Bellefaire Residential Treatment Center, undated). (Mimeographed.)

showed some improvement during the time they were in the institution, and 46 percent showed significant improvement. Seventy-four percent of the subjects were considered to have gained maximum benefit at discharge. When the subjects were interviewed during the follow-up contact, 57 percent of them believed that they were considerably helped by the experience, and another 28 percent recognized some help gained.

Ratings based upon the manner in which the subjects adapted to their environment, as well as upon measures of ego functioning reflected in such areas as self-attitudes, energy, control, growth, and identity, showed that 56 percent of the subjects achieved at least minimal age-related adaptability with respect to intrapsychic functioning, and 74 percent achieved this level with respect to performance in social relationships and social situations. Eleven areas of social functioning were examined, including such situations as participation in family life other than meals, running away from place of residence, consummated friendships, inclusion in social groups or cliques, dating patterns, involvement in full-time work or school, stability of work or school situations, performance in school, participation in school, the presence or absence of disciplinary actions in the community, and economic stability.

On the average, the children in the sample performed adequately in at least 70 percent of the social areas cited above. A child was considered successful in social achievement if there were 60 percent or more positive accomplishments in situations applicable to him. On this basis, 64 percent of the subjects were succeeding according to societal standards. These investigators also reviewed the living situations of the subjects to determine whether they were experiencing supportive interpersonal situations and supportive cultural environments which might positively influence their adjustments. It was found that 46 percent of the youngsters were experiencing supportive interpersonal situations

and 54 percent were experiencing supportive cultural environments.

In their total living situations, 68 percent of the subjects were judged to be living within predominantly supportive contexts. An interesting finding was that of the ten cases where the subjects were considered to be performing inadequately at discharge but who, contrary to expectations, were actually performing adequately at follow-up, nine were in predominantly supportive environments. Conversely, of those eight subjects who were considered adequate at discharge and were inadequate at follow-up, seven were in predominantly stressful environments.

Child Behavior in Institutional Settings

Child psychiatrists, psychologists, and child welfare workers have long been hard pressed to develop satisfactory classification systems of child behavior disorders of the sort daily encountered in their practices. This lack of an adequate descriptive typology has impeded a variety of important professional activities, not the least of which has been the area of research. Obviously, research in child welfare requires that investigators be able to describe adequately the disorders of children known to child welfare agencies.

A study of the behavior disorders of children in ten residential treatment centers has been reported by Fanshel, Hylton, and Borgatta.[77] A behavioral check list had been developed by Hylton for use in a study of institutional costs; this was designed to allow key staff members who knew the children in these centers to make judgments about their observable behavior.[78] Information was thus collected

[77] David Fanshel, Lydia Hylton, and Edgar F. Borgatta, "A Study of Behavior Disorders of Children in Residential Treatment Centers," *Journal of Psychological Studies*, Vol. 14, No. 1 (March 1963), pp. 1–23.

[78] Hylton, *op. cit.*

about 316 children for 76 descriptive categories on a five-point response scale running from "never" to "very often." These ratings were subject to factor analytic procedures and ten factors emerged with relatively clear identification. These included, among others, physical aggression, sexual activity, intellectual inability, compulsive cleanliness, lethargy, and self-destructive behavior. When comparing the ratings of the same child known to three types of staff members, the findings indicated that administrators tended to perceive more pathology in the children than did the social workers, and social workers more than psychologists, psychiatrists, and teachers.

Sklarew studied the differences in adjustment of boy and girl adolescents at a children's institution.[79] He was interested in the effect of prior separations from parents upon the children's adjustment at the institution. He found, among other things, that boys who had been separated from their families during their first ten years of life tended to engage in running-away behavior more often than those who had not experienced such separation, but this was not true for girls. Separated boys also had a greater tendency to engage in disruptive behavior at the institution. With respect to a general adjustment rating, based upon judgments derived from existing case records, it was found that there were more ratings indicative of good adjustment among nonseparated boys than among separated boys. In contrast, the separated girls tended to have more ratings indicating good adjustment than the nonseparated girls did. The differences in the adjustment of children with respect to effects of prior separations point up the need to keep the second-order sex differences visible in the analysis of such data.

Pringle undertook a study of children who had spent the major part of their lives away from their own parents in residential care in England.[80] From a larger study of 188 children who were "in care" and living in large children's homes, contrasts were made between children who were found to be "severely maladjusted" and those who were "notably stable." Her criteria for selection required that children be included whose first removal from home had occurred before the age of 5 years and who continued to live apart from their parents for more than half of their lives. These were children of average intelligence and their classification into "maladjusted" or "stable" categories was based upon the ratings made by child welfare staffs and teachers and upon individual psychological testing. Eleven "severely maladjusted" and five "notably stable" children were identified for study. The life histories of the maladjusted children showed that their first separations from their mothers occurred at a rather early age, all but two children having had this experience by the time they were 1 year of age. For the stable group, the separations had occurred between the ages of 2 to 4 years. These findings coincide with those on young adult adjustment and early separation found by Maas.[81]

Both groups in the Pringle study had experienced a number of different placements, but the maladjusted children had more changes in their environment, partly because their difficult behavior led to repeated breakdowns in fostering arrangements. The most marked difference between the two groups was in the amount of contact maintained with parents or parent substitutes. All the stable children had experienced a dependable or lasting relationship with a parent or parent substitute outside the institutional environ-

[79] Bruce H. Sklarew, "The Relationship of Early Separation from Parents to Differences in Adjustment in Adolescent Boys and Girls," *Psychiatry*, Vol. 22, No. 4 (November 1959), pp. 399–405.

[80] M. L. Kellmer Pringle, "Emotional Adjustment Among Children in Care," *Child Care* (London), Vol. 15, No. 1 (January 1961), pp. 5–12.

[81] *Op. cit.*

ment. Only one child in the maladjusted group had known such a contact.

Adoption

In 1962, about 121,000 children in the United States were legally adopted. This is the number of children named in adoption petitions by the courts. Of these, 52 percent were adopted by nonrelatives. There are approximately 1.5 million adopted children under 18 years of age in this country at the present time.[82]

Research in the field of adoption is concerned with the characteristics of couples chosen by agencies to assume the adoptive parent role. Within the group who become adoptive parents, who are the couples who are able to care for the so-called "hard-to-place" children, e.g., the physically handicapped child, the older child, the Negro child, and so on? Research in adoption is also concerned with the criteria used by caseworkers in the selection of couples; the consistency shown in the professional judgments that have to be made in this area of work; the dynamics of adoptive family life; and the adjustments of adoptive families. The manner in which adoptive families may differ in family interaction from biological families is of interest as well as the identification of any special hazards in adoption that may not be present in the natural family situation.

Do adopted children uniformly reveal certain maladjustments because of the particular hazards they have to overcome, such as multiple parents, illegitimate birth, and so on? When adopted children are compared with biological children with respect to patterns of adjustment, what differences are revealed? Researchers are also interested in the adjustment of adopted children as this is related to sex, age at

adoption, family composition, and so on. The relationship between measures of parental attitudes and measures of social adjustment of adopted children is of interest. Finally, there is much to be gained in attempting to identify the kinds of emotional disturbances associated with adoption and in examining data dealing with the prevalence of disturbance in adopted children, as revealed by their presence in the patient loads of psychiatric clinics.

Adoption of "Hard-To-Place" Children

There has been considerable effort on the part of child welfare agencies across the country to promote the adoption of Negro children who face the hazard that they will spend all of their childhood years in foster care. The quest is for Negro couples who will make suitable adoptive parents.

Fanshel undertook a content analysis of case record material available on 224 Negro couples who had approached a social agency out of an interest in adoption, and compared them with 183 white couples who had approached the same agency.[83] He confirmed what has been viewed as a fairly common pattern among child welfare agencies: the Negro couples failed to sustain the application procedures at the same level of successful completions as the white couples. While only one couple in five of the Negro applicants succeeded in adopting a child, two couples in five of the white applicants went on to do so. Examination of socioeconomic status by ethnic group revealed that the Negro sample was characterized by considerable economic disadvantage and this appeared to be an important variable in influencing the outcome of adoption applications. The cogency of this variable for *both* groups was revealed by the fact that only 17 percent of the white couples, when the head

---

[82] U.S. Department of Health, Education, and Welfare, Children's Bureau, *Facts About Children: Adoptions in the United States* (Washington, D.C., 1963).

[83] David Fanshel, *A Study in Negro Adoption* (New York: Child Welfare League of America, 1957).

of the family was in a lower-status occupation, went on to adopt a child, compared to almost half of those in middle-status and higher-status occupations. However, while Negro and white blue collar workers did poorly, it turned out that Negro applicants in this occupational stratum actually did somewhat better than their white counterparts.

A factor that seemed to be particularly operative with the Negro couples was that quite often the female applicant would come to the agency without being escorted by her husband. In these instances, the Negro applicants were less apt to sustain the application process. Fanshel identified a number of major reasons listed by caseworkers for the withdrawal of Negro couples: inability to establish infertility, evidence of psychological unreadiness, failure to involve the spouse, financial problems, and objection to the agency study process. The major reasons cited by caseworkers for white couples withdrawing from adoption planning were psychological unreadiness, resort to independent adoption, and dissatisfaction with the kind of child offered to them.

A number of projects developed in large metropolitan areas have reported the problem of recruiting Negro parents to be a rather formidable one. In order to understand more about the attitudes of Negroes toward the institution of adoption, Negro couples in Baltimore and Washington were interviewed. Deasy and Quinn reported upon a field survey covering 484 respondents.[84] A telling finding was that of the sample of respondents who were partners in childless marriages, some 43 percent stated that the possibility of adopting a child had never been considered. Of the remainder, only one in ten was now thinking about adoption as a means of having a family.

While the investigators assumed that attitudes toward adoption might be differentiated according to the socioeconomic status of the respondents, as Fanshel's study had suggested, the differences they found among three levels of socioeconomic status did not seem to be as remarkable as expected, although there were some differences. For example, of the ten families in the study who had adopted children legally, nine were in the top two socioeconomic groups and only one was in the bottom. Also, while the majority of those in the top groups said they would choose a child through an agency, those in the bottom group would choose either an agency child or a relative's child in equal numbers. More striking was the finding that the respondents in Washington, D.C., seemed to be both better informed with respect to agency practice and more critical than those in Baltimore. They also showed more inclination to use agency resources. Summarizing their findings, Deasy and Quinn state: "Our respondents think of agencies as a prime source of adoptive children and express no great fear of involvement with them. Yet there seems to be a basic lack of motivation to adopt."[85]

Development of Adopted Children

In recent years, there has been increasing interest in the significance of experiences of adopted children during early infancy. In particular, there has been concern about the effect upon the adopted child of the quite radical procedure of being transferred from a foster family to an adoptive home. The question has arisen whether this removal of the child from one setting to another wreaks havoc upon his normal development. As one specialized form of maternal deprivation, this is an area meriting particular research effort.

A significant piece of research with a child development focus has been under-

---

[84] Leila Calhoun Deasy and Olive Westbrooke Quinn, "The Urban Negro and Adoption of Children," *Child Welfare*, Vol. 41, No. 9 (November 1962), pp. 400–407.

[85] *Ibid.*, p. 407.

taken by Leon Yarrow.[86] While the study is still in progress, data have already been reported about observations of infants in interaction with adoptive mothers, and from interviews with the latter. Children who remained in only one home during the first six months of life were included in this analysis. Yarrow reports that perhaps his most striking finding is the degree to which the child's progress during the first six months appears to be influenced by maternal stimulation. The amount of achievement stimulation (oriented toward developmental progress), social stimulation (oriented toward eliciting social responses), and the quality of stimulus-adaptation (the extent to which materials and experiences given to the infant were adapted to his individual capacities) were highly related to tests of the child's intelligence with correlations ranging from .65 to .72. He suggests that mothers who give much intense stimulation and encouragement in advancing developmental skills tend to be successful in producing infants who make rapid developmental progress.

The high relationship between stimulus adaptation and IQ scores suggests that "it is not simply the amount of stimulation per se that influences developmental progress but the appropriateness of the stimulation to the child's individual and developmental characteristics." [87] Yarrow also found that highly related to the infant's capacity to maintain equilibrium and avoid disorganization under stress was the quality of the infant's relationship with the mother, as reflected in the following maternal variables: emotional involvement, physical involvement, sensitivity, adaptation to the individuality of the infant, and acceptance. Of significance was the fact that little association was found between the variable of maternal con-

sistency and such aspects of infant behavior as developmental progress, social initiative, and the capacity to handle stress.

Several other important developmental characteristics of adopted infants as these relate to the types of environments presented by the adoptive families have been explored by Yarrow and have great interest for the practitioner. When he analyzed the reactions of the infants immediately after the change in mother figure, he found that this could be considered a traumatic event.

. . . it is associated with immediate disturbances in behavior, such as blunted social responsiveness, excessive clinging to the mother, excessive crying, unusual apathy, disturbances in adaptation to routines, sleep and feeding, and developmental regression, e.g., a drop in I.Q. or loss of abilities previously present.[88]

His data showed that the severity and pervasiveness of disturbance was heightened with increasing age. A few infants showed disturbance as early as 3 months; 86 percent of the infants who experienced changes in mother figures at 6 months of age showed definite disturbances in behavior. Every one of the children placed at or after 7 months reacted with marked disturbance. With respect to the question of whether these changes in mother figures will have long-term effect on the children's personality development, Yarrow suggests that this may be a very difficult kind of issue to resolve. There are so many intervening events and conditions that may take place between a specific traumatic event and later personality development that it is difficult to trace out the effect of the former. His work suggests that reactions to separation cannot be easily differentiated at a later point in time from the effects of subsequent maternal rejection.

Gardner, Hawkes, and Burchinal conducted a longitudinal study concerned with children who suffered an unusual kind of

[86] Leon J. Yarrow, "Research in Dimensions of Early Maternal Care," *Merrill-Palmer Quarterly of Behavior and Development*, Vol. 9, No. 2 (April 1963), pp. 101–114.

[87] *Ibid.*, p. 106.

[88] *Ibid.*, p. 111.

mothering in a "home management house" for a period of one college quarter, or about three months, prior to adoption.[89] During the period of residence in this type of home, the care of each infant was provided by a number of different student mother-figures, each student having responsibility for the baby for a few days at a time. Twenty-nine of some sixty-two children who had lived under such circumstances were located in a follow-up study when they were from 8 to 17 years old and in the third through twelfth grades. A group of comparison subjects were selected on a matched-pair basis. The matched child was of the same age and sex and had lived with his own biological family from birth. The subjects were compared on the three major scoring categories of the California Test of Personality: personal adjustment, social adjustment, and total adjustment—the latter representing a favorable balance of elements of the other two.

The results indicated that there were no significant differences between pairs of adopted children and the control children in social adjustment and total adjustment. However, in the case of personal adjustment scores, the results favored the children who had not been subjected to unusual mothering; statistically, the difference approached significance. There were no differences, however, between the two groups on the Children's Form of the Manifest Anxiety Scale. Indeterminate results were also developed from the protocols of the Rosenzweig Picture-Frustration Study Test. In selecting these psychological tests, the investigators sought to focus upon a variety of dimensions of personality processes such as school achievement, personal and social adjustment, anxiety level, and response to frustration. They made the comment: "In none of these variables could differences be attributed to the factor of discontinuity of mothering in early childhood." [90]

Adjustment of Adoptive Families

Amatruda and Baldwin reported on a study undertaken to evaluate adoption practices in the state of Connecticut.[91] They reviewed a series of both agency and independent adoptions that had been studied at the Yale Clinic of Child Development. Under a new state law, it had become mandatory to have a social agency investigation of independent adoptions after the placements had been made, and it was also necessary to have a physical and mental examination of the child before the end of the probationary period of one year.

These investigators studied children who had been known to the Yale Clinic for examinations in compliance with the law. In reporting upon their research, Amatruda and Baldwin noted that of one hundred babies placed independently, seventy-five were judged "reasonably good" babies who could be placed with reasonable safety in selected homes. However, almost one out of four babies was considered a poor adoption risk for one reason or another, such as mental retardation of varying degrees or serious personality defects. In examining the families who adopted these babies, seventy-five were considered adequate, offering a reasonable amount of security and stability, a happy home life, and a decent upbringing.

While the investigators did not provide the reader with an opportunity to examine the rating procedures, they did report a rather intensive type of search for factors

---

[89] D. Bruce Gardner, Glenn R. Hawkes, and Lee G. Burchinal, "Noncontinuous Mothering in Infancy and Development in Later Childhood," *Child Development*, Vol. 32, No. 2 (June 1961), pp. 225–234.

[90] *Ibid.*, p. 233.
[91] Catherine S. Amatruda and Joseph V. Baldwin, "Current Adoption Practices," *Journal of Pediatrics*, Vol. 38, No. 2 (February 1951), pp. 208–212.

that might affect the upbringing of the child. Of the independent placements, in only forty-six instances were the "good" babies and the "good" families together. In twenty-six of the fifty-four remaining cases, the situation was regarded as dubious when a baby was seriously "overplaced" (a child of low but normal mental ability placed in a home where the cultural standards and expectations were higher than the child could meet). In the remaining twenty-eight cases, the family and baby together seemed involved in a situation so undesirable that it was recommended to the court that the adoption not be allowed.

In inspecting one hundred agency placements, Amatruda and Baldwin found that seventy-six of the babies placed through the agencies were "good" babies in "good" homes. The babies were judged to be normal by physical and developmental examinations and it was felt that the homes lacked any of the undesirable factors characteristic of "poor" families. In sixteen cases overplacements had been made, and in eight cases the situation was so poor that it was advised that the adoptions be terminated. Thus, the agency placements were more successful according to the somewhat inexact criteria of these researchers.

The investigators pointed out a major difference between the two types of placement. Of one hundred infants placed independently, seventy-nine were under 3 months of age; of the one hundred infants placed by agencies, only fourteen were under 3 months of age. Despite this, it was the view of these investigators that independent placements entail a far greater risk, both to the child and to the adoptive parents.

Studies of the adjustment of adoptive couples have been reported by Kirk.[92] This investigator has developed a theory about adoptive family life that assumes that most childless couples entering into adoption

are confronted with a number of disabilities. These disabilities he has identified as a role handicap, which is ostensibly reinforced by the attitudes of other people. In a mail survey questionnaire, Kirk asked some 1,500 adoptive parents whether they had ever encountered attitudes displayed by the general public that indicated disapproval or misunderstanding of adoption. Varying proportions of respondents reported encountering painful experiences, such as having individuals comment to them: "Isn't it wonderful of you to have taken this child"; "This child looks so much like you he could be your own"; "He is certainly lucky to have you for parents"; and "Tell me, do you know anything about this child's background?"

Kirk further develops his theory by suggesting that adoptive parents deal with their role handicap and feelings of alienation with two types of coping mechanisms: those that serve the adopters in denying that their situation is different from that of biological parents ("rejection of difference"); and those that serve the adopters in facing up to the difference ("acknowledgement of difference"). Kirk presents empirical data to show that a high degree of "acknowledgement of difference" was associated with a high degree of empathy with the child and a readiness to think about the child's natural parents. Also, the higher the degree of "acknowledgement of difference," the more likely it was that the adopter would feel his situation to be especially satisfying. Kirk's work represents one of the few attempts to develop a theory about the adoptive family as one having special dynamics that set it apart from the biological family. It will, no doubt, stimulate a number of empirical studies.

There has been little research about adoptive parents' reactions to the supervisory period after the child is placed for adoption. A study by Gochros of fifty-seven adoptive couples in Minnesota focused upon their reactions to the availability of case-

---

[92] David H. Kirk, *Shared Fate* (New York: Free Press of Glencoe, 1964).

workers in the postplacement period, prior to the legal consummation of the adoption.[93] He found that while a number of the families suffered from some tension in adjusting to the adoptive parent role, they were not particularly oriented to the caseworker as a person potentially helpful in relieving them of stress. The caseworkers tended to see themselves primarily in the role of aiding parents with their "feelings," while the parents themselves were inclined to view the caseworkers as benevolent probationers and not particularly available for help with any general emotional upset related to adoption. The lack of role consensus was seen as interfering with the full potential use of the caseworker during the postplacement period.

Emotional Disturbance in Adopted Children

There has been increasing interest displayed in the professional literature over the issue of whether adopted children are more prone to emotional disturbance than are children who have been reared by their natural parents. A number of investigators have expressed the view that the adopted child's position is inherently more hazardous than that of his peers raised under more typical family arrangements. The adopted child is seen as needing to integrate the emotionally charged knowledge that he once had another set of parents who procreated him and then made the decision to give him up. He also has to make peace with the matter of knowing that his coming into being was the product of behavior commonly regarded as deviant and immoral. Psychoanalytically oriented investigators have also suggested that the adopted child, in addition to all

this, has to cope with the fact that his own parents are not biologically related to him, and the feeling is strong that this knowledge can create problems of identity confusion as well as other aberrations in personality as the child goes through the Oedipal phase of development.

Concern about the emotional adjustment of adopted children was recently touched off by Schechter, a psychiatrist in private practice in California.[94] In a published report, he noted that during the years 1948 to 1953 some 120 children were seen by him in private practice. Of this number, sixteen (13 percent) were adopted. He considered this a very significant departure from what one would expect considering the small ratio of adopted children in the general population. Moreover, he was not only struck by the greater number of adopted children involved in treatment, but also thought the symptomatology worthy of note. He commented that in most cases the feature of the child's adoptive status played a significant role in the underlying dynamics of the problem. Schechter observed that a major question that arose in the treatment of these children was the timing and period of telling the child that he was adopted. He suggested that for many of these children the immature ego could not cope with the knowledge of the rejection by the original parents and that this represented a severe narcissistic injury.

Further information on the problems of adopted children in psychiatric treatment settings has been published by Toussieng of the Menninger Clinic.[95] His data cover a five-year period from 1955 through 1960 and were based upon intensive diagnostic outpatient studies performed at the Chil-

[93] Harvey Gochros, "Not Parents Yet: A Study of the Post-Placement Period in Adoption." Unpublished doctoral dissertation, Columbia University School of Social Work, 1963.

[94] Marshall D. Schechter, "Observations on Adopted Children," *A.M.A. Archives of General Psychiatry*, Vol. 3, No. 7 (July 1960), pp. 21–32.

[95] Povl W. Toussieng, "Thoughts Regarding the Etiology of Psychological Difficulties in Adopted Children," *Child Welfare*, Vol. 41, No. 2 (February 1962), pp. 59–66.

dren's Service at the clinic. Thirty-nine out of 357 individual children examined were adopted; that is, children not related by blood to either parent. This was some 11 percent of the entire patient load for that period. Fifteen of these children were adopted before they were 1 month old, ten were adopted before the age of 6 months, and five between the ages of 6 and 12 months. Only one child was more than 5 years old when adopted. Twenty of the children were adopted through adoption agencies, seven were adopted through physicians, four through courts, and one through a lawyer. Seven were adopted through other kinds of channels. With respect to diagnoses, twelve of the children showed findings impressive enough to warrant a primary or secondary diagnosis of "chronic brain syndrome." Severe emotional disturbances and personality disorders were overrepresented among the adopted children. This type of disorder was characteristic of 41 percent of the adopted children in contrast to almost 34 percent of the 318 nonadopted children studied at the service in the five years covered by the study.

With respect to the proportion of adopted children known to psychiatric facilities, Dukette points out that a number of investigators, like Toussieng, have incorrectly based their comparisons on the proportion of the total number of children born in 1953 to the number for whom adoption petitions were filed in that year as reported by twenty-nine states.[96] The more appropriate comparative figure would be the total number of adopted children and nonadopted children in the general population for the age range represented by the children who are patients at clinics.

Another study of a child guidance center population (in Pittsburgh) has been re-ported by Sweeny, Gasbarro, and Gluck.[97] A total of 292 closed cases were studied and it was found that 21 were legally adopted. The adopted sample thus represented 7.2 percent of the total cases closed in the period covered by the study, September 1959–December 1961. This compared with a local estimate indicating that 0.12 percent of the children 18 years of age and under, living in Allegheny County in 1959, were adopted.

The researchers felt that the difference between the presence of adopted children in the general population area served by the center and the incidence of adopted children in the center's case load was striking and appeared to be quite significant. With respect to the characteristics of the children receiving treatment, there did not seem to be any gross difference in the incidence of boys and girls between the adopted and nonadopted children. However, the non-adopted sample in treatment had more younger children, while the adopted sample was distributed rather evenly over the age range above 6 years. The income levels of both samples appeared very similar. More important, the types of symptoms occurring in both samples were considered quite comparable. Symptoms reported most frequently for both sets of children included anxiety, feelings of inadequacy or inferiority, fighting with teachers, fighting with parents, and poor school achievement.

Yet another effort to shed some light on the prevalence of emotional disorders among adopted children, and the nature of these disorders as compared to nonadopted children, was undertaken by Borgatta and Fanshel.[98] They succeeded in gaining the

---

[96] Rita Dukette, "Thoughts Regarding the Etiology of Psychological Difficulties in Adopted Children," *Child Welfare*, Vol. 41, No. 2 (February 1962), pp. 66–71.

[97] Dolores M. Sweeny, Diana T. Gasbarro, and Martin R. Gluck, "A Descriptive Study of Adopted Children Seen in a Child Guidance Center," *Child Welfare*, Vol. 42, No. 7 (July 1963), pp. 345–349, 352.

[98] Edgar F. Borgatta and David Fanshel, *Behavioral Characteristics of Children Known to Psychiatric Outpatient Clinics* (New York: Child Welfare League of America, 1965).

co-operation of thirty outpatient psychiatric clinics serving children in various parts of the United States; these represented 25 percent of the clinics originally invited by mail to participate. These facilities were drawn from a broad array of geographic representation where the agency ostensibly had minimally a half-time social worker and a half-time psychiatrist or psychologist. A behavior-rating instrument containing seventy behavioral items was filled out by the clinician who had major treatment responsibility in the case. The agencies were asked to locate clinicians who had an adopted child in their case load. With this basis for selection of clinicians, the study sample comprised 607 children of whom 56, or 9.4 percent, represented unrelated adoptions. A second survey of case loads covering *all* clinicians indicated that 5.5 percent represented unrelated adoptions.

When adopted and nonadopted children were compared on an over-all rating of their general competence (or ego functioning) by the clinicians, only a very small difference, not statistically significant, occurred favoring the adoptive cases. However, looking at a second method of assessment, a comparison was made of the classification by diagnostic category of the two types of children. It was found that only 4 percent of the adopted children were classified as psychotic, whereas 14 percent of the nonadopted were so classified. This difference was statistically significant. Thus, if reporting of cases as psychotic is considered a criterion of severity of disorder, it would appear that proportionately more of the adopted children showed better mental health. Further, examining the two types of children by profile scores, it was found that adopted cases more often involved problems of the child showing defiance of the parents and an unwillingness to assume responsibility and have a proper task orientation, but less often involved problems of overinhibited behavior.

One recent study that runs counter to those reporting an inordinately high incidence of adopted children coming to psychiatric clinics is reported by Goodman, Silberstein, and Mandell at the Staten Island Mental Health Center.[99] The charts of 593 children seen at the clinic between 1956 and 1962 were examined. Of this total, fourteen cases or 2.4 percent were found to be extra-familially adopted children. The children under study were brought to the clinic 1.4 times as frequently as would be expected on the basis of their existence in the community. The authors believe the magnitude of the problem is not sufficient to warrant social consequence: "Our findings suggest that child care agencies might postpone their anxieties pending further investigation."

As can be seen from the studies cited above, the issue of emotional disturbance in adopted children as measured by attendance at psychiatric clinics is not a simple one. The last research word on this subject has yet to be said.

Follow-up Studies of Adopted Children

Some of the early basic studies of the adjustment of adopted children were reported by Skeels, Harms, and Skodak.[100] They followed up a group of children who had been placed in adoptive homes in Iowa during the 1930's. These children came from a large congregate institution and suffered from "inferior social histories."

[99] Jerome D. Goodman, Richard M. Silberstein, and Wallace Mandell, "Adopted Children Brought to Child Psychiatric Clinic," *A.M.A. Archives of General Psychiatry*, Vol. 9, No. 5 (November 1963), pp. 451–455.

[100] Harold M. Skeels and Irene Harms, "Children With Inferior Social Histories: Their Mental Development in Adoptive Homes," *Journal of Genetic Psychology*, Vol. 72, Second half (June 1948), pp. 283–294; and Marie Skodak and Harold M. Skeels, "A Final Follow-Up Study of One Hundred Adopted Children," *Journal of Genetic Psychology*, Vol. 75, First half (September 1949), pp. 85–125.

The children were so defined because their mothers had been classified as mentally retarded on a standard test of intelligence, with an IQ of 75 or less, or their putative fathers had very low occupational positions. A follow-up of the children placed with adoptive parents indicated that the children consistently and unmistakably showed results on intelligence tests that were superior to their natural parents, and actually showed a higher pattern of intelligence than found among children in families like their adoptive families. The authors concluded that the implications of their study for placing agencies would support a policy of early placement of children with so-called inferior backgrounds in adoptive or foster homes offering emotional warmth and security and an above-average educational and social setting.

One of the earliest efforts to conduct a follow-up study of adopted children was undertaken in 1947 by the Free Synagogue Child Adoption Committee in New York City.[101] Taking advantage of the fact that ninety-five adopted children out of 291 who had been placed in adoptive homes for the period 1941–45 had been retested for intelligence by the agency psychologist three and one-half to twenty-two months after placement, it was decided to conduct a follow-up of about fifty of these children who were at least 4 years old. While the original study group of ninety-one was by no means a random sample—geographic factors had some importance in their selection—it was nevertheless thought that this did not negate the usefulness of the study. Fifty families out of fifty-seven who were approached agreed to participate in the follow-up.

Research procedures included an office interview, usually with the mother, home observation of about three hours' duration, and psychological testing of the child. The home observations provided reports on (1) the amount of affection shown the child, (2) admiration or criticism of the child, (3) ease or tension of the parents toward the child, (4) time spent with the child by both parents, (5) methods of discipline, (6) the degree of freedom permitted the child, and (7) the marital relationship. The fifty cases were classified by the study worker and two caseworkers—not members of the agency staff—into three groups according to the attitudes of the parents: successful, fairly successful, and unsuccessful.

There was perfect agreement among the three raters on forty-three cases out of fifty. Twenty-six cases were rated as successful, eighteen as fairly successful, and six as unsuccessful. The evaluative classification of the families proved to have no significant relationship with the age of the parents, but couples with longer durations of marriage tended to provide a high proportion of the successful cases. It was also found that the median income of the unsuccessful families was substantially higher than those in the more positive outcome categories. The psychologist's re-examination of the intelligence of the children showed a rise in intelligence quotient of 9.8. Comparing "successful" versus "unsuccessful" homes for gains in IQ's of the children resulted in inconclusive findings.

In the field of adoption, there has been interest in determining whether psychological tests administered to infants available for adoption will predict subsequent intelligence scores achieved in later childhood and adulthood. Wittenborn attempted to assay this issue with a follow-up study of adoptive families and their children who had been known to the staff of Dr. Arnold Gesell at the Yale Clinic of Child Development.[102] These children had been known to the clinic for the period 1942–1947. They had been administered the Yale Examination for Infant Development. The examination provided a standardized pro-

[101] Child Adoption Research Committee, *A Follow-Up Study of Adoptive Families* (New York, 1951).

[102] J. Richard Wittenborn, *The Placement of Adoptive Children* (Springfield, Ill.: Charles C Thomas, 1957).

cedure for the clinical evaluation of an infant's progress in such developmental areas as gross motor co-ordination, fine motor co-ordination, linguistic, adaptive, and personal-social behaviors. Analysis of his data led Wittenborn to the following interesting observation:

We can observe despite our use of all available features of the infant examination and of many different criteria of development that we find no means of refuting an hypothesis that "the infant examination has no useful predictive validity." Although we cannot prove that the hypothesis of no predictive validity is true, it describes our data.[103]

By way of further findings from Wittenborn's research, the data he collected did not reveal any evidence of a significant relationship between early institutional care of an infant and subsequent measures of development. The information that was available about the child's background also failed to show any significant correlation with the ultimate success of the adoption. In contrasting the initial developmental measurements of infants placed through independent means and those placed through social agencies, Wittenborn found that the independently placed youngster had fewer physical deviations and slightly higher classifications on the infant examination. These infants were generally considered more adoptable than the agency placed children. At the time of the follow-up study, the independently placed children had slightly fewer low IQ's than the agency-placed children. While the follow-up study seemed to favor the independently placed children somewhat, this appeared related to the fact that agencies were willing to seek adoptive placements for handicapped children. The findings run counter to those previously cited by Amatruda and Baldwin favoring agency-placed children. While both studies were conducted at the Yale Clinic of Child Development they appear to have concerned different samples of children adopted at different time periods.

The most ambitious follow-up study of adopted children reported to date is that of Witmer and her colleagues.[104] They undertook to follow up children who were adopted independently in the state of Florida during the period 1944–1947. Research data covering 484 such adoptions were obtained. The basic concern of the investigators was to determine—through studying the adjustment of these children—how successful the independent adoption process was in achieving the purpose of adoption law. They also wished to ascertain whether certain factors are predictive of adoption outcome, especially those that are present and can be recognized at the time adoption decisions are made.

Detailed interviews were conducted with the adoptive parents and these were focused upon the respondents' experiences with adoption and their perceptions of their children's social and emotional adjustment. The 484 children who were included in the study represented 73 percent of the 665 children whom the investigators tried to locate and who were found to be still living in the state of Florida. The two- to three-hour interviews were most often held with the adoptive mother. Of interest, as a methodological procedure, was the decision of the investigators to develop a topical outline of points to be covered in the interview, while leaving the interviewers free to follow their own modes of obtaining information and to ask questions in whatever sequence seemed preferable. The purpose of this type of interviewing procedure was to secure the advantage of the caseworkers' skills in helping the parents to report material of a sensitive nature—material that might normally be withheld because of defensive behavior.

In order to obtain objective measures of the child's adjustment, it was decided to administer group tests in the child's classroom under the guise of a child development study. The tests were given to the

---

[103] *Ibid.*, p. 71.

[104] Helen Witmer *et al., Independent Adoptions: A Follow-Up Study* (New York: Russell Sage Foundation, 1963).

child and four other children, one of whom constituted a "control" child of the same sex and race as the adopted child and came from a home of comparable socioeconomic status as judged by the father's occupation. A considerable array of information was gathered: the children filled out a sociometric test through which an indication of the popularity of the youngsters and their controls was obtained. The California Test of Personality was used to evaluate social and emotional adjustment from the children's own viewpoint. Teacher ratings were obtained about the subjects' attitudes and behavior at school and the school records were examined for information about each child's intelligence and school achievement.

Witmer and her colleagues found that, by and large, the intelligence ratings of the adopted children and their controls were similar, and they were functioning at about the same level, as indicated by achievement tests. On the sociometric test, however, the control children seemed somewhat more popular than the adopted children and this difference was statistically significant. The California Test of Personality also showed some tendency for the adopted children to rate a bit lower in their adjustment than the controls who were of the same sex and comparable socioeconomic levels. The authors indicated that these findings suggest a possible slight relationship between adjustment and the status of being adopted. However, the children's showing on the test was not very far out of line with expectations.

Concerning teacher ratings, there were some slight differences favoring the control children with respect to qualities of leadership and evidence of aggressive maladjustment. There was no notable difference, however, between the two groups with respect to withdrawn behavior. The most telling difference between the adopted children and their controls concerned measures developed by the investigators from teachers' comments. The teachers had been asked whether "there is anything unusual about this child, such as special assets, problems, or unusual circumstances," and whether the child had any problems such as retardation, juvenile court record, truancy, and so on. Coding these comments revealed that 31 percent of the adopted children were either somewhat maladjusted or seriously maladjusted contrasted with only 19 percent of the control children. However, when the investigators introduced the variable of the subject's age at the time of adoption, it was found that children placed at less than 1 month of age, constituting three-fourths of the sample, showed the same distribution of adjustment categories as the control children. Other differences between adopted children and their controls on the measures used by the investigators also tended to disappear when the variable of age at the time of adoption was introduced into the analysis.

The findings of the Florida study were summarized as follows:

Most of the adoptions were working out well. The proportion of poor outcomes, however, was not inconsiderable and the comparison with the control children was a bit in favor of the non-adopted children.[105]

Another major finding was that most of the overt characteristics of the adoptive applicants that were the easiest to determine and on which independent observers were most likely to agree gave little indication of the kind of home afforded the children in later years. The authors noted: "While a number of these overt indicators showed statistically significant associations with adoption outcome, their influence was usually either indirect or else too slight to counteract the force of other, less tangible factors." [106] Thus, parents' age at placement, socioeconomic status, parents' education, and mother's employment did not seem to have a major bearing upon the child's subsequent adjustment.

The research literature is very sparse about the adult status of adopted children.

[105] *Ibid.*, p. 256.
[106] *Ibid.*, p. 349.

To help develop knowledge in this area, Jaffee and Fanshel undertook a follow-up study of adults, 21 to 30 years of age, who had been adopted before the age of 3 from four New York City agencies.[107] The task of locating these families after a hiatus of many years was a formidable one and the development of a sample of one hundred subjects required drawing more than twice this number of names from rosters prepared by the co-operating agencies.

Depth interviews held with the adoptive parents were tape-recorded and these were subsequently codified. While the data are still being analyzed, some preliminary findings have emerged. One of the most striking is that, contrary to expectations, children who were placed at a somewhat older age showed fewer problems in their social relationships as they grew up in their adoptive homes than did children placed at a very young age. Part of the explanation for this finding appears to reside in the characteristics of adoptive parents willing to accept older children.

Decision-Making in Child Welfare

In recent years, a major interest has developed in studying the decision-making processes engaged in by caseworkers when performing such important tasks as selecting adoptive parents, selecting foster parents, allocating children to various types of facilities, and so on. One of the approaches favored by researchers in studying professional judgments is to determine whether caseworkers show reliability when asked to make the critical decisions normally confronting them in practice. For example, given the full details of a couple's background, current living situation, and reasons for wanting to adopt a child, would a representative group of workers tend to arrive at the same decision in selecting or rejecting the couple's application?

[107] Benson Jaffee and David Fanshel, "A Follow-Up of Adoption" (report in progress).

Selecting Adoptive Parents

Research that experimentally examines the basis for adoptive parent selection was reported by Brieland in 1959.[108] He developed a study that confined itself to the problem of screening applicants for home study. Brieland arranged to have recorded on sound tapes consecutive intake interviews with five couples approaching a private, nonsectarian, statewide agency holding membership in the Child Welfare League of America. The interviews were conducted by the same male caseworker whose trial tape recordings were regarded as of sufficiently good voice quality for the purposes of the research.

The content of the interviews followed the same general order and included such topics as the couple's general interest in a child, including sex, age, coloring, and background; their prior experience with children; their attitudes about telling the child of his adoption and giving him information about his background; their attempts at having children of their own; the manner in which their interest in adoption developed; the general life experiences of both partners; their educational history; their marital interaction; and so on. The tapes were played on sixteen different occasions to a total of 184 caseworkers in thirteen states. The aim was to obtain and analyze the judgments of these workers concerning the capacity for adoptive parenthood of the five couples whose interviews had been taped. A day and one-half were required in each agency for evaluation of the tapes. The pattern of worker-judge acceptances were:

Couple A: 164 acceptances to 20 rejections
Couple B: 147 acceptances to 37 rejections
Couple C: 124 acceptances to 60 rejections
Couple D: 113 acceptances to 71 rejections
Couple E: 129 acceptances to 55 rejections

[108] Donald Brieland, *An Experimental Study of the Selection of Adoptive Parents at Intake* (New York: Child Welfare League of America, 1959).

Brieland notes that the results for the total sample are statistically significant at the .001 level of confidence. However, he questions whether this represents a satisfactory level of reliability, since the data reveal considerable disagreement. Using the criterion of consensus as a way of validating the individual casework-judges' decision, Brieland found that of the 184 worker-judges, 43 agreed completely with the majority, 65 agreed on four decisions, 53 on three, 21 on two, and 2 agreed with the majority in only one of the five cases. Thirty-three workers not only did not accept at least one of the two couples most often accepted by the consensus, but also accepted at least one of the couples rejected by the consensus.

It would appear from this research that for many couples approaching an adoption agency, the matter of whether or not they would be accepted by the agency for home study would depend on which caseworker was assigned to interview them. Various agencies showed wide internal differences in the decisions to accept or reject couples. Of note was the fact that workers who had completed many home studies of adoptive applicants did not differ from those with less experience. Also of interest was the finding that the worker-judges tended to make fewer comments in the margin of the transcripts in the second half of the transcript than in the first half. Had the drop in the number of comments been accounted for by fatigue, there would have been a larger number of comments on a case that was heard early in the day than on one heard late in the day; no such relationship was found. Brieland came to the conclusion that the first half of the interview apparently sets the tone and pervades the final decision at intake. His work suggests that an evaluative response-set is established fairly early in the judgment process and further stimuli presented on the tapes fail to alter the over-all impressions of these caseworkers.

Research such as Brieland's tends to be somewhat unflattering to professionals,

since it suggests that chance factors help shape vital decisions made about couples. This research has been challenged by some child welfare workers, however, on the grounds that many agencies do not make firm decisions on the basis of the first interview and that the experimental decision-making process does not adequately replicate the kinds of judgments caseworkers have to make in real-life situations. The research has, nevertheless, had the beneficial effect of pointing up the need for agencies to explicate the criteria by which adoptive parents are selected.

Selecting Foster Parents

The problem of establishing the reliability and validity of decision-making in the selection of foster parents has been intensively studied by Wolins.[109] As part of his over-all project, this investigator was interested in deriving the variables used by caseworkers to evaluate foster home applicants. Using as his subjects child welfare workers in two public and two voluntary child welfare agencies—153 caseworkers in all—Wolins sought to determine the factors that influenced the worker-judges in ranking foster parent applicants. Seven cases were prepared for this study, using abstracted material from case records obtained from several child welfare agencies. Wolins conceived of the information made available to caseworkers in case records as perhaps containing too much volume or too little volume of material. He also conceived that worker judgments would be affected by the relevance of the material that was made available to them. He noted:

We knew from theory that too much material (or too much irrelevant content) blocks or distorts judgment. We can think of that condition as a blocked or a too fine sieve. Reduction and selection of content is needed, but too much reduction will produce such a

[109] Martin Wolins, *Selecting Foster Parents* (New York: Columbia University Press, 1963).

coarse sieve as to permit all judgments to flow through without discrimination. A very long case record with substantial amounts of extraneous material (a tight sieve) and a very sparse record (a coarse sieve) should produce discrepancies in decision. A case record somewhere between the two should yield most reliability. But how much and what kind of information should a case record include? [110]

In asking worker-judges in the four participating agencies to rank the seven cases, Wolins found that there was high intra-agency agreement and also considerable similarity among the agencies. Child welfare staff in each agency who ranked the seven cases achieved about 50 percent perfect agreement. This agreement was regarded as surprisingly high. However, Wolins found that reliability of decision-making differed according to the status position occupied by the decision-maker. He found that those who were engaged in making such decisions in their regular practice—the homefinders and their supervisors—tended to make decisions more reliably than others. Staff at both extremes—students, supervisors, and senior workers—were less consistent in their decision-making than the homefinders. He concluded that decision-makers apparently developed a consensus because they met and acted together and came to share a common point of view.

A very cogent finding of the Wolins study was that volume and relevance of material affected the agreement of judges about cases. He found volume related to reliability, but from an inverse standpoint. Judges achieved the best agreement about cases with 40 percent of the material culled from the original record. They did poorest with the full case record or with 80 percent of the record and continued to do quite poorly with 60 percent of the record. There appeared to be a middle ground—40 percent of the process record—that constituted a maximum base for reliable decision-making. Further, when cases were trimmed to remove noninformational material (ma-

terial not considered relevant for decision-making either by child welfare workers or by the research staff of the project), the reliability of the judgment was affected. Thus, compact case records that had considerable reduction in the quantity of informational items present and contained only crucial material showed a reliability measure constituting 81 percent of a perfect score, contrasted with 40 percent of a perfect score with the full case material, and 29 percent when crucial informational items were deleted.

Wolins suggests that "the most reliable decisions are made with relatively little volume, although probably not with little content." Put another way, the more material the worker-judge is given to absorb, the more chance there is for him to show disagreement. When quantity of material is reduced, even if only by random selection, caseworker-judges show higher agreement. When it is reduced selectively by the elimination of noninformational material, a marked increase in reliability among workers results.

A further interesting finding of Wolins' study is that a two-hour training session with worker-judges failed to show the kind of agreement in ranking cases for which he had hoped. Subsequently, he found that more thorough training of caseworker-judges resulted in a gratifying improvement of interworker agreement. His work suggests that the training of caseworkers to use rating instruments, if limited to short periods, has the effect of possibly dislodging them from their own moorings while failing to provide a substitute frame of reference. Longer training sessions, however, establish a more adequate framework for the task of decision-making. What is not known, however, is whether such elaborate training procedures merely serve to "brain-wash" potential raters so that the high reliability, rather than reflecting the normal process of decision-making in child welfare practice, tends to produce a group of research subjects who have been coached to respond to the same types of

[110] *Ibid.*, p. 62.

stimuli in similar fashion. In other words, the question arises whether the reliability that is being measured is a reflection of professional cognitive processes or whether it represents instead an artifact of the experimental situation.

An important further component of Wolins' study was the attempt to develop a schema from the judgments made by workers on the basis of case materials. He developed a series of scales composed of the items workers utilized in their decision-making processes. These items were constructed in the form of an attitude questionnaire, enabling Wolins to present it to large samples of workers, foster parents, and foster parent applicants. The scales developed from these items were of the Guttman type and covered such attitudinal dimensions as ambitiousness, rationalism, nondifferentiation, possessiveness, bossiness, conformity, selflessness, rigidity, impermeability, authoritarianism, planfulness, and martyrdom. The development of twelve Guttman-type scales from the material caseworkers used to rate foster parents represents a creative application to child welfare practice of this attitude-scaling procedure developed for other purposes in the social sciences.

Wolins' questionnaire was utilized with 343 workers in eight county welfare departments in California, Minnesota, and New York. The workers were asked to give their images of the "good" and "bad" foster homes by filling out the questionnaire as they thought a "best" family and a "poorest" family would approach the task. From the responses of these workers, Wolins built up the image of the workers' ideal foster family as one that was goal oriented—having a general idea of where it was going and general rules for getting there. He also found that a proper display of parental authority, capacity for self-sacrifice on a moderate level, a somewhat conforming attitude, and several other identifiable orientations were characteristics of the "best" foster family, as conceived by caseworkers in these agencies.

There was impressive agreement among these workers in formulating ideal images.

When the instrument was filled out by real-life foster-fathers and foster-mothers of some 1,649 families who had been rated "superior," "adequate," or "inferior" by their current caseworkers, it was found that the attitude questionnaire did not discriminate well among these three types of families. This was a disappointing failure considering the effort that went into the development of the instrument. By way of explanation, Wolins suggests that in the counties where supply and demand pressures were relatively low, and the administrative milieu affecting caseworkers was generally favorable, quite respectable predictions were made. In other words, when workers are faced with the pressure of children "piling up" in placement without sufficient numbers of foster homes available for them, they will feel constrained to depart from their idealized image of a good foster home.

Question also arose as to what variables included in Wolins' study yield the best predictions of who will be selected as foster parents. Six hundred and twenty-eight applicant families in seven of the eight counties that participated in his study filled out the questionnaire, "Family Life in America." How did these variables combine to predict who will be selected? Wolins comments:

A family has a high chance of being accepted if it has enough of the following characteristics. The father of the family regards children as distinct individuals. The mother is farm reared and is not excessively planful, ambitious, possessive, or self-sacrificing. Both parents are fairly flexible in their notion of means and the pursuit of goals. They have several children of their own, are reasonably well educated, and are not too old. The more of these qualities a family has, the better are its chances of acceptance. Thus possession of nine of these positives resulted in 80% acceptance, eight produced 73% acceptance, six yield 57%, and so on.[111]

---

[111] *Ibid.*, p. 149.

Institution or Foster Family?

Another experimental study of caseworkers' judgments in foster care placement is that reported by Briar.[112] His research concerned one of the decisions frequently made by social workers in child placement: the choice between institutional and foster family placement. He wished to test the hypothesis that social workers would more frequently recommend institutional placement for a child with serious emotional disturbance than for a child who is mildly afflicted. He also hypothesized that their placement recommendations would be affected by the natural parents' expressed preference for one type of care as opposed to another. These hypotheses stemmed from Briar's examination of the diagnostic criteria that seemed to be specified in the child welfare literature. The sample of decision-makers in this study consisted of forty-three caseworkers engaged in child placement and representing five different agencies. Three of the agencies were residential treatment centers with small foster family programs; the fourth agency was a sectarian family agency with a large foster family program; and the fifth agency was the child welfare division of a public welfare department in which nearly all the children in foster care were placed with foster families.

Case materials were prepared in which a 10-year-old boy was alternately described as either being seriously emotionally disturbed or mildly emotionally disturbed; in a second case situation, a 10-year-old boy was described whose parents were either strongly opposed to foster family care or strongly opposed to institutional placement. Worker-raters were assigned on a random basis to two groups, each receiving different versions of the two types of cases. They were asked to make a rating, among other judgments that were requested of them,

about the prognosis for foster home placement and institutional placement for the child in question.

Briar found that there does, indeed, appear to be a relationship between the degree of emotional disturbance in the child and the social worker's placement recommendations for the child, but the direction of this relationship is variable and appears to lack reliability. He also found that in making their placement recommendations, the subjects in this study were influenced by the natural parents' expressed preference for one type of placement over another, with the greatest influence in relation to the expressed negative attitudes toward foster family care. He found no relationship between the age, sex, marital status, experience, and training of the worker and his clinical judgments and recommendations.

A particularly telling finding reported by Briar was that for at least one of the cases in this study, the social workers' placement recommendations were directly related to the placement patterns in their own employing agencies. In other words, when the social worker was employed in an agency that emphasized foster family care, he tended to recommend foster family care; when employed in an agency that was largely committed to institutional care of children, he tended to recommend this type of care.

Fanshel has challenged some of the bases for Briar's research, particularly his assumption that practice principles dictate the placement of disturbed foster children in institutional care and that natural parents' preferences are the overriding criterion in determining type of placement for children.[113] Question was also raised about the ability of the investigator to present, through limited case illustrations, a true facsimile of the real-life situation confronting social workers in child welfare practice.

[112] Scott Briar, "Clinical Judgment in Foster Care Placement," *Child Welfare*, Vol. 42, No. 4 (April 1963), pp. 161–169.

[113] David Fanshel, "Commentary on 'Clinical Judgment in Foster Care Placement,'" *Child Welfare*, Vol. 42, No. 4 (April 1963), pp. 169–172.

Neglect and Abuse of Children

According to several investigators, the physical abuse or neglect of children constitutes a leading child welfare problem in the United States today. Every community requires protective services to safeguard the welfare of children who are reported to be neglected, abused, and exploited, or who live under other kinds of noxious conditions. Protective services may include casework services undertaken in behalf of the child in his own home, or include legal actions aimed at removing the child from a home judged unfit.

Jeter, in her recent survey of child welfare programs in the United States, points out that protective services ranked third in the number of children served among services provided by public agencies and seventh among services provided by voluntary agencies.[114] She estimated that over 45,000 children were receiving protective services from public agencies on one day in 1961. For the children living in foster care and served by public agencies, the predominance of neglect, abuse, or exploitation was very pronounced as a cause of placement. Forty-three percent of these children in care suffered from various forms of neglect or abuse. For the children served by voluntary agencies, the estimate was that 17 percent suffered from neglect, abuse, or exploitation.

The Massachusetts Society for the Prevention of Cruelty to Children, a statewide private agency that provides professional casework services, recently undertook to determine the number of cases of physical abuse to children reported to its eighteen district offices during one year. Through this inquiry, 134 cases involving about two hundred abused children were reported.[115] In a more intensive study of a somewhat reduced proportion of these cases, it was found that relatives accounted for 24 percent of these referrals, legal authorities for 23 percent, neighbors for 22 percent, and, more significantly, hospitals and doctors referred *only 9 percent* of the cases (although they had been involved in over 30 percent of them).

Examination of residential data on these families revealed that the majority had lived in their communities for substantial periods of time and had not moved about extensively. They did not, however, show even a moderate degree of integration within their communities as evidenced by the paucity of reports of group associations; 50 percent had no formal group association, and 28 percent had only one group association (which was most frequently the church). Further, a good portion of these families were described as not being fully accepted within their communities. While most of them were self-supporting, some 90 percent had serious social problems. For example, marital discord was characteristic of 40 percent of the families; financial difficulties, 22 percent; other conflict, 15 percent; faulty community relationships, 14 percent. In almost half the families, premarital conception had occurred. In 86 percent of the cases, the abusing adults were the parents of the children, and they were usually living with the abused children. Child abuse was committed about equally by the fathers and mothers, who were described as being young at the time of the marriage and relatively young at the time of the abuse.

Three distinct types of parental personality characteristics were identified. The first was described as being related to *hostility* and *aggressiveness*, and included parents who appeared to be continually angry at someone or something. The anger

114 Helen Jeter, *Children, Problems and Services in Child Welfare Programs*, Children's Bureau Publication No. 403 (Washington, D.C.: U.S. Department of Health, Education, and Welfare, Children's Bureau, 1963).

115 Harold D. Bryant *et al.*, "Physical Abuse of Children—Agency Study," *Child Welfare*, Vol. 42, No. 3 (March 1963), pp. 125–130.

was described as continuous and uncontrolled. The second group of parents showed rigidity of personality, including *compulsiveness* and *lack of warmth*. The third group of parents showed strong feelings of *passivity* and *dependence*. A fourth grouping included a significant number of abusing fathers who were fully or partially unable to support their families because of a physical disability.

Another picture of the widespread nature of problems of abuse of children in the United States was revealed in a publication of the Children's Division of the American Humane Association.[116] Combed from the newspapers of the country for a year's period were 662 cases of child abuse, found in almost all of the states in the Union. The majority of the children, some 55 percent, were youngsters under 4 years of age. A serious aspect of these cases was that 25 percent of the children afflicted by this abuse died as a consequence. This research pointed up the fact that fathers initiated the violence for 38 percent of the injuries and were responsible for 22 percent of the child deaths. Mothers inflicted 28 percent of the injuries and were responsible for 48 percent of the deaths. Three out of four of the children who were killed had suffered at the hands of one or both parents.

As part of a larger study, Leontine Young studied 180 families identified in seven communities of different size, where problems of neglect and abuse of children were identified.[117] All of the families were reported to come from the active files of public child welfare departments, except for those coming from one private agency in a large city that handled only cases of child neglect and abuse. Information was obtained from case records. These records contained repeated observations by case-workers, supplementary reports by schools and other persons knowing the family, official medical reports, and reports of psychiatric and psychological examinations.

The 180 families were divided into four groups for the purpose of tracing the effect of family patterns upon child care: those involving severe and moderate neglect, and those involving severe and moderate abuse. For severe neglect, the criterion was inadequate feeding. For moderate neglect the criterion was lack of cleanliness, lack of adequate clothing for the children, or failure to provide medical care. When either or both of the parents beat the children violently and consistently, "so that time after time the results of the beatings were visible," the classification was severe abuse. When parents beat their children only now and then, and the beatings tended to be less violent, the classification of moderate abuse was used. When a family both neglected and abused their children, the case was classified as abuse. A fifteen-page case-reading schedule was devised to cover a wide range of information.

In describing some of her findings, Young notes that "physical torture of the children was present in 69.7 percent of the severe abuse cases, but in only 25 percent of the families classified as showing moderate abuse." Such severe behavior appeared in only one family in the cases of severe neglect and not at all in moderate neglect. A similar pattern of differentiation was revealed for the item "consistent denial of normally accepted activities" to children. Young found that 69 percent of the families in the severe abuse category showed this pattern and 56.3 percent of those in the moderate abuse category. In the neglect cases only about 10 percent of the families of those in both the severe neglect and in the moderate neglect categories were said to have demonstrated this pattern. Gross parental expressions of hostility and aggression toward children, involving such things as the parents bluntly stating that they hated the children, was

[116] American Humane Association, Children's Division, *Protecting the Battered Child* (Denver, 1962).

[117] Leontine Young, *Wednesday's Children* (New York: McGraw-Hill Book Co., 1964).

true of almost four-fifths of the families in severe abuse, half of those in moderate abuse, two-fifths of the severe neglect cases, and one-fifth of the cases showing moderate neglect.

The families in Young's study were described as being chiefly members of the lower socioeconomic group, limited in education, unskilled in occupation, and given to frequent changes of jobs and periods of employment. Their housing tended to be overcrowded, dirty, and in poor repair. They were burdened with health problems, and many of them were alcoholics or heavy drinkers. There was an occasional middle-class family in the sample of this study and Young notes: "There is nothing here to substantiate an assumption that neglect and abuse of children are confined solely to this group [lower-class families] and this economic and social class." [118]

Some suggestion of why these parents fail comes from the finding that almost 50 percent of them came from homes where they, too, were physically neglected or abused—homes much like their current ones. Fifty-five parents grew up in institutions or foster homes. Only a tiny minority of these parents seemed to have any positive relationship with a member of their own family—either with a parent or with a relative.

Elmer reported on a study of fifty children, formerly known to a hospital in Pittsburgh, whose diagnoses included multiple bone injuries. [119] These were children who, when seen at the hospital, had X-rays that revealed, in addition to the recent fracture, signs of older healing fractures indicating that they had suffered prior multiple bone injuries. The purpose of the follow-up study of these children was to help develop criteria for making professional judgments about the probability of physical abuse when such fractures come

to the attention of medical authorities. These judgments are difficult to make because abusive acts are usually perpetrated in the child's own home without witnesses being present. While Elmer recognized that bone fractures represent only one type of injury suffered by abused children, it seemed to be a good starting point for research in this area.

A major finding of Elmer's study was that the incidence of death among these children was high; seven out of the fifty children were known to have died, and at least three other children sustained additional injuries after discharge from the hospital. Thirteen other children showed ongoing physical defects that were of a quite serious nature. Elmer notes that the variable of age was by far the most striking item of information: the largest group, seventeen, was composed of infants under 3 months of age when multiple bone injuries were found; the smallest group, nine, was composed of infants from 3 to 6 months old.

Work with parents who abuse or neglect their children creates special demands upon social workers. Billingsley undertook a study of the activities and role performance of workers in a protective agency and contrasted these with the staff of a family agency. [120] He found family service workers spent more time in client-centered activity and less time in collateral contacts than was true of protective service workers. The family service workers tended to report greater work satisfaction. Personnel turnover seemed to be a greater problem in the protective agency. With respect to working styles, the orientation of the family service worker tended to be more psychodynamic, whereas the workers offering protective services seemed more alerted to sociocultural aspects of their clients' situations.

One of the critical questions facing child

---

[118] *Ibid.*, p. 74.

[119] Elizabeth Elmer, "Identification of Abused Children," *Children*, Vol. 10, No. 5 (September–October 1963), pp. 180–184.

[120] Andrew Billingsley, "The Role of the Social Worker in a Child Protective Agency," *Child Welfare*, Vol. 43, No. 9 (November 1964), pp. 472–479.

welfare workers in situations involving neglect or abuse of children is whether it is in the child's interest to remove him from the home and place him in foster care or to allow him to remain with his family. This is often a difficult decision to make and, unfortunately, there has been little research undertaken in this area thus far.

A beginning effort in this direction was undertaken in 1961 by Bernice Boehm.[121] As one phase of her study, an analysis was undertaken of two hundred protective cases drawn from the public and private social agencies in Minneapolis and St. Paul. Half of the cases were situations in which it had been found necessary to place the child away from his family. The remaining half were situations where the social workers perceived the family as meeting minimum standards of adequacy of child care and it was considered that the family could be worked with.

Q-sort ratings by caseworkers knowing the families in the study were obtained to explicate the criteria utilized in the decision to remove children from their homes.[122] From initial correlations emerging from the Q-sort material, the following appear to represent some of the basic dimensions along which workers' perceptions of these families were organized: (1) the organization of family living (i.e., from a home management standpoint of cleanliness of home, physical care of children, regularity of mealtime and bedtime, stable use of income, and encouragement of school attendance); (2) the child's behavior (i.e., his self-confidence, relationships with other children, nervousness and irritability, mood,

and so on); (3) the father's role in the stability of family life; (4) the parents' recognition of their own problems and their ability to use outside help; (5) volatility (i.e., degree of violence and quarrelsomeness in family life); (6) strength of mother in maternal role; and (7) child's tendency for deviant behavior.[123] Six of these dimensions were found to discriminate between situations in which children were placed away from their families and those where this action was not considered necessary.

Day Care and Maternal Employment

A 1958 study by the U.S. Bureau of the Census, undertaken in co-operation with the U.S. Children's Bureau, revealed that there were over five million children under 12 years of age whose mothers were working full time.[124] There were many other youngsters whose mothers were employed part time or not on a regular basis. The effects of the absence of working mothers upon the development of their children have been the object of study by an increasing number of investigators.

Siegel and her colleagues sent questionnaires to the mothers of kindergarten children in seventeen schools in two large suburban communities.[125] From an 86 percent return (917 questionnaires), it was possible to explore the relationship between maternal employment and the adjustment of children in kindergarten. Matched pairs

---

[121] Bernice Boehm, "An Assessment of Family Adequacy in Protective Cases," *Child Welfare*, Vol. 41, No. 1 (January 1962), pp. 10–16.

[122] The Q-sort technique is a method for collecting data in which a respondent is given a series of items, usually printed on cards, each containing a descriptive phrase. Typically a fair number of items are used and the respondent is asked to distribute them along a single continuum ranging, for example, from "most true of this case" to "least true."

[123] Dr. Boehm graciously made available the analysis of the Q-sort data. The descriptions were permitted the writer by Dr. Boehm.

[124] Henry C. Lajewski, *Child Care Arrangements of Full-Time Working Mothers*, Children's Bureau Publication No. 378 (Washington, D.C.: U.S. Department of Health, Education, and Welfare, Children's Bureau, 1959).

[125] Alberta Engvall Siegel *et al.*, "Dependence and Independence in Children of Working Mothers," *Child Development*, Vol. 30, No. 4 (December 1959), pp. 533–546.

of working and nonworking mothers were selected and their children were observed during the free period of the day during kindergarten. In all, twenty-six matched pairs were obtained, with the observers not knowing which member of any pair represented the child of a working or nonworking mother. These investigators reported that they did not find differences between the children of working and nonworking mothers with respect to dependent and independent behavior. Those significant differences that did emerge in the analysis were so few that it was felt they represented chance findings only. It was suggested, however, that a mother's employment has different consequences for the two sexes.

Siegel's findings tended to be supported by research undertaken by Burchinal in a study of seventh- and eleventh-grade school children in Cedar Rapids, Iowa.[126] No difference was found in the children's perceptions of family relationships for those whose mothers had been employed during the past thirty months and those whose mothers had not. Maternal employment did not appear to be related to the children's reports of the degree to which they had regular jobs at home, their feeling of the legitimacy of the amount of work they were required to perform, whether they were provided an allowance or whether they had to earn the allowance by working at home. Except for eleventh-grade girls, there appeared to be no significant relationship between maternal employment during the thirty months and the school adjustment of the children. It was found, however, that for eleventh-grade girls whose mothers had been employed during the prior months, there was a less positive attitude toward school than for corresponding girls whose mothers were not employed,

but the difference was not statistically strong.

In a systematic review of research on the effects of maternal employment, Stolz was impressed with the number of different and opposing findings that have emerged from a number of studies.[127] She comments: "One can say almost anything one desires about the children of employed mothers and support the statements by some research study." Citing many conflicting findings about the linkage between employment of mothers and such phenomena as delinquency rates, adjustment of elementary school and adolescent children, achievement in school, and the development and adjustment of preschool children, she suggests that some of this confusion may be due to the lack of control over pertinent variables, such as socioeconomic status and intactness and size of family. Another factor that may have influenced the results of some of these studies may be the time of data collection. Many changes have taken place in the cultural milieu in the United States after World War II and these changes may account for some of the shifts in findings that have been reported.

The research of Hoffman has pointed up the need to differentiate among various types of working mothers.[128] She suggests the importance of investigating the attitude of the mother toward her work as an important intervening variable in studies of the effects of maternal employment. Her findings suggest that the mother who likes working is relatively high in positive affect toward the child, uses mild discipline, and tends to avoid imposing upon the child a battery of household tasks. The working mother who dislikes working, on the other hand, seems to be less involved with the

[126] Lee G. Burchinal, *Maternal Employment, Family Relations and Selected Personality, School-Related and Social-Development Characteristics of Children*, Research Bulletin 497 (Ames, Iowa: Agricultural and Home Economics Experiment Station, Iowa State University, 1961).

[127] Lois Meek Stolz, "Effects of Maternal Employment on Children: Evidence from Research," *Child Development*, Vol. 31, No. 4 (December 1960), pp. 749–782.
[128] Lois Wladis Hoffman, "Effects of Maternal Employment on the Child," *Child Development*, Vol. 32, No. 1 (March 1961), pp. 187–197.

child altogether and yet makes appreciable demands upon him for help with household tasks. Hoffman found that the child of the first type of mother tends to be nonassertive and somewhat ineffective, whereas the child of the second type of mother tends to be assertive and hostile. While both groups of children with working mothers show indications of maladjustment, it appears they show different syndromes. Hoffman points up the need for studying some of the intervening variables that link maternal employment with child adjustment, such as the effect of employment on parent-child relationships, family structure, or other aspects of family life.

While there have been a number of studies that have explored the effects of mothers' outside employment upon their children, there have been relatively few reports including as subjects the mother substitutes used by working mothers. Perry reports on interviews conducted with 104 nonemployed mothers, 104 employed mothers, and 82 mother substitutes.[129] Three unidimensional scales measuring children's nervous symptoms, antisocial tendencies, and withdrawal tendencies were created for the purpose of measuring the developmental progress of the subjects.

Perry's findings indicated no significant difference in adjustment on the scales between the children of employed mothers and those of nonemployed mothers. Reasons given by the mother substitutes for assuming the task of caring for other persons' children were: (1) it permitted the mother substitute to remain at home with her own children; (2) it provided her children or herself with companionship; (3) it was easier than other jobs; and (4) a general liking for children or those in her care. There was little disagreement between the employed mothers and the mother substitutes on procedures of child care. Eighty-seven percent of the mother substitutes stated that there had been no disagreement with the parents on such problems. The employed mothers were asked their judgment of the mother substitutes' attitudes toward their children. In general, it was shown that the employed mothers had conceptions of the desirable characteristics of mother substitutes that were fairly well met in the arrangements they had made.

Determining Need for Day Care

The importance of the increased population of working mothers in the United States for the field of social welfare stems from the service needs that may be linked with this phenomenon. Communities throughout the United States are confronted with the task of making decisions about services for the care of children whose mothers may be employed or absent from the home for other causes. Communities face problems in determining the quantity, location, and kind of services these children need.

One attempt to place the social planning aspects of day care on a more scientific basis was reported by Wiener, who used Wichita, Kansas, as a testing ground for determining what kind of research method might best be employed to determine the need for day care services.[130] Of particular importance was his finding that the choice of survey method employed by an investigator might affect the representativeness of the sample and, as a result, the findings as to the number of children in need. He found, for example, that estimates based upon school and industrial surveys for preschool children were not similar to residential survey estimates, probably because of the sampling inadequacy for the preschool children who were covered by the former types of survey. Wiener also

[129] Joseph B. Perry, "The Mother Substitutes of Employed Mothers: An Exploratory Inquiry," *Marriage and Family Living*, Vol. 23, No. 4 (November 1961), pp. 362–367.

[130] Jack Wiener, *Survey Methods for Determining the Need for Services to Children of Working Mothers* (Washington, D.C.: U.S. Department of Health, Education, and Welfare, Children's Bureau, 1956).

makes the point that a questionnaire survey will probably underestimate the need for child care facilities unless there is provision for follow-up interviews with the mothers who have failed to return the forms. He also found that survey findings of the number of children requiring child care services would vary markedly depending upon the criteria used to determine the need for a day care service. While some mothers reported that their biggest problem was to provide care for their children while they worked, they did not always indicate they would use a community child care facility if one were provided.

A most ambitious three-stage study of day care arrangements in the United States has recently been completed by Ruderman for the Child Welfare League of America.[131] The study covers seven communities in different regions; these vary widely with respect to size, demographic characteristics, available day care resources, and patterns of community welfare organization. Attempting to view daytime child care within the context of the contemporary American scene, this study is the largest cross-sectional survey study yet undertaken under social work auspices. In the first stage, a mail questionnaire was sent to leadership groups in each of the seven communities. These included professional social workers, board members of social agencies, members of business groups, labor, and clergy. The return rate reported by Ruderman for the questionnaire was better than 60 percent (n=2,100). In general, it was found that day care was regarded by the majority as a service of only moderate priority, although social workers ranked it higher than did board members of agencies, the clergy, businessmen, and labor officials.[132]

The second stage of the league's day care study involved depth interviews with some three hundred mothers in each of the seven communities, and two hundred additional interviews in the suburban area of one community—all selected through area probability sampling methods. The interview covered family composition, background data, divisions of responsibility in the family, and considerable detail about the day care arrangement currently in use in the family and the mother's assessments of the arrangement. The third stage involved an examination of the community's day care resources, including an inventory of these facilities. A random sample of the facilities was selected for special study by day care consultants. Data in this study are currently being analyzed and written up. It is anticipated that the final report of this study will have considerable value for those responsible for the development of day care resources in communities across the United States.

Social Policy and Child Welfare

Some of the research cited in this review has dealt with the effects upon personality development of various types of child care arrangements for children deprived of adequate parents. Such studies are increasingly reported in the professional literature, and it is anticipated that there will be no diminution of such research during the years ahead. Such research is necessary for the rational development of child welfare services that can best restore children to normal functioning.

At the same time, there is a need to examine child welfare from a macroscopic point of view—to locate problems and services within the larger fabric of American society and to plan within the framework of long-range perspectives for community services. Investigators such as Kahn have done yeoman service in pulling together various types of social trend data to pro-

---

[131] Florence A. Ruderman, "The Child Welfare League's Day Care Project: Research and Action," *Child Welfare*, Vol. 40, No. 5 (May 1961), pp. 24–27.

[132] Florence A. Ruderman, "Report on Stage I of the Day Care Project: Community Opinions on Day Care," preliminary report (New York: Child Welfare League of America, 1962). (Mimeographed).

vide a context within which services for children might better be co-ordinated and mobilized on behalf of children.[133] He has undertaken the very urgent task of attempting to make sense out of the varied findings coming from a variety of research projects and to spell out their implications for service to children. The fact remains clear that no individual investigator in child welfare research has been able to integrate his particular project with the many others currently extant, and until this integration takes place much of the research that has been reported will not be utilized. In reacting to the research that has been accomplished in child welfare, Kahn underscores the need for early, concise case planning and evaluation of children's needs at critical points in their life situations.

Kahn makes a particular plea for case accountability. A community that intervenes in family life by separating children from parents, even on a temporary basis, has the obligation to follow up on plans, appraisals, and objectives so that they can be implemented before the child is damaged by having to wait for help, or for other reasons. He notes:

Accountability involves honest reporting as to whether the agency's system is capable of attaining community objectives. Thus, a community has a problem if family agencies offer little or no direct work with children in their own homes; if most foster boarding care in a state is public, while most adoption is private; if child guidance "treats" but child welfare does not. These and comparable situations demand organizational and professional solutions, and it is in the nature of agency responsibility (or the responsibility of co-ordinating bodies) to initiate them.[134]

Kahn's work and that of others point up the fact that services for children may well be shaped by social attitudes held by key community leaders as much as by individual factors in case situations. These attitudes were shown to be operative in the previously cited study by Ruderman of day care needs. In similar fashion, Nettler undertook to assess the attitudes of community leaders in Houston, Texas, about child welfare problems.[135] He found that board members tended to be more punitive, more voluntary-minded, and to perceive less inadequacy in services than did child welfare personnel, educators, ministers, pediatricians, and other professional persons. He also found them to be less deterministic, i.e., tending to see deviant behavior less as a product of present and past experiences and more as an idiosyncrasy of the individual. The tendency was to see deviant behavior in children as a consequence of "free will" rather than something linked to specific experiences.

Cross-Cultural Studies

As part of the over-all effort to obtain some perspective on child welfare services in the United States, a number of investigators have been looking into the methods of care provided in other cultures as one way of developing a more balanced viewpoint. Thus, there has been considerable interest in the consequences of group care for children living under the group conditions provided by the *kibbutz* in Israel. Rabin, for example, gave a number of projective tests to children reared in a *kibbutz* and those reared in conventional family and social settings. He reported:

From the data presented, it was concluded that the Kibbutz adolescent is at least as well adjusted as his non-Kibbutz counterpart; there is some evidence that he is more spontaneous and at least as intelligent. The Kibbutz adolescent does not seem to differ from the control with respect to positiveness of at-

[133] Alfred J. Kahn, "Child Welfare: Trends and Directions," *Child Welfare*, Vol. 41, No. 10 (December 1962), pp. 459–476; and Alfred J. Kahn, "The Social Scene and the Planning of Services for Children," *Social Work*, Vol. 7, No. 3 (July 1962), pp. 3–14.

[134] Kahn, "The Social Scene and the Planning of Services for Children," p. 13.

[135] Gwynn Nettler, "Ideology and Welfare Policy," *Social Problems*, Vol. 6, No. 3 (Winter 1958–1959), pp. 203–212.

titude to parent; also he tends to be less in conflict with them and to involve them less in his fantasy productions. He is more rigidly concerned with taboos on premarital sexuality, less self-motivated and less "ambitious" in our conventional sense.[136]

In order to increase understanding about the effect of group care in a variety of cultures and translate these findings for use in the United States, Wolins has undertaken to study children reared away from their families in the Soviet Union, Poland, Yugoslavia, and Israel.[137] He reports on a preliminary analysis of psychological protocols of children reared in a *kibbutz,* and supports the findings of other investigators. There exists a strong sense of group identification among these children, a sense of security within the group, and the absence of success strivings and a willingness to assume social responsibilities.

One can predict that there will be an increasing number of studies of child welfare facilities abroad whose main aim will be to help social planners on the American scene reassess, in the light of current unsolved problems, the traditional attitudes toward group care facilities. Kahn, for example, has made the following points about children in foster care who are replaced with disturbing frequency:

The research literature would seem to suggest that: 1) children certainly do need warm, intimate primary relationships with adults to grow up satisfactorily. 2) The congregate institutions of the 1930's were inadequate in this regard and the attempts to substitute foster care were justified. 3) There is, however, no evidence of the superiority of many of the types of foster homes now in use over large "family groups" in agency sponsored group homes or smaller institutions with relatively high staff-child ratios and relatively small cottage groupings. 4) It is highly likely that the latter types of facilities are far superior to currently used large congregate facilities in which children live in unstable

temporary large groups and are cared for by three shifts of counselors at a low staff-child ratio, facilities which are justified as "temporary shelter" even though children wait in them for foster homes or residential treatment for months or years. In short, every facility called "institution" or "group home" need not look like the Mexican one in Rene Spitz's "Hospitalism" studies, on which a generation of child care workers has been reared. Moreover, few foster homes are as good as the ideal types of the professional literature.[138]

Future Perspectives

It is obvious from the range of studies cited in this review that child welfare research has, in the past decade, begun to emerge as an area of increasing productivity. The total panorama of the child welfare scene is now becoming the object of multifarious research endeavors. Yet, it is obvious that much of the research spadework for building a knowledge base for child welfare has only partially been undertaken. Some of the basic questions that will need special research attention include the following:

1. What is the nature of maternal deprivation as it affects children who come to the attention of child welfare agencies? It is obvious from the previously cited literature of Bowlby, Ainsworth, and Yarrow that there is still a great deal to be learned about the effects upon children of being separated from their natural parents and receiving some form of substitute care. Relatively little is known about the significance of constitutional factors in children and how these are affected by different kinds of living experiences. Some children in the same settings withstand almost total parental deprivation without any serious distortions in personality and social adjustments, while other youngsters in family settings seem to be almost destroyed by the experience. It is obvious that more research will be required to shed light upon this complex problem, and specific aspects of personality and social interaction will have to

---

[136] Albert I. Rabin, "Culture Components as a Significant Factor in Child Development," *American Journal of Orthopsychiatry,* Vol. 31, No. 3 (July 1961), pp. 493–504.

[137] Wolins, "Some Theory and Practice in Child Care: A Cross-Cultural View."

[138] Kahn, "The Social Scene and the Planning of Services for Children," p. 9.

be studied to spell out the effects of such deprivation. For example, intelligence, cognitive development, value orientations, self-image, and identification are aspects of the child's total personality. These will need to be analyzed more precisely in future deprivation studies. Also, as Yarrow and others suggest, there are a variety of types of deprivation that children encounter and each will have to be singled out for its unique consequences.

2. What kinds of restitutive forces can be mobilized by the community on behalf of children who have suffered damage as a consequence of parental deprivation? What is the role of various treatment agencies in this area? Can the kinds of disturbances shown by these children be classified so as to mobilize more effectively specific treatment efforts? The large question is which consequences of deprivation experienced by children known to child welfare agencies are reversible and which lead to deficiencies that can never be overcome.

3. What can be learned about some of the major actors involved in the child welfare services that are now being offered children? Can more be learned about the motivations of foster parents, particularly those who can tolerate and not exacerbate the behavior of emotionally disturbed children? What can be discovered about finding adoptive parents for the so-called "hard-to-place" child? What kinds of individuals can best give service to emotionally disturbed children in treatment institutions, including residential treatment centers? What roles do the social caseworker, the group worker, and other professionals play in the ongoing life of the child deprived of his parents?

4. Can the organization of services for needy children be established on a more rational basis, in which the goals of service can be better explicated and meshed within a network offering a variety of types of care? How can the larger society be mobilized on behalf of this sizable group of children?

For almost all these questions, as this review of child welfare research has shown, only beginning answers have been found. Across the board there is need for more refined, differentiating, and contingency-linked answers.

NEIGHBORHOOD CENTERS

By WILLIAM SCHWARTZ

From Williamson's 1929 personnel study of the agencies that "have a common function of dealing with individuals in groups" to Vinter's analysis of group work and recreation services in Detroit thirty years later, it has been pointed out many times that group work is practiced not in a unified field of service but in a loose assortment of agencies with diverse traditions and purposes.[1] Even as this inquiry is limited to the "neighborhood center" segment—excluding the psychiatric and medical hospitals and clinics, institutions, camps, family agencies, public recreation facilities, and other settings in which group work is practiced—there still remains an array of different objectives and client groups, as well as a wide gamut of commitments ranging over the fields of education, recreation, social service, psychotherapy, and social reform.

Yet whether or not one can define the field precisely, these agencies—*building centered* like the settlements, "Y's," Jewish Centers, and Boys' Clubs; and *program centered* like the Boy Scouts, Camp Fire Girls, and the B'nai B'rith Youth Organization—operate in the heart of the American urban neighborhood and are historically connected, in varying degrees, with the field of social welfare and the profession of social work. As such, they have a potential as yet only barely realized for affecting deeply the scope and quality of the social welfare performance where it is most needed. Much will depend on the extent

[1] Margaretta Williamson, *The Social Worker in Group Work* (New York: Harper & Brothers, 1929); Robert D. Vinter, "New Evidence for Restructuring Group Services," in *New Perspectives on Services to Groups: Theory, Organization, Practice*, selected group work papers from the 1961 National Conference on Social Welfare (New York: National Association of Social Workers, 1961). *See also* William Schwartz, "Group Work and the Social Scene," in Alfred J. Kahn, ed., *Issues in American Social Work* (New York: Columbia University Press, 1959), pp. 110–137.

to which these agencies can follow both the field and the profession into a closer working relationship with science and research.

To this end, it becomes useful periodically to review past research, to reveal some of the work currently in progress, and to draw some implications for further study. An attempt should also be made to assess related research from allied fields, but here the problem of relevance is a difficult one. When agency purposes are so all embracing and ill defined, when the client group is almost unlimited, and when the "client" concept itself includes not only the people but the vehicles in which they move together (the family, the group, the neighborhood), the relevant scientific data are encyclopedic. Nevertheless, additional references will be pointed out in this review for those interested in particular lines of inquiry.

In choosing agency studies for inclusion, an attempt has been made to be as comprehensive as possible, while neither overstating nor underplaying the achievements to date. Following Zimbalist, "research" has been defined here as any effort to collect and analyze data in a planned attempt to answer questions or test hypotheses arising out of the planning and practice of relevant agencies.[2] Published accounts have been favored, but many mimeographed documents describing some important work and a number of studies in progress are also included. Student research has been drawn in where possible, but any systematic review of this work would require a special effort similar to those of Van der Smissen in the field of recreation and Gordon in his analysis of thesis titles in social work.[3]

Although there have been a few research reviews relevant to some aspects of group work practice, this seems to be the first attempt to draw together a fairly inclusive summary of neighborhood center research as such; it may thus be expected to suffer from the crudeness of a first try. Some background material was particularly helpful: historical and technical discussions by Zimbalist, Kahn, Tyler, and Greenwood; group work research reviews by Vinter, Konopka, Northen, Klein, and Zander; summaries of unpublished work by two research committees of the professional association; and some more specific agency materials from Hillman, Brown, Sanua, Eaton and Harrison, and the Boy Scouts of America.[4]

---

[2] Sidney Eli Zimbalist, "Major Trends in Social Work Research: An Analysis of the Nature and Development of Research in Social Work, as Seen in the Periodical Literature, 1900–1950," p. 12. Unpublished doctoral dissertation, George Warren Brown School of Social Work, Washington University, 1955.

[3] Betty Van der Smissen, "A Bibliography of Research (Theses and Dissertations Only) Related to Recreation" (Iowa City: State University of Iowa, 1962) (mimeographed); and William E. Gordon, *The Focus and Nature of Research Completed by Graduate Students in Approved Schools of Social Work, 1940–1949, as Indicated by Thesis and Project Titles* (New York: American Association of Schools of Social Work, 1951).

[4] Zimbalist, *op. cit.;* Alfred J. Kahn, "The Design of Research," in Norman A. Polansky, ed., *Social Work Research* (Chicago: University of Chicago Press, 1960), pp. 48–73; Ralph W. Tyler, "Implications of Research in the Behavioral Sciences for Group Life and Group Services," in *Social Welfare Forum, 1960,* proceedings of the National Conference on Social Welfare (New York: Columbia University Press, 1960), pp. 113–126; Ernest Greenwood, "Social Science and Social Work: A Theory of Their Relationship," *Social Service Review,* Vol. 29, No. 1 (March 1955), pp. 20–33; Robert D. Vinter, "Group Work with Children and Youth: Research Problems and Possibilities," *Social Service Review,* Vol. 30, No. 3 (September 1956), pp. 310–318; Gisela Konopka, "Group Work with Children and Youth: Unanswered Questions," *Social Service Review,* Vol. 30, No. 3 (September 1956), pp. 300–309; Helen Northen, "What is Researchable in Social Group Work?" in *Social Work With Groups, 1959,* selected papers from the National Conference on Social Welfare (New York: National Association of Social Workers, 1959), pp. 149–160; Alan F. Klein, "Role and Reference Group Theory: Implications for Social Group Work Research," in Leonard S. Kogan, ed., *Social Science Theory and Social Work Research* (New York: National As-

The studies will be discussed in five sections: (1) clients and their problems; (2) the agency as a vehicle of service; (3) neighborhood and community problems related to the function of the centers; (4) the worker and the practice of group work; and (5) the measurement of outcome. Some final comments will be directed to implications for future research.

The Client

The traditional approach of the neighborhood centers to those they serve has been that of an organization to its "members," rather than a social agency to its "clients." The complex historical issues involved in the use of these terms have been discussed by Reynolds and more recently by Vinik, and they are not within the scope of this review.[5] It should be noted, however, that

the membership concept creates interest in certain kinds of problems—notably those of recruitment, dropout, and factors involving the interests of current and potential members. These are, of course, important to social agencies as well as membership groups, but the latter emphasis sometimes invests the research effort with a kind of "market research" quality, when the investigation is designed to uncover the "buying habits" of a target population so that the product—or program—can be fashioned to meet consumer demand.

In addition to these studies of member participation, needs, and interests there is a body of work directed to certain special problems and populations and to the group itself as an instrument of service—a concept sometimes expressed in the term "the group as a client."

Participation Factors

The studies on hand reveal a number of factors that seem to affect the process of client selection in the neighborhood centers. The clearest case seems to have been made for the fact that agency membership, in both the building-centered and the program-centered organizations, tends to be drawn from the higher, rather than the lower, socioeconomic groups in the community. These findings are similar to those reported by Cloward on the clientele of the private family agencies.[6] The Survey Research Center of the University of Michigan, in studies of the general population of boys

sociation of Social Workers, 1960), pp. 32–45; Alvin F. Zander, "Current Research in Group Work," in *Toward Professional Standards* (New York: American Association of Group Workers, 1947), pp. 37–50; American Association of Group Workers, Research and Study Committee, "Selected Studies and Research Projects in Group Work, 1948–1953" (New York, 1954) (mimeographed); National Association of Social Workers, "Inventory of Research of Group Work Practice, 1955–1960" (New York, undated) (mimeographed); Arthur Hillman, *Neighborhood Centers Today: Action Programs for a Rapidly Changing World* (New York: National Federation of Settlements and Neighborhood Centers, 1960), chap. 7; Susan Jenkins Brown, *The Helen Hall Settlement Papers: A Descriptive Bibliography of Community Studies and Other Reports, 1928–1958* (New York: Henry Street Settlement, 1959); Victor D. Sanua, "Social Science Research Relevant to American Jewish Education: Fifth Bibliographic Review," *Jewish Education,* Vol. 33, No. 3 (Spring 1963), pp. 162–175; Allen Eaton and Shelby M. Harrison, *A Bibliography of Social Surveys: Reports of Fact-Finding Studies Made as a Basis for Social Action* (New York: Russell Sage Foundation, 1930); and Boy Scouts of America, "Bibliography of Studies on Scouting" (New York, 1962) (mimeographed).

[5] Bertha Capen Reynolds, *Social Work and*

Social Living (New York: Citadel Press, 1951); and Abe Vinik, "Role of the Group Service Agency," *Social Work,* Vol. 9, No. 3 (July 1964), pp. 98–105.

[6] Richard A. Cloward and Irwin Epstein, "Private Social Welfare's Disengagement from the Poor: The Case of Family Adjustment Agencies" (New York: Research Center, Columbia University School of Social Work, 1964). (Mimeographed.) To be published in Arthur Pearl and Frank Riessman, eds., "Poverty and Low Income Culture: Ten Views," by the National Institute of Mental Health.

11 to 13 and 14 to 16 years of age, undertaken for the Boy Scouts of America, found that those who were most involved in organizations tended to live in the smaller central cities, had more possessions, better educated parents, more autonomy within the home, and were punished less by their parents.[7] In a study of Boy Scout membership, the Survey Research Center verified the greater participation of boys from higher-status families, and also found that Negro membership was about proportional to its percentage in the general community —a significant finding in view of the greater need and lower social status of this segment of the population.[8] In yet another SRC study, this time for the Girl Scouts, Douvan and Kaye found that the unaffiliated segment of a large general sample of adolescent girls—about 25 percent— was predominantly from the lower socioeconomic group.[9] Again, a study of the Girl Scout membership by the SRC produced verification and an additional finding that lower-income children tended to drop out sooner, with reasons less often related to loss of interest.[10] Many years before, in 1937, Young's *Report of the Girl Scout Program Study* had pointed out that

the proportion of Girl Scouts to all girls in all communities is much larger in the middle and upper income groups, although admittedly large numbers of girls from low income groups are to be found in Girl Scouting . . . Where Girl Scouts are found in lowest proportions, there the percentage of foreign born is greatest and the delinquency and dependency rates are the highest.[11]

In other settings, studies of youth memberships show some agreement. Lippitt's "game-board" interviews of 1,117 Camp Fire Girls in a nationwide sample disclosed that the agency served a high economic group—92 percent native born, 98 percent white, and 79 percent Protestant.[12] Sanua, in a demographic study of four Jewish community centers, found a broad distribution on the Hollingshead-Redlich class scale, but generally high-status educational, religious, and professional characteristics.[13] Jacobs, in a study of the membership of eleven recreational agencies in the Germantown section of Philadelphia, found that the membership was again roughly equal to the racial composition of the area but that the nonwhite members were a distinctly younger group.[14] Even the Boys' Clubs of America, serving primarily a working-class group, found that a high proportion of its members were from the more stable segment of the population—native born, predominantly white, from a high proportion of intact families, and almost 100 percent of Catholic or Protestant religious affiliations.[15]

[7] Survey Research Center, Institute for Social Research, University of Michigan, *A Study of Boys Becoming Adolescents* (Ann Arbor: Survey Research Center for the National Council, Boy Scouts of America, 1960) ; and S. B. Withey and E. Douvan, *A Study of Adolescent Boys* (Ann Arbor: Survey Research Center, Institute for Social Research, University of Michigan, 1955).

[8] Survey Research Center, Institute for Social Research, University of Michigan, *A Study of Boy Scouts and Their Scoutmasters* (Ann Arbor: 1960).

[9] E. Douvan and C. Kaye, *Adolescent Girls* (Ann Arbor: Survey Research Center, Institute for Social Research, University of Michigan, 1957).

[10] Survey Research Center, Institute for Social Research, University of Michigan, *The Program of the Girl Scouts of America* (Ann Arbor: Survey Research Center for the Girl Scouts of America, 1958).

[11] Charles H. Young *et al., Report of the Girl Scout Program Study* (New York: Girl Scouts of America, 1937), p. 16.

[12] Rosemary Lippitt, *They Told Us What They Wanted—Report of the Camp Fire Girls Program Study* (New York: Camp Fire Girls, 1946).

[13] Victor D. Sanua, "Preliminary Research Findings in Jewish Community Centers," *Journal of Jewish Communal Service*, Vol. 40, No. 2 (Winter 1963), pp. 143–152.

[14] Jerome H. Jacobs, "Who and Where? A Survey on Recreation in Germantown," Special Report No. 10 (Philadelphia: Health and Welfare Council, 1961). (Mimeographed.)

[15] Boys' Clubs of America, *Needs and Interests of Adolescent Boys' Club Members* (New York, 1960).

Other studies cite findings that might reasonably be considered class related. Some small studies of dropouts in three New York City settlements revealed a preponderance of member comments directed to factors of association ("the crowd is too rough," "too many non-Jews," and so on); agency demands and procedures ("the rules are too strict," and so on); and other possible indicators of a drift toward class homogeneity and agency-client norm discrepancies.[16] The New York City Youth Board, investigating the high agency dropout rate of 15- to 19-year-olds, received responses from sixty agencies, in which high importance was ascribed to rigid agency requirements and to "workers who act like policemen or preachers."[17] Ellsworth, in a study of young adults, found that the YMCA members in his population had little concept of the "deeper meaning of Y membership" and were "least in accord with staff in relation to program."[18]

There are some scattered data suggesting other factors that affect participation. On *area of residence,* an early study of New York City settlements, a recent self-study of thirteen Los Angeles settlements, and some other studies have found that the great majority of neighborhood center members live within a few blocks' radius of the agency.[19] On *age,* it has been suggested

that the ages 11 to 13 are optimal for membership in organized club groups, that organized group participation decreases progressively as age increases, and that there is a "slow evolution" of attitudes and concerns in boys 11 to 13 years of age, when "the pace of change is more often set by school grade rather than by age."[20] On *membership motivation,* it has been found that both children and adults tend to join an agency because of specific activity interests rather than a general commitment to agency philosophy and objectives.[21]

Needs and Interests

Field-generated knowledge about client needs is scanty and substantively diffuse, emerging largely from broad population surveys and opinion studies. Many of the researches mentioned in the previous section have yielded information, more or less penetrating, in this area. The Survey Research Center found that four out of every twenty boys in the 11- to 13-year-

---

[16] Canio J. DeVito, "A Study of Drop-outs," unpublished master's thesis, New York School of Social Work, Columbia University, 1955; Melvin M. Kuwamoto, "A Study of Seventeen Dropouts," unpublished master's thesis, New York School of Social Work, Columbia University, 1955; and Sheila Pekowsky, "Where Have They Gone?" unpublished master's thesis, New York School of Social Work, Columbia University, 1954.

[17] New York City Youth Board, *Reaching Teenagers Through Group Work and Recreation Programs,* Monograph No. 1 (New York, 1954).

[18] Allen S. Ellsworth, *Young Men and Young Women: New Insights on Becoming Adult* (New York: Young Men's Christian Association, 1963), pp. 3–4.

[19] Albert J. Kennedy, Kathryn Farra, and

associates, *Social Settlements in New York City: Their Activities, Policies, and Administration* (New York: Columbia University Press, 1935); and Margaret Hirschfeld, "Neighborhood Centers" (Los Angeles: Welfare Federation of Los Angeles Area, 1961) (mimeographed).

[20] Lippitt, *op. cit.;* Boys' Clubs of America, *op. cit.;* Alvin Zander *et al.,* "Straight from the Boy on Why Scouts Drop—And What to Do About It." in *Scouting for Facts with a Local Council* (New York: Boy Scouts of America, 1945); Douvan and Kaye, *op. cit.;* and Survey Research Center, *A Study of Boys Becoming Adolescents,* p. 206.

[21] Boys' Clubs of America, *op. cit.;* Kennedy, Farra, and associates, *op. cit.;* Stanley W. Harris, "The Expressed Interests of Two Hundred Jewish Teen-Agers," *Journal of Jewish Communal Service,* Vol. 32, No. 4 (Summer 1956), pp. 406–415; Ellsworth, *op. cit.;* and Harry Specht, "Jewish Young Adults and the Jewish Communuity Center," unpublished doctoral dissertation, Florence Heller School for Advanced Studies in Social Welfare, Brandeis University, 1963.

old group chose a glamour figure as their hero, but "by the time these boys are 14–16, that figure is more than cut in half."[22] They found, too, that the younger boys seemed more likely to refer openly to their anxieties about war, accidents, and disasters.

The Metropolitan Chicago YMCA, in an opinion survey of 30,000 adolescents in the Chicago area, reported that two out of every five boys expressed an active fear of failure, and three out of five expressed doubt that their minds work normally.[23] Lippitt, in her previously cited study of grouping preferences among the Camp Fire Girls, found that respondents wanted to be in the middle of their age range, preferring companions either one year older or younger.

Some data point to a kind of continuing struggle between clients and agency staff to define the germane needs and interests of the clients. Thus, almost all of the program and interest studies noted above found desires on the part of the children for more active programs, fewer "social" themes and conversations, more autonomy, less dependency, and more member-direction. Such desires, increasing with age, might account for a great part of the organizational dropout rate in adolescence.

Zander and Hogrefe's research on five hundred dropped Boy Scouts from ten communities traced differential dropout patterns relating to age, scout rank, tenure, economic group, and other factors.[24] Similarly, Harris found that his B'nai B'rith adolescents had less interest in community service activities as they grew older; that their greatest interest lay in concrete, informal, active programs; that "Jewish content activities rated last for the boys and second to last for the girls"; and that interest declined as program emphasis moved from local to national concerns.[25] Sanua's Jewish Center mothers "did not perceive the center as an agency which fosters Jewish identification for their children," and had little objection to non-Jewish members and leaders in the program; in his study of adolescents, he found the term "Jewish" identified as a religious rather than a cultural concept.[26]

The divergence between client and staff perceptions of need is dramatically illustrated in some studies of the relationship between young adults and the neighborhood agencies. Ellsworth, Olds and Josephson, Rosenthal and Schatz, and Specht have all noted that young adults are a most difficult age group to involve in organized agency activity, and they have commented that staff workers tend to ascribe this reluctance to such young adult characteristics as superficiality, restlessness, and narrow horizons rather than to inadequate provision for their developmental needs.[27] Ellsworth found his YMCA members "least in accord with staff in relation to program."[28] Olds and Josephson called particular attention to the discrepancy between organizational aims and what staff workers perceive as the "merely social" interests of young adults, and Specht pointed out that Jewish Center personnel "appear to frown on the types of programs which are geared to meet the courtship needs of young adults."[29]

---

[22] Survey Research Center, *A Study of Boys Becoming Adolescents*, p. 207.

[23] Sears, Roebuck and Company, National Personnel Department, Psychological Services Section, "The Youth of Chicagoland: A Study of Its Attitudes, Beliefs, Ideas, and Problems," a study conducted for, and in conjunction with, the Young Men's Christian Association of Metropolitan Chicago (Chicago, undated). (Mimeographed.)

[24] Alvin Zander *et al.*, *op. cit.*

[25] Harris, *op. cit.*, p. 408.

[26] Sanua, *op. cit.*

[27] Ellsworth, *op. cit.*; Edward B. Olds and Eric Josephson, *Young Adults and Citizenship* (New York: National Social Welfare Assembly, 1953); William Rosenthal and Harry A. Schatz, *Young Adults and the Jewish Community Center* (New York: National Jewish Welfare Board, 1956); and Specht, *op. cit.*

[28] Ellsworth, *op. cit.*, p. 4

[29] Specht, *op. cit.*, p. 444.

Special Problems and Populations

A number of studies have been generated by the agencies' concern for particular clients with special problems. The bulk of this work seems to be concentrated in three categories: (1) the research on cultural identification and "belongingness," with which the Jewish Centers have been particularly concerned; (2) the studies emerging from the various "reaching-out" programs aimed at street-club adolescents who do not lend themselves easily to service within agency walls; and (3) the newer work with handicapped people whom agencies have undertaken to integrate into their ongoing programs.

Identification and belongingness. Space does not permit an adequate summary of studies on the identification problems associated with minority group membership. While the research is still sporadic, the group survival emphasis of the Jewish Centers has stimulated some interesting work, much of it generated by Kurt Lewin's field theory on belongingness.[30] Aside from references already made to studies by Sanua, Harris, and Specht, fruitful lines of research have been opened by Hurwitz, Chein, Canter and Rothman.

Hurwitz studied the self-perceptions of Jewish Center children in twenty-four groups and found differences among children designated as "orthodox oriented," "center oriented," or "community oriented." [31] His orthodox-oriented children, closely related to their religion, seemed more secure when younger, but developed more intense antagonisms toward nonobservant elements in their own culture as they grew older; the center-oriented children, defined as those who tried to live in two cultures, generated more rebellion against the culture of the parents as the difference in cultures became more marked; and his community-oriented children, fairly well adjusted to the American culture, tended to accept anti-Semitic positions along with other majority group values, thus demonstrating most clearly Lewin's concept of "self-hate."

Chein, commenting on the Hurwitz study in what he calls an "action research perspective," points out that what these three groups have in common is the fact that their Jewishness is for them "a source of confusion, ambivalence and divergent goals." He concludes that, for the Jewish child:

the help he most needs in finding himself is not *teaching*, but assistance in unravelling his own problems in the order and within the psychological settings in which they present themselves.[32]

In a later collaboration, Chein and Hurwitz studied 166 boys in fourteen different Jewish Centers in metropolitan New York, comparing attitudes of group members by age, socioeconomic grouping, and the extent to which they were exposed to Jewish observances in their homes.[33] They found significant differences, which they summarized as follows:

If we were to reduce these patterns to a single statement, it would be the following: with increasing acculturation (a process that probably goes on—though perhaps in different ways—with aging, with improved socio-economic status and, as a rule, with a perceptible decrease in Jewish environment) there is an increasing desire for social and cultural integration with the general community. In the case of the age and socio-economic breakdowns, this desire for social integration is clearly associated with increased defensiveness and feelings of insecurity.[34]

Canter surveyed the sociopsychological

---

[30] Kurt Lewin, *Resolving Social Conflicts* (New York: Harper & Brothers, 1948), Part 3.

[31] Jacob I. Hurwitz, "On Being a Jew: Perceptions, Attitudes, and Needs of Jewish Children," *Jewish Center Worker*, Vol. 9, No. 2 (May 1948), pp. 6–12.

[32] Isidor Chein. "The Problem of Belongingness: An Action Research Perspective," *Jewish Center Worker*, Vol. 9, No. 2 (May 1948), p. 16.

[33] Isidor Chein and Jacob I. Hurwitz, "The Reactions of Jewish Boys to Various Aspects of Being Jewish" (New York: National Jewish Welfare Board, 1949, reissued 1959). (Mimeographed.)

[34] *Ibid.*, p. 6.

research relevant to the problems of training workers in the Jewish settings, and he abstracted a number of "developmental tasks" of the Jewish adolescent.[35] He studied the effects of the Christmas holiday in the life of adolescents in the B'nai B'rith Youth Organization, and examined over one thousand records kept by workers on twenty-five groups that met at the Irene Kaufman Center in Pittsburgh between 1944 and 1946, defining and analyzing "situations of a Jewish nature" and the problems they create for both the member and the worker.[36] Rothman challenged some of Lewin's assumptions about the relationship between ingroup identification and outgroup association, and has developed an instrument designed to identify and measure the "belongingness" variable itself.[37]

Interest in the problems of minority group members vis-à-vis the larger culture is, of course, not restricted to the Jewish agencies; settlement and other neighborhood workers are continually concerned with these problems in the lives of Negroes, Catholics, and the various ethnic groups they serve. However, no evidence of any systematic study of these issues in these settings could be found.

The "hard-to-reach." Despite the traditional claim that the work of the neighborhood centers is related to the prevention of delinquency, it was not until the relatively recent movement of staff out of the buildings and into the streets that the agencies undertook their first serious engagement with nonconforming youth. It was at this point that they began to tap the street-work tradition of Aichhorn, Thrasher, Shaw, and Whyte; and to focus with some purpose on the body of delinquency research and the theoretical work of Cohen, Cloward and Ohlin, Kobrin, Miller, and others.[38] Typically, however, the centers have over the years produced some excellent service and very little research of their own. As Hogrefe and Harding put it: "Doing something with gangs has been easier than measuring the effectiveness of what was done."[39] It was not until the emergence of the more recent, well-financed, multifunction community-based projects

[35] Irving Canter, "What Research Tells Us About Training for the Jewish Component in the Practice of Group Work in Jewish Settings," *Journal of Jewish Communal Service*, Vol. 39, No. 3 (Spring 1963), pp. 266-285.

[36] Irving Canter, *Christmas in the Life of a Jewish Teenager* (Washington, D.C.: B'nai B'rith Youth Organization, 1960); and Irving Canter, "How the Jewish Center Members are Relating to Their Jewishness: A Study of Group Process Records," *Jewish Center Worker*, Vol. 11, No. 1 (February 1950), pp. 10–16.

[37] Jack Rothman, "Construction of an Instrument for Measuring Minority Group Identification Among Jewish Adolescents: An Exploratory Attempt," *Journal of Jewish Communal Service*, Vol. 34, No. 1 (Fall 1957), pp. 84–94; and Jack Rothman, "In-Group Identification and Out-Group Association: A Theoretical and Experimental Study," *Journal of Jewish Communal Service*, Vol. 37, No. 1 (Fall 1960), pp. 81–93.

[38] August Aichhorn, *Wayward Youth* (New York: Viking Press, 1935); Frederick M. Thrasher, *The Gang* (2d rev. ed.; Chicago: University of Chicago Press, 1936); Clifford R. Shaw, *The Jackroller* (Chicago: University of Chicago Press, 1930); William Foote Whyte, *Street Corner Society* (Chicago: University of Chicago Press, 1955); Oliver Moles, Ronald Lippitt, and Stephen Withey, *A Selective Review of Research and Theory on Delinquency* (2d ed.; Ann Arbor: Survey Research Center, Institute for Social Research, University of Michigan, 1959); Albert K. Cohen, *Delinquent Boys: The Culture of the Gang* (Glencoe, Ill.: Free Press, 1955); Richard A. Cloward and Lloyd E. Ohlin, *Delinquency and Opportunity: A Theory of Delinquent Gangs* (Glencoe, Ill.: Free Press, 1960); Solomon Kobrin, "The Chicago Area Project—A 25 Year Assessment," *Annals of the American Academy of Political and Social Science*, Vol. 322 (1959), pp. 19–29; and Walter B. Miller, "Lower Class Culture as a Generating Milieu of Gang Delinquency," *Journal of Social Issues*, Vol. 14, No. 3 (1958), pp. 5–19.

[39] Russell Hogrefe and John Harding, "Research Considerations in the Study of Street Gangs" (New York: Commission on Community Inter-relations of the American Jewish Congress, 1947), p. 1. (Mimeographed.)

that most of the continuous empirical work began.[40]

One of the earliest studies was produced by the Central Harlem Street Clubs Project, an action-research venture that leaned heavily on the analysis of case materials.[41] It developed some important insights into worker techniques, street club structure, the dependency needs of "hardened" youth, and the problems of working with those who withdraw into the use of drugs. The pioneer work of the New York City Youth Board has also been of great interest to the practitioner, although a good deal of its published material leans heavily on program description and interpretation rather than research.[42]

Some of the more theoretically oriented studies on the "hard-to-reach" have been published by Miller of the Boston Delinquency Project and by Short and his associates, working with the Program of Detached Workers of the YMCA of Metropolitan Chicago, and later followed up in the Youth Studies Program of the University of Chicago.[43] Miller has summarized

his findings on the relationship between gang delinquency and lower-class culture:

1. Following cultural practices which comprise essential elements of the total life pattern of lower class culture automatically violates certain legal norms. 2. In instances where alternate avenues to similar objectives are available, the non-law-abiding avenue frequently provides a relatively greater and more immediate return for a relatively smaller investment of energy. 3. The demanded response to certain situations recurrently engendered within lower class culture involves the commission of illegal acts.[44]

Short and his associates have tested hypotheses derived from the theoretical positions of Cohen, Miller, and Cloward and Ohlin—"hypotheses concerning the values of gang, non-gang lower-class, and non-gang middle-class boys." They found that:

. . . contrary to expectation, the data indicated no differences between gang, lower-class, and middle-class boys, both Negro and white, in their evaluation and legitimation of behaviors representing middle-class prescriptive norms . . . The samples differed most in their attitude toward the deviant behaviors, tending to form a gradient, with gang boys most tolerant, middle-class boys least tolerant.[45]

Short's project has also yielded data on the use of outgroup aggression by gang leaders as a means of reducing threats to their status; the sociological, cultural, and

---

[40] *See* Martin Gold and J. Alan Winter, *A Selective Review of Community-Based Programs for Preventing Delinquency* (Ann Arbor: Institute for Social Research, University of Michigan, 1961).

[41] Paul L. Crawford, Daniel I. Malamud, and James R. Dumpson, *Working with Teen-Age Gangs*, a report on the Central Harlem Street Clubs Project (New York: Welfare Council of New York City, 1950).

[42] New York City Youth Board, *Reaching the Fighting Gang* (New York, 1960).

[43] Walter B. Miller, "The Impact of a Community Program on Delinquent Corner Groups," *Social Service Review*, Vol. 31, No. 4 (December 1957), pp. 390–406; Miller, "Lower Class Culture as a Generating Milieu of Gang Delinquency"; Miller, "Preventive Work with Street-Corner Groups: Boston Delinquency Project," *Annals of the American Academy of Political and Social Science*, Vol. 322 (1959), pp. 97–106; Robert A. Gordon *et al.*, "Values and Gang Delinquency," *American Journal of Sociology*, Vol. 49, No. 2 (September 1963), pp. 109–128; James F. Short, Jr., "Street Corner Gangs and Patterns of Delinquency: A Progress Report,"

American Catholic Sociological Review, Vol. 28, No. 2 (Spring 1963), pp. 13–32; James F. Short, Jr., and Fred L. Strodtbeck, "The Response of Gang Leaders to Status Threats: An Observation on Group Process and Delinquent Behavior," *American Journal of Sociology*, Vol. 48, No. 5 (March 1963), pp. 571–579; James F. Short, Jr., Fred L. Strodtbeck, and Desmond S. Cartwright, "A Strategy for Utilizing Research Dilemmas: A Case from the Study of Parenthood in a Street Corner Gang," *Sociological Inquiry*, Vol. 32, No. 2 (Spring 1962), pp. 185–202; and James F. Short, Jr., Ray A. Tennyson, and Kenneth I. Howard, "Behavior Dimensions of Gang Delinquency," *American Sociological Review*, Vol. 28, No. 3 (June 1963), pp. 412–428.

[44] Miller, "Lower Class Culture as a Generating Milieu of Gang Delinquency," p. 18.

[45] Gordon *et al.*, *op. cit.*, p. 109.

personal concomitants of illegitimate father-hood; and the behavioral dimensions of group delinquency based on data collected from 598 members of sixteen delinquent street clubs with assigned workers.

There have also been reports on the Hyde Park Youth Project, which studied case-finding, street club work, and community self-help in co-operation with the Hyde Park Neighborhood Center in Chicago; the Huntington-Gifford project in Syracuse, New York, which developed instrumentation to measure individual movement and "group tone"; the ongoing five-year project of the Seattle Atlantic Street Center, designed to demonstrate and evaluate social work effectiveness in serving boys of junior high school age in the central area of Seattle; the Neighborhood Youth Association in Los Angeles, working with school referrals of acting-out adolescents; and the work of the Wesley Community Centers in San Antonio with Mexican-American conflict gangs.[46] Promising research projections have been published for New York's Mobilization for Youth, Harlem Youth Opportunities Unlimited, Cleveland's Community Action for Youth, and other such projects that are under way in Boston, New Haven, and elsewhere throughout the country.[47] There is hope that the

pattern of building research designs into project proposals, encouraged by the federal grant system, will soon begin to produce a substantial body of research emerging directly from the practice of social work with working-class children not amenable to the routine ministrations of the neighborhood centers.

The handicapped. Contrary to the tradition that the neighborhood agencies were somehow assigned to the "normal" client, leaving the handicapped and afflicted to the "special settings," the centers have recently begun to undertake projects designed to help those with special physical and emotional illnesses to use the agency as a bridge to the general community. Again, there is not yet any significant production of research data, but there are signs that some important investigations are in progress.

The integration project for orthopedically handicapped children of the Mosholu-Montefiore Community Center of the Associated YM-YWHA's of Greater New York has already produced some first documents, including a study of the social and recreational patterns of these children by Schwartz and Holmes's "scale of deviance, in which individual and group factors are taken into consideration . . . to predict 'how deviant' a deviant individual will be, when cast into a particular social milieu, here represented by the various children's groups."[48] Cole and Podell surveyed

[16] Charles H. Shireman, *The Hyde Park Youth Project* (Chicago: Welfare Council of Metropolitan Chicago, 1955–1958); Norman R. Roth, *Reaching the Hard-to-Reach* (Syracuse, N.Y.: Huntington Family Centers, 1961); Seattle Atlantic Street Center, "Effectiveness of Social Work on Acting-Out Youth: Second Year Progress Report," September 1963 to August 1964 (Seattle, 1964) (mimeographed); Helen Northen, "Social Group Work: A Tool for Changing Behavior of Disturbed Acting-Out Adolescents," in *Social Work with Groups, 1958*, selected papers from the National Conference on Social Welfare (New York: National Association of Social Workers, 1958); and Buford E. Farris and William M. Hale, *Mexican-American Conflict Gangs: Observations and Theoretical Implications* (San Antonio, Tex.: Wesley Community Centers, undated).

[47] Mobilization for Youth, *A Proposal for*

the Prevention and Control of Delinquency by Expanding Opportunities (New York, 1961); Harlem Youth Opportunities Unlimited, *Youth in the Ghetto: A Study of the Consequences of Powerlessness and a Blue-Print for Change* (New York, 1964); and Greater Cleveland Youth Services Planning Commission, *Community Action for Youth* (Cleveland, 1963). For other projects in progress, *see* Gold and Winter, *op. cit.*

[48] Associated YM-YWHA's of Greater New York, "Progress Report on 'A Study of the Problems of Integrating Physically Handicapped Children with Non-Handicapped Children in Recreational Groups'" (New York, 1963) (mimeographed); Arthur Schwartz,

agency staff attitudes toward working with physically handicapped children and discovered reactions likened to minority group stereotyping.[49]   At New York's Greenwich House, Quartaro and Pierson studied the experience of settlements with narcotics addicts and found that most of the agencies simply excluded them for fear of alienating the community, and because of repeated failures in practice and lack of adequately trained personnel.[50]

The Henry Street Settlement has reported a project in "preventive psychiatry," and in Chicago, Bunda has issued promising preliminary reports on the Girl Scouts of Chicago project for integrating 7- to 18-year-old girls with mental and physical handicaps into the ongoing program of troops and camps.[51] Parnicky and Brown, at the Bordentown, New Jersey, YMCA, have reported a study designed to probe the reactions of institutionalized retardates in their first experiences in the community, suggesting that it may soon be possible to develop an "index of readiness for community placement." [52]

The Group As Client

There is a large and fast-growing literature of research on the small group, and all of it is in some way relevant to those agencies whose primary interest lies in the group as a medium of service.   Interestingly enough, the body of research on the small group has been built up in many settings—the army, the factory, the school, the laboratory—with the virtual exception of the neighborhood centers, where thousands of groups meet every day in the year.   Several researchers have expressed concern about this and tried to relate the center practitioner to this body of work, both as consumer and producer.[53]   It is impossible to review here even a representative segment of this research. Some helpful introductions, surveys, and bibliographies have been provided by Terauds, Altman and McGrath, Berelson and Steiner, Hare, Schwartz, and many others.[54]

Social and Recreational Patterns of Orthopedically Handicapped Children (New York: Associated YM-YWHA's of Greater New York, 1962) ; and Douglas Holmes, "A Consideration of Deviance in Conducting Programs for Clinical Populations in a Community Center Setting," paper presented at the National Conference on Social Welfare, Los Angeles, May 29, 1964 (mimeographed), p. 14.

[49] Minerva G. Cole and Lawrence Podell, "Serving Handicapped Children in Group Programs," *Social Work*, Vol. 6, No. 1 (January 1961), pp. 97–104.

[50] Peter Quartaro and Arthur Pierson, "A Survey of Settlement House Experience with Narcotics Addicts" (New York: Greenwich House, undated). (Mimeographed.)

[51] Harry Joseph, Annelise Thieman, and Evelyn Hamilton, "Preventive Psychiatry at the Henry Street Settlement: A Five-Year Experimental Project," *American Journal of Orthopsychiatry*, Vol. 22, No. 3 (April 1952), pp. 557–569; and Bertha Bunda, "Project for Working with Exceptional Girl Scouts," Progress Reports Nos. 1–5 (Chicago: Girl Scouts of Chicago, 1961–64) (mimeographed).

[52] Joseph J. Parnicky and Leonard N.

Brown, "Introducing Institutionalized Retardates to the Community," *Social Work*, Vol. 9, No. 1 (January 1964), p. 83.

[53] *See*, for example, Edgar F. Borgatta, "What Social Science Says about Groups," *Social Welfare Forum, 1957*, proceedings of the National Conference on Social Welfare (New York: Columbia University Press, 1957), pp. 212–237; Klein, *op. cit.*; Edwin J. Thomas, "Theory and Research on the Small Group: Selected Themes and Problems," and Robert D. Vinter, "Small-Group Theory and Research: Implications for Group Work Practice Theory and Research" in Leonard S. Kogan, ed., *Social Science Theory and Social Work Research* (New York: National Association of Social Workers, 1960), pp. 91–108 and 123–134.

[54] Anita Terauds, Irwin Altman, and Joseph E. McGrath, *A Bibliography of Small Group Research* (Arlington, Va.: Human Sciences Research, 1960) ; Bernard Berelson and Gary A. Steiner, *Human Behavior: An Inventory of Scientific Findings* (New York: Harcourt, Brace, and World, 1964), chap. 8; Paul A. Hare, *Handbook of Small Group Research* (New York: Free Press of Glencoe, 1962) ; and William Schwartz, "Small Group Science and Group Work Practice," *Social Work*, Vol. 8, No. 4 (October 1963), pp. 39–46.

There are several lines of research from related fields of practice that should be mentioned, however briefly, for their importance to the work of the centers. The social influence and "behavioral contagion" studies, conducted in the camp setting by Lippitt, Polansky, Redl, and others, pointed strongly to the social origin of children's behavior.[55] They have noted:

The fact that it has proved possible in this study to make a number of generalizations about the behavior of individuals in groups almost independently of any real knowledge of the internal working of the individuals concerned, but solely in terms of functioning group positions, is seen as indicative of the necessity for an interest in *groups* as having dynamic reality in the same sense as do personalities.[56]

The games and activities studies of Gump, Sutton-Smith, Redl, and others, also in the camp context, have explored the effects of games on the group experience of children and have produced some clear results enabling the authors, as Gump has observed, to "look forward to the day when workers will . . . have more accurate expectations regarding the impulses a given activity is likely to provoke and gratify, the defenses or control measures it will likely call forth, and the interaction it will stimulate."[57] Attention is also called to

the prolific work of the Sherifs in the areas of intergroup relations and adolescent group behavior—particularly the well-known "Robbers Cave Experiment," in which intergroup friction among camp groups was experimentally induced by heightening ingroup feeling and dissipated by creating "superordinate goals," leading to the conclusion that "the limiting condition determining friendly or hostile attitudes between groups is the nature of functional relations between them, as defined by analysis of their goals." [58] Aside from their substantive contributions, these studies did much to establish the camp setting as a research laboratory; McNeil has reviewed some aspects of this relationship between social research and the field of camping.[59]

Also in the category of related research, Lippitt has summarized the conclusions about group morale drawn from the Lewin, Lippitt and White studies of leadership and group behavior in which the effects of complete freedom, authoritarianism and disciplined freedom are seen to produce varying effects upon the "climate" of the

[55] Ronald Lippitt *et al.*, "The Dynamics of Power: A Field Study of Social Influence in Groups of Children," *Human Relations*, Vol. 5, No. 1 (February 1952), pp. 37–64; Norman A. Polansky, "On the Dynamics of Behavioral Contagion," *The Group*, Vol. 14, No. 3 (April 1952), pp. 3–8, 21, and 25; and Norman A. Polansky, Ronald Lippitt, and Fritz Redl, "An Investigation of Behavioral Contagion in Groups," *Human Relations*, Vol. 3, No. 4 (November 1950), pp. 319–348.

[56] Polansky, Lippitt, and Redl, *op. cit.*, p. 348. Emphasis in original.

[57] Paul Gump, "Observational Study of Activities for Disturbed Children," in *Group Work and Community Organization, 1953–54*, papers presented at the National Conference of Social Work (New York: Columbia University Press, 1954), p. 22; Paul Gump

et al., "Activity Setting and Social Interaction: A Field Study," *American Journal of Orthopsychiatry*, Vol. 25, No. 4 (July 1955), pp. 755–760; Paul Gump and Brian Sutton-Smith, "The 'It' Role in Children's Games," *The Group*, Vol. 17, No. 3 (February 1955), pp. 3–8; and Fritz Redl, "The Impact of Game Ingredients on Children's Play Behavior," in Bertram Schaffner, ed., *Group Processes* (New York: Josiah Macy, Jr. Foundation, 1959), pp. 33–81.

[58] Muzafer Sherif and Carolyn Wood Sherif, *Groups in Harmony and Tension: An Integration of Studies on Intergroup Relations* (New York: Harper & Brothers, 1953); Muzafer Sherif and Carolyn Wood Sherif, *Reference Groups: Exploration into Conformity and Deviation of Adolescents* (New York: Harper & Row, 1964); and Muzafer Sherif *et al.*, *Intergroup Conflict and Cooperation: The Robbers Cave Experiment* (Norman, Okla.: University of Oklahoma Press, 1961), p. 208.

[59] Elton B. McNeil, "The Background of Therapeutic Camping," *Journal of Social Issues*, Vol. 13, No. 1 (January 1957), pp. 3–14.

group.[60] Kolodny and Waldfogel have summarized the research carried on by the Department of Neighborhood Clubs of the Boston Children's Service Association, a unique structure of group services in a case-work setting and one that has been extremely sensitive to the need for research.[61] Luck has studied the intensity of children's peer relationships within groups in a child guidance clinic, isolating differences in learning problems, psychological remedial work, size of groups, and types of program activity.[62]

In the same area of related research, Somers compared four small-group theories with respect to their ideas on the individual in the group, relationships among members, the relationship between group activities and group process, the group's relations with its environment, and longitudinal growth and decay in group life.[63] A particularly provocative study by Mann and Mann indicated that group interaction produced more personality and behavior changes among members in "task-oriented" groups than in self-directed "role-playing" groups.[64] This study suggests a line of in-

vestigation that may ultimately challenge the vague "personality" emphasis in agency work and replace it with one more clearly focused on the common and concrete tasks that bind group members to each other.

Moving closer to work emerging from the practice problems of the centers themselves, one finds a few problems that have attracted the interest of students of group process, but no continuous body of work on any single theme, with the possible exception of the work with street clubs. Spergel has developed a "typology of gangs within a sociocultural framework," with special reference to the "anomie tradition" as it has been developed by Cloward and Ohlin.[65] Spergel found that he could identify the "racket," "conflict" and "theft" subcultures in the neighborhoods he studied, and relate the emergence of these subcultures to certain distinguishable neighborhood conditions under which they tended to flourish.

Short's work at the YMCA of Metropolitan Chicago, previously mentioned, has yielded data on the structure of the gang, with the study by Short and Strodtbeck revealing several dimensions of gang behavior.[66] They found, for example, that although intragroup aggression was high, gang norms were not generally supportive of internal aggression aimed at the establishment of individual dominance, even by the leaders themselves. They found, too, as had Whyte before them, that gang leaders were cautious not to use their leadership arbitrarily but were sensitive to the needs and tolerances of group members. There was evidence that the relationship between leaders and staff workers was often such as to stabilize the leadership structure and reduce the need for status-asserting forms

[60] Ronald Lippitt, "The Morale of Youth Groups," in Goodwin Watson, ed., *Civilian Morale*, Second Yearbook of the Society for the Psychological Study of Social Issues (Boston: Houghton Mifflin Company, 1942), pp. 119–142.

[61] Ralph Kolodny and Samuel Waldfogel, "Summary of Research Carried on by the Department of Neighborhood Clubs, Boston Children's Service Association, 1955–1958." Unpublished paper, Boston, Mass., undated.

[62] Juanita M. Luck, "A Study of Peer Relationships," *The Group*, Vol. 17, No. 3 (February 1955), pp. 13–20.

[63] Mary Louise Somers, "Four Small Group Theories: A Comparative Analysis and Evaluation of Selected Social Science Theory for Use as Teaching Content in Social Group Work." Unpublished doctoral dissertation, School of Applied Social Sciences, Western Reserve University, 1957.

[64] John H. Mann and Carola Honroth Mann, "The Relative Effectiveness of Role Playing and Task Oriented Group Experiences in Producing Personality and Behavior Change," *Journal of Social Psychology*, Vol. 51, Second Half (1960), pp. 313–317.

[65] Irving Spergel, "An Exploratory Research in Delinquent Subcultures," *Social Service Review*, Vol. 35, No. 1 (March 1961), pp. 33–47.

[66] "The Response of Gang Leaders to Status Threats: An Observation of Group Process and Delinquent Behavior."

of intragroup aggression. Yablonsky obtained data on thirty New York City street clubs over a four-year period and developed a typology that yielded the concept of the "near-group," located on a continuum from group to mob and distinguished by characteristics such as diffuse definitions of membership, limited membership responsibility, self-appointed leadership, limited goal consensus, shifting stratification systems, norms in conflict with the larger society, and indeterminate size varying with circumstances.[67]

Studies of organized groups in, and related to, neighborhood center programs have focused on various dimensions of group life. On the *role of the member* in youth clubs, Maas contrasted the ways in which this role is filled by lower-class and middle-class urban adolescents.[68] He studied ten paired groups in action, noting "collaborative," "aggressive," and "digressive" interactions and their direction—toward adult leader, peer president, or other members. He found that the role relationships between members and adult leaders in the lower-class clubs were similar to those between the members and their own peer leaders in the middle-class clubs, where the adult seemed less important to the members.

On *indigenous leadership*, Lowy examined leadership patterns in adolescent groups and secured some verification for the idea that leadership is not identical with office-holding, that it varies with group size and group events, and that it cannot be regarded as a personality characteristic in the old tradition of youth work.[69] On *group*

size, Hare arranged 150 Boy Scouts in discussion groups of different size and found that, as the size of the group increased from five to twelve, consensus resulting from discussion decreased when time was limited, leaders had less influence, skill was a more important factor, there was an increase in factionalism, and amount of expression decreased, as did degree of member satisfaction.[70]

On *group-influenced attitudes*, Kelley and Volkart, also working with a Boy Scout population, found that a speech criticizing the scout emphasis on camping had more impact on those who placed less value on their membership, and that this feeling was expressed more readily under private rather than public conditions.[71] Avigdor, working with groups of children in a New York City settlement, found a relationship between the traits chosen by children for group stereotyping and the functional relations between groups.[72]

On *group cohesion*, French compared the reactions of organized social and athletic clubs with those of unorganized undergraduates to frustrating situations, represented by the need to solve insoluble problems.[73] He discovered that the organized groups manifested more frustration and aggression, but because the cohesive forces were also stronger, this did not in turn create more group disruption. The unorganized groups showed lower motivation, hence less frus-

[67] Lewis Yablonsky, "The Delinquent Gang as a Near-Group," *Social Problems*, Vol. 7, No. 2 (Fall 1959), pp. 108–117.

[68] Henry S. Maas, "The Role of Member in Clubs of Lower-Class and Middle-Class Adolescents," *Child Development*, Vol. 25, No. 4 (December 1954), pp. 341–351.

[69] Louis Lowy, "Indigenous Leadership in Teen-Age Groups," *Jewish Center Worker*, Vol. 13, No. 1 (January 1952), pp. 10–15.

[70] Paul A. Hare, "A Study of Interaction and Consensus in Different Sized Groups," *American Sociological Review*, Vol. 17, No. 3 (June 1952), pp. 261–267.

[71] Harold H. Kelley and Edmund H. Volkart, "The Resistance of Change to Group-Anchored Attitudes," *American Sociological Review*, Vol. 17, No. 4 (August 1952), pp. 453–465.

[72] Rosette Avigdor, "The Development of Stereotypes as a Result of Group Interaction." Unpublished doctoral dissertation, New York University, 1952.

[73] John R. P. French, Jr., "The Disruption and Cohesion of Groups," *Journal of Abnormal and Social Psychology*, Vol. 36, No. 3 (July 1941), pp. 361–377.

tration and aggression but more tendencies toward disruption.

On *group development*, little has been done until very recently to elaborate or document Bernstein's *Charting Group Progress,* published in 1949.[74] A significant contribution has now been made by Garland, Jones, and Kolodny, whose "Model for Stages of Development in Social Work Groups," emerging from the work of the Department of Neighborhood Clubs of the Boston Children's Service Association, is a long step forward in analytic sophistication.[75] Distilled from the experience of practice, the model deals with a client population close enough to that of the neighborhood centers to offer valuable assistance in their work.

The Agency

As the centers have responded to changing times, new functions have tended not to displace the old but to move in alongside them. As a result, the agencies present a kind of agglomeration of services and objectives; one may almost read their histories in a cross section of their current issues, their interpretations to the public, and their internal problems. Such a situation poses questions for historical and empirical research on which little has yet been done, although there are signs that some of the newer work on the study of organizations is being noted with interest by agency personnel.[76] Studies on hand are best presented in three categories: those dealing with the clarification of *agency function* or purpose, work on the problems of *agency structure*, and research on *agency program* that defines the nature of the service itself.

Functions

Several studies bear on the question of whether a given agency will be perceived by board, staff, client, and community as a social service or part of a social movement, an issue with which the ideologically oriented agencies in particular have been increasingly concerned.[77] In 1948, Janowsky set out to clarify the "fundamental purpose of the Jewish Center" in an extensive study of agency history, records, reports, opinions, and programs in Jewish Centers throughout the country.[78] He emerged with the conclusion that "the Jewish Center is one of the agencies Jews join in order to satisfy their distinctive Jewish needs." [79] Perhaps because the Janowsky study failed to distinguish clearly between philosophical questions and empirical ones, it has precipitated a good deal more heated debate than scientific research and follow-up.

In 1960, Dodson undertook a study of the Young Women's Christian Association as "part of an effort by the YWCA to redefine its relationships to the YMCA in light of changes that are taking place in both organizations and stemming at least in part from changes in American life." [80] Dodson

---

[74] Saul Bernstein, *Charting Group Progress* (New York: Association Press, 1949).

[75] James A. Garland, Hubert E. Jones, and Ralph L. Kolodny, "A Model for Stages of Development in Social Work Groups." Unpublished paper, Boston, Mass., undated.

[76] *See* Peter M. Blau and W. Richard Scott, *Formal Organizations* (San Francisco: Chandler Publishing Co., 1962); Alvin W. Gouldner, "Organizational Analysis," in Kogan, ed., *op. cit.,* pp. 46–63; and Mason Haire, ed., *Modern Organization Theory* (New York: John Wiley & Sons, 1959).

[77] *See* William Schwartz, "Small Group Science and Group Work Practice."

[78] Oscar I. Janowsky, *The Jewish Welfare Board Survey* (New York: Dial Press, 1948).

[79] *Ibid.,* p. 7.

[80] Dan W. Dodson, *The Role of the YWCA in a Changing Era: The YWCA Study of YMCA-YWCA Cooperative Experiences* (New York: National Board of the Young Women's Christian Association of the U.S.A., 1960), p. 76.

reaffirmed the need for an independent women's organization, pointed up the balance between local service programs and national purposes, and tried to bridge the gap between movement and service: "The art of lacing together involvement in service and intelligent action is perhaps the greatest social frontier of all." [81]

The most sophisticated of these organizational analyses is undoubtedly that of Zald and Denton in their recent study of "the transformation of the YMCA from an evangelistic social movement to a general service organization." [82] Their structural analysis points up the agency's dependence on a paying clientele, its federated structure, factors of professional ideology and lack of it, and the range of programs and services legitimized by concepts of character development. In addition, Zald and Denton develop some general propositions about organizational change, which they feel can be helpful in the analysis of other agencies. They suggest, for example, that

organizations that are dependent on some form of enrollment economy (a form of competitive market place) are forced to recognize quickly the environment changes affecting the demand for services. On the other hand, organizations protected from the market place, such as religious organizations, welfare organizations, or social movements, may soon find themselves poorly adapted to the changing order. [83]

Meeting community needs. Another body of research on function is comprised of the numerous self-studies and surveys designed to determine the extent to which a given agency, or group of agencies, is "meeting the needs" of its community. In these studies, the primary emphasis is generally on the service, rather than on the ideological, components of agency work;

attempts are made to elicit neighborhood problems, measure the agency's facilities against them, or evaluate the agency's role in the community. One of the earlier and more comprehensive of these was the Kennedy and Farra study of 1935, designed to appraise the "activities, policies and administration" of eighty New York City settlements, the major concentrations of which they found in areas of declining population. [84] More recently, the National Federation of Settlements and Neighborhood Centers published its *Review and Revision*, a self-study that drew information by questionnaire from 288 member agencies in all parts of the country concerning the attitudes and opinions of board, staff, and members on common agency and neighborhood problems. [85]

In Los Angeles, a self-study by thirteen community chest-supported settlements was designed to "define the modern role of the neighborhood center in Los Angeles" and included "an attempt to formulate practice theory by relating agency objectives and goals to program activities." [86] The study produced a carefully worded statement on the settlement function, but "encountered great difficulties" in fulfilling its task of relating the nature of the service to specific community problems. This, of course, is the heart of the functional problem, and the one on which the least progress has been made—the development of a statement of agency purpose directed at the social and individual problems they are meant to address, as hospitals address the cure of illness, schools the propagation of learning, and the courts the administration of the law.

It is impossible to review here even a

---

[81] *Ibid.*, p. 106.

[82] Mayer N. Zald and Patricia Denton, "From Evangelism to General Service: The Transformation of the YMCA," *Administrative Science Quarterly*, Vol. 8, No. 2 (September 1963), p. 216.

[83] *Ibid.*, p. 234.

[84] Kennedy, Farra, and associates, *op. cit.*

[85] National Federation of Settlements and Neighborhood Centers, *Review and Revision: A Report of the Self-Study Committee of the National Federation of Settlements and Neighborhood Centers* (New York, 1960).

[86] Hirschfeld, *op. cit.*, p. 7.

small part of the single-agency studies in this self-study category; most of them have been helpful to their sponsors in some measure but have not lent themselves to generalization or been built one upon the other into a body of work useful to the field as a whole. Several have aspects that could be so used if the attempt were made. New York's University Settlement and the Educational Alliance re-evaluated their functions in a changing neighborhood; the Alliance found some interesting differences about agency function among board, staff, and members.[87] For example, board and staff ranked "developing the total personality" first in their priority of functions, while the members ranked this item seventh; on "promoting Jewish loyalty," staff put the item second, members fourth, and board seventh; and on the item "combat delinquency," members thought it should be first, board fourth, and staff fifth.

In Chicago, the Erie Neighborhood House studied various aspects of life in its neighborhood, each having some bearing on the agency's service to adolescents. They found certain neighborhood attitudes toward youth that had implications for their use of local volunteers as group leaders.

The new awareness of the hostile attitude of the more conforming group toward the less conforming teen-agers provided knowledge which clarified our administrative problem. Among the changes now in process we are trying to select leadership which can freely move toward the teen-agers without loss to their own sense of self-esteem.[88]

Scheidlinger compared the various forms taken by the Boy Scout movement in different cultural groups and concluded that "the institution of Scouting has become a tool for inculcating into the young a total system of integrated behavior patterns considered desirable by the particular national or social group which is making use of the Scout program." [89] Lewin's comparison of the Boy Scout organization with the Hitler Youth movement examined the goals and practices of two highly organized youth groups in a democratic and totalitarian state.[90] Proceeding by content analysis of literature aimed at both members and leaders, he found significant differences in what he called the "experience context" of his "ends" items: for ends recommended as a member of the national community, the Hitler Youth literature had 66 percent to the Boy Scouts' 25 percent; for those ends recommended for the sake of personal growth and satisfaction, the Boy Scouts had 47 percent, the Hitler Youth 15 percent. There was marked agreement between the two organizations on the emphasis on learning by doing and on the strong emotional appeal, particularly to the sense of patriotism.

Structure

Studies about the relationship between agency structure and its impact on clients are generally beyond the present level of research sophistication. The work of Cloward and his students, however, provides a foretaste as to where such a line of research

[87] New York University Center for Human Relations, *Building Neighborliness*, Human Relations Monograph No. 8 (New York: National Council of Christians and Jews and University Settlement, 1957); and Nathan E. Cohen, *A Summary of the Survey of the Educational Alliance*, summary prepared by Emanuel Fisher (New York: Educational Alliance, 1950).

[88] Robert Armstrong and Edna Raphael, "Relating a Neighborhood Study to Programming," *The Group*, Vol. 17, No. 3 (February 1955), p. 21.

[89] Saul Scheidlinger, "A Comparative Study of the Boy Scout Movement in Different National and Social Groups," *American Sociological Review*, Vol. 13, No. 6 (December 1948), p. 750.

[90] Herbert S. Lewin, "A Comparison of the Aims of the Hitler Youth and the Boy Scouts of America," *Human Relations*, Vol. 1, No. 2 (November 1947), pp. 206–227.

may lead.[91] Cloward's research proposal represents the convergence of three different viewpoints:

. . . the leisure-time agency as an organization, direct social relations between individuals, and the community setting. Seen in this way, an agency is, first of all, a formal structure with definite goals, program, and organizational machinery; it is also a social framework within which people are in constant interaction. The interplay between "structure," "interaction" and "community characteristics" has implications for agency policies and for what happens to them as they are translated into action.[92]

He projects a number of specific questions for research meant to "identify and understand the ways in which unintended consequences arise." Further, these consequences "are not haphazard, but can be systematically located." [93] Among the major sources of such consequences, he suggests the "formal structure of the agency," and it was this formalization variable that was taken up in a student project aimed at comparing two sets of agencies differentiated by defined differences in degree of formalization "in order to ascertain what consequences or functions the operation of these agency structures have [sic] for the client group that they are serving." [94] Cloward's students found that the agencies they had defined as more highly formalized served fewer members, had larger budgets, employed more paid staff workers, and allocated larger proportions of service to group and club structures. In these more formalized agencies, members perceived themselves as having more voice in decision-making, tended to carry personal problems to workers lower in the administrative hierarchy, and were more likely to share such problems with staff. This important inverse relationship between degree of formalization and the social distance between client and practitioner staff has been discussed by Cloward in a general summary of the findings of this study and its implications for future research.[95]

Material pertinent to the structure of boards of directors and the government of agencies can be found in the Glaser and Sills reader on leadership in voluntary associations.[96] Among the studies sampled here is one by Arsinian and Blumberg exploring sources, status, and expectations of volunteers in the YMCA.[97] Their group of ninety-three volunteers, about evenly divided between board members and club leaders, was examined on factors of age, sex, marital status, religion, education, occupation, community activities, community residence, previous "Y" experience, church activity, and parental family activity in community affairs. Both board and volunteer staff members tended to be active in other organizations, to have had satisfactory "Y" experiences in their own backgrounds, and to have come from families

---

[91] Richard A. Cloward, "Leisure-Time Agencies and Adolescents: A Proposal for Research" (New York: New York School of Social Work and Bureau of Applied Social Research, 1955) (mimeographed); Richard A. Cloward, "Agency Structure as a Variable in Service to Groups," in *Group Work and Community Organization, 1956,* papers presented at the National Conference of Social Work (New York: Columbia University Press, 1956); and Greta Anhisiger *et al.,* "Some Consequences of Agency Structure for Teen-Age Perceptions and Participation," unpublished master's thesis, New York School of Social Work, Columbia University, 1956.

[92] Cloward, "Leisure-Time Agencies and Adolescents: A Proposal for Research," p. 10.

[93] *Ibid.*

[94] Anhisiger *et al., op. cit.,* p. 1.

[95] "Agency Structure as a Variable in Service to Groups."

[96] William A. Glaser and David L. Sills, eds., "The Government of Private Organizations: A Social Science Reader for Leaders of Voluntary Associations" (2 vols.; New York: Bureau of Applied Social Research, Columbia University, 1963). (Mimeographed.)

[97] Seth Arsinian and Arthur Blumberg, "Volunteers in the Y.M.C.A.," in *ibid.,* Vol. 2, pp. XI:2–15.

with a tradition of community activism. Board members were older, more educated, more likely to be married, higher on the status ladder in occupation, and had lived for a longer period in the same community. Group leaders were more likely to be female, non-Protestant, and with more previous participant experience in the YMCA.

In another study, Reece collected data from a representative 25 percent of all YMCA board members throughout the country in 1960; he found the typical "Y" board member to be male, white, in a high-status professional or managerial occupation, and generally inactive as a program participant or client.[98] One of the factors that generally has operated to obscure the study of boards is the common confusion engendered by combining, in a single category called "volunteer," those who govern the agency with those who may lead a group without compensation, offer a single lecture, or help out from time to time with clerical chores.

Fierman's survey of intake practices in 1952 is one of the very few evidences of agency interest in the intake process.[99] One might speculate that this general lack of interest in how persons are introduced to neighborhood center programs is related to other issues affecting the practice of social work in the neighborhood centers— for example, uncertainties about the "member" as "client," ambiguities surrounding agency function, and a historic reluctance to impose conditions on the offering of service. Finally, a nostalgic reference is in order to a 1941 study reminiscent of another era—Stoney's "Rooms of Their

Own," in which he examined the origins and structure of twenty-eight "cellar clubs" in the Henry Street Settlement neighborhood in New York City.[100]

Programs

Most of the national agencies and federations have produced periodic program studies, more or less objective and varying considerably in their interest in generalized knowledge. Reference has already been made to several of these general surveys and inquiries.

In this category is Hillman's survey conducted for the National Federation of Settlements and Neighborhood Centers, presenting thirty-three case studies of programs under way in various parts of the country.[101] In addition, his final chapter on "Research as a Function of Settlements" reviews some settlement research in progress and suggests some lines of inquiry on family life, neighborhood organization, and other subjects related to the work of the settlements.

Weisman has studied the reactions of 231 adolescents in eleven groups meeting in four centers, developing data on member attitudes, activity preferences, member perceptions about agency power distribution, and reciprocity of feelings between members and group leaders.[102] She also studied groups ranked as "effective" and "ineffective," comparing them on variables of participation, member-leader communication, group climate, involvement in decision-making, and program achievement. In contrasting her Type I ("high-effective") groups with those of Type II ("low-effective"), she found that (1) there was

[98] Sanford M. Reece, *YMCA Boards and Committees of Management: A Study of the Membership, Structure and Practice of YMCA Boards* (New York: National Council of the Young Men's Christian Association, 1963).

[99] Frank Fierman, "Intake Policy and Procedure for the Jewish Community Center," *Jewish Center Worker*, Vol. 13, No. 2 (May 1952), pp. 27–30.

[100] George Stoney, "Rooms of Their Own" (New York: Henry Street Settlement, 1941). (Mimeographed.)

[101] Hillman, *op. cit.*

[102] Celia B. Weisman, *A Study of Jewish Community Center Teen-Age Programming* (New York: National Jewish Welfare Board, 1960).

more reciprocity of feeling between members and group leaders in the Type I groups; (2) Type I leaders underestimated the degree to which they were liked by their members, while Type II leaders overestimated this factor; (3) Type I leaders underestimated the positive feelings members had about each other, while Type II leaders overestimated them; and (4) Type I leaders perceived more power concentrations than the members did, while the reverse was true in the Type II groups. In examining the rankings of program activities, she found that "a great discrepancy emerges when it is found that there is a very low correlation between the supervisors' and executive directors' actual rankings and the members' perceptions of the agency ranking." [103]

Among the studies produced by the Research and Statistical Service of the Boy Scouts of America was the well-known "Boys in Wartime," which examined the attitudes of scouts and their leaders toward the war and their part in it.[104] Of particular interest was the extent to which the scouting program seems to have created, along with the high morale and active participation in the national war effort, many highly stereotyped reactions to the nature of the enemy, the differences between the Germans and the Japanese, and the aims of the war. Also significant was the fact that, while scouts and nonscouts were generally similar in the frequency of their intolerant responses, this was not true in the poor environments of the metropolitan areas; in these populations, the scouts were twice as intolerant as the nonscouts.

An "experience survey" conducted by Chein *et al.* at the Commission on Community Interrelations of the American Jewish Congress was designed to crystallize the major issues and develop hypotheses regarding the content of Jewish school curricula and Jewish Center programs.[105] In interviews with sixty-four leading Jewish educators and group workers, they addressed themselves to the general question: "Taking into account the fact that the Jewish child has a dual role to play, and all that this implies, what should the major emphases of Jewish schools and group work agencies be in their dealings with Jewish children?" [106] Respondents were differentiated on their central viewpoints, specific goals, over-all emphasis, and the extent to which non-Jewish experiences should be provided. This technique, aimed at crystallizing the experience of working practitioners, seems ideally suited to the task of clarifying and dramatizing the research issues in an area where little systematic work has yet been done.

There is a sizable segment of the group work literature devoted to what was once called "casework–group work"—an enterprise devoted to improving the service to individuals both by interagency referral and by instituting improved modes of personal service within the agencies.[107] Linderman, for example, reported a project in which eight Pasadena neighborhood centers experimented with the use of the Social Service Exchange for children under 18 and found that about half of the cases they registered were previously known to other social agencies in the community.[108] However, the material that generally emerged

---

103 *Ibid.*, p. 47.
104 Boy Scouts of America, "Boys in Wartime: Special Research Supplement," in *Scouting for Facts* (New York, 1942).

105 Isidor Chein *et al.*, "Basic Issues in Jewish Education and Group Work" (New York: American Jewish Congress, 1950). (Mimeographed.)
106 *Ibid.*, p. 3.
107 *See*, for example, Saul Scheidlinger, "Patterns of Case Work Services in Group Work Agencies," *The Group*, Vol. 8, No. 1 (November 1945), pp. 1–7; and Gertrude Wilson, *Group Work and Case Work—Their Relationship and Practice* (New York: Family Welfare Association of America, 1941).
108 Wanda Taylor Linderman, "An Experiment in Casework–Group Work Cooperation," *The Group*, Vol. 8, No. 1 (November 1945), pp. 11–13.

from this type of research effort was largely descriptive and hortatory, and interest seems to have dried up in recent years.

The Community

The interest of the centers in their neighborhoods and in the social problems of the larger community has been reflected in three main lines of research: the community survey, which had its moments of glory in the first two decades of the twentieth century; the study of specific social problems of immediate concern to the big city settlements in particular; and the development of indices for measuring the community's need for group work and recreation services.

The Community Survey

The early social survey was a process for effecting social improvement by means of a large-scale, one-time investigation of a community's social welfare needs. . . . Major emphasis was placed throughout upon publicizing the survey and its findings and conclusions as widely and effectively as possible, so as to arouse the community to action and implementation of its recommendations.[109]

Zimbalist and Eaton and Harrison have described and documented the centers' historic interest in the social survey; in its day, it commanded considerable community attention and produced some action on social problems of great urgency.[110] Over the years, the traditional survey approach, primarily designed to make a strong case for action on social issues, fell into decline. "Because of the many changes and extensions of use which the term 'survey' has undergone over the years, it no longer appears to provide a meaningful referent in social work research." [111]

The community study nevertheless remains an important part of the catalogue of techniques used by social welfare councils and other planning bodies, both public and private, to study conditions bearing on the need for social services. Every community has its own local landmark survey, which it uses as a continuous point of reference.[112] Some recent efforts may be noted: the "self-portrait" of the Greater Mission District in San Francisco, developed by the Mission Neighborhood Centers; the New York City Youth Board's studies of delinquency trends in New York City between 1953 and 1962; Jacobs' recreation survey of the Germantown area in Philadelphia; the Bergen County, New Jersey, study of Jewish population trends and community needs; and two larger surveys by Wolins in Berkeley and Jenkins in New York City.[113]

The Jenkins study, sponsored by the research department of the Community Council of Greater New York, is one of the most comprehensive efforts undertaken in recent years to develop the relationship between recreational needs and services in

---

[109] Zimbalist, *op. cit.*, p. 179.
[110] *Ibid.*, chap. 7; and Eaton and Harrison, *op. cit.*
[111] Zimbalist, *op. cit.*, p. 200.

[112] Helen Hall, "Community Studies," in *Group Work and Community Organization 1953–1954*, papers presented at the National Conference of Social Work (New York: Columbia University Press, 1954); and Jean M. Maxwell, "Group Work and Community Surveys," *The Group*, Vol. 11, No. 4 (Summer 1949), pp. 9–17.
[113] Mission Neighborhood Centers, "A Self-Portrait of the Greater Mission District in Southeastern San Francisco" (2 vols.; San Francisco, 1960) (mimeographed); New York City Youth Board, *Ten-Year Trends in Juvenile Delinquency in New York City: Offenses for Ages 7 Through 20 Years, 1953–1962* (New York, 1964); Jacobs, *op. cit.*; YMHA of Bergen County, *A Survey of the Jewish Population of Bergen County* (New York: National Jewish Welfare Board, 1963); Martin Wolins, *Welfare Problems and Services in Berkeley, California* (Berkeley: Berkeley Council of Social Welfare and School of Social Welfare, University of California, 1954); and Shirley Jenkins, *Comparative Recreation Needs and Services in New York Neighborhoods* (New York: Community Council of Greater New York, 1963).

a large and enormously complex metropolis. Also in New York City, Cloward and the staff of the Institute of Public Administration studied and made recommendations to the city government on "the organizational and administrative relationships involved in services rendered by the various agencies, departments, commissions, officers and boards of the City of New York dealing with child and youth problems."[114]

Selected Social Problems

In her "descriptive bibliography" of the Helen Hall Settlement Papers, Brown notes:

. . . over the years, settlements have done sampling or surveying repeatedly—to obtain information about the most pressing social and economic problems of their neighbors at the moment when the facts might serve best, whether it was unemployment, medical care, public relief policies, or milk consumption, to name just a few of the fields in which we have investigated the needs or attitudes of neighborhood families.[115]

Among the best of the early examples were Lenroot's "Children of the Depression," published in 1935, and *Case Studies of Unemployment*, compiled by the Unemployment Committee of the National Federation of Settlements under the chairmanship of Helen Hall and edited by Marion Elderton in 1931.[116] Elderton's 150 case studies were selected in a survey conducted between June 1928 and March 1929, with the co-operation of 104 neighborhood houses in thirty-two cities and

the District of Columbia. Coming as it did before the actual onset of the Great Depression, the study was a striking demonstration of the potential ability of the neighborhood agencies to serve as a barometer of impending problems and to dramatize them in terms drawn from their own firsthand experiences with people where they live.

More recently, agencies have produced other studies of current social problems. Caplovitz, under the sponsorship of three New York City settlements, has researched the consumer practices of the poor, examining buying habits, modes of installment purchase and other aspects of the "peddler economy." [117] The Union Settlement Association, studying the impact of a new low-cost housing project in New York's East Harlem, found that the new community showed little evidence of neighborhood feeling; it was not an integrated community, with only the barest representations of white, single, middle-income, and aged populations.[118] The most stable families resented the impersonal treatment and invasions of privacy in project living more than they appreciated the improved physical facilities. Also studied were friendship selection, participation in organized activity, management problems, and the characteristics of the "problem tenant."

In another East Harlem study, the East Harlem Project of the James Weldon Johnson Community Center, in co-operation with the New York City Commission on Human Rights, examined the effects on parents and children of a busing program designed to take minority group children, mostly Negro, from an overused, segregated school facility to underused

---

[114] Richard A. Cloward, *The Administration of Services to Children and Youth in New York City* (New York: Institute of Public Administration, 1963). The quotation above is from the letter of transmittal sent with the recommendations.

[115] Brown, *op. cit.*, p. 4.

[116] Katherine Lenroot, "Children of the Depression: A Study of 259 Families in Selected Areas of Five Cities," *Social Service Review*, Vol. 9, No. 2 (June 1935), pp. 212–242; and Marion Elderton, ed., *Case Studies of Unemployment* (Philadelphia: University of Pennsylvania Press, 1931).

[117] David Caplovitz, *The Poor Pay More: Consumer Practices of Low-Income Families* (New York: Free Press of Glencoe, 1963).

[118] Ellen Lurie, *A Study of George Washington Houses, A Federally Aided, Low Cost Housing Project in East Harlem: The Effect of the Project on its Tenants and the Surrounding Community* (New York: Union Settlement Association, 1955–1956).

schools in white neighborhoods.[119] Parents who had given permission to have their children transported had relatively high educational achievement of their own and higher educational aspirations for their children, although of fifty-two fathers in the home, forty-one were in the manual labor class. Parents' motivation for giving consent was expressed primarily as wanting improved educational opportunities and relief from overcrowding, with a "chance to integrate" as a low-order choice. They also reported changes in their children as a result of the new experience, noting improvements in "work habits" and "interest in school."

Urban sociologists and others unaffiliated with settlements have shown a continuing interest in social problems of immediate relevance to the tasks of the neighborhood centers. For example, Handlin, Deutschberger, and Fellin and Litwak have studied changing neighborhoods and newcomer integration.[120] Komarovsky, Mann, and Dotson have worked on patterns of voluntary association and "neighborliness."[121] White and others have ex-

amined social class differences in the use of leisure time.[122] The list is long and cannot appropriately be reviewed here, but examples are cited to suggest some of the areas of knowledge to which the centers can make a contribution from their experience, and upon which they can draw for a firmer knowledge base for their practice.

Measuring Need

Carter has called attention to the problems involved in studying the need for welfare services in the community, stressing the importance of relating such research to a theoretical context:

Research on need for services is guided by content theory, but we do not always clarify this in our written reports. . . . The point is that we are not conducting research unaffected by theory, although in most instances the theory is speculative rather than verified, implicit rather than explicitly stated, and fragmentary rather than systematized.[123]

Among the index-building studies she cites as having been both based on and productive of theory is the Youth Project Yardstick.[124] The Yardstick research was developed by the research department of the Welfare Council of Metropolitan Los Angeles, on a request from the Los Angeles Youth Project for an index that would serve as an administrative tool in identifying areas needing service. Here the research

---

[119] East Harlem Project and the New York City Commission on Human Rights, "Releasing Human Potential: A Study of East Harlem-Yorkville School Bus Transfer" (New York, 1962). (Mimeographed.)

[120] Oscar Handlin, *The Newcomers: Negroes and Puerto Ricans in a Changing Metropolis* (Cambridge: Harvard University Press, 1959); Paul Deutschberger, "Interaction Patterns in Changing Neighborhoods: New York and Pittsburgh," *Sociometry*, Vol. 9, No. 4 (November 1946), pp. 303–315; and Phillip Fellin and Eugene Litwak, "Neighborhood Cohesion Under Conditions of Mobility," *American Sociological Review*, Vol. 28, No. 3 (June 1963), pp. 364–376.

[121] Mirra Komarovsky, "The Voluntary Associations of Urban Dwellers," *American Sociological Review*, Vol. 11, No. 6 (June 1946), pp. 686–698; Peter H. Mann, "The Concept of Neighborliness," *American Journal of Sociology*, Vol. 60, No. 2 (September 1954), pp. 163–168; and Floyd Dotson, "Patterns of Voluntary Association Among Urban Working-Class Families," *American Sociological Review*, Vol. 16, No. 5 (October 1951), pp. 687–693.

[122] R. Clyde White, "Social Class Differences in Uses of Leisure," *American Journal of Sociology*, Vol. 61, No. 2 (September 1955), pp. 145–150.

[123] Genevieve Carter, "The Concept of Measurability of Need for Social Work Services," in *Group Work and Community Organization, 1953–1954*, papers presented at the National Conference of Social Work (New York: Columbia University Press, 1954), pp. 64–65.

[124] Genevieve Carter and Elisabeth R. Frank, *The Youth Project Yardstick: Measuring Youth Services Needs*, Special Report Series No. 36 (Los Angeles: Welfare Council of Metropolitan Los Angeles, 1953).

problems are identified as extracting criteria from the practitioners, obtaining agreement among experts, and translating the criteria into quantitative symbols that could be expressed in an index. Seven years earlier, Sorenson had developed, in the same project, an Index of Relative Social Need, substantiating the fact that the Los Angeles Youth Project boundaries were identical with the "areas of greatest need" and using five major factors—the presence of minority groups, the absence of professional and managerial occupations, unemployment in 1940, contract rents, and delinquency rates.[125]

The later Yardstick researchers cited the Sorenson study as having represented considerable progress at the time, but tried in their own work to overcome some of the shortcomings, perceived by them as overly gross area units, overweighting of economic factors, the overgeneralized nature of the "social need" concept, and the crudeness of the ranking method used to distinguish areas.[126] The weighting procedures used by Carter and Frank were designed with the aim of producing a composite index, comparable, for example, to the consumer price index of the Bureau of Labor Statistics.

The "yardstick" can then be applied by a new worker or by a lay leader in Youth Project territory with the same results as those a practitioner could deduce from his years of experience in directing special services to needy areas.[127]

Several other attempts at index construction have been made, generally under the auspices of community-wide groups and councils. Jenkins' study of recreation needs and services in New York City proposed

. . . to provide information on selected neighborhood characteristics and on existing recreation and group work programs, and to analyze these data to determine comparative neighborhood needs for group work and recreation services.[128]

In the process, she utilized two main concepts: "one is the index, as the tool which relates all data to the city-wide average; and the other is the concept of comparative need, based on the relationship of the various indexes to each other." [129]

Similarly, White, for the Welfare Federation of Cleveland, set out to develop "criteria for determining what constitutes need for community-subsidized leisure-time services," and to evolve a method "for measuring relative need among various geographic areas of the community." [130] The White study emphasized four points: (1) the relativity of the "need" concept; (2) the distinction between "growth" needs and "social" needs; (3) the partialization of objectives needed in the field of recreation; and (4) the self-study aspects, involving the importance of the community processes set in motion by the study itself.

Reference should also be made here to the "guideposts" effort of the Group Work and Recreation Division of the Hennepin County Community Welfare Council, and to the New York City Youth Board's *Indices of Social Problems.*[131]

Future efforts to quantify and measure the need for group work and recreation services will owe much to those who can

---

[125] Roy Sorenson *et al.*, *Recreation for Everybody* (Los Angeles: Welfare Council of Metropolitan Los Angeles, 1946).

[126] Carter and Frank, *op. cit.*, p. 12.

[127] Carter, *op. cit.*, p. 69.

[128] *Op. cit.*, p. 1.

[129] *Ibid.*, p. 3.

[130] Virginia Kann White, "Measuring Leisure-Time Needs: A Report of the Group Work Council Research Project" (2 vols. and appendix; Cleveland: Welfare Federation of Cleveland, 1955), p. 6. (Mimeographed.)

[131] Community Welfare Council, "Guideposts for the Location of Group Work and Recreation Services In and Near Minneapolis, Hennepin County, Minnesota (Minneapolis, 1955) (mimeographed); and New York City Youth Board, *Indices of Social Problems: Selected Socio-Economic Characteristics of New York City by Borough and Health Area* (New York, 1962).

begin to specify what is meant by both the "needs" and the "services." It is in this sense that there is a critical interplay between the agencies' ability to clarify what they do and the community's efforts to plan for its people.

Vinter, from his research for the Policy Committee on Services to Groups of the Metropolitan Detroit United Community Services, has challenged the ambiguities surrounding current references to both needs and services:

The indeterminacy of needs contributes to vagueness in formulating service objectives and confusion in designing service programs. Given such unclear purposes as "character-building" or "personality development," it becomes extremely difficult to plan for their implementation through the strategic allocation of services within metropolitan areas, and impossible to determine how effectively particular services accomplish these general aims.[132]

Vinter concluded that "the view that all these services constitute a unitary field— such as 'group work and recreation'—was mainly due to the absence of criteria for differentiating among the diverse services being offered." [133] His attempt to identify "the outcomes deliberately intended in the provision of services" produced a classification of group services into three major fields—"socialization," "rehabilitation," and "facilities provision"—roughly equivalent to the leisure-time, clinical, and public recreation settings.[134]

The Worker

The major factor affecting the study of professional practice in the neighborhood centers is that the professionally educated group workers, of whom the centers garner about three-fourths of the available pool, do not serve the clients directly but manage the agencies as administrators and super-

visors.[135] Pernell, summarizing the data from Wilson's study of members of the Group Work Section of the National Association of Social Workers in 1956, noted:

. . . the social group worker who wants to use his knowledge and skill in direct services aimed toward effecting the social adjustment of individual members of agency groups, has a much better chance of finding the opportunity to do so in the "special setting" than in the traditional.[136]

The fact that the agency's service to clients is carried out by people not formally educated in the work has left the method of work largely undocumented and unstudied; what research exists has, for the most part, been inspired by administrative curiosities rather than technical ones.

For present purposes, studies will be reported in three different sections: (1) factors defining the population of paid and full-time professionals; (2) data on the body of volunteer practitioners; and (3) findings related to the study of group work practice—the worker-group encounter and the nature of the helping process.

The Professionals

General characteristics. The Wilson study mentioned above is still the most comprehensive analysis on record of professional group work personnel in all

---

[132] Vinter, "New Evidence for Restructuring Group Services," p. 58.

[133] *Ibid.*, p. 54.

[134] *Ibid.*, p. 51.

[135] Gladys Ryland, "Employment Responsibilities of Social Group Work Graduates" (New York: Council on Social Work Education, 1958) (mimeographed); Robert D. Vinter, "Group Work: Perspectives and Prospects," in *Social Work With Groups 1959*, selected papers from the National Conference on Social Welfare (New York: National Association of Social Workers, 1959), pp. 128–148; and Gertrude Wilson, "The Practice of Social Group Work" (New York: National Association of Social Workers, 1956) (mimeographed).

[136] Ruby Pernell, "Members and Their Positions," in Gertrude Wilson, ed., "The Practice of Social Group Work: Summary of the Report" (New York: National Association of Social Workers, 1957), pp. 18–19. (Mimeographed.)

settings. Acting for the Committee on Practice of the Group Work Section of the National Association of Social Workers, she analyzed responses from 665 section members—about 25 percent of the total—to questions dealing with their backgrounds, selected characteristics, conditions of work, their agency policies and programs, the use of their time, and their observations on certain issues of practice. Her data are not rendered in strict accord with the "neighborhood center" definition used here, since she includes the field service personnel of the national agencies in a separate classification. Her "traditional settings" category, however, consisting of personnel from the local group-serving agencies and representing two-thirds of her sample, is close enough to give some of the salient characteristics of the professional group in the neighborhood centers.

According to Wilson's data this professional group is about evenly divided between men and women, with a slight shading toward the latter; 38 percent were under 35 years of age, 57 percent under 40; 6 percent were in "direct service" jobs, 33 percent were listed as supervisors, 61 percent as administrators; 43 percent reported that they spent no time in direct service to clients, or "social group work" activity, while 13 percent said that they spent 25 percent to 54 percent of their time in direct service. Pernell's summary of the characteristics of the average professional worker in the traditional settings points out that "In taking this job, she found she was presenting both experience and educational qualifications beyond the level required by the agency. . . ." [137]

In contrast to the neighborhood centers group, Wilson found that her "special settings" respondents were more apt to be women (55 percent); they were younger, with 57 percent under 35 and 69 percent under 40; they were closer to practice, with 45 percent in direct service positions, 32 percent supervisors and 23 percent ad-

ministrators; and they spent more of their time in direct service—only 20 percent reporting no time thus spent, and 36 percent indicating that they used 25 percent to 54 percent of their time working directly with clients.

The Wilson study produced a great deal of additional data, too voluminous to report here; further aspects of the work will be discussed below. Main and Macdonald, in a more limited attempt to develop similar information, studied the responses of 151 members of the Chicago Area Group Work Section of NASW in 1962, seeking information about "the functions that social group workers are performing, their perceptions of these functions, and something of their professional aspirations for themselves and for social group work practice." [138] It may be significant, or it may simply be a regional characteristic, that in this more recent study a much smaller proportion of the total sample—54 percent, as against Wilson's 67 percent—were employed by what Wilson called the "traditional" agencies.

Like Wilson, Main and Macdonald found a slightly higher proportion of women—54 percent—and a large percentage of members with ten or more years of experience, raising some question about the absence of younger workers from the professional association. Also like Wilson, they found a great diversity of named functions and few clear distinctions among responsibilities designated as administrative, supervisory and practitioner: "nearly everybody seemed to be giving attention to practically everything." [139] Of those employed in direct service agencies, thirteen respondents classified themselves as practitioners, thirty-one as supervisors and fifty-two as administrators.

The Main and Macdonald study also

---

[137] *Ibid.*, p. 18.

[138] Marjorie W. Main and Mary E. Macdonald, "Professional Functions and Opinions of Social Group Workers," *Social Service Review*, Vol. 36, No. 4 (December 1962), p. 421.

[139] *Ibid.*, p. 427.

reveals some confusion within the profession itself as to the importance of direct practice. Asked where they would place new workers if there were personnel shortages, 101 out of 143 responded that they would put them into direct service positions. On the other hand, when those in the direct service agencies were asked to select the job to which they aspired, without reference to salary or preparation, over two-thirds selected supervisory and administrative positions. Further, when the respondents were asked in which of eight aspects of practice they considered the recent graduate to need the *most* further preparation and the *least*, there was a bipolar response, with fifty-two calling for direct work with groups as a top-priority area of further training and fifty-five stating that this was the area of least need. The authors concluded:

[Although] efforts are being made to distinguish the goals of social group work practice from the more inclusive goals of the multipurpose agencies with which they are identified, the present findings indicate the existence of widely divergent expectations of the social group work practitioner.[140]

Further data on allocation of time appear in two other studies. Adler and Kleinstein found that, of the 43 percent of agency time spent on program activity at the Jewish Community Center of Los Angeles, 17 percent was devoted to direct work with clubs. In the Los Angeles self-study mentioned earlier, Hirschfeld reported that 9 percent of the workers' total time was spent in direct leadership, 11 percent in free play and mass activity, 14 percent in routine office work, and 26 percent in preparation and planning.[141]

The National Jewish Welfare Board, in a preliminary study of full-time professional workers in the Jewish community centers, found a dramatic increase of professional staff during the past decade, serving to create a worker population that is young, mobile, and relatively inexperienced.[142] In the only psychological study of worker characteristics in group work that could be found, Koepp tested a sample of graduate and undergraduate social work students at the University of Wisconsin with Form D of Rokeach's Dogmatism Scale and found that social group work candidates were more authoritarian than those in corrections, child welfare, and psychiatric social work.[143] Such studies must be replicated in other regions, of course, for their findings to have any more than very limited significance.

Mobility. There are several studies of professional mobility in the neighborhood centers. In her 1929 examination of 11,877 full-time positions in the leisure-time agencies, Williamson had no access to precise figures on turnover, but she was able to determine that mobility was higher among workers than executives, and higher among men than women.[144] She also disclosed the major reasons for leaving advanced by the executive group—long hours, inadequate salaries, better offers in other fields, return to school for further study, the feeling that their professional status was not accepted, and the difficulties they encountered in working with volunteers. In 1954, the Girl Scouts' "Exit Study" explored factors causing resignations of professional workers in Girl Scout Councils from November 1951 through July 1953 and came up with many of the same reasons, adding factors

---

140 *Ibid.*, p. 432.

141 George M. Adler and David Kleinstein, "Our Professional Time—How Do We Use It?" *The Group*, Vol. 13, No. 1 (October 1950), pp. 11–15; Margret Hirschfeld, "Neighborhood Centers" (Los Angeles: Program Division, Welfare Federation of the Los Angeles Area, 1961) (mimeographed).

142 National Jewish Welfare Board, "Educational and Experience Background of Full-Time Professional Workers in Jewish Community Centers—1962: A Preliminary Report" (New York, 1964). (Mimeographed.)

143 Edwin F. Koepp, "Authoritarianism and Social Workers: A Psychological Study," *Social Work*, Vol. 8, No. 1 (January 1963), pp. 37–43.

144 *Op. cit.*

related to problems with supervisors and difficulties in staff relationships.[145]

Vinter studied a group of 125 full-time workers who had left their positions in member agencies of the National Federation of Settlements and Neighborhood Centers between January 1955 and January 1956, and he elicited identifying information, previous work history, plans on taking and leaving the position, and reasons for leaving.[146] He found that they were educationally superior to the remaining workers, with 62 percent having undertaken or completed graduate study, as against 45 percent of all settlement workers. Over 40 percent had left their positions within the first two years, while another group of almost 25 percent had been in their jobs for more than four years. Vinter concluded that, to the extent that his group is a representative sample, it appears that the greatest turnover occurs in the first few years after taking a position.

He also reported that the greatest salary differences were those between executives and assistant executives; that workers tended to express their commitment to settlements as a whole, rather than to a particular agency; that salary inadequacies were given as a relatively minor reason for leaving; and that "work content"—degree of satisfaction inherent in the work to be done—was given as the major reason for leaving by the highest percentage of respondents.

Herman sought the "personal" and "institutional" determinants of job mobility among Jewish Center workers. Studying agency reports, work histories, and questionnaire responses from over three hundred workers in seven professional group work categories, he developed his findings along several dimensions.[147] His description of the field disclosed that less than one-tenth of the Jewish Centers employ one-third of all Jewish Center professional personnel, with the jobs of executive director, program director, and program assistant accounting for almost 85 percent of all positions. The center worker is young—the median age being just under 35. The analysis of "amount of job movement" disclosed that the mobility of center workers declines with age, but remains high among those 30 to 50 years old. The study of "movement propensity" yielded the conclusion that the center worker is "poised for flight," with almost 40 percent reporting that they expected to leave their jobs within two years and more than 25 percent actively seeking new employment at the time of the study. The "significant determinants" of this condition are described as "level of aspiration," "perception of the road to advancement," "salary increase," and "status anxiety," wherein the worker perceives "movement as being associated with advancement." [148]

Herman makes an important contribution to future work in this area with his analysis of three "patterns of job movement": (1) horizontal change, involving movement from one agency to another without change in job title; (2) vertical change, describing movement upward in the job hierarchy in the same agency; and (3) diagonal change, with a difference in both agency and job title. He found that horizontal movement was the most common form of job change, encouraged by differences in salary for the same job title in the

[145] Girl Scouts of the U.S.A., "An Exit Study of Local Professional Workers in Girl Scouting" (New York, 1954). (Mimeographed.)

[146] Robert D. Vinter, "Report of the Personnel Turnover Study," *The Round Table* (Journal of the National Federation of Settlements and Neighborhood Centers), Vol. 21, Nos. 5–6 (May–June 1957), pp. 1–5.

[147] Melvin Herman, *Occupational Mobility in Social Work: The Jewish Community Center Worker* (New York: National Jewish Welfare Board and the Research Institute for Group Work in Jewish Agencies of the National Association of Jewish Center Workers, 1959).

[148] *Ibid.*, p. 72.

larger agencies, by the prestige attached to these agencies, and by the condition of status anxiety.

The Volunteers

Whatever reservations one might have about the use of volunteer and other untrained personnel in the neighborhood centers, it seems clear from a study by Pins that the practice has helped cast the centers as a major recruiting agent for the social work profession.[149] Studying factors affecting the choice of social work as a career, Pins found that 76 percent of the students entering schools of social work in the fall of 1960 had first learned about social work from a prior work experience in the field; that 74 percent of this first-year class ascribed their career choice to these work experiences; and that the group service agencies had provided this volunteer and part-time work for the largest number of these students—36 percent of the total, with public assistance next at 31 percent. This recruitment role yields only a small return of workers to the centers themselves: of the 2,771 entering students in the United States and Canada at this time, only about 10 percent, or 272, had elected the specialization in social group work. The centers, then, are apparently well suited to introduce young people into the social work arena but may not promise the kind of professional experience that would attract them into the field of service in which they began.

The centers' historic stake in voluntarism has produced a rich descriptive and philosophical literature, but there has been little systematic study of the volunteer's role in the administration of a social service. However, the few reportable studies offer some interesting data and some promising clues for future work. Findings have been developed on the group characteristics of those who volunteer, some motivational factors, and the analysis of volunteer performance.

General characteristics. Thursz, for the B'nai B'rith Youth Organization, and Arsinian and Blumberg, for the Young Men's Christian Association, have studied the characteristics of volunteer group leaders.[150] Although Thursz's sample was a very large one, and Arsinian and Blumberg's group leader sample very small, the similarities are worth mentioning. Both found an older population than they had expected—one-half of the BBYO sample was between 26 and 40 and 93 percent were over 21. One-half of the "Y" group was between 30 and 47. Both had a high married population—80 percent for the BBYO and 61 percent of the "Y" leaders. Both had a high proportion of leaders— about one-third—who had been educated at the college level and above. Both had a high proportion of leaders in the middle- and upper-status occupations. Both found a very high percentage of "satisfied customers"—that is, group leaders who had themselves come through a satisfying agency experience as a participant or "client."

Thursz also found that volunteer qualifications were higher in the small cities than in the large metropolitan agencies, while Arsinian and Blumberg developed additional data identifying the volunteer leader as one who is more active in other community activities, has lived in his community a relatively long time, and comes from a family with a tradition of community service. The figure on length of residence, it may be added, replicates a finding of Sills in his study of the March of Dimes volunteers.[151]

---

[149] Arnulf M. Pins, *Who Chooses Social Work, When and Why?* (New York: Council on Social Work Education, 1963).

[150] Daniel Thursz, *Volunteer Group Advisors in a National Social Group Work Agency* (Washington, D.C.: Catholic University of America Press, 1960); and Arsinian and Blumberg, *op. cit.*

[151] David L. Sills, *The Volunteers: Means and Ends in a National Organization* (Glencoe, Ill.: Free Press, 1957).

Motivation. Both the BBYO and YMCA studies found evidence that might support a theory that the motive for volunteering is more closely related to what Arsinian and Blumberg called a "trait of volunteerism" than to a desire to implement the purposes of a particular agency. Almost half of Thursz's respondents "gave as their motive for volunteering a self-oriented or self-fulfilling reason," while only 25 percent gave "motives which can be classified as organization-centered." [152] Arsinian and Blumberg's leaders indicated that they derived their satisfactions from certain social and psychological factors, rather than from factors closely related to a "high regard for the purposes of the Y.M.C.A.," such as "wholesome Christian activities," "religious reasons," and the like. The researchers were led, in conclusion, to ask: "Would these people just as readily volunteer in some other agency?"

The problem of motivation is sharply raised in Schwartz's small comparative study of paid and volunteer club leaders at the East Bronx Community YM-YWHA in New York City.[153] He found the two groups to be similar in age, education, and work experience, but strikingly different in three major respects, exclusive of performance. In each of four fields of prior experience—school, natural group, camp, and agency—he found that "the paid workers presented a personal history of group activity and participation that far outweighed that of the unpaid leaders." [154] Second,

the paid workers were more oriented to social work and group work as a future career. Finally, the paid workers tended to fall into what was designated as a *"mission-*centered" category, denoting strong value systems and the desire to transmit them, while the volunteers fell mainly into the *"self-*centered" group, marked by underelaborated responses, difficulties in self-involvement, and fearfulness of, though eager to try, the group experience. On this aspect of the study Schwartz concluded that "it might be stated, in essence, that the paid workers were attempting to *duplicate* a successful experience, while the unpaid leaders were trying to achieve one." [155]

Richards and Polansky investigated the question of why the participation of women in voluntary organizations tends to vary with their class position.[156] Working from the perspective of girl scouting and its concern about the paucity of volunteer leadership in working class neighborhoods, the authors state that they realized early that it would be a mistake to assume that the agency program was appropriate, and that only adaptation and intelligent public relations were needed.

They compared samples of working-class and middle-class women in two different neighborhoods, found markedly greater participation by the latter, and proceeded to search for determining factors. They found few differences in what they called "reality factors"—family size, outside employment, spatial mobility, and chronological age; greater differences emerged in family participation and activity patterns—significantly lower in the working class families, even among the adolescents. Their most impressive results came in the area of "general morale and personality," with the working class women more often describing their health as poor and producing re-

[152] Thursz, *op. cit.*, p. 330.

[153] William Schwartz, "Group Leaders—Paid and Volunteer: A Comparison of Background Characteristics and Performance" (New York: East Bronx Community Y.M.-Y.W.H.A., 1949) (mimeographed); and William Schwartz, "A Comparison of Background Characteristics and Performance of Paid and Volunteer Group Leaders," *Jewish Center Worker*, Vol. 12, No. 1 (January 1951), pp. 32–44.

[154] Schwartz, "A Comparison of Background Characteristics and Performance of Paid and Volunteer Group Leaders," p. 38.

[155] *Ibid.*, p. 40. Emphasis in original.

[156] Katherine Richards and Norman A. Polansky, "Reaching Working Class Youth Leaders," *Social Work*, Vol. 4, No. 4 (October 1959), pp. 31–39.

sponses characterized as "depressive." They concluded:

> . . . larger numbers of working-class women . . . appear to feel defeated, alienated, powerless to help themselves and others. Moreover, if you look at their backgrounds, they come to adult life with less ingrained self-expectation of participating, and less experience in their own adolescent years.[157]

Performance. The Baden Street Settlement in Rochester, New York, has used volunteers as case aides in a family-visiting program designed to make more agency and community services available to "hard-to-reach" families who "would respond to a less formal and less demanding relationship."[158] First reports showed that the aides perceived their roles as satisfying, that concrete modes of practice were being worked out, and that marked success had been demonstrated in 38 percent of the cases, with the "health problems" group being the most productive of movement. Later reports pointed to reduced figures on neglect petitions, arrests, truancies, and evictions, with "only slight changes" in welfare status and growth in financial independence.[159]

In St. Louis, McAllister evaluated the work of 102 "program volunteers" in fourteen group-serving agencies, using supervisory ratings on "enrichment of experience," "creative learning," "emotional adjustment," and "social adjustment."[160] His highest-rated volunteers were women

over 30 from the metropolitan area, with superiority in education and experience.

Schwartz's previously cited comparison of parttime paid and volunteer club leaders revealed no differences in the quality of their actual work with clients "even on the simplest levels."[161] The paid workers, however, showed marked superiority on those performance criteria that required not professional skill but motivation and ability to learn, scoring higher on the criteria related to reliability, flexibility, and participation in supervision.

> Faced with a job whose difficulty and complexity became clearer week by week, and with groups whose reactions they could not understand and whose failure to "move" they regarded as a personal rejection, the responses of the paid leaders as a whole differed considerably from those of the unpaid. . . . It was at this point that the leaders' ability to accept responsibility for what was happening and to subject their own values to critical examination was vitally important. In the main, the unpaid workers found this too difficult. . . . In an interesting manner, the *"mission*-centeredness" [of the paid workers] played a salutory role in this regard. While this quality tended strongly to increase their manipulativeness, it also seemed to make them extremely sensitive to this very tendency, which was sharply out of line with their own intellectual conception of the leader's role.[162]

The Method

The state of practice research in group work can be judged by the fact that discussions on the subject are still apt to begin and end with a study conducted outside the field more than twenty-five years ago. The Lewin, Lippitt, and White research, dealing with the effects of "authoritarian" and "democratic" leadership behaviors on the social climate of children's groups, impressed both group workers and teachers

[157] *Ibid.*, p. 38.
[158] Baden Street Settlement Staff, *Final Evaluation of the Volunteer Case Aide Demonstration Project* (Rochester, N.Y.: Baden Street Settlement and Junior League of Rochester, 1959), p. 4.
[159] Baden Street Settlement Staff, *Patterns of Change in Families Assigned to the Volunteer Case Aide Program* (Rochester, N.Y.: Baden Street Settlement, 1960).
[160] William A. McAllister, "Program Volunteers and Their Job Performance," *Smith College Studies in Social Work*, Vol. 23, No. 1 (January 1952), pp. 93–119.

[161] "A Comparison of Background Characteristics and Performance of Paid and Volunteer Group Leaders," p. 40.
[162] *Ibid.*, p. 42. Emphasis in original.

with its unique interest in the details of practice, its experimental daring, and its direct confrontation of the worrisome issue of permissiveness and laissez-faire as factors in group leadership.[163]

Lippitt and White summarized these experiments, showing "the interdependencies of leadership role, group composition, group history, and membership personality structure in this study of four experimental clubs of preadolescent boys."[164] Aside from reassuring group workers on several of their working articles of belief, this research also developed data—in terms more specific than had yet been made available —on group patterns of aggressiveness and passivity engendered by the behavior of the worker and the group's history of previous relations with adult control. Of equal importance were the research implications: ". . . it was found in this exploratory study that the process of small-group life could be experimentally manipulated in a satisfactory way for scientific study and could be recorded adequately for meaningful quantitative analysis."[165]

Unfortunately, the study remained a conversation piece instead of becoming a stimulant to research in the neighborhood center field. Moreover, the social sciences have not since yielded any comparable bonanza of data on professional leadership in the

small-group context. Steiner's recent review of group dynamics research states:

. . . the term "group dynamics" refers to the interpersonal transactions which occur in groups, and to the antecedents and consequences of those behaviors. Unfortunately, many studies of group phenomena have examined the presumed antecedents and consequences without giving careful attention to the mediating interpersonal transactions.[166]

It is these "mediating interpersonal transactions," involving the professional worker in his client group, that have remained largely undocumented and unstudied. Some work, nevertheless, has been done, and some lines of inquiry are beginning to take shape. There is interest, for example, in clients' and workers' perceptions of each other as they interact. Maas, pointing out that "group life . . . depends partly on the nature of the leader's perception of members' behavior in the group," undertook "an exploratory study of factors related to the modification of such perception."[167]

He examined the work of twenty-two college juniors leading youth groups in neighborhood agencies over an eight-month period: ten groups were designated as "open," with informal, unstructured membership and activities, and twelve were "closed" groups, with elected members and more formal programs and procedures. Leaders were characterized as "x-type"—those who tended to project blame—and "y-type"— those who tended to introject responsibility. "Desirable" changes in leader perceptions were defined as a decrease in "j-reactions" —perceptions distorted by moral judgments—or an increase in "c-reactions"—

[163] Kurt Lewin, Ronald Lippitt, and Ralph K. White, "Patterns of Aggressive Behavior in Experimentally Created 'Social Climates,'" *Journal of Social Psychology*, Vol. 10, No. 2 (March 1939), pp. 271–299; Ronald Lippitt, "An Experimental Study of Authoritarian and Democratic Group Atmosphere," in Kurt Lewin, Ronald Lippitt, and Sybylle Escalona, eds., *Studies of Topological and Vector Psychology I* (Iowa City: University of Iowa Press, 1940), pp. 45–198; and Ronald Lippitt and Ralph K. White, "An Experimental Study of Leadership and Group Life," in Eleanor E. Maccoby, Theodore M. Newcomb, and Eugene L. Hartley, eds., *Readings in Social Psychology* (New York: Henry Holt and Company, 1958), pp. 496–511.

[164] *Op. cit.*, p. 510.

[165] *Ibid.*, p. 511.

[166] Ivan D. Steiner, "Group Dynamics," in Paul R. Farnsworth, Olga McNemar, and Quinn McNemar, eds., *Annual Review of Psychology*, Vol. 15 (Palo Alto, Calif.: Annual Reviews, 1964), p. 440.

[167] Henry S. Maas, "Personal and Group Factors in Leaders' Social Perception," *Journal of Abnormal and Social Psychology*, Vol. 45, No. 1 (January 1950), p. 54.

perceptions with causal inferences. Using diary content analysis, group observation, and the California Test of Personality, Maas found the personal and group factors related to the workers' perceptual changes: x-type leaders (the projectors) showed more desirable changes when they led open groups; y-type leaders (the introjectors) showed more desirable changes when they led closed groups; reverse placements produced more undesirable changes; and the members' demands on leaders were greater in the open groups. Maas concluded that x-types were probably less frustrated in the open groups, while the y-types probably functioned with less anxiety in closed, well-structured groups.

In 1958, the Group Work Section of the Southern Pennsylvania Chapter of the National Association of Social Workers published a research proposal focusing on intragroup perception variables and their relationship to measures of "social functioning" and "relationship competence" in groups led by social group workers.[168] In casework practice research, Polansky, Thomas, and Kounin have studied the expectations of the client vis-à-vis the "potentially helpful person," with special emphasis on the client's experienced "freedom to communicate" and "freedom to reveal one's feelings."[169] "This particular index [freedom to reveal feelings] correlated significantly with every other dimension having to do with satisfaction with the interview, and it was about the only

one that did."[170] Along similar lines, Wormby has studied adolescent perceptions of the "potentially helpful person."[171]

Other lines of interest have been developing. Vinter has suggested, in an approach similar to the "planned change" emphasis of Lippitt, Watson, and Westley, that study be directed to the worker's means of influence, defining "direct" means as "those interventions utilized to effect change through immediate interaction with one or another group member," and "indirect" means as "those interventions utilized to effect modifications in group conditions which subsequently affect one or more members."[172] Schwartz has called attention to the need for an operational definition of practitioner skill: "The difficulty in defining skill in human relations is the problem of describing an act in its own terms, rather than in terms of its results."[173] Along these lines, there had been, in Schwartz's leader-comparison study mentioned earlier, a formulation of a set of criteria for measuring performance of group leaders. Later, in work with a professional committee, an instrument was designed for the identification of worker responses in group situations; and there have been recent indications that the interest in operational analysis is being carried forward in graduate classrooms, student re-

---

[168] "Group Workers Design Practice Research," *NASW News*, Vol. 4, No. 1 (February 1958), pp. 9–10.

[169] Norman A. Polansky, "Small-Group Theory: Implications for Casework Research," in Kogan, ed., *op. cit.*, pp. 109–162; Norman A. Polansky and Jacob Kounin, "Clients' Reactions to Initial Interviews," *Human Relations*, Vol. 9, No. 3 (August 1956), pp. 237–264; and Edwin J. Thomas, Norman A. Polansky, and Jacob Kounin, "The Expected Behavior of a Potentially Helpful Person," *Human Relations*, Vol. 8, No. 2 (May 1955), pp. 165–174.

[170] Polansky, "Small-Group Theory: Implications for Casework Research," p. 113.

[171] Marsha Wormby, "The Adolescent's Expectations of How the Potentially Helpful Person Will Act," *Smith College Studies in Social Work*, Vol. 26, No. 1 (January 1955), pp. 10–59.

[172] Ronald Lippitt, Jeanne Watson, and Bruce Westley, *The Dynamics of Planned Change: A Comparative Study of Principles and Techniques* (New York: Harcourt, Brace and Company, 1958); and Vinter, "Small-Group Theory and Research: Implications for Group Work Practice Theory and Research," p. 128.

[173] William Schwartz, "Toward a Strategy of Group Work Practice," *Social Service Review*, Vol. 36, No. 3 (September 1962), p. 277.

search, and, most important, in the agencies themselves.[174]

There have been studies stemming from an interest in what might be called self-definition. This line of research raises questions about what group work is and what it is not, where it should be practiced, and what activities are consistent with its historic goals and functions. In this category is Wilson's attempt to draw reactions and discussion from her respondents to a distinction she had made between "social group work" and "work with groups"— producing 69 percent agreement that such a distinction was valid and a fascinating symposium revealing many of the confusions in the profession's own thinking about its practice.[175]

The quest for definition is also reflected in Wilson's earlier practice study at the Educational Alliance in New York City.[176] A good deal of the value of this account lies in its close examination of research problems in the agency context and in the internal effects of the study process. And also to be included in this category is Hartford's "Search for a Definition," undertaken for the Committee on Practice of the former Group Work Section of NASW as part of a project designed to compile a number of "working definitions of social group work" drawn up by leading professionals.[177]

Finally, there are a few studies related to the tasks of leadership training, when such tasks demand a synthesis of knowledge about the practice of group work. Kolodny and Johnson have reviewed the contributions of social research to leadership training in group work and concluded that social scientists have dealt more with the method and structure of the training process than with the content of practice.[178] For those interested in the body of research related to leadership, Bass has provided the most recent comprehensive account.[179]

At the Treasure Island Camp of the Philadelphia Boy Scout Council, Lippitt and Hogrefe worked as part of the camp staff and produced one of the first close explorations of the leadership training process in action.[180] Bavelas, in a co-operative project of the Child Welfare Station of the State University of Iowa, the Iowa WPA and the Home Camp of the Des Moines Jewish Community Center, conducted an experiment designed "to test under controlled conditions the efficiency of certain methods for rapid retraining of leaders in a particular field." [181] Bavelas reported highly successful training effects on the morale, involvement, and productivity of both the leaders and the children's groups they led, ascribing these effects to a "democratic" training experience in which the trainer had stressed "attitudes

---

[174] William Schwartz, "Identification of Worker Responses in Group Situations," memorandum to Gertrude Wilson *et al.*, Chicago, 1958, (mimeographed); and United Neighborhood Houses, Pre-Teen Delinquency Prevention Project, "Recording Devices: Guiding and Documenting Work" (New York, 1963) (mimeographed).

[175] "The Practice of Social Group Work."

[176] Gertrude Wilson, "Measurement and Evaluation of Social Group Work Practice," *Social Welfare Forum, 1952*, proceedings of the National Conference of Social Work (New York: Columbia University Press, 1952), pp. 205–219.

[177] Margaret E. Hartford, "Social Group Work 1930 to 1960: The Search for a Definition," Cleveland, 1960. (Mimeographed.)

[178] Ralph L. Kolodny and Edwin Johnson, "The Contributions of Research and Experimentation in the Social Sciences to Leadership Training in Group Work," *The Group*, Vol. 14, No. 4 (June 1952), pp. 13–16 and 26.

[179] Bernard M. Bass, *Leadership, Psychology, and Organizational Behavior* (New York: Harper & Brothers, 1960).

[180] Ronald Lippitt and Russell Hogrefe, "Camp as a Laboratory for Scoutmaster Training," in *Scouting for Facts* (New York: Boy Scouts of America, 1944).

[181] Alex Bavelas, "Morale and the Training of Leaders," in Goodwin Watson, ed., *Civilian Morale* (Boston: Houghton Mifflin Company, 1942), p. 146.

versus techniques," "'sensitizing' the leaders," "broadening and restructuring the goal region," "development of techniques," "integration of work with broader social objectives," and "sensitivity of morale to leadership."

Many have tried to explain the paucity of practice research in the neighborhood centers and many have discussed remedies. Vinter has tied the problem closely to the need for practice theory; by contrast, Polansky has suggested that a concrete "how to" approach should not be shunned because it seems superficial at the outset.[182] "Theory," he stated, "does not always come from posing 'theoretical questions.' " These approaches are not, of course, mutually exclusive; on the contrary, any point of departure for a systematic search is valid, and future study will depend a great deal on the growing ability of professionals to think their way from the specific to the general and the general to the specific.

Evaluations and Outcomes

Since the study of outcomes is so closely tied to the clarity of expectations, one might foresee that evaluation research would present particular difficulties for the neighborhood centers. It is hard to measure "character changes," even if agency personnel were to believe their own claims that this is the business they are in; so, too, with "socialization," "maturity," and similar abstractions. Thus, along with the need to limit and operationalize their goals, there is the added problem of clarifying the essential service of the agency, so that an open contract can be established with each client. It would, for example, seem a more practical enterprise to measure success in

imparting a new skill, if that was what the client had come for, than to try to determine whether he had, without his knowledge or co-operation, become more social, more independent, or more mature. This is not to say that experiences do not have complex effects and side-effects, or that these cannot be measured; but the demands of rigorous inquiry would seem to call for some ability at the outset to distinguish between one's vision of the product and the by-product.

There is evidence that the processes of concretizing and clarifying are under way, and the problems of evaluation may soon seem less formidable to neighborhood center professionals. The studies on hand fall into three categories: the "movement" studies of individuals and groups, the evaluations of program effectiveness, and the work dealing with the impact of agencies in their neighborhoods.

Movement Studies

Northen has reported a project in which a professional research committee evaluated fourteen summaries of individuals in group experience.[183] Using Hunt's family agency movement scale, an instrument that will probably be a point of departure for movement research for some time to come, the committee concluded that it had found ten cases of progress, two of regression, and two of no change.[184] The study throws light on the problems of studying individual growth in the group work context and serves also to illustrate the major problem of overstated and global objectives: "The general goal of all social group work is to effect changes or adaptations in an individ-

[182] *See* Vinter, "Small-Group Theory and Research: Implications for Group Work Practice Theory and Research"; and Norman A. Polansky, "Comments on Papers by Vinter and Konopka," *Social Service Review*, Vol. 30, No. 3 (September 1956), pp. 318–321.

[183] Helen Northen, "Evaluating Movement of Individuals in Social Group Work," in *Group Work Papers 1957* (New York: National Association of Social Workers, 1958), p. 28–37.

[184] J. McV. Hunt and Leonard S. Kogan, *Measuring Results in Social Casework: A Manual on Judging Movement* (New York: Family Service Association of America, 1950).

ual's attitudes, relationships, and behavior to the end that he may develop greater personal adequacy and improved social adjustment." [185] Such statements are generally based on the historic "Definition of the Function of the Group Worker," a document prepared by a professional committee in 1948 under the leadership of Grace Coyle.[186] The definition was indeed a landmark, but its major achievement was in its summary expression of philosophy and purpose, rather than its precision of language for use in research.

There is some work in progress on the more precise identification of client problems, clearly marking the areas in which an agency might reasonably expect to measure the effects of its service over time. From the casework perspective, Purcell has developed "a preliminary classification system for the identification and evaluation of problems encountered in the course of social work and counseling." [187] He addressed himself to the task of categorizing the "systems" with which clients need to cope—such as educational, employment, welfare, family, and housing—thus not only sharpening the client's problems and the worker's focus but also synthesizing the social and psychological aspects of the difficulties at hand. In a similar approach, a rare instance of convergence in social work, the United Neighborhood Houses' Pre-Teen Delinquency Prevention Project has emphasized the client's specific tasks as he tries to negotiate the various systems of demand and relationship with which he needs professional assistance.[188]

In a laboratory study, Maas studied the effects of group work services on the behavior of 7-year-old boys in two clubs under the supervision of a social group worker.[189] In a forty-five-minute experimental situation calling for intragroup planning and co-operation, he found that the members of Group A, composed of boys "with no social group work experience," displayed more ego-centered behavior, intragroup hostility, dependence on the worker, and inability to collaborate in planning than did those in Group B, consisting of boys who were "members of an organized club in a YMCA (Indian Guide) social group work program" for six months prior to the study.

"If these ten boys," Maas stated, "were well matched on all relevant factors except their prior participation in a social group work program, some of the effects of one social work program seem to have been dramatically demonstrated." [190] Maas then asked: "How were they matched?" and proceeded to discuss the "five concepts and fifteen factors" used in the studies, building on a biological concept ("organism"), two psychological concepts (the "self" and "personality"), and two social concepts ("membership and reference group" and "social role"). What is important about these concepts and their constituent factors is that they are shown to be interdependent within a conceptual framework. Earlier formulations, such as Bernstein's "Individual Evaluation Chart" in *Charting Group Progress*, as well as similar devices, had suggested important factors for observation but had not yet gone beyond the simple listings or inventories of discrete and unrelated items.[191]

The study of group movement is still

---

[185] Northen, "Evaluating Movement of Individuals in Social Group Work," p. 29.

[186] American Association of Group Workers, "Definition of the Function of the Group Workers," in Dorothea F. Sullivan, ed., *Readings in Group Work* (New York: Association Press, 1952).

[187] Francis P. Purcell, "A Suggested Classification for Problems in Social Functioning" (New York: Mobilization for Youth, 1964). (Mimeographed.)

[188] *Op. cit.*

[189] Henry S. Maas, "Evaluating the Individual Member in the Group," in *Group Work and Community Organization, 1953–1954*, papers presented at the National Conference of Social Work (New York: Columbia University Press, 1954), pp. 36–44.

[190] *Ibid.*, p. 38.

[191] *Op. cit.*, p. 15.

virtually untouched within the field. Group workers were enthusiastic about Cattell's early offering of the "syntality" construct, which "defines for the group precisely what personality does for the individual," but they have not yet been able to produce the body of narrative and descriptive data against which this and subsequent work might be applied.[192]

The previously cited Garland, Jones, and Kolodny "Model for Stages of Development in Social Work Groups" is an encouraging example of what can be done through a disciplined examination of case materials. The United Neighborhood Houses' Pre-Teen Delinquency Prevention Project has completed preliminary work on a design for a "Group Problems Inventory," designed to abstract from group records and staff discussion the tasks and problems that a *collective* may be said to have had—and with which "it" has been given certain specific kinds of professional help. Finally, it should be added that whatever inadequacies a sophisticated observer might properly find in Bernstein's early inventory of group characteristics, it still contains a number of ideas that have never been adequately explored.

Program Evaluation

Several of the street club projects have addressed themselves to studies of their own effectiveness. The most thoroughgoing of such attempts seems to have been that of the Boston Delinquency Project, reported by Miller to have taken "as its principal target of change the value system of the group itself."[193] He described a

"definite and measurable impact" on patterns of group behavior, incidence of recorded acts of law violation, commitment rates, and the dynamics of community relational systems. He also pointed to certain factors that militated against effects that would represent "the true potential of this method and its developed operating rationale."

In Chicago, Gandy reported on the efforts of the Hyde Park Youth Project to provide intensive staff services to youths with high delinquency potential. He reported:

... comparison of the frequency of individual antisocial behavior at the outset of the staff service and termination indicated that the youths who were participating in little or no antisocial behavior when staff service was first provided continued to avoid delinquency. The staff was least successful with youths who, at time of first contact, already had a history of antisocial behavior.[194]

In Minneapolis, Wright and Magoffin studied the effects of the "Floating Worker Service" on the social adjustment of adolescent delinquents in six groups, using controls.[195] They found that school records on ten items of adjustment favored the six groups served, but official delinquency records favored the control groups. Generally speaking, one must still agree with Miller's judgment in 1959: "The corner-group method of attempting to prevent 'gang' delinquency is in fairly wide use, but little substantial evidence as to its effectiveness is available."[196]

Studies have illustrated the kind of work that can be done by local centers in collaboration with skilled researchers. The

---

[192] Raymond B. Cattell, "New Concepts for Measuring Leadership in Terms of Group Syntality," in Sullivan, ed., *op. cit.*, pp. 387–417. *See also* the section in this review on "The Group As Client," pp. 154–158.

[193] Miller, "The Impact of a Community Program on Delinquent Corner Groups"; and Miller, "Preventive Work with Street-Corner Groups: Boston Delinquency Project," p. 98.

[194] John M. Gandy, "Preventive Work with Street-Corner Groups: Hyde Park Youth Project, Chicago," *Annals of the American Academy of Political and Social Science*, Vol. 327 (1959), p. 107.

[195] Charles F. Wright and John Magoffin, "Floating Worker Service Study" (Minneapolis: Community Welfare Council of Hennepin County, 1959). (Mimeographed.)

[196] "Preventive Work with Street-Corner Groups: Boston Delinquency Project," p. 97.

Horace Mann-Lincoln Neighborhood Center and the Commission on Community Interrelations of the American Jewish Congress conducted an experiment designed to test the effects of interracial club experience and certain prescribed leadership behaviors on the reduction of intergroup prejudice among children.[197] Although they produced no significant findings on the experimental leadership variables, they did find marked differences on subsequent projective test responses between the neighborhood center children and the control non-neighborhood center group, with the former showing more avoidance of segregation patterns.

At the Friends Neighborhood Guild in Philadelphia, Lewis evaluated the effects of a training program for housekeepers rated poor by housing personnel and social service staff. Lewis found no evidence for the "hard-core" or "life-pattern" explanations currently in vogue. The poorly rated housekeepers were of average intelligence, optimistic, capable of warm interpersonal relationships, and their housekeeping patterns were susceptible to changing circumstances. He found clear improvement in the group that received training, as against a control group whose only stimulus for change was the threat of eviction.[198]

Other outcome studies in progress have been reported at the Goodrich-Bell Neighborhood Center in Cleveland and the Lighthouse Settlement in Philadelphia, both studying the effects of "intensive" group work on given populations; at the Child-Parent School of the University Settlements in Philadelphia, in an early-detection project; and at the Oakland (California) YWCA, studying the formation of community-based groups for on-leave mental patients.

Agency Impact

By far the most popular instrument of agency evaluation is and has been the "self-study," in which the major emphasis is frequently on the study process itself as an educational device for clients, board, and staff. Often, too, the search for information is broad and comprehensive, rather than focused on any particular problem, hypothesis, or outcome. Serotkin has described this process in some detail.[199]

In the 1940's, Reed directed himself to the question of the effectiveness of the neighborhood centers in preventing delinquency, beginning with the hypothesis that "the group-work agencies worked more largely with youths from families which by reasons of better fortune and character were less productive of delinquency and that this might be the reason that fewer group-work youths got into court."[200] He studied randomly selected samples of 1,679 children served by the Cincinnati group-serving agencies in April 1942, and 246 cases from the juvenile court files of 1941. The samples were proportionate for sex and race. He found that the group work agency youth were younger and had a smaller proportion of Negroes, a significantly smaller percentage of them lived in the highly depressed areas, and they tended to come from more stable and socially adequate families than the court sample, rated by Social Service Exchange registration and other criteria. He also found that the

[197] Russell Hogrefe, Mary Catherine Evans, and Isidor Chein, "The Effects on Intergroup Attitudes of Participation in an Inter-Racial Play Center," paper presented at the 55th annual meeting of the American Psychological Association, Detroit, 1947.

[198] Harold Lewis, "Implication of Evaluation," in "Housekeeping—A Community Problem: Summary of Workshop" (Philadelphia: Friends Neighborhood Guild, 1961). (Mimeographed.)

[199] Harry Serotkin, "The Evaluation of Recreation and Informal Education Agencies," in *Social Welfare Forum, 1953*, proceedings of the National Conference of Social Work (New York: Columbia University Press, 1953), pp. 250–265.

[200] Ellery F. Reed, "How Effective are Group Work Agencies in Preventing Delinquency?" *Social Service Review*, Vol. 22, No. 3 (September 1948), p. 340.

highest proportion of the group work youth lived in both the highest and lowest economic areas and that they represented a more secure group in all economic areas.

Two years later, the group work names were checked against court files, showing a lower delinquency rate, fewer repeated offenders among those with court records, and higher delinquency rates as they grew older. Reed concluded that the study raised serious questions about the agencies' screening-out processes, with age and socio-economic factors rendering them favorable to lower delinquency rates.

Several years later, Reed repeated his study, this time restricting his attention to a single, highly deteriorated section of Cincinnati.[201] He compared the social and economic status of families served by the leisure-time agencies with the general population of the area. Gathering data on 5,675 client youth, he found again that the agencies were serving an above-average group for that area of the city. He also found that, under these conditions, the Social Service Exchange registration rates, being pervasive, were poor indicators of social status and stability; more suitable were figures on delinquency, public assistance, and other factors.

More recently, Brown and Dodson studied the impact of the Louisville, Kentucky, Red Shield Boys' Club on the delinquency rates of its neighborhood.[202] Because the Boys' Club had been established in 1946, they did an ex post facto statistical study of the period 1944 to 1954 and found that the area's delinquency figures had decreased markedly—from one in nineteen in 1946, to one in thirty-nine in 1954. At the same time there was an increase in the city as a whole—from one in twenty-nine to one in eighteen. Comparable neighborhoods used as controls had also increased. In their discussion of results, the authors pointed up other neighborhood factors that may have affected the outcome: commercial expansion, leadership structure, intergroup relations, organizational activity, and others. They suggested that the same social stabilizers that had led to the establishment of the agency may also have contributed to the improved delinquency situation.

In general, it is probably safe to predict that a number of other difficulties will have to give way before the neighborhood centers can make any real progress in evaluation research. To repeat an earlier injunction:

Despite the impatience of those who would like to move as quickly as possible into studies of outcome and effectiveness, our main progress for a time will probably be in studies of process and of limited effects . . . our major tools are still the group record, the life-history, the critical incident, and other techniques for codifying and conceptualizing the experience of practice.[203]

Some Final Observations

One is tempted to conclude by offering one's own list of research priorities, urging study of certain crucial questions and exploration of certain neglected areas of knowledge. The fact is, however, that the list of possible questions is endless. Further, few of these questions are, in any absolute sense, more important than others. While such lists, reflecting one person's theoretical stance and sense of urgency, are for him a logical way to proceed, they rarely stimulate research by others. The field has produced many such agendas for research, each marking out problems of unquestioned importance and then taking its place in the realm of unfinished business.

[201] Ellery F. Reed, "Families Served by Group Work Agencies in Deteriorated Area Compared with the General Population of That Area," *Social Service Review*, Vol. 28, No. 4 (December 1954), pp. 412–423.

[202] Roscoe C. Brown and Dan W. Dodson, "The Effectiveness of a Boys' Club in Reducing Delinquency," *Annals of the American Academy of Political and Social Science*, Vol. 312 (1959), pp. 47–52.

[203] Schwartz, "Toward a Strategy of Group Work Practice," p. 278.

Heuck's "A Challenge to Group Work" in 1946 showed awareness of the need for scientific study, and the responses to her challenge were written by personages no less important than Lewin, Slavson, and Trecker, each of whom specified particular problems of knowledge and methodology to be pursued.[204] A year later, Zander published a comprehensive review and prospectus for future research.[205] In 1955, Coyle projected a number of "proposed areas for concentration and study," and subsequent research agendas have been put forward by Hurwitz, Konopka, Vinter, Northen, Hillman, Schwartz, and others.[206] Thus, there is no lack of research problems —only of research. Rather than proliferate questions for study, it may be more profitable to attempt some brief assessment of the factors that impede the scientific effort, as well as some positive indicators for the future.

A major obstacle to research in this field is the failure of most of the centers to institutionalize the process of raising and formulating the questions that emerge from agency practice. This lack of "official curiosity" creates an atmosphere in which research becomes a kind of hobby, pursued independently and sporadically by an oc-

casional staff member if he has the time, rather than a formal responsibility stemming from the job analysis of the agency itself. A second problem, stemming partly from the first, is the absence of any systematic logging or recording of agency practice. Despite, or perhaps because of, the heavy recording emphasis in the formal training of group workers, the agencies have never given more than lip service to the discipline of documenting their work with people. The problem goes beyond the narration of events or the recording of "process"; even the development of uniform statistical procedures, such as common definitions of units of service, remains about as it was twenty-five years ago, when the U.S. Children's Bureau made a valiant but short-lived effort in this direction.[207]

Finally, mention should be made of the fact that the profession upon which the centers depend is itself badly trained in the skills of research. Social workers still tend to view systematic inquiry as an alien task, rather than as part of their professional equipment. This alienation increases the dependence of the agencies on outside experts. Also, the research interest, when it appears, is often expressed in a kind of perfectionism—wherein a study design is either very intricate and ambitious or it is not "research" at all. Such a perspective discourages the use of limited but consistent modes of study through which the agencies can, within their resources, systematically scrutinize their practice and build up their findings over the years.

On the credit side, the achievement to date, though not as rich as one might expect from a century of practice, is not as poor as many have supposed. There are

---

[204] Julia F. Heuck, "A Challenge to Group Work," *The Group*, Vol. 8, No. 3 (March 1946), pp. 1–4; Kurt Lewin, "The 'Challenge' Should Be Met," *The Group*, Vol. 8, No. 3 (March 1946), pp. 4–5; S. R. Slavson, "Problems of Research," *The Group*, Vol. 8, No. 3 (March 1946), pp. 8–10; and Harleigh B. Trecker, "A Methodology for Research in Group Work," *The Group*, Vol. 8, No. 3 (March 1946), pp. 6–8.

[205] *Op. cit.*

[206] Grace Coyle, "Proposed Areas for Concentration and Study," *The Group*, Vol. 17, No. 5 (June 1955), pp. 7–10; Jacob I. Hurwitz, "Systematizing Social Group Work Practice," *Social Work*, Vol. 1, No. 3 (October 1956), pp. 63–69; Konopka, *op. cit.*; Vinter, "Group Work with Children and Youth: Research Problems and Possibilities"; Northen, "What is Researchable in Social Group Work?"; Hillman, *op. cit.*, chap. 7; and Schwartz, "Toward a Strategy of Group Work Practice."

[207] *See* Frances Adkins Hall, *Statistical Measurement in Group Work: A Manual on Statistical Records for Use by Staff Members* (Washington, D.C.: U.S. Department of Labor, Children's Bureau, 1939); and Louis J. Owen, "The Group-Work-Reporting Project of the United States Children's Bureau," in *Proceedings of the National Conference of Social Work, 1938* (Chicago: University of Chicago Press, 1939).

small bodies of work and growing signs of activity in key areas of concern: class factors in client selection; the relationship between agency structure and service; the "need" perceptions of worker and client; conflicting concepts of agency function among board, staff and clientele; modes of leadership and professional impact on group life; the cultural identification and "belongingness" work of the Jewish Centers; the developing attention to the details of the helping process in the group context; and the many other lines of inquiry discernible in the work reviewed above. There is a developing literature on the experience of center research and the nature of the ongoing relationship between agency service and the discipline of study.[208]

Similarly, there is a growing body of experience in action-research collaboration between the professional practitioners and the social scientists.[209] From the profession, there is a growing technical literature projecting new and more sophisticated attempts to theorize about the practice of social work with groups and to take on some of the research problems inherent in the study of group service in action.[210]

Ultimately, much will depend on the developing relationship between the neighborhood centers and the social work profession. When the agencies continue to clarify their conceptions of service, they will be increasingly less occupied with questions of faith and doctrine and more with the problems of science. Within these settings, a maturing profession can then be asked to turn its attention to the systematic pursuit of the knowledge it needs in order to practice.

---

[208] *See* Irving Canter, "Pittsburgh's Adventure in Research," *Jewish Center Worker,* Vol. 9, No. 2 (May 1948), pp. 19–22; Ralph L. Kolodny, "The Research Process—An Aid in Daily Practice," *The Group,* Vol. 16 No. 1 (October 1953), pp. 17–20 and 24; Eli Picheny, "Research Comes to the Center," *Jewish Center Worker,* Vol. 9, No. 2 (May 1948), pp. 17–19; and Wilson, "Measurement and Evaluation of Social Group Work Practice."

[209] *See* Isidor Chein, Stuart W. Cook, and John Harding, "The Field of Action Research," *American Psychologist,* Vol. 3, No. 2 (February 1948), pp. 43–50; William Schwartz, "Action Research in a Group Work Setting: A Record of a Cooperative Experience," unpublished master's thesis, New York School of Social Work, Columbia University, 1948; and James F. Short, Jr., "Notes on Action-Research Collaboration: Research Design and Some Not-So-Technical but Vital Problems" (Seattle: University of Washington, undated) (mimeographed).

[210] *See* Gordon Hearn, *Theory Building in Social Work* (Toronto: University of Toronto Press, 1958) ; William Schwartz, "The Social Worker in the Group," in *Social Welfare Forum, 1961,* proceedings of the National Conference on Social Welfare (New York: Columbia University Press, 1961), pp. 146–171; David F. De Marche and Michael G. Iskander, "On-Lookers," *The Group,* Vol. 12, No. 3 (June 1956), pp. 7–12 and 17–18; Hans L. Epstein and Arthur Schwartz, "Psycho-diagnostic Testing in Group Work," *Rorschach Research Exchange,* Vol. 11 (1947), pp. 23–41; Norman A. Polansky *et al.,* "Problems of Interpersonal Relations in Research on Groups," *Human Relations,* Vol. 2, No. 3 (July 1949), pp. 281–291; Vinter, "Small-Group Theory and Research: Implications for Group Work Practice Theory and Research"; and Vinter, "Group Work with Children and Youth: Research Problems and Possibilities."

SOCIAL PLANNING

By ROBERT MORRIS

Social welfare planning in modern industrialized society is going through a major transition from co-ordinating and rationalizing established services to developing new approaches to the solution of major social problems. As part of its equipment for this task, community organization and social planning share with the other social work methods a limitation in research investment. Community organization has been built upon the narrowest definitions of locality—primarily the neighborhood and the city—and of the social problems perceived through the experience of social agencies. It has also suffered from a commitment to limited forms of citizen consensus. For a long time, social welfare policy was interpreted to mean the governing policies of welfare agencies, and especially those of local voluntary agencies.

In the current transition, research is slowly moving toward (1) analysis of the national as well as the local community and the interrelationships between the two; (2) an attempt to understand welfare problems as a function of society involving total populations; (3) planning for the solution of

social problems that have complex causes; and (4) study of social policy and decision-making in social change. These redefined tasks increase the scale of research and lead to demands for sharpening and refinement of methodology that have begun to develop while earlier research mechanisms and practices are still widely maintained. Methodologically, these practices are limited by over-reliance upon measures of need in the form of agency service statistics; reliance upon descriptive and single-community case studies; and inadequate provisions for the analyses of quantitative data. Substantively, such practices are hampered by inadequate concepts by which to organize systematic study of the complexities of planning in urban society. This is noticeable in the limited research attention given to social and institutional change, to the latent functions of institutional systems, and to class influences (social, economic, and political) on the direction of planning enterprises.

Rapid progress in developing new approaches has been made difficult by the admittedly ill-defined character of the subject,

185

comprising as it does elements of social action, co-ordination, management of social resources, financing, analysis of social need, as well as rationally organized steps to achieve social policy goals. Such elements are frequently grouped under the loose term, "community organization," which, at its broadest, covers any attempt by an organization, or a group of organizations, to deal with functional problems of a community. In its narrowest sense, the term is limited to interaction among specified social welfare agencies. It is also difficult to separate clearly the study of planning processes from the substantive content of the particular social problem.

To such natural ambiguities can be added the limited social welfare investment in research, which is too often devoted to daily administrative tasks and concealed in general administrative budgets that are traditionally kept as low as possible. Social work functions with the lowest investment in research and development of any major enterprise in the United States—perhaps less than .003 percent of the sums being planned for.

Any attempt to assess developments in this ill-defined yet fast-changing field must rely on an arbitrary selection, for a commonly accepted framework into which research can be fitted is lacking. The selections here have been limited to work that seems to illuminate the planning process, to the exclusion of research that advances specific solutions to real problems.[1] The production of knowledge has been uneven and the resulting picture is full of gaps and blind spots, but movement along the lines outlined can be discerned.

---

[1] Reference should be made to valuable contributions made by Alfred J. Kahn and Henry S. Maas, among others, to planned solutions for child welfare problems that have also contributed to understanding social planning processes. *See,* for example, Kahn's *Planning Community Services for Children in Trouble* (New York: Columbia University Press, 1963); and Maas's and Richard E. Engler's *Children in Need of Parents* (New York: Columbia University Press, 1959).

This analysis summarizes developments in research conducted by social workers or social scientists studying social problems in a population rather than in an agency context; or studying multiple organizations rather than single agency administrations. With some exceptions, it is limited to work published in the past five years and deals with the study of (1) social welfare need, (2) communities, (3) social planning structures, and (4) the processes of planned change.

Assessing Social Welfare Needs

If social planning has as its objective the reduction of a social problem, then its research has initial responsibility for illuminating the character or shape of a social problem. Social problems, however, assume different shapes when viewed by contributors, varying cultural groups, professional or specialized agencies, and consumers. What is identified as a problem by one social class or cultural group may not be seen as such by others, and a problem for society may not be a problem for an individual. Professional staff with specialized responsibilities often view problems differently than do equally qualified professional staff, who seek a more comprehensive and general view. Such differences are expressed in differing forms of provision, differing proposals for the solution of problems, and differing rates of client utilization. Fundamental to all such practical difficulties is the limited capacity to trace out a clear causal chain.

Research in social planning has begun to introduce new means for more effective and efficient study of the need to overcome such handicaps. These include the analysis of need in total populations without regard for conventional distinctions between those in need and the contributors; the introduction and increased use of probability sampling on a national as well as urban scale; and the attempt to correlate multiple variables in the search for especially significant factors or persistent patterns. The results have been dramatic. The volume of dysfunction or of social problems in metropolitan populations is now seen to be very much more extensive than was previously revealed through agency applications alone. Existing social provisions reach only a small proportion of need—perhaps only a minor fraction of it —however defined. Social agencies are increasingly viewed as only one of a variety of means by which a population seeks to deal with widespread problems, but understanding about utilization factors is still limited to imperfect studies of attitudes. The simple one-to-one correlation between a social need and a service to fill it is almost destroyed. New evidence suggests that cultural class and professional bias persists in the provision of services and results in seriously unbalanced service provision.

These more complex studies have also begun to uncover additional explanations for the persistence of social problems, notably in the field of educational preparation, with its great significance for shifting emphasis in prevention planning. Economic and social class, age, psychological development, and ethnic background all continue to appear as possible causal factors, but they are not necessarily associated with conventional predictions about social need. When a social need becomes a problem or an unmet need requires attention remains unclear. Efforts to develop technical shortcuts for measurement of need through indices have thus far been no more successful than in the past.

Service Statistics

A common approach to the study of need, to which the bulk of social work research manpower is still committed, is based on the annual accumulation of service reports from direct-service agencies.[2] Annual re-

ports of the U.S. Department of Health, Education, and Welfare, and of the major local community councils, provide a rough measure of agency effort expended and are valuable for the maintenance of support activities. They do not provide adequate data about prevalence or unmet need, which is essential for comprehensive planning as distinguished from mere co-ordination. This regular reporting is occasionally supplemented by a community survey combining analysis of applications, case loads, and professional staff judgments about needs. Common, too, are quantitative studies of specific problems such as delinquency and emotional disturbance in children, conducted by direct-service agencies or sponsored by community planning councils. Characteristic of such studies is the one conducted by Martin and Nurco for the Baltimore Health and Welfare Council.[3] Agencies and institutions working with children were asked by questionnaire to "nominate" children for placement in a variety of defined residential psychiatric placements. One hundred and twenty-six agencies reported 1,004 children whom they would recommend for such care at a statewide rate of eight per ten thousand. Although this number far exceeds available facilities, the lack of standardization in psychiatric terminology and the absence of evidence about family or agency readiness to act make it difficult to assess the precise meaning of the nominations or to translate them into significant plans.

A report by Ives is similar.[4] Based on a public school census of exceptional children, the study identified 24,000 socially maladjusted or emotionally disturbed children in a three-county area around Chicago, with only 50 percent of them under the care of either a voluntary child care

[2] *See*, for example, Robert Elkin, ed., *Inventory of Research, 1961–62* (New York: National Association of Social Workers, 1962).

[3] William A. Martin and Adelaide Nurco, *Residential Psychiatric Treatment for Children in Maryland* (Baltimore: Health and Welfare Council, 1961).

[4] Kenneth H. Ives, *Emotionally Disturbed Children* (Chicago: Welfare Council of Metropolitan Chicago, 1961).

agency or a youth commission. Although such work uncovers the gross disparity between available community resources and needs, the data are limited by their reliance on agency sources and unstandardized administrative interpretation.

Sampling Approaches

To overcome these limitations, a few studies have attempted to examine social needs (including health) from an epidemiological base or by probability sampling of population. Jaco sought to identify the crude annual incidence of new psychiatric cases in a specified time interval in a region.[5] This study elaborated the standard agency service reporting by inclusion of private fee-charging, proprietary facilities, and identification of annual rates of new cases. Substantial social data were also gathered in order to locate differences in problem distribution according to urban-rural characteristics, marital status, occupation and education, and subcultural differentiation (Anglo-American, Spanish-American and nonwhite populations). In some respects earlier findings were substantiated, such as the increasing incidence of psychosis with age and with urbanization, the low incidence of psychosis among married couples, and an increase among divorced or single persons. The findings, however, are at sharp variance with other studies in the significantly higher incidence of psychosis among females, among Anglo-Americans compared with nonwhites and Spanish-Americans, and among employed professionals compared with manual and agricultural workers.

Srole extended the study of need to a metropolitan population by interviewing a random sample of the total population.[6]

Utilizing indirect measures of positive mental health functioning, he found much more poor mental health functioning than had been expected. Using selective measures, the report estimated that 23.4 percent of this urban population suffered from marked, severe, or incapacitating symptoms. These prevalence rates were correlated with cultural and social characteristics and resource utilization. With a much larger base, the data succeeded in substantially widening the gap between presumed need and community resources and thus served to throw doubt upon the potential of present resources for dealing with the problem. The value of such data, therefore, lies in the revelation of the complexity that confronts and perhaps overwhelms planning in mental health, but it does not provide immediately useful guides for the purpose.

Utilization and Provision

Evidence about extensive need is complemented by evidence of imbalance found in comprehensive studies of service provision in metropolitan areas. Taber, in a study conducted for the Institute of Gerontology at the State University of Iowa, described and analyzed a system of social provision for older persons in one standard metropolitan statistical area with a population of 137,000.[7] Questionnaires were completed by employees of all income maintenance, health care, counseling, and personal service agencies, whether voluntary, sectarian, nonsectarian, proprietary, or governmental in auspices. Program administrators were interviewed and annual and special reports reviewed. Individual clients were identified to eliminate

[5] E. Gartly Jaco, *The Social Epidemiology of Mental Disorders* (New York: Russell Sage Foundation, 1960).

[6] Leo Srole *et al.*, *Mental Health in the Metropolis: The Midtown Manhattan Study*, Vol. 1 (New York: McGraw-Hill Book Co., 1962).

[7] Merlin Taber, Frank Itzin, and William Turner, *A Comprehensive Analysis of Health and Welfare Services for Older Persons in One County* (Iowa City: State University of Iowa, 1963).

duplication. This comprehensive attempt to identify *total* social provision for a major age sector of the population revealed unexpected imbalances in the service network and in the use rates of professionally valued services. Two-thirds of the population over 60 years of age received some socially provided *income*, but only 266 out of a total of nearly 15,000 received socially provided *care*, and only 1,200 utilized socially provided *service*. The disparity between service use and care (usually within a custodial institution) is striking in light of the high proportion of social resources usually allocated for custodial care. More puzzling is the limited provision of non-income services for a population expected to have a high rate of need for care and welfare service. Only a few more than 300 out of a total of 15,000 elderly were in receipt of recreation, counseling, casework, or other personal services. Nongovernmental agencies provided services to only 5 percent of the persons in receipt of any service, although this 5 percent received 70 percent of all professional time available. Either the need is much less than experience would predict, or income provision satisfies most other needs, or, more likely, the service network simply does not reveal need adequately.

Weakness in planning to deal with such questions is highlighted by the finding that some of the important programs (the general hospitals, Veterans Administration, Old Age and Survivors Insurance, and private nursing homes) were generally not considered a part of the community system of social provision, and their administrators were not likely to be engaged by the existing social planning mechanisms. The lack of coherence in community planning is thus reinforced by the absence of a structure broad enough to comprehend the problem.

Lambert studied a sample of 297 non-institutionalized persons over 65 years of age living in their own homes in a well-to-do community with organized health and welfare resources.[8] The sample was selected on a probability basis to represent a universe of 9,389 persons. Differentials of age, sex, income, employment, and education were reviewed and personal interviews conducted to secure information about health-related needs and attitudes toward participation in community service. The study confirmed previous reports by identifying a third of the residents with health-related problems. However, it seemed to contradict other research in the *limited amount of unmet need* identified. Recognizing this to be a middle-class community, Lambert was not able to report any useable evidence of *unmet* needs of which respondents were aware. Although the study did not reveal how long current arrangements through family and friends could be expected to last, it opened up investigation of the difference between prevalence of a social problem and unmet need. In an attempt to explain the difference, the study linked multiple indicators of health need: (1) the use of, as well as the perceived need for a prosthesis; (2) diminished mobility and patient-perceived causation; (3) observed, as well as client-perceived need for home health care; and (4) the client's perception about his health status compared with the perception of others about his health. By combining these elements, three groups in the study population were identified: (1) those believing their health to be good or fair, and with no expressed need for care; (2) those perceiving their health as poor and having diminished mobility; and (3) those with diminished mobility and expressed health needs but perceiving their health to be comparatively good. These groupings were reduced to percentages of the study group and then projected to the total population. For an aged population of under 9,000, the group with both perceived

[8] Camille Lambert, Jr. *et al.*, "Re-opening Doors to Community Participation: How Realistic?" *Social Service Review*, Vol. 38, No. 1 (March 1964), pp. 42–50.

needs and poor health was estimated at approximately 1,500 or just under 17 percent. This figure exceeded community provision of service, but the study did not establish its reliability as an indicator of effective demand or need. Contrary to earlier studies, the identification of persons with the greatest presumed need could not be predicted by an increase in age and the distribution among those 65 to 79 years old and those over 80 was not statistically significant, thus disassociating the concept of age from the concept of need.

Morgan and his colleagues extended quantitative analysis and sampling to a national scale and at the same time combined synthesis of social and economic data with a search for causation.[9] This complex study of poverty, income, welfare, and public policy was conducted through a cross-section study of 2,800 families drawn from a national sample of dwelling units, with adequate representation of middle, high and low incomes. A supplementary sample of low-income families was drawn from a federal agency survey of consumer finances. The study set a high standard in its skillful blend of quantitative analysis and social-psychological interpretation. It selected *family income* as a unit for analysis, but correlatively assessed the *determinants* of family income, such as decisions about employment of the wife and children. Multiple analyses permitted selection of most significant factors in the production of poverty from the score of explanations conventionally advanced. While such factors as ill health, old age, motivation, and cultural disadvantage were considered, the data suggest very strongly that educational disadvantage is probably the most powerful factor in the persistence of poverty. The implications for shifting emphases in community planning is unmistakable and is already reflected in the work of the President's Committee on Juvenile De-

linquency and Youth Crime and the Office of Economic Opportunity.

The study introduced a useful new instrument—"the welfare ratio"—the ratio of the gross disposable income of the family unit to the estimated budget requirements of the family unit. As with all such indicators, the social problem was inferred but a strong link between the fact and the inferred social problem was not forged. Thus the data revealed that nearly nine-tenths of all money transfers were within systems to which the individual contributed, usually on an involuntary basis. Beneficiary families were therefore financing their own benefits to a much greater extent than hitherto realized, but it is not at all clear how this affects the persistence of poverty. The data also add to the growing evidence of limitations in welfare mechanisms. Economic lack was more objectively measured than mental or emotional ill-health, but only 23 percent of the persons identified by the "welfare ratio" benefited from public assistance and only 50 percent benefited from any income maintenance program.

Indices

The costliness of population-wide studies has for many years prompted a search for less costly indices of need based upon secondary analysis of census data. Illustrative of such a search is the work of the Recreation, Informal Education, and Group Work Division of the United Community Services of Metropolitan Boston.[10] The metropolitan area was divided into planning segments with roughly equal populations of 55,000 persons each. An index of need was derived from such data as total population, youth population, percent of population change during ten years, income, housing density, educational level, child dependency, race, delinquency rates,

⁹ James N. Morgan *et al.*, *Income and Welfare in the United States* (New York: McGraw-Hill Book Co., 1962).

¹⁰ United Community Services of Metropolitan Boston, *Profile for Planning* (Boston, 1962).

number of public housing units, foreign-born white, and total population over 65. In addition, the adequacy of existing services was appraised by a professional jury in terms of facilities, leadership, program use, participation and cost. As with all such index efforts, fundamental but untested assumptions were made; namely, that the data fed into the index had some visible relationship to the service need under study. Thus, the number of dependent children per thousand in an area was assumed to bear some relationship to that area's relative need for, or willingness to use, recreation services. Cultural and ethnic differentiation in choice was identified but the assumption is yet to be established that, for example, a given ratio of Negroes in an area bears any relationship to the readiness to utilize facilities. The scores for appraising available services were heavily weighted by arbitrarily assigned and untested measures drawn from national agencies, and jury judgments were unstandardized.

Perception of Need

Lack of technical readiness to construct suitable indexes of need is shown in recent studies of the gross differences in perception that separate professional staff, agencies, and consumers, and thus affect utilization patterns. The work of Miller and Polansky, to be discussed later, has been supplemented by studies such as those conducted by Varon, who interviewed in depth a small sample of the former clients of a protective service agency and the residents of the same community who had never been clients.[11] Varon found that community attitudes, those of clients and nonclients alike, generally viewed the protective service agency as punitive and not helpful to families. However, residents who rejected

the working-class character of this particular subcommunity were more accepting of the agency. The manifest obstacles thrown up by such client perception to an understanding of social need through agency experience require no comment.

Lambert introduced evidence that use of agency services is uneven in a low-income, culturally homogeneous population whose members have similar health problems.[12] Based upon a probability sample drawn from a universe of low-income families with school-age children, located through school records, the research established that eligibility measures for use of clinic resources do not discriminate effectively between low-income families who will or will not use the service. Alterations in eligibility standards could predict an increase in usage but will not significantly alter the balance between eligible families who will use the service and the one-third of eligible families who will not. The difference in dental condition and the difference in attitude to health matters among clinic and nonclinic families do not explain differences in utilization. The proportion of ineligible low-income families who seek to use the clinic regardless of eligibility is also unaffected by alterations in eligibility standards. Cultural differences could not be associated with any pattern of use. As a result, orientation toward health care and utilization of public facilities seems imperfectly correlated with economic status or cultural conditioning.

These findings are consistent with other studies previously recorded, which indicate that social welfare facilities are only one of a variety of resources utilized by persons with limited incomes to meet their needs. This work, however, introduces the

[11] Edith Varon, "The Client of a Protective Agency in the Context of the Community." Unpublished doctoral dissertation, Brandeis University, Waltham, Mass., 1961.

[12] Camille Lambert, Jr., "Interpersonal Factors Associated with the Utilization of a Public Health Dental Clinic." Unpublished doctoral dissertation, Brandeis University, Waltham, Mass., 1961. *See also* Lambert *et al.*, "Public Clinic Care and Eligibility," *American Journal of Public Health*, Vol. 53, No. 8 (August 1963), pp. 1196–1204.

view that, once utilized, the clinic experience tends to become a habitual mode for
meeting needs by some clients. Once eligibility is terminated, other forms of meeting
needs come into play, but not automatically,
so that perceptions of community resources
obstruct the development of new patterns.

Research into the dimensions of social
need has clearly entered a new phase—
spotty and incomplete, but challenging conventional planning notions about the relationship between needs and resources. The
scale of presumed need is evidently much
greater than expected, while patterns of
resource utilization are less than predicted
(or less certainly predictable).

Expanded study and more varied experimentation are needed along the lines already illustrated.

Studying the Community

The second major concern of planning research is the character of the community
in which social problems arise; not to explain why these problems exist but to
illuminate those forces that constitute the
planning environment. The development
of modern industrial society has rapidly
overtaken the simple view of community
in which face-to-face association among
individuals and the control of social conditions could be reasonably well identified in
close-knit and small-scale geographical
areas. The development of interdependent
national societies has broken apart this
relatively simple means of examining the
sense of community. In its place stand an
extraordinary variety of informal face-to-
face associations extending over wide dis-
tances, a great complex of formal organizations with impersonal relationships, and
networks of influence that spread from
small communities to all parts of the national state through both governmental and
voluntary channels. For social work research, much of this vast canvas remains
untouched and fragments of data do not

yet provide the outlines of a coherent
picture.

A start has been made toward understanding the distribution of influence, the
varieties of influence patterns, and the
dynamics of decision-making. Substantial
progress has been made in understanding
the subtleties of formal as well as informal
community action and the different functions performed by various class groupings
within each community. Unfortunately,
these developments have, with minor exceptions, been focused upon the smallest
geographical entities, and have not yet begun to examine the penetration of national
and regional community forces into the
welfare life of local communities. However, a theoretical framework for understanding these associations has been finally
produced for welfare purposes. As a result,
tentative hypotheses are now available concerning the conditions for effective community action under varying circumstances
—hypotheses that remain to be tested in
future work.

A significant start has also been made
in trying to understand the subelements
of the general community that are of particular significance for social welfare.
Social welfare institutions are now examined as subsystems, although it is not
yet clear whether there is one or more
than one system working side by side.
Neither is it yet clear whether social work
organization has wholly distinctive patterns of influence and decision-making.

The neighborhood has received fresh
attention in studies that point to the limited utility of certain formal organizations,
while rediscovering how individuals inhab-
iting homogeneous neighborhoods inform-
ally organize themselves for the performance of functions differing substantially
from those of the external community.
Since the latter generally organize intervening welfare services, the foundation is
laid for a constructive neighborhood approach.

The study of citizen participation in welfare policy, one of the central tenets of social work doctrine, is only on the threshold of more significant analysis. Descriptive studies have been extended to include an analysis of social, economic, and educational class factors. Work has been started on the selection of welfare agency policymakers, while analyses of working-class attitudes begin to uncover reasons for the difficulties encountered in efforts to combine many distinct groups in a common voluntary purpose.

The Local Community

Warren's study, *The Community in America*, has introduced a concept that links many aspects of community together coherently.[13] Without claiming finality, it combines a complex frame of reference with pragmatic utility. Methodologically, it relies upon reanalysis of four earlier community studies conducted by sociologists or social psychologists in El Cerrito, Middletown, Crestwood Heights, and Springdale, supplemented by the author's experience in small and rural communities in New York State.[14] In Warren's book, a local community is examined as a system of formal and informal units and subunits performing major social functions horizontally within a defined locality. These units and subunits are influenced by

vertical extra-local units, which in turn, are parts of intersecting systems through which each locality links itself to the larger society. Social welfare organizations can be examined by the extent to which they fulfill some general purposes, such as production, distribution and consumption, socialization, social control, social participation, and mutual support. The analysis, in revealing how such functions are altered by general social or economic trends, becomes a tool for understanding how a community functions dynamically. It interweaves formal and informal types of organization, social purpose (not agency program, which is a means to an end), authority and control patterns in decision-making, and input of resources by a scheme that accounts for the interdependence of communities through several spatial levels. The work is valuable not so much for specific findings, as for the formulation of a theoretical framework by which the community in America can be studied more efficiently.

Another significant line of general community study has been directed at decision-making processes in urban areas. Using the insights of political science, Banfield and Dahl have separately studied welfare decision-making processes in public welfare and housing in Chicago, and in urban renewal and education in New Haven.[15] Earlier studies in this genre conducted by Floyd Hunter suggested a stable concentration of power in pyramidal form in which a few individuals, sharing interests, could further or obstruct community action by combinations of passivity and open intervention.[16] The Dahl and Banfield data introduce a different picture of metropolitan functioning, in which many specialized

[13] Roland Warren, *The Community in America* (Chicago: Rand McNally Co., 1963). For another way to view the community, *see* Irwin T. Sanders, *The Community: An Introduction to a Social System* (New York: Roland Press, 1958).

[14] Leonard Olen and C. P. Loomis, *Cultural and Contemporary Rural Community: El Cerrito, Mexico* (Washington, D.C.: U.S. Department of Agriculture, 1941); Robert S. Lynd and Helen Merrill Lynd, *Middletown in Transition* (New York: Harcourt, Brace, 1937); John R. Seeley, Alexander Sim, and Elizabeth W. Loosely, *Crestwood Heights* (New York: Basic Books, 1956); and Arthur J. Vidich and Joseph Bensman, *Small Town in Mass Society* (Princeton: Princeton University Press, 1958).

[15] Edward C. Banfield, *Political Influence* (Glencoe, Ill.: Free Press, 1961); and Robert C. Dahl, *Who Governs?* (New Haven: Yale University Press, 1961).

[16] Floyd Hunter, *Community Organization: Action or Inaction?* (Chapel Hill: University of North Carolina Press, 1956).

groups are organized for the furtherance of their separate interests. Power and authority to make key decisions are widely dispersed among these groups, and no formal or centrally rational process of planning leads to choice and decision. Instead, the various interests form temporary coalitions and engage in ad hoc negotiation and bargaining, during which exchanges of preference and favor occur in order to achieve specified ends.

Banfield's accumulated case studies produced a model of how influence is structured and how it works in action, built around the opposing forces for centralization and decentralization. Civic leaders, as distinguished from political figures, are usefully typed and analyzed as advisers, negotiators, and publicists. Community affairs are dealt with through various influences such as control, ad hoc associations, and power—temporarily concerted to produce action.

To this model Dahl added a careful analysis of information about leadership and population characteristics, group preferences, and economics. These are woven into decision-making in urban redevelopment, public education, and political nominations, so that leadership in welfare can be compared with that in other fields. There is little evidence that basic community processes differ significantly when welfare issues are at stake. However, both studies expand awareness of how dispersion of power and influence in a population functions. The stereotype that a socioeconomic elite maintains some influence in all major community decisions is significantly altered by the discovery that each influence center, even if stable, is aroused by some subjects, such as education, and not at all by others, such as urban renewal. Specialization of leadership is traced and three major patterns of leadership functioning are analyzed —each revelant for welfare: (1) division of agreed spheres of influence; (2) executive-centered coalitions (a new concept derived from government); and (3) rivalry among autonomous forces. Within these

patterns, political behavior is distinguished from civic behavior by the influence over resources that characterizes each: social standing; cash, credit or wealth; legality, popularity, and control over jobs; and control over sources of information.

These findings about dispersed influence have major implications for social planning agencies, which have tended to rely upon slow-changing constellations of leadership assembled in relatively static or stable agencies. The dispersed influence view points to a more flexible organization capable of readily altering leadership groupings for various purposes. This line of study also opens up the possibility that some day planning methods can be organized, with predictable outcomes, in relation to social conditions.

The differences among Hunter, Dahl, and Banfield are substantial, but it is not yet clear whether this is due to Hunter's study of voluntary welfare as distinguished from Banfield's and Dahl's use of local government, to differences between political science and sociological methods, or to historic differences among the four cities studied. A larger sample of urban areas may produce evidence of typical patterns of leadership and decision-making that may one day be used to create different planning mechanisms, each suited to a pattern.

Welfare agencies as a subcommunity. Whether or not the aggregate of social welfare agencies and organizations in a community, by themselves, constitute a functional system may be a matter of some debate, although certain interconnections and identities of interest cannot be denied. Until recent years, social work research in this area has been limited to one-dimensional descriptions of health and welfare agencies or services—board makeup, volume of services, sources of income and expenditures—that do not illuminate how this aggregate functions as a system.

Two major avenues exist for studying the welfare system: the confrontation of

agencies through the budgeting and allocation process of the United Fund or a legis-
lature; and the systems of referral and
exchange of cases. While the former has
not been systematically studied anywhere,
the latter has been observed by Levine and
White, who developed the concept of "exchange" as a framework for studying interorganizational relationships in one city.[17]
They defined organizational exchange as
any voluntary activity between two members (organizations) having consequences
for the realization of their respective goals
or objectives. The concept can be used to
determine the extent of integration and
co-ordination that may be achieved and,
at the same time, to explicate factors accounting for the presence or absence of
exchange and co-ordination.

The elements that may be exchanged
were defined as referring patients or clients; exchanging labor services through
volunteers or loaned personnel; and giving
or receiving other resources, including
funds, equipment, and technical information. Elements in the exchange—case referrals, exchange of resources, joint activities, and written or verbal communications
—were measured on a five-point scale after
gathering data by questionnaire. This device distinguishes patterns of exchange
among subunits of the welfare system, such
as rehabilitation, educational, and preventa-
tive health agencies, and also identifies exchanges between direct and indirect service
institutions. The study is distinguished
from earlier study of referrals between
social agencies by the introduction of exchange units, which extend the typical relation from cases to include funds and
other resources; and by the concept of
utility, which explains variations in exchange according to utility for agency
function.

Whereas former studies have highlighted

either the limited amount of referral or
the difficulties in securing action at the receiving end of the referral system, the
Levine and White method offers a way to
understand the reasons for difficulty in
functioning. The relative independence
or interdependence of the parts of the welfare system were found to be contingent
upon three related factors: (1) the accessibility of the organizations to elements from
outside the local exchange system; (2) the
objectives of each organization; and (3)
the degree to which consensus exists
among the members of the system regarding their respective domains. Except for
Levine's work, most analyses of co-ordination, integration, and growth have de-
pended upon a confrontation of opinions
held by various individuals and organizations concerning efficient and desirable
patterns of relationship. There is now available a simple and relatively objective instrument that may lead to more rational
arrangements among agencies and between
groups of agencies.

The Neighborhood

The neighborhood, viewed as one of the
basic building blocks in social planning
theory, has long held a favored position
in social work research. This is consistent
with the early identification of social planning with depressed neighborhoods, and
with the profession's conviction about individual participation in the resolution of
social ills. Major attention has been given
to descriptions of specific action projects
based upon the support and organization
of small neighborhood populations, as in
Abrahamson's study of the Hyde Park-
Kenwood Area of Chicago, but these have
not yet produced satisfactory knowledge
about how American neighborhoods function internally or in relation to their surrounding community.[18]

[17] Sol Levine and Paul E. White, "Exchange
and Interorganizational Relationships," *Administrative Science Quarterly*, Vol. 5, No. 4
(March 1961), pp. 583–601.

[18] Julia Abrahamson, *A Neighborhood
Finds Itself* (New York: Harper & Brothers,
1959).

Recent work has begun to explore the role and effectiveness of typical formal neighborhood groups, such as community councils and block clubs. The deviant cultural patterns of residents in homogeneous areas are freshly seen as having positive functional values that affect the intervention plans of agencies organized in the larger community and hamper efforts to establish communication between metropolitan agencies and local residents. The viability of neighborhood life has been confirmed by the vitality of informal association despite declining participation in formal organization.

Turner has studied a specific instrument of neighborhood welfare organization— the block club.[19] It is one of the few social work studies that has attempted to test the effectiveness of a specific social organization by systematically specifying and managing the variables that may influence effectiveness. The work began with certain central propositions: block club organizations can be tested by (1) their effect on the quality of relationship among residents; (2) variations in the acceptance and enforcement of community norms; and (3) variations in social influence. Blocks in Cleveland were selected that varied in length of the street, population density, owner-occupancy rates, land-use patterns, race, and prevalence of street problems. The block residents were further classified according to lower-middle class and working-class characteristics and their block organizations were rated by expert panels as to their relative effectiveness and ineffectiveness. Data were collected within blocks by a method of random sampling among the residents, but the total number of interviews completed was less than one hundred.

While the Turner study has opened up promising avenues in methodology, it has not substantially added to knowledge. The general conclusion of the research is that block clubs are most likely to attract like-minded residents who already have a greater capacity for social relationships and a greater sense of their own power. The relative effectiveness of various groups for achieving results in varying conditions is not established. A presumably middle-class area requires less external help to bring such organization into being. Such conclusions, although not new, may influence the allocation of scarce community planning resources, for they begin to distinguish sectors which, at least relatively, need external help least.

Most neighborhood study is still descriptive, as illustrated by Sridharan, who reviewed thirty neighborhood councils in urban areas by interviews, participation in meetings, and review of records.[20] Characteristic of many such descriptions, the design is heavily biased by preconceptions, without built-in mechanisms for testing objectively either the results of community council activity, or variations in perception about its work, so that it sums up perceptions held by persons most heavily invested in their continuing activity.

Miller sought to understand the neighborhood through the behavior of its people rather than through institutional organization.[21] This is one of a series of studies dealing with "the poor" in America which antedates the "antipoverty" program of 1964. Using the cultural approach to "customary behavior," he found that his community was built primarily upon a female-based household. When this finding was related to other characteristics, such as peer street groups, serial marriage, and antisocial behavior, the neighborhood

[19] John B. Turner, "A Study of Block Clubs As an Instrument of Community Organization." Unpublished doctoral dissertation, Western Reserve University, Cleveland, 1959.

[20] K. V. Sridharan, "An Area Approach to Social Welfare Planning." Unpublished doctoral dissertation, Ohio State University, Columbus, 1959.

[21] Walter B. Miller, "Implications of Urban Lower-Class Culture for Social Work," *Social Service Review*, Vol. 33, No. 3 (September 1959), pp. 219–236.

was found to be internally consistent, self-sustaining, and serving a positive function for its residents. The activities of the street gangs, the devotion to toughness, and the prevalence of illegitimacy cannot be considered only from the point of view of the surrounding middle-class communities that support welfare agencies in the area. The neighborhood pattern of behavior was not only "deviant" in that it was at variance with that of the external community; it served the subcommunity in a positive and constructive fashion—in its survival. A foundation is thereby made for planning and construction of more effective approaches than have yet been tried.

A similar culturally organized study conducted for the Community Service Society of New York by Cattell supports Miller's general conclusion.[22] Interviews and a study of published records concentrated upon the functioning of a Chinese community and its relationship to the organized health and welfare services provided by non-Chinese and nonlocal resources, such as the Community Service Society and the city of New York. Attitudes toward health and illness, and welfare services and the welfare obligations of the subcommunity were probed. The findings constitute another illustration of the persistence of subgroup cultures in the American scene and the chasm separating the perception of problems by these subcommunities and that of the surrounding population. While the work identifies the power elements within the subcommunity that control its linkage to the general society, it does not throw light upon how, if at all, the ties between the two communities can be improved.

Urban neighborhoods are not always as culturally cohesive as New York's Chinatown, but the internal functioning of heterogeneous neighborhoods is little understood. The absence of formal organization often leads to the impression of anonymity and disorganization, with which the neighborhood orientation of most welfare planning fumbles. Greer and Kube have illuminated the extent to which neighborhood and personal interaction have been affected by growing urbanization.[23] They randomly selected small samples of residents in four sections of Los Angeles for interview. The widely separated districts were rated on the Schevky and Bell scale to establish degrees of urbanization.[24] Economic, residential, and background characteristics of each of the residents were identified and information secured about their characteristic modes of social participation. While the authors found that the proportion of respondents participating in local but formal groups decreases with urbanization, they also found a significantly high level of *informal* interaction on a neighborhood base, so that "neighboring" rather than neighborhood group participation emerged as the characteristic of the city. While respondents differed slightly in the extent to which they felt attached to the neighborhood in which they were residing, approximately 84 percent generally liked the areas in which they lived. Measures of anomie were seldom above 10 percent, although the usual correlations were found between anomic responses and low occupation, education, and family income. The decline in participation in formal organization at the neighborhood level, accompanied by a surprising maintenance, and even increase, in informal face-to-face primary relationships, calls for new methods by metropolitan agencies to re-establish neighborhood linkage based on something other than formal groups.

[22] Stuart H. Cattell, *Health, Welfare and Social Organization in Chinatown, New York City* (New York: Community Service Society of New York, 1962).

[23] Scott Greer and Ella Kube, "Urbanization and Social Structure: A Los Angeles Study," in Marvin Sussman, ed., *The Community Structure and Analysis* (New York: Thomas Y. Crowell Co., 1959).

[24] The scale is reported in Eshbef Schevky and Wendell Bell, *Social Area Analysis* (Stanford, Calif.: Stanford University Press, 1955).

Citizen Participation

The concept of the citizen is central to planning. It is a key link between agency and community, and may determine both policy and structure. Full participation of the citizen, as an individual and a representative, has long been a cardinal social work principle, but research focused on the citizen in planning has usually been limited to descriptive studies of membership on welfare agency, community council, and United Fund boards of trustees, which reveal the distribution of board membership among professional, employer, housewife, and employee categories. Single community surveys have occasionally reported on the distribution of individuals involved in particular acts of community decision-making without fully probing its significance, although Angell early attempted to correlate participation in welfare activities with various social class, economic, and cultural characteristics.[25]

Descriptive data uniformly reveal that employers, professional men and women, managers, and housewives (usually with husbands in the other mentioned categories) hold a disproportionate share of board positions, although other occupational groups have some representation. Recent studies have sought to uncover the dynamics of citizen participation: the social, economic, and other class factors operating in welfare policy-making, and the effect of these factors on policy choices.

No systematic work has yet been undertaken to determine whether alternate patterns of participation affect decision-making or improve the likelihood of successful planning results. Much recent discussion seeks to engage poor and underprivileged groups in community action. While this aim is ideologically desirable, its effect on planning is not yet measurable.

Seeley has dealt with the subject extensively for the Community Chest in one community.[26] Campaign leaders in the Community Chest movement in Indianapolis were classified on an estimated social status scale, ranging from "top-top" leaders to "the poor" or "lower class." Elder statesmen were found high in the upper-middle class and young campaigners low in the upper-middle class—a finding consistent with the fund-raising pattern. These classifications were effectively associated with attitudes toward welfare, philanthropy, and the resulting welfare policies. Agency attempts to bring conflicting views, associated with differing social status, into one organization had two dysfunctional results: a blurring of organization goals and a concentration of power in one class at the expense of others.

Willie studied the extent of participation in community welfare decision-making in Syracuse.[27] By examining the variety of participants in a series of community welfare decisions in one city, he was able to separate the larger number of participants in various welfare activities from those centrally involved in choice and decision. His finding, that approximately 1 percent of the population of Syracuse is consistently involved in major decisions, conforms to the general view that participation at key levels is extraordinarily narrow in the field of welfare, although the extent of the narrowness is startling. It is not clear whether this 1 percent is coherent and stable enough to suggest less dispersion of power in social welfare than Dahl and Banfield found in Chicago and New Haven. Kravitz amplifies these findings in a study of four cities with a heavy concentration of executives of large industry and locally owned businesses.[28]

[25] Robert C. Angell, *The Moral Integration of American Cities* (Chicago: University of Chicago Press, 1951).

[26] John R. Seeley *et al.*, *The Community Chest* (Toronto: University of Toronto Press, 1957).

[27] Charles Willie, "Trends in the Participation of Businessmen in Local Voluntary Affairs," *Sociology and Social Research*, Vol. 48, No. 3 (April 1964), pp. 289–300.

[28] Sanford Kravitz, "Sources of Leadership Input for Social Welfare Planning." Unpublished doctoral dissertation, Brandeis University, Waltham, Mass., 1963.

Polansky's early study sought to understand the difficulty in securing wide participation from other than middle-class college-educated families by examining the difficulties encountered by the Girl Scouts in recruiting an adequate number of club leaders from lower- and working-class families.[29] Using depth interviews with small samples of actual and potential club leaders drawn from different class strata, Polansky concluded that working-class mothers tended to have a more pessimistic view about the future and a more pessimistic view about their capacity to influence future events. He concluded that this is a basic obstacle to the extensive involvement of families with lower economic and social status and lower education.

Litwak, however, examined the same question through the relationship between individual affiliation in voluntary neighborhood groups and level of industrial organization, and found no lower-class bar.[30] From a survey of 920 white married women living in suburban Buffalo, with at least one child under 19, he concluded, contrary to other findings, that modern industrial organizations tended to encourage participation in voluntary associations at least at the local level. He also found that new workers in industry, once they adjusted to the community, tended to reduce their participation, provided they had developed a positive orientation to the neighborhood of residence. Where they lack such positive neighborhood orientation, however, their participation in voluntary associations remains high. If substantiated by other study, the conclusions are especially significant for they suggest that working class participation in voluntary associations may be a substitute for other more satisfying forms of activity rather than being a positive expression of civic mindedness.

The Polansky and Litwak findings cannot yet be correlated with those of Seeley, Willie, and Kravitz, since organizational tradition in welfare planning, as distinct from welfare service, is masculine dominant. Further study of working-class attitudes is needed, correlated with cultural background and corrected for upward aspiring segments of the working class who now populate middle-class and managerial groups. The explanation for class bias in welfare leadership clearly needs to be sought out, and some study along these lines is dealt with next. The full extent to which social class status is consistently associated with biased trends in agency policy has not yet been verified, although this is generally suspected; nor have there been studies of the effectiveness of alternate means for linking leadership decisions to the wishes of a wider public, although this is widely claimed.

Developments along these lines can be discerned, but a more basic problem has not yet been broached systematically—the national community and the ways it is increasing its influence on social policy formation. Research development requires attention to such national and regional communities, as well as to the metropolitan community. With the beginning elements of a theoretical framework, and hypotheses for decision-making patterns, extensive replication of community studies is now needed in an effort to test both theory and hypothesis.

Analyzing the Structure of Planning Organizations

Studies of the structure of planning organizations need to be distinguished from studies in administration, in order to concentrate on planning among institutions and on the relationships between planning agencies and the objects of their planning. Studies of this character necessarily focus

---

[29] Norman Polansky and Catherine Richards, "Reaching Working Class Youth Leaders," *Social Work*, Vol. 4, No. 4 (October 1959), pp. 31–40.

[30] Eugene Litwak, "Voluntary Associations and Neighborhood Cohesion," *American Sociological Review*, Vol. 26, No. 2 (April 1961), pp. 258–271.

on technical and professional aspects of planning research, rather than on general community issues. The main purpose is to evaluate the various structural and organizational forms and their effectiveness for carrying out planning tasks in the contemporary community. This requires a relaxation of preconceptions about uniformities of organization appropriate for all planning situations. The general functioning and malfunctioning of organizations need to be reviewed objectively and factors in such performance isolated.

Current research has made a start in mapping this subject matter, although the results to date appear fragmentary. Work has begun not only in identifying the class distribution of policy-makers in planning organizations, but in tracing selectivity in leadership input and the direction of influence on agency policy. Alternate forms of planning organization to handle internal and external conflict are now being studied, as are patterns of resource control and patterns of interorganizational association as they influence agency objectives.

An urgent need remains for the development of objective research instruments and measures of function, and for the systematic accumulation of comparative case studies. Typologies of complex organizations for planning need to be elaborated, as for example in variations of open and closed decision-making systems. The influence of power needs elaboration—its location within a planning organization, its patterns of input, and the linkage between decision-makers and the group influences from which they emerge. Other subjects requiring attention are the structural patterns at national and regional levels that supplement work at the metropolitan community level, and the linkages between planning organizations at various levels.

Seeley's study of *The Community Chest* is the most extensive effort to understand a social agency functioning in its living environment.[31] The survey staff of nine lived

in Indianapolis for three years, relying on the methods of social anthropology supplemented by extensive statistical analyses of the fund-raising experience of Community Chests in forty-one cities, and of non-Chest fund-raising agencies in Indianapolis. Formal aims, latent aims and values of policy-makers and professional staff, selection of organization leadership, economic potentials, and community cultural inheritance were related to organization accomplishments. Seeley analyzed especially well the dilemma of a voluntary welfare agency that must rely on vague and ambiguous aims to retain the loyalty of contradictory community interests in the name of a not yet existent "community" goal. This was, in turn, located in the context of the state, its character, and the history of its philanthropy. The underlying nature of the organization and the obstacles to logical solution were fully identified so that, for the first time, the gap between community necessity and professional doctrine was confronted. Conclusions about alternate forms of organization, more consonant with community realities, were limited to the community studied, but the method for evaluating organization malfunction is widely useful.

Loring used observational techniques to study patterns of council organization when the purposes are citizen participation in planning, not fund-raising.[32] The concept of horizontal and vertical linkage within a metropolitan area was used to unite groups on different planes, and three primary structural models were identified as being efficient at each level: the metropolitan, the district, and the neighborhood. Unfortunately, the work virtually ignored the dynamics of group conflict in such representational organizations, with the result that the five criteria for evaluating structural

---

[31] Seeley *et al., op. cit.*

[32] William C. Loring, Frank L. Sweetser, and Charles F. Ernst, *Community Organization for Citizen Participation in Urban Renewal* (Cambridge, Eng.: Cambridge University Press, 1957).

soundness remained general and vague: (1) inclusion of all elements; (2) citizens group representation at all levels (city, district, and neighborhood); (3) adequate horizontal relations between groups on each plane; (4) adequate vertical links between groups on different planes; and (5) liaison between citizens groups and government officials. While predictions were made about the effective results of such organization, the generality of criteria and the absence of objective results limited the utility of such characteristic prescriptions.

Other studies have begun to select a few elements assumed to be related to organization effectiveness and to test them through intercommunity analysis. While only a few such elements have thus far been studied, they indicate that some long accepted concepts are unsupported by outcome studies of effectiveness. Morris and others have studied levels of control in planning agencies in seven cities.[33] The variables in organization were evaluated against progress in generating new programs and services for the elderly. Data were secured by participant-observers in local demonstrations and by research staff field visits utilizing structured questionnaires. Organization types were classified by the levels at which responsibility was lodged for initial development of proposals and for final action. It was hypothesized that the further removed the initial planning unit was from final authority, the less influential would be its recommendations. Contrary to expectations, it was found that the formal structure of planning, at least for the elderly, was not a significant factor in the rate of program alteration or expansion. The study concluded that the degree of interest identified in the central policy authority was more significant than the unit to which it assigned initial planning respon-

sibility. The limited sample revealed that the downward distribution of key leadership did not appear to make any significant difference in the extent to which recommendations made to superior authority were acted upon.

Patterns of resource control were explored by reviewing patterns of relationship developed between voluntary planning councils and governmental agencies in several efforts to launch new programs. Analysis led to the conclusion that voluntary planning agencies, dependent upon private philanthropy in a stable economy, were not efficient in meeting large-scale new problems. When such a planning agency is prepared to draw upon public resources, its willingness is customarily limited to support for private agency operation that requires no adjustment in policy control. The conclusion suggests a modification of the traditional view of a shared partnership between public and voluntary resources and substitution of an association in which some responsibility and authority is redistributed in relation to primary loci of support.

Rein considers the form of interagency association appropriate to a service agency's objectives.[34] Effective and ineffective affiliates of a national organization (Planned Parenthood Federation) were first identified, using ratings of affiliates built upon the concepts of resource possession (clients and funds). The ratings were correlated with the degree of affiliate integration within local networks of health and welfare agencies, using as criteria membership in the local community council and the proportion of referrals received from health and welfare agencies. These measures were tested by intensive case

[33] Robert Morris and Ollie A. Randall, "Determining Factors in the Planning and Organization of Community Services for the Elderly," *Social Work*, Vol. 10, No. 1 (January 1965), pp. 96–102.

[34] Martin Rein, "An Organizational Analysis of a National Agency's Local Affiliates in Their Community Contexts: A Study of the Planned Parenthood Federation of America" (unpublished doctoral dissertation, Brandeis University, Waltham, Mass., 1962); and Rein, "Organization for Social Change," *Social Work*, Vol. 9, No. 2 (April 1964), pp. 32–41.

studies of four selected affiliates. The rating of effectiveness, as measured through affiliates' procurement of resources, clients and money, was found to bear no measurable relationship to integration in the social welfare community network. In fact, affiliates with the least linkage to community planning organizations, such as welfare councils, had strikingly superior success in procuring clients and funds.

Such efforts at evaluation inevitably raise the question whether any common basis exists for evaluative measurement. Olshansky indirectly produced limited evidence from his effort to develop systematic measures of effectiveness of a planning organization.[35] Lacking any formalized theory by which a standard for evaluation could be applied, it was assumed that some body of concepts, not yet stated in systematic form, might exist in practice and could provide the foundation for uniform evaluation efforts. Preliminary work revealed the insufficient definition of operational planning goals, the subjective ways in which the appropriateness of objectives are viewed by planning organization, and the lack of recorded data. The author therefore sought to transform nonobjective opinions for measuring movement into a set of uniformly and systematically transmissible judgments about what constitutes successful planning. Pre-testing elicited seven factors considered to be significant in evaluating success. Sample summary case histories using these factors were submitted to a selective sample of experienced social work community organizers. Factors that produced sufficiently strong agreement among judges were then utilized in a larger mail inquiry to eighty-eight executives of large welfare councils affiliated with United Community Funds and Councils of America. Responses were in reply to a focused questionnaire with forced responses to specific alternatives outlined.

In the view of professional raters, only three factors seemed to have a strong capability for differentiating between successful and unsuccessful planning efforts: (1) the extent to which the planning organization itself is motivated by community-wide factors (orientation to community-wide rather than agency factors seems more frequently to be associated with successful efforts); (2) the attitudes of participating agencies toward the planning effort are determinative (are the agencies more or less community centered?); and (3) the amount of direction given to the planning by the planning organization. The third element appears to be a negative indication, in that its absence seems to indicate failure, but its presence does not necessarily predict success. The two positive indicators appear to be culture-bound in that they reflect the current values of the profession. While this work exposes the very preliminary state in which evaluative research in planning finds itself, the existence of even three evaluative elements upon which professional personnel agree may be considered promising for future work.

Representation, Power, and Influence

Although studies of the structural effectiveness of organizations have been limited, yet critical, their impact has been supported by progress in studying power and influence in the decision-making of community organizations. Work in this area has done much to make clear the distance between organization reality and the ideals of professional standards, which assume that community planning organizations are widely representative of all interests. Early work by Hunter reopened the door to an appreciation of the power structure in American communities.[36]

Illustrative of the new wave of interest is Kravitz's study of five communities, con-

[35] Bernard Olshansky, "An Approach to Evaluating Research in Social Planning." Unpublished doctoral dissertation, Brandeis University, Waltham, Mass., 1961.

[36] Floyd Hunter, *The Community Power Structure* (Chapel Hill: University of North Carolina Press, 1953).

ducted in 1961, with established United Funds and Welfare Councils but with differing patterns of local organization.[37] One of his major conclusions was that welfare councils were uniformly, if unwittingly, selective in the leadership permitted to rise to influence in policy matters. Trustee leaders believed to hold decisive influence in the approval or disapproval of projects in the field of aging were identified by reputational methods and eighty-one were interviewed. Their social characteristics and attitudes toward planning in specified fields were determined by depth interviews. A general model of leadership input for local welfare planning organizations emerged and was characterized as "selective." Regardless of historical origins, social or economic characteristics, and extent of local organization, leadership input in general seemed to conform to the following elements:

1. Key decision-making was generally retained by three types of individuals—socially influential persons representing early settlement; persons with economic influence because of independent wealth or significant managerial positions in large corporations; and a scattering of representatives neither socially nor economically influential but holding authoritative positions in social agencies very similar to those supported by the other two groups.

2. While a great many other persons in community life were involved in various planning processes, they were uniformly kept at secondary levels of influence.

3. Despite a long history of efforts to enlarge the range of representation, such associations had significantly little representation from minority and ethnic groups that did not control social agencies, and from individuals or organizations primarily committed to the pursuit of one cause—such as aging—rather than to a more balanced theory of resource distribution.

Taber's study tends to support this view about "selectivity" by noting the virtual exclusion of major service systems—notably the social insurance agencies and proprietary health institutions—from planning structures in Iowa.[38] The findings are by no means conclusive but the hypotheses do offer significant clues for future study: (1) voluntary planning associations may have achieved a homeostasis in their participation which limits their capacity to absorb additional leadership elements that in any way threaten the existing balance of consensus; (2) such associations appear to have a limited capacity to develop new programs or to achieve major readjustments in resources in the light of new needs; their primary value lies in the maintenance and stability of programs rather than in innovation and development.

Measuring the Methods and Processes of Planned Change

Study of planning methods has a special relevance for social work practice. It increasingly seeks to identify effective and efficient practices for the attainment of planning purposes; that is, what works effectively under what conditions. Recent research expresses the shift from passive to more active concepts of planning responsibilities, captured in the term "planned change." As with previous subjects, current work is still fragmentary but lays the foundation for more incisive study. Research has identified the existence of a common practice base and has isolated for further study troublesome issues such as the contradictory concept of participant-change agent. Planning goals have been outlined and more usable baselines for measurement have been evolved. Various processes have been distinguished, as in the distinction between planning for co-ordination among agencies and planning for the production of new services and resources. Above all, tools for planning and research are evolving, especially in work on agency

---

[37] Kravitz, *op. cit.*

[38] Taber, Itzin, and Turner, *op cit.*

exchange units and critiques of priority systems.

There have been, however, very few comparative studies conducted that permit critical evaluation of planning conditions, objectives, and practices. While a start has been made to distinguish the processes of allocating and generating economic resources, professional roles in planning are still treated in omnibus fashion.[39] Original work is also required, but is nowhere in sight, to improve the means for predicting and forecasting social conditions. Lacking such improved predictive means, planning will continue to remain addressed to today's conditions without accounting for the changes through which society is moving.

A beginning focus for studies of change would be the definition of baselines for measurement, or goals for planning. As indicated by Olshansky, planning goals tend to remain general, making it difficult to use them as a base for measurement or study. Lacking research, useful experience is nonetheless accumulating, especially in the attempts of many welfare councils to develop more exact goals.

The growing interest in priority determination as a way to select goals for future allocation of resources led Lagey to study by questionnaire 73 communities, selected from 136 North American Community Chests and Councils, that served urban populations of 300,000 or more.[40] Approximately one-third of the Chests and Councils in the sample used priority systems. Most of them were not satisfied with the results although they continued to experiment by modifying current plans. Of those using such systems, 75 percent believed that their participant agencies *in general* accepted the priorities but with strong reservations. About 15 percent of the respondent councils did not believe that priorities worked at all. There remains, however, a great deal of uncertainty about scope of the subject matter included and the classification of agency or field of service.

An attempt to improve on these defects is represented by the Indianapolis Community Council Long-Range Plan.[41] Using standard methods previously described by Lagey, the judgment of citizen committees was used to identify targets for community welfare services, projected fifteen years into the future. Data about community trends and forecasts were assembled regarding population and economic growth, age distribution, ethnic distribution, housing, personal incomes, and public expenditures for the fifteen-year period. Five major fields of service were selected, such as adjustment services for families, with subunits for programing, such as family counseling and family life education. Recommendations for future development were derived from this background and based upon four alternatives: curtailment, maintenance of the status quo, normal development, or accelerated development. The resulting guides are presumably to be used by policy-makers, budget committees, and public officials during the next fifteen years. A yardstick of *normal* development, meaning annual budget increases from 3 percent to 8 percent a year, was developed, taking into account such factors as general population growth, the rise in real salaries and wages, past trends in public and private expenditures, as well as an improvement in service techniques. Accelerated growth would therefore be growth greater than 8 percent a year. Sources of financing were assigned among United Funds, other private sources, fees, and tax funds.

---

[39] The Council on Social Work Education and the National Association of Social Workers have sponsored an extensive study of community organization curriculum and practice, directed by Arnold Gurin of Brandeis University, which will stimulate study of such issues.

[40] Joseph C. Lagey and Beverly Ayres, *Priority Determination Plans* (Vancouver, B.C.: Community Chests and Councils of Vancouver, 1960).

---

[41] Community Service Council of Metropolitan Indianapolis, *A Long-Range Plan for 1975* (Indianapolis, 1961).

This approach is significant even though founded on unstandardized lay judgments and derived from diverse secondary sources of information. It provides measurable baselines, specifies growth rates and resources over a fifteen-year period, and identifies specific target agencies. A separate study is now in progress, under the auspices of Western Reserve University, to determine the extent to which such baselines and long-range planning recommendations are, in fact, utilized in annual planning decisions of agencies, civic bodies, and the United Fund.[42]

Even with measurable goals and baselines, studies of planning processes have been limited by an absence of a usable theoretical framework. The attempt to study systematically a logical sequence of planning was given new impetus by the publication of Lippitt's *Dynamics of Planned Change*.[43] Lebowitz sought to test this model by examining the efforts of five community welfare councils to secure specific changes in their communities.[44] The effort represents a valuable beginning in that the model is based upon a noncoercive, nonauthoritative system for planning that corresponds to the welfare council reality. The Lippitt model was found to have certain limitations in its application to community welfare councils. It is difficult to view the councils as organizations in the personalized terms of change agents. The council system does not provide for clear specification of the primary client to be served, and the traditional welfare council system operates under conditions that inextricably bind the change

agent and the client to each other. In effect the change agent is a part of the system to be changed. This introduces both realistic and conceptual difficulties that have yet to be studied.

Robertson studied the responses of two voluntary organizations to a joint effort of change.[45] Unstructured interviews, a review of working records, and correspondence were resorted to in an attempt to reconstruct the history of this operation. The inferences drawn from such data were further tested against independently derived knowledge about individuals and organizations. The findings support other fragmentary evidence, and a great wealth of practice wisdom about forces that obstruct rational planning: struggles for power between individuals and organizations, the search for status and recognition, and ideological conflicts. Robertson concluded that in voluntary systems of association, agencies tended to accept symbolic modifications rather than substantial changes in their relationships. There was also evidence that implementation of specific goals to any substantial extent is achieved by independent activity of powerful individuals, a finding that affects premises about consensus underlying current community planning theory.

Morris studied the efforts of six community planning organizations in six different communities shortly after they had actively attempted to bring about the coordination of services between a general hospital, a home for the aged, and other community services.[46] The study was

[42] This study, not yet completed, is directed by John Turner, Western Reserve University, assisted by Harold B. Chetkow, Community Services Council of Metropolitan Indianapolis.

[43] Roland Lippitt, *Dynamics of Planned Change* (New York: Harcourt, Brace, 1958).

[44] Milton Lebowitz, "The Process of Planned Community Change: A Comparative Analysis of Five Community Welfare Council Change Projects." Unpublished doctoral dissertation, Columbia University, 1961.

[45] Mary Ella Robertson, "A Study of Planning and Implementing Processes in Social Welfare by Two Voluntary Associations." Unpublished doctoral dissertation, University of Pittsburgh, 1962.

[46] Robert Morris, "Community Planning for the Aged," *Selected Biennial Round Table Conference Papers, 1963* (Chicago: American Public Welfare Association, 1964), pp. 98–103; and Robert Morris, "Basic Factors in Planning for the Coordination of Health Services," *American Journal of Public Health*, Vol. 53, Nos. 2 and 3 (February and March 1963), pp. 248–259 and 462–472.

based upon depth interviews conducted by teams of social workers, public health workers, or social scientists using structured interview guides. Informants were selected by reputational methods for their role in final decision-making. Conditions among the communities were standardized on several dimensions: planning bodies with comparable structures and procedures, comparable community value orientations, comparable ranges of services already organized for the subject (in this case chronic illness), similarity in economic conditions, and recency of the planning effort. Uncontrolled variables included such factors as history of interagency relationships, geographic location, volume of public versus voluntary services, and the power centralized in the hands of the planning agency. The study was limited to an examination of factors considered central for only one type of goal—co-ordination among existing agencies. Policy-making control centers in each of the affected agencies were determined by an examination of economic, social, and religious ratings. Change was defined as "any alteration of specified working relationships between two institutions, established as the goal by a community planning organization and adopted by the affected agencies and operationally effective within ten years of the initial planning." [47]

The study concluded that successful as compared with unsuccessful planning efforts for co-ordination can be accounted for by two pre-existing conditions: simultaneous crisis in the functioning of the agencies to be co-ordinated and previously established informal and social interaction among trustees of the agencies involved. Once these conditions are met, the direction of the planning effort can be modified by four planning tools: (1) a planning structure committed to interagency co-operation and thus holding the confidence of participants; (2) individual leadership with negotiating

skill and with high status to bridge antagonistic boards of trustees; (3) the conduct of expert studies (an incidental influence); and (4) the discriminating use of incentives (primarily to encourage movement along lines of agency aspiration). The findings are useful as a basis for further study in order to test the indicated lesser value of expert studies and incentives (common planning tools today), and the increased value of individual negotiation skill.

The effort to study planning to create new resources, as distinguished from co-ordination, is represented by a retrospective study conducted by Miller into the processes by which thirty rural areas carried through plans for the construction of new hospitals under provisions of the Hill-Burton Hospital Construction Program.[48] Analyses were made of the pre-existing community situation, steps leading to the initiation of action, the organization of support, and the community organization methods to mobilize resources.

The relationships between volunteer or informal organizations and formal administrations of government received special attention. Conclusions suggest that organizing skill of an administrative character, while valuable, is not associated with success. Similarly, styles of work and methods of organization can successfully vary and no single style was found more effective than any other. Although a number of decision-making capacities were dealt with, there was a general finding that authority in the process of planning for health in rural areas was held by relatively few people with three characteristics: (1) money or the ability to influence those with money, *and* awareness of this capacity; (2) middle age; and (3) activity in many phases of community life.

Miller's study is unique in social work for its identification of regional variations in the types of persons occupying leadership positions. In the South, they are

[47] Morris, "Community Planning for the Aged," p. 99.

[48] Paul A. Miller, *Community Health Action* (East Lansing: Michigan State University Press, 1953).

likely to be official government office-holders; in the Middle West, professional persons; in the Northwest, business or executive leaders; and in the Northeast, citizens *not* holding public office.

Litwak and Hylton developed more effective research tools in a study of interaction among agencies.[49] For purposes of inter-organizational analysis, partial conflict was assumed to be a regular part of all relationships, as was organizational autonomy while authority remained relatively unstructured. Agencies were classified by their dependence upon local exchange, as seen in their financial and service interdependence or independence. This standardized unit permitted both description and evaluation of co-ordinating efforts. The methods used refined the study of conflicts of agency interest and produced a rational basis for separating co-operative efforts in a planning council from conflict situations in a budgeting agency. Three measures were developed to predict the feasibility of co-ordination efforts: extent of interdependence among agencies, agency awareness of interdependence, and standardization. The work is a milestone in its use of simple and relatively objective instruments, similar to those of Levine and White, and forecast more rational planning arrangements.

Professional Practice in Community Planning

The limited research in planning is nowhere more evident than in the area of professional practice. Single-case reports seldom rise above one-dimension descriptions that lack systematic use of quantitative or evaluative measures. Observations by Miller and Morris, incidental to other research, suggest that planning success is not necessarily correlated with professional skill, but

such stimuli to study effective practice conditions or characteristics have not yet been acted upon.

The potential for such research is confirmed by Olshansky, who found that a common set of principles apparently underlies the practices of community organization staff in a variety of settings.[50] Lebowitz's study of planned change develops the role of the community organization worker in a standard welfare council as the "participant change-agent."[51] This concept, which may ultimately prove to contain a fatal contradiction, describes the present stance of much practice and is therefore a useful point of departure for future study. It attempts to unite two widely recognized phenomena: (1) that planning does involve the introduction of change by one organization into another; and (2) the new ideas for change are seldom tolerated or well received unless the introducer is an intimate part of the organization to be changed or is at least accepted by it. With the use of this concept, however, the introducer of change must become engaged in the affairs of the organization to be changed. It remains to be tested whether this process results in the abandonment of change objectives through co-optation by the basic organization or target organization or whether it is possible to sustain the thrust of innovation. Selznick has documented in single-case studies the extent to which new representatives introduced into an organization ultimately alter its line of development.[52] For community organization, it becomes important to determine the extent to which, for example, welfare council staff can or must become involved in the internal work of constituent agencies in order to effect change.

Rainman's empirical study of community organization practice was based on

---

[49] Eugene Litwak and Lydia F. Hylton, "Interorganizational Analysis," *Administrative Science Quarterly*, Vol. 6, No. 4 (March 1962).

[50] *Op. cit.*
[51] *Op. cit.*
[52] Philip Selznick, *TVA and the Grass Roots* (Berkeley: University of California Press, 1959).

interviews of a sample of fifty community organizers drawn from the membership lists of the National Association of Social Workers and the Association for the Study of Community Organization.[53] The major findings support Olshansky in identifying common practices and functions even though the community organizers were employed in a variety of agencies and were not limited to the welfare council proto-type. Educational backgrounds differed significantly although over 50 percent held degrees in social work. Despite the difference in background there was a significant uniformity in the tasks performed and the perceptions of these tasks.

A number of recent articles have attempted to develop practice prototypes distinguishing between models of enablement, innovation, and change, but they derive from generalized experience rather than from explicit studies of practice.[54] Nevertheless, they do provide models that may serve as the framework for future study of practice.

It is noteworthy that limited theoretical models produced by Ross and Lippitt, although available for some years, have not been tested by outcome studies.[55] A preliminary step in this direction was attempted by Webb, who applied Lippitt's concept of planned change to one community organization effort in rehabilitation in one city.[56] While the cycle of change sequence postulated by Lippitt was found applicable, there was no testing of practice behavior.

Conclusions

More significant than specific research findings has been the emergence of a more rigorous and scientifically based method of study. Observation and description of current practice have been used to frame hypotheses about planning problems that are rooted in such theoretical concepts as organization, system, and decision-making. This has made possible the framing of sharper research questions and analysis, which can lead to the accumulation of evidence necessary for research development. Equally significant, new investigative approaches have been developed, among which may be noted: (1) systematic cross-section case study conducted simultaneously in several matched communities; (2) units of exchange as a means of studying agency interrelationships; (3) the extension of probability sampling to total populations in order to study the incidence and prevalence of social conditions; (4) the enrichment of case methods of study by combining observation, social and political theory, demographic analysis, studies of participant behavior, attitude surveys, and statistical measures of organization effort.

Research in social planning is on the threshold of a new era, but entry will depend upon a new value being accorded the systematic penetration of the mysteries of community and social policy formation. For such work, confidence in the planned evolution of welfare systems is essential.

[53] Eva Schindler Rainman, "Community Organization: Selected Aspects of Practice." Unpublished doctoral dissertation, University of Southern California, 1962.

[54] *See*, for example, Robert Morris and Martin Rein, "Goals, Structures and Action Strategies for Planned Community Change," *Selected Papers, 1962* (New York: Columbia University Press, 1962); National Association of Social Workers, "Defining Community Organization Practice" (New York, 1962) (mimeographed); Martin Rein, "Organization for Change," *Social Work*, Vol. 9, No. 2 (April 1964), pp. 32–42; and Jack Rothman, "An Analysis of Goals and Roles in Community Organization Practice," *Social Work*, Vol. 9, No. 2 (April 1964), pp. 24–31.

[55] Murray G. Ross, *Community Organization: Theory and Principles* (New York: Harper & Brothers, 1955); and Lippitt, *op. cit.*

[56] Robert M. Webb, "Some Community Organization Principles in Practice," *Social Work*, Vol. 4, No. 3 (July 1959), pp. 84–91.

1½M/SWR/4-66